City politics in Canada

City Politics in Canada offers a new perspective on Canadian municipal politics. Its concern is not with the mechanics of government, but with the practice of politics at the local level. Its focus, moreover, is on seven specific political systems at the heart of what are arguably the most important metropolitan areas in Canada. This book marks the beginning of an effort to specify what is distinctive about Canadian politics at the municipal level, in relation to practice at other levels and in other countries.

The essays that form the core of *City Politics in Canada* were commissioned from leading authorities on local politics in the cities concerned: Montreal, Toronto, Ottawa, Halifax, Vancouver, Winnipeg, and Edmonton. The result is a set of accessible and highly informative essays, each written from a different perspective and based on a different approach to the subject, but each contributing to a general portrait of Canadian city politics.

Warren Magnusson's introductory essay is itself a sketch for such a portrait. Especially designed for readers who are new to the subject, this essay reviews the development of local government and politics in Canada as a whole. It explains those features of municipal politics that the authors of the case studies have had to take for granted, and it sets the context for comparative analysis. Such analysis is Andrew Sancton's concern in his concluding essay. He bases his observations on the studies in this book, and pays particular attention to the way in which the pattern revealed differs from the American and the British. As he says, Canadian city politics is almost exclusively about boosterism, land development, and the enhancement of property. This is its unifying and distinguishing feature – a feature that is clarified by the analyses in each chapter of *City Politics in Canada*.

WARREN MAGNUSSON is assistant professor in the Department of Political Science at the University of Victoria. ANDREW SANCTON is assistant professor in the Department of Political Science at the University of Western Ontario.

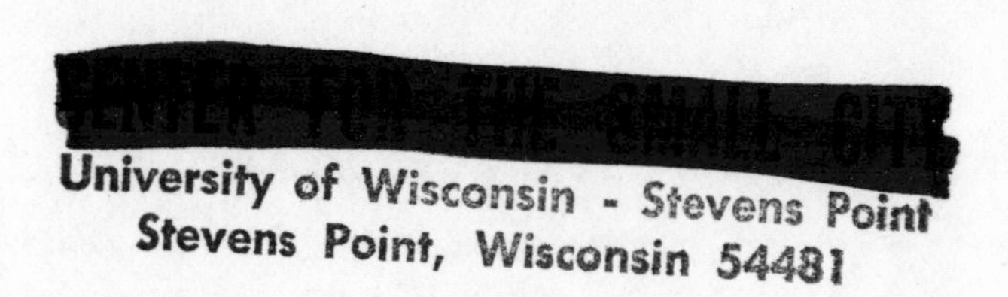

WARREN MAGNUSSON
and ANDREW SANCTON
editors

City politics in Canada

University of Toronto Press
TORONTO BUFFALO LONDON

Toronto Buffalo London
Printed in Canada

ISBN 0-8020-2497-1 (cloth)
ISBN 0-8020-6520-1 (paper)

Canadian Cataloguing in Publication Data

Main entry under title:
City politics in Canada

Includes index.
ISBN 0-8020-2497-1 (bound). – ISBN 0-8020-6520-1 (pbk.)

1. Municipal government – Canada – Case studies.
I. Magnusson, Warren, 1947– II. Sancton, Andrew, 1948–

JS1708.C47 352.071 C83-098071-7

Contents

Preface

Finding out about city politics in Canada is not easy. Library shelves are filled with ambitious government reports, tantalizing case studies, detailed local histories, useful textbooks, and the occasional lively biography of a prominent politician. Rare, however, are books that treat our cities' politics comprehensively, in their full historical and economic context. Those of us who teach urban politics in Canadian universities know this gap to be a serious problem. How can we expect our students to be involved in the subject if the material they are expected to read is so often abstract or incomplete?

This book began in 1978–9 when, for one year, we were both teaching at the University of Western Ontario. The initial idea was to write a systematic comparison of city politics in Montreal and Toronto. Challenging as this might have been, we soon realized that, if we wanted our book to be widely read and used, we would have to go beyond the confines of central Canada. This we could not do ourselves.

Initial encouragement came from two men to whom we consequently owe a huge debt: Errol Sharpe and Peter Saunders, now main partners in Fernwood Books. These fervent advocates of Canadian scholarly publishing were encouraging from the very beginning. It was on the basis of their support that we were able to recruit our first contributors. It was also through them that we made first contact with our publisher.

Informed students of Canadian urban politics are more likely to be familiar with the names of our contributors than with ours. This testifies to our extreme good fortune in finding people who know a great deal about their particular city, were able to work according to schedule in a collective enterprise, and were willing to do much of their work with no guarantee that Magnusson and Sancton could really put together an acceptable finished product. Perhaps they knew that, with Virgil Duff as our editor, we were in capable hands. We made this discovery soon enough and are grateful indeed.

For help with incidental expenses, we are pleased to acknowledge financial support from both the University of Victoria and Western. Our secretaries and colleagues in both places, particularly Allan O'Brien at Western, were helpful and encouraging. For ourselves and our contributors, we would like to thank the many people who read all or part of this book in manuscript and helped by their comments and suggestions to improve the final product.

Our greatest debt is to L.J. Sharpe of Nuffield College, Oxford. He knew little about this project, and as a result he (and everybody else named here) cannot be held responsible for its shortcomings. As our common supervisor for graduate research, he helped us discover that studying local politics leads to all the central questions in political science and sometimes helps answer them. If this book reflects Jim Sharpe's intellectual influence, it is the kind of book we wanted it to be.

Warren Magnusson
Andrew Sancton

CITY POLITICS IN CANADA

WARREN MAGNUSSON

Introduction: The development of Canadian urban government

Canadians have learned to understand their country as one of infinite variety, but this conception has had little impact on the study of municipal politics and government in Canada. The standard texts in the field portray a pattern of politics and government that is common to the country as a whole.[1] In the study of municipal affairs, regional variations in Canada's political culture and political economy – which have attracted so much attention among students of federal and provincial politics – have been largely ignored. Whether students of municipal government have a sense of the unity of things that others have lost or whether they simply have been blind to regional and local variations is a matter for argument. Such an argument can hardly be settled, however, without examining and comparing municipal political systems in different Canadian communities. Remarkably little effort in this direction has been made. While studies of the provinces have multiplied, even the largest and most important of our municipal polities have received little attention from serious political scientists. Everyone's understanding of Canadian politics has suffered as a result: a whole level of activity has been neglected.

No single book could remedy this problem, but the present text makes a small beginning. It brings together for the first time profiles of municipal government and politics in seven major cities in all parts of the country. Each of these essays is original. In method and emphasis they vary considerably, but they reflect a common effort to provide general accounts of specific municipal polities. As such, they invite the sort of comparative analysis that would specify the uniformities and diversities of Canadian local politics and deepen understanding of our whole political system. In the final chapter of this book, Andrew Sancton has drawn some of the conclusions that emerge from our own reflections on these studies, and he has attempted to place the Canadian experience in an international perspective. These conclusions are not the only ones conceivable: any analysis based on a few case studies must be highly tentative. We hope this volume will stimulate the work necessary to fill the gaps within and between the studies it presents and make a more definitive analysis possible. If it does that, we will have accomplished one of our main aims.

For specialists in the study of Canadian municipal politics, the essays that follow will need no further introduction. However, we hope that most of our readers will not be in that class: we may attract the attention even of a part of the army of specialists in Canadian politics who have never read anything about municipal government. For them especially, and for the students who will be using this volume as a text, it may be useful to sketch the development of urban government and politics in Canada. The rest of this introductory essay is devoted to that purpose. No effort has been made to duplicate the detailed descriptions of urban forms or local government structures that are readily available elsewhere.[2] The intention is instead to provide general historical description and analysis of a sort which is lacking in other texts. Of course, the danger of such a description is that it will suffer from the over-generalization this volume is supposed to counteract. For the reader the only remedy is to treat the introduction strictly as such – as a way into case studies which correct many of its errors and inaccuracies. This is a place to begin and not to end.

THE ORIGINS OF CANADIAN LOCAL GOVERNMENT

We too often make the facile assumption that local government is everywhere and always an instrument of the local community. Such autonomy is more often the exception than the rule. It is true that the United Kingdom, which conquered Canada in 1759, was heir to a tradition that stressed the importance of local self-government – a tradition that contributed to the revolt of the American colonists in 1776. Nevertheless, the British system of local government was as much as anything a device for imposing unwanted responsibilities (and taxes) upon local communities. The ancient parishes were granted their civil powers in exchange for keeping the King's Peace, maintaining his highways, supporting his churches, and caring for his indigent subjects. The county courts and borough corporations, improvement commissions and turnpike trusts, were allowed even greater powers, but always in exchange for services to the king and his people – and a tacit promise to refrain from charges on his treasury.[3] In France, the royal administration was even more concerned to make local authorities into central agencies. This was certainly true in New France, where local government (such as it was) appeared to both its officers and subjects as an instrument for extracting labour and taxes from reluctant colonists and regulating activities at odds with imperial policy. The displacement of the French imperial power by the more 'liberal' but alien British did little to convince French Canadians that local government institutions could have a different character.[4] It was not only in Lower Canada, however, that municipal institutions were regarded with hostility and suspicion. In Newfoundland – where the Royal Navy made a sporadic effort until 1833 to suppress the 'outlaw' settlements established on the island – municipal government was widely perceived as a device for forcing the fishermen to pay unwanted taxes for unneeded services. That attitude has survived to the present day.[5]

The contrary theory – that local government is the bedrock of liberal democracy – found its first expression in this country in the townships of Upper and Lower Canada that were settled by American loyalists. Municipal autonomy was one of the demands of the early Reformers, and the Baldwin Act, which granted it to Upper Canada in 1849, was hailed as a 'charter of municipal freedom.'[6] Locally elected officials would thereafter be able to raise money for local improvements without recourse to the provincial legislature and design those improvements to meet local, not provincial, requirements. The 'liberty' at stake was the freedom for positive municipal government, and 'democracy' the responsiveness of that government to the people who were dominant locally.

As originally conceived, municipal councils were police authorities with powers that were justified in terms of the need for public order and safety. This conception of their role was essentially negative, but it involved them in everything from issuing fire regulations and attempting to prevent contamination of the water-supply to controlling brawls in the taverns and keeping pigs from wandering at will. From the beginning of municipal government in Europe, the local authorities had been interested primarily in protecting and promoting commerce and industry.[7] The medieval boroughs that were the original municipalities in England were designed as commercial ventures. From the early days of English settlement in North America, the nascent towns aspired to borough status in recognition of their commercial importance, and they sought the powers that went with that status as a means of promoting their own development.[8] The rural towns and townships had no less economic a conception of their functions. In the early nineteenth century the common objection to existing municipal corporations in Britain and the United States was that they were organized and acted like private companies. Local government reform was designed to put them under the control of the whole propertied class and force them to act like public corporations.[9]

Canadian municipal councils were born in the Victorian 'age of improvement,' and it was natural for them to regard themselves positively as development authorities, responsible for the construction (as well as the regulation) of new communities in the wilderness. Capital for urban improvements was scarcer in Canada than England, but property-owners here generally were not burdened with 'rates' for poor relief. The convenient (if unrealistic) assumption was made that churches and charities could look after anyone so feckless as to be without work in a labour-short continent.[10] Education had to be locally financed, but this function was not assigned to the municipal councils. The problem of religious education in the schools generally had been solved by establishing separate Protestant and Catholic systems and by making the school boards independent of the municipal councils.[11] This left the latter free to concentrate on 'police' and 'improvement' functions, which were the nineteenth-century equivalents of modern 'environmental' and 'development' concerns.

Canadian municipalities had a narrower range of functions than many American ones, but what they had under their control was believed to be the essential part of municipal business. The municipality was widely regarded as a special sort of joint-stock company, with functions that did not properly extend to matters liable to be a drain on local resources.[12] The central authorities often had other ideas, but where the proponents of municipal autonomy were successful, local councils were protected from unwanted burdens. This was the case in Upper Canada from 1849, and the principles applied there by the Baldwin Act were gradually extended to other parts of British North America. The municipal councils established in Upper Canada were not the first to be created in Canada: Saint John, New Brunswick, was incorporated as a 'city,' on the English model, in 1784.[13] The arrangements in the Baldwin Act were not particularly innovative: they followed a precedent set in the state of New York that had already been followed in the American Midwest.[14] Nevertheless, the Baldwin Act created, for the first time in Canada, a uniform system of municipal institutions that applied to the whole of a province. Despite recent changes, the system remains essentially intact in Ontario, and the other provinces have not departed greatly from the Ontario model.

The Baldwin Act system was based on several principles. The first of these was that the municipal councils were the creatures of the provincial legislature and were subject to its sovereign authority.[15] This was in defiance of the idea, advanced by extreme proponents of local self-government, that the right of the community to govern itself arose directly from the people and could not be abridged or denied even by an ostensibly sovereign authority.[16] The legislature asserted instead that the municipalities were its own creation and could be altered or abolished at will: thus, a community that was recognized as a municipality one day could be denied that status the next. Local constitutions were to depend not on local decision, but on provincial legislation. The powers of the municipal councils were strictly defined by the provincial legislature and strictly interpreted by the courts, in accordance with the doctrine of *ultra vires*.[17] Moreover, these powers had to be exercised in accordance with regulations developed and applied by the legislature and its executive or administrative agents. It was not until the twentieth century that the provinces subjected the municipalities to close administrative control, but the principle of provincial supremacy was firmly established, even in the 'charter of municipal freedom.'

The second great principle of the Baldwin Act was that the powers of a municipality should vary with its size and character.[18] Urban and rural areas were to be separated from one another administratively, because the urban communities demanded improvements and forms of regulation required by their density of settlement that the rural communities did not need and were certainly unwilling to finance. It was assumed that the larger urban communities would need even greater powers than the smaller ones to cope with their problems and fulfil their ambitions. Thus, there was from the beginning a recognition that the governments of cities would be different from the governments of other polities at the municipal level – more complex, more ambitious, more powerful, and certainly more expensive. Such status was granted as a concession from rural leaders fearful of civic expansion and exploitation, and these fears contributed to continuing provincial restraints on municipal activism.

Further restraints were implicit in the third great principle of the Baldwin Act: that the municipal councils should be elected by and from the local property-holders. Whatever the democratic rhetoric, it was assumed that only *men* who had houses, farms, or businesses of their own should be entitled to vote. Moreover, this property had to be of a certain value.[19] The general view was that participation in municipal affairs ought to be even more closely restricted to the propertied classes than participation in politics in general. The rationale for this was that most of the functions of municipal government were related to real property and were supported by taxes upon it. This definition of the municipal role was as much an effect as a cause of the restrictions on the municipal franchise, since it corresponded so well with the interests of the propertied class, which dominated every level of government. These people were obviously not interested in creating welfare agencies at the local level, and they had remarkable success in institutionalizing a system that virtually precluded municipal government from assuming that role. The implicit assignment of the municipal councils to functions of property management was the fourth great principle of the local government system that became established in Canada.[20]

TRADITIONAL URBAN POLITICS

Comparatively little has been written about local politics in Canada in the nineteenth century, but what little evidence there is suggests that it followed a pattern the contemporary British and Americans would have found familiar.[21] Every form of political organization depended on 'patron-client' relationships.[22] In the absence of twentieth-century social security, the ordinary man was heavily dependent on help he could get from people in stronger positions. Workmen depended on the 'favour' of employers for jobs and on churches and lodges for assistance in times of financial distress. The smaller merchants, jobbers, and manufacturers looked to the larger ones for their patronage. That patronage was in turn dependent on the success of the great businessmen in securing advantages such as a railway, a government contract, or an adjustment in the tariff. In a comparatively open political system, the *quid pro quo* for the patronage of the great was political support, since without it the advantages necessary for continued patronage could not be sustained.

Political organization depended, to a large extent, on the efforts of men of substance, who came together for mutual advantage. They were of use to one another because each could count on the support of his clients in politics as well as in business. Of course, the power of any patron was never as complete as he would like, and there were little men who were not exclusively attached to any one patron. The many lodges and fraternal orders of nineteenth-century cities offered an alternative form of patronage and mutual aid. The loyalty these organizations could command could be turned to political (and economic) advantage by their leaders. The support of the lodges was traded in return for benefits – jobs and contracts – that could be of advantage to their members. Since men of substance often associated themselves directly with the lodges, 'personal' patronage and 'lodge' patronage frequently overlapped. There was also an overlap between the churches and the lodges, because the latter had a definite ethnic-religious base and there were organizational links between particular churches and fraternal orders.

Religious sentiments and loyalties were of potentially overwhelmingly importance. Whenever religious issues were directly introduced (as they were with respect to education), parties could be expected to divide on religious lines. Even when religion was not so apparently at issue, people could be mobilized politically by appealing to their common religious outlook. Moreover, the sense of religious brotherhood found its secular counterpart in a belief that patronage should first be extended to one's co-religionists. Thus, the clientelist system was shaped and buttressed by religious loyalties. Since religion and ethnicity were so closely linked, the loyalties concerned were also of a 'national' character. For some, at least, ethnic appeals were of greater significance than religious ones, and the lodges (as well as many patrons) depended on both for securing their own solidarity. Again, patronage was expected to follow the principle of 'helping one's own.'

Although there were 'parties' in nineteenth-century Canadian politics, they were not the centralized, disciplined organizations we know today.[23] Governments were formed in the provinces and later in the Dominion by bringing factional leaders into loose coalitions that might or might not hold together long enough to keep a cabinet in office for a reasonable term. There were a number of discernible political tendencies and some fairly stable political alliances, but 'party' was a matter of self-identification that a politician could take as seriously or lightly as required. What counted most for the politician were local, not national, alignments. To win a seat in Parliament without the support of a local political machine was impossible. A great man could count on his own following, but he needed the support of other notables and their followers to be successful. The lodges, the churches, and the political clubs brought men together in a setting where deals could be struck. An organization could be formed with sufficient support to put a man forward for Parliament – in competition, usually, with one or more candidates put forward by competing organizations. The overt political contest might take the form of a 'party' fight, but the contestants might also declare their neutrality with respect to party issues or compete in their declaration of support for the same party or national leader. Larger political events certainly had their impact on these local contests, but success for a politician did not necessarily depend on unswerving loyalty to a single party or leader: such loyalty was a constraint on political manoeuvre.

The national parties remained shaky alliances of local organizations until late in the nineteenth century. When finally they solidified themselves under Macdonald and Laurier, they became more detached from municipal politics.[24] Previously, any political organization could be expected to seek control of the municipal council as well as of the available parliamentary seats. However, as commitment of the organization to a national party came to mean more in terms of loyalty to leaders and policies, the obstacles to using it for every form of political activity became greater. The issues and interests involved in municipal affairs were not the same as the ones that arose at the federal or provincial level and created different political divisions. These divisions were a threat to party unity, and there were diminishing returns for the parties in attempting to mediate these disputes for the sake of controlling municipal councils. Politicians at the municipal level also found that non-partisanship allowed for greater freedom of action. Not only did it permit political alliances across party lines, but it also strengthened the municipality in its dealings with senior governments and outside business: leaders could claim that they had support from both local parties for their actions. Thus, at a time when the major parties were establishing their hegemony over federal and provincial politics, their grasp was being loosened at the municipal level: so began the divergence between partisan federal and provincial politics and non-partisan municipal politics that has since characterized the Canadian political system.

Some of the heat was taken out of municipal politics in the nineteenth century by the separation of the school boards from the municipal councils and the effective assignment of charitable functions to the churches and other voluntary institutions. The municipalities were thus prevented from intervening in matters that touched on religious sensibilities or ethnic differences. Nevertheless, the municipal councils were still the 'police' authorities and as such had some control over the regulation of social behaviour. This meant licensing the taverns and controlling the liquor trade, protecting the quiet of the sabbath, and regulating prostitution, gambling, and other amusements. No such regulation was possible without confronting the divergent standards of permissible behaviour within the community. Since these standards varied from one religious or ethnic group to another, there was potential here for explosive political conflict; however, local élites were generally concerned to prevent such conflicts from becoming overt.[25]

Most of the open disputes in municipal politics related to urban improvements. Any works to be undertaken by a municipal council were necessarily controversial, because jobs and contracts were at stake. Even if there was agreement on what should be done, there were likely to be differences about who should do it. The letting of a contract was a serious business, since the fortunes of so many people – great and small – depended on municipal favour. To most contemporaries, there was nothing untoward about seeing that favours were allocated in a favourable way. Given the looseness of political alliances, arrangements had to be made to ensure that each of the groups supporting the people in power received a reasonable share of the benefits of municipal government. This could be extraordinarily complicated. Different contractors had each to be given a part of the works in progress; jobs in the municipal departments had to be allocated among competing claimants; the demands for improvements in one part of the city had to be balanced against similar demands in another. Delicate compromises could easily be overturned by an emergent group or an obstreperous leader making demands for a piece of the action. Technical innovations had a similar effect because they made possible costly – and immensely lucrative – contracts for the provision of services and stimulated intense competition for the potential rewards.

These technical innovations were both a cause and an effect of the rapid urban and industrial development in the nineteenth century. Although Canadian cities were by no means international leaders, they were caught up in the general expansion, and their efforts to cope had the effect of disrupting carefully wrought political arrangements. Each city was involved in a great competition with its rivals in Canada and abroad. Success – which meant increasing prosperity, growing opportunities, and the prestige and power of a metropolitan position – depended on attracting new trade and industry. In turn, this meant establishing favourable conditions for business. During the nineteenth century, these conditions became increasingly dependent on civic improvements: street paving, water-supply, sewerage, cleaning, lighting, gas supply, tramways, electricity, streetcars, telephones, etc. Each of these improvements had to be made under municipal franchise, if not by direct municipal enterprise.[26] It was agreed that the council had the responsibility to see that the community did not lag behind its competitors. However, business expansion depended on giving the entrepreneurs favourable tax concessions or 'bonuses,' which depleted the revenue that would be used to support further improvements.[27] Since other taxpayers could be expected to protest against bearing an extra burden, the councils were caught between a shortage of revenue and a demand for expansionist policies.

To the extent that municipal leaders were divided on issues of economic policy, the relevant cleavage was between the 'boosters' and the 'cutters.' The latter demanded stringent economies, to save the ratepayers from excessive burdens.[28] The former insisted on the need for expansion and promised to use the city's resources to stimulate growth. With growth, there would be an expansion in the tax base, and the revenue problem would supposedly solve itself. Of course, this never happened, because each phase of development brought new demands for public investment. During times of economic expansion, the boosters had the upper hand, since everyone was generally optimistic and civic revenues were increasing as business improved. When the boom collapsed, however, the municipal corporations often found themselves badly over-extended: in the face of imminent bankruptcy, the demand for cuts was inevitable. Economies were practised (or advertised, at least) until the next round of expansion began, and the cycle repeated itself.

What separated the boosters from the cutters was more an attitude of mind than an ideology: the same man might be a booster one year and a cutter the next, according to the mood of times (and his own economic interest). However violent the disputes might have been, they were contained within limits defined by common assumptions about the appropriate role of municipal government. The cutters did not deny that municipal councils should support the expansion of local business; they simply questioned the extent of the investment and pointed to the need for lightening the burden on the rates (which inevitably fell on business) and protecting the municipal credit. The boosters were as convinced as the cutters that money should not be wasted on projects that would fail to contribute to the expansion of business. A broader conception of public spending was hardly at issue.

The containment of municipal politics within these bounds was of extraordinary importance for the future. A form and conception of municipal government, which reflected the interests of the propertied class, was firmly established before the franchise was extended to people without real property. This helped to inhibit political change in face of the democratization of the franchise that occurred in the late nineteenth century and afterwards. It is significant that the universal franchise was more successfully resisted municipally than at any other level of government: in many provinces it was not generally established until the 1970s.[29] This reflects the persistence of the ideas and interests that linked municipal government to the management of real property. Whatever changes have occurred in the twentieth century, we can still see at work the mechanisms of traditional local politics, whereby significant social and economic cleavages are overcome by ideological appeals to the good of the community as a whole and by the practical politics of clientelism. These processes are most obvious in smaller communities, where the conservatism of municipal politics is legendary.[30] However, they are also at work in the cities, despite (or because) of the movement for reform that began there at the end of the last century.

THE FIRST WAVE OF MUNICIPAL REFORM

A new attitude towards local government became apparent after 1870 on both sides of the Atlantic. In Britain, Joseph Chamberlain brought international publicity to the city of Birmingham with his Radical program of civic improvement – a program that was carried into effect with the aid of rigorous party discipline.[31] The growing labour movement found in Chamberlain's 'civic gospel' a congenial doctrine, for the gospel emphasized the need for a broader conception of municipal functions and a more vigorous pursuit of the civic good. That good was conceived ostensibly in terms of the health and welfare of the city's inhabitants. Although many of Chamberlain's own supporters believed that the city's responsibilities in this regard should be narrowly construed, that was not a necessary conclusion. Since the 1840s, the local 'sanitary authorities' had been charged with the duty of protecting the public from hazards to health, and this function was joined in the cities and boroughs to the traditional municipal duties.[32] The Chamberlain Radicals insisted that the health of the city depended on more than the prevention of disease. They looked for a program of public works that would improve the safety, efficiency, convenience, beauty, and purity of the city, for the benefit of all concerned, including even the lower orders. Moreover, they accepted that direct municipal enterprise might offer a superior method for providing the necessary works, since the council could see that things were done for the profit of the city and not for the profit of the entrepreneur. It was a short step from this position to the Fabian belief in 'gas and water socialism.'

By the 1890s, this sort of 'municipal socialism' was on the political agenda in Britain.[33] Rather than franchising private monopolies to provide such services as gas and water, the socialist municipal councils were prepared to take over these functions themselves. The concept of a public utility – and hence the scope for municipal ownership – were given the widest extension, so that the municipalities might begin to provide trams, develop subways, open restaurants, provide parks and recreation grounds, support theatres and museums, and so on. The idea was attacked that everything the local authorities did had somehow to be in the service of business. Instead, they were to devote themselves explicitly to the service of the working man and the ordinary consumer. This was the most radical change involved in the development of municipal socialism, for it was traditionally supposed that the needs of business – for lower taxes or better services – should take absolute precedence. What was implied was a radical shift of power, and it was this, more than the actual programs at issue, that stimulated the fierce partisan struggles that came to characterize British urban politics.[34]

In terms of the extension of municipal functions, three features of the development in Britain were of note.[35] The first was the increase of 'municipal trading' – i.e. municipal ownership of public utilities. There was a gradual drift in this direction from the late nineteenth century until the Second World War, when many of these utilities passed from private and municipal to national ownership. The second was the gradual integration of non-municipal local authorities with the existing municipal councils. Whereas health, education, and welfare had been under independent local boards in the nineteenth century, by 1929 these functions had all passed under municipal control. The municipal councils came to resemble the national government in the range of their functions. The third feature of this development was the emergence of housing and planning as central activities of local government. For the British local councils it was no longer simply a matter of effecting a few improvements, promoting growth, and curbing the 'nuisance' of urban development. They increasingly assumed the main responsibility for providing working-class housing and social amenities. They also asserted the right, and acquired some of the necessary powers, to control the physical development of the entire city. The assumption (of the socialists at least) was that the development of cities and the quality of working-class life should not be determined exclusively by the market, but that a rational plan should be the basis for both. Asserting this goal and achieving it were two different things, but the conception of municipal government that followed from this idea became common in the twentieth century.

Not surprisingly, the American revolution in municipal thinking had little of the socialist impetus of its British counterpart. Indeed, the pressure for reform after 1870 came mainly (as it originally did in Britain) from elements of the business community.[36] As the years progressed, middle-class professionals played an increasingly important role, but municipal reformers generally remained sympathetic to business. In this sense, at least, the American reformers remained at the stage the Birmingham Radicals had reached in the 1870s. The most distinctive feature of the American municipal movement was its vigorous attack on partisan politics. Rather than mobilizing partisan bias for the sake of reform, as Chamberlain's supporters had done, the American progressives attacked the party system as the basis for corruption and inefficiency. What they were attacking were the clientelist relationships that characterized nineteenth-century municipal politics. The party machines of the great American cities had systematized these relationships for the benefit of the 'bosses' and 'ward-heelers.' They relied on a mass clientele of immigrant workers and traded the favours of municipal government for appropriate pay-offs from the business community. The money so extracted, together with jobs and services of municipal government, helped to keep the immigrant clientele of the parties reasonably content – while yielding a substantial return to the party managers. The trouble with this system was that it alienated the middle and upper classes from municipal government: the party bosses supplanted the great families as patrons of the lower orders and seized for themselves a political and economic position that was widely resented.[37]

As a political movement, municipal reform developed in reaction to the party machines. Although at first the demand was simply for putting good men in office, the conviction gradually spread that major structural reforms were required in municipal government. These were intended both to wreck the party machines and to put in their place a new set of machinery for administering local affairs. The aim was to transform the municipalities into efficient bureaucratic organizations, staffed by people who were selected and promoted on merit. At the top of each of these organizations would be a kind of board of directors, elected at large by the municipality's shareholders. In the later versions of this model, the directors would be served by a chief executive officer, who would have full administrative responsibility for the efficient operation of the corporation.[38] The hope was to eliminate all the patronage positions in municipal government and so to destroy the organizational basis of the party machines. By eliminating the division of the city into wards, it was hoped that the practice of distributing services as favours to people in particular neighbourhoods could eventually be overcome: councillors elected at large would, in theory, be obliged to look to the needs of the city as a whole. The aim was to have a municipal council that allocated funds and developed public services in accordance with a rational plan, which in turn was based on a disinterested conception of the civic good.[39]

Later critics have claimed that the middle- and upper-class bias of the American reformers led them to a narrow conception of the civic good and made them underestimate the services to the lower class provided by the party machines.[40] This is certainly correct, but many of the reformers were sympathetic to the development of modern social services, which provided to the poor help of a more appropriate kind than the machines could offer. The welfare state, in its contemporary form, owes much to the efforts of these early reformers. The same is true of the apparatus for civic planning. The reformers were concerned not only with improving the honesty and efficiency of municipal government, but also with using its powers creatively. This meant developing social services, and planning the City Beautiful and the City Efficient.[41] For the latter purposes, the reformers were prepared to accept devices for land-use control that were pioneered in Europe – and that their conservative critics suspected as un-American innovations. The most important of these devices was zoning, which was first applied generally in 1916, in New York City.

To a considerable extent Canadian municipal reformers followed the American lead, despite the fact that conditions in the two countries were often dissimilar.[42] Municipal reform, like agrarian protest, was a continental movement, and Canadian reformers linked their organizations with their larger American counterparts. They naturally looked south for guides to action, hoping to avoid American mistakes as well as to learn from successes. When the campaign for municipal reform reached national proportions in the United States in the 1890s, most Canadian cities were extremely small.[43] There were none of more than 50,000 in western Canada, and only a few in the East. Montreal itself, which was much the largest city, had only a few hundred thousand residents, including those in the outlying suburbs. Big-city problems had thus hardly emerged. Even so it was not hard to anticipate their arrival, especially with the boom of development on the Prairies. That boom gave a spurt to the commercial and industrial centres of central Canada and created cities from nothing on the Prairies and the Pacific coast. Since the immigrants came from all over Europe, and even from the Orient, Canadian cities began to attain the polyglot character of their American counterparts. This affected some of them more than others: Toronto, like the cities of the Maritimes, retained its 'British' character, while Montreal and the new cities of the West became quite diverse. Even in the most homogeneous cities, however, there were the traditional divisions – British and French; English, Scottish, and Irish; Protestant and Catholic; high church and low. Moreover, the growth of the cities and the development of manufacturing brought the crowding and deteriorated housing characteristic of the American slums.[44]

Immigrant ghettos were one consequence of a process of segregation that was carried to its logical extreme in the big cities.[45] The physical separation of the rich from the poor, of houses from places of work, and of stores and offices from factories and warehouses was made possible by the new means of transportation and communications developed in the latter part of the nineteenth century. It was one of the attractions of these means that they allowed for the segregation (and hence more efficient organization) of economic activities and the sorting of classes into separate residential communities. Residential segregation, which was sought by people with property, had the unintended effect of weakening control from above over the industrial working class. The new modes of commercial and industrial organization tended, in any case, to separate workers from their employers and create more favourable conditions for union organization. This raised the spectre of a Marxian class struggle.[46] However, the fine sorting of individuals within complex bureaucratic organizations and physically differentiated cities led to a fragmentation of interests and identities. Class solidarity was not easy to achieve under these conditions. Churches, schools, and the new media of mass communications helped to overcome class antagonisms and make pluralism socially integrative, by instilling a common culture and teaching people to express their differences within the existing order. That order was naturally integrative, in so far as it provided for individual or group advancement.

Reformers in this period were greatly concerned to create the conditions for social unity, in the face of what they regarded as the disintegrative effects of urban and industrial development. Uplifting the poor was an obvious priority, but the late Victorian reformers were reluctant to offer material assistance that might corrupt the lower orders. Moral regeneration was instead the priority:[47] the poor were to be denied the pleasures of drink and gaming and general carousing and encouraged on the paths of sobriety and righteousness. Reformers attempted to achieve this by a mixture of stringent regulation and friendly counsel. Of course, neither strategy was particularly effective, but the effort at least had the effect of sensitizing the reformers to the problems faced by the poor in the cities. As they discovered, even the 'respectable' working man found it hard enough to find decent housing or to clothe and feed his family, when jobs were uncertain, wages low, and rents constantly rising under the pressures of demand. The more enlightened reformers gradually realized that something else must be done, besides changing the habits of the poor, to overcome the conditions of the slum.

The municipalities came under particular pressure to act. However, it seemed clear to most reformers that structural changes were required to make municipal governments effective. There was even a moral case for it. People were corrupted by the sight of a council that dispensed its services and awarded contracts as favours in return for favours. A reformed municipality would instead provide a public example of honest and efficient government: everyone would have before them a purified vision of the bourgeois order, with men succeeding strictly by virtue of their contribution to the community. Of course, there were more practical reasons for structural reform, which appealed as much to conservative businessmen as to social reformers. Reorganization of municipal government on the new American model promised economy and efficiency in the provision of traditional services to business. The social reformers may have wanted to broaden the scope of municipal activity, but they accepted that social improvement depended on economic progress, which in turn depended on public support for business. Honesty and efficiency in local government were thus the general priority.

If this was a narrow vision of municipal reform, it was sufficient to inspire many efforts to improve the quality of municipal administration and alter the structures of local government.[48] These efforts had a great impact on Canadian municipal government. Most important, perhaps, was the stimulus given to professionalization and bureaucratization. This had the ultimate effect of disrupting the traditional patron-client relationships of municipal government and making the weak dependent instead on the paternal care of professional civil servants. This helped to free politicians from some of the burdens of office, and it enabled reformers who were ill-disposed to patronage to compete more successfully in municipal elections. However, the decline of patronage weakened political control of the administrative system. The reformers claimed to compensate for this by clarifying lines of command and concentrating political authority in the hands of small groups of public representatives who could wield effective authority over each of the operations at hand. This meant reducing the size of municipal councils or transferring much of their authority to boards of control or boards of commissioners.[49] It also meant hiving off certain functions that were little related to the core of municipal activity, or that required a special sort of competence or interest, and leaving these matters to be administered by independent or semi-autonomous agencies. The precedent for this had been set in school boards, and the same arrangement was made in various cities for public health, childrens' aid, parks, recreation, public transit, electricity, and a host of other functions.[50] This protected many activities from the vagaries of municipal politics – for the benefit of those whose interests were served by the agencies concerned.

Despite any compensating measures there is no doubt that municipal reform strengthened the position of civil servants in relation to their political masters. Thus, the development of new activities and the extension of the old was increasingly dependent on professional attitudes. The growth of municipal government in the succeeding years was partly the consequence of professional ambitions, which themselves were encouraged by growing professional competence.[51] However, this bureaucratic expansionism was kept in check by external political pressures. There was the traditional business insistence that municipal activity should contribute to the expansion of the local economy, and there was the equally traditional pressure by ratepayers for cuts in municipal taxes. The net effect was to channel the bureaucratic advance in the traditional direction and to contain the forays into other fields. As a result, Canadian municipal government was more conservative than the rhetoric of reform sometimes suggested.

It is true that there was an expansion in municipal ownership of public utilities in the era of 'reform' that lasted until 1920. This was partly in reaction to the corruption involved in franchising private monopolies and partly in consequence of the demand for cheaper services, which came as much from business as from ordinary consumers.[52] There were also certain moves towards municipal planning, although few of these had much effect. Zoning became popular, but essentially as a means for protecting residential and commercial amenities and so of enhancing the value of private properties.[53] Health and housing regulations were improved but little came of any plans for slum clearance or public housing development.[54] Although some reformers pressed for bolder action, conservative pressures were still too strong (even within the movement for reform) to allow for a massive extension of municipal activity. Part of the problem was that the municipal governments had a narrow revenue base. Quite apart from the fact that their authority to tax was limited,[55] the municipalities were still in competition with one another for new industrial or commercial developments. Thus, there were genuine fears about the effects of raising taxes to support extended services. Reformers who were interested in new activities had to show that these would not be a drain on the municipal treasury. This was a difficult thing to do, especially with respect to expensive ventures such as public housing.

The modernization of administrative structures that occurred as a result of this wave of municipal reform had the effect of increasing the capacity of the local authorities, but not of changing their basic orientation. The functions of fostering and regulating urban development were bureaucratized, routinized, and to a considerable extent de-politicized. This was necessary if the process of development were to continue in accordance with the logic of the market and not be so greatly distorted by partisan concerns. The appeal of municipal reform to the business community can be explained in terms of the promise it gave of effective, inexpensive, non-partisan municipal support for urban growth. When reformers began talking of using the powers of municipal government for new purposes, their support from the business community – and the ordinary home-owner – began to melt away. Thus, the legacy of municipal reform in Canada was not the promised extension of functions, but administrative modernization, structural modification, and political neutralization. The old idea that municipalities were essentially joint-stock companies belonging to the local property-holders was not overthrown but reinforced. This helped to preserve the traditional character of local government and politics and inhibit the tendency towards municipal socialism. What was not so apparent at the time is that the municipalities were shutting themselves out from much of the subsequent growth of the Canadian state.

THE TRIUMPH OF THE CENTRAL AUTHORITIES

The seeming inability of the municipal authorities to perform the functions demanded of modern governments became the central concern of reformers in the middle decades of this century. It was the Great Depression that brought this concern to a head. For every level of government the Depression created problems that at first were overwhelming, but the central authorities emerged from the economic crisis (and the war that followed) in a stronger position than ever, in relation both to the municipal councils and to private business. Even the provinces were weakened by comparison to the federal government, and thirty years had to pass before they recovered their relative position. The municipalities never experienced a comparable revival, despite the fact that efforts were made to extend their powers, improve their financial position, and increase their political and administrative capacity. Some would say that the provinces used their sovereign authority to prevent the emergence of vital, modern local governments, which might eventually demand recognition as authorities equal in constitutional status to the federal and provincial governments. However, the relative decline in the importance of municipal government is largely the result of features of modern society that are not the product of political decisions and cannot easily be altered by government action.

In the nineteenth century, cities were relatively autonomous socially, economically, and politically. This autonomy was gradually destroyed by the railway, telegraph, and telephone – and finally by the automobile, radio, and television. What once were distinct civic societies were gradually knit together, so that the bounds between one local community and another seemed increasingly arbitrary. Not only did the cities overspill their boundaries and make suburbs of the surrounding townships, and not only were the villages and towns converted into satellites of the greater cities; but also the cities themselves were merged with one another, sometimes physically, but more often commercially and socially. This was most apparent within regions or provinces, but by the middle of this century it seemed proper to talk of a national urban system, in which the cities were merely nodes of development.[56] Indeed, the Canadian urban system could, in some ways, best be understood as a sub-system of the American: how it developed depended on decisions in New York and Washington – or in Hollywood, Detroit, Pittsburgh, and Houston.

If this conception of Canadian cities is correct, and they are but nodes of development in a larger urban system, then the functions of local government are bound to be minor. To the extent that any government can control such a system, only one with extensive territorial jurisdiction is likely to be successful. Even the federal government is in a weak position as a controlling authority, because the Canadian economy (and Canadian society) are so much an appendage of the American. This is one of the reasons why there has been such concern about the shift of power from Ottawa to the provinces, for the provinces seem even less capable than the federal government of wresting control of their future from the Americans. Even so, the provinces are generally large enough and distinct enough to make a credible claim to sovereignty: the same cannot be said of the municipalities. Municipal boundaries tend to make artificial divisions between city and suburb, centre and satellite, town and country, metropolis and hinterland. The areas they define are rarely self-contained, in terms of the daily activities of their inhabitants, and the people concerned are liable to identify more strongly with the wider society than with their own municipalities. This is particularly true of urban areas.[57] Thus the will for municipal independence is weak and is undermined by a sense of functional incapacity.

If, as is usually the case, a city's boundaries are tightly drawn around the core of its built-up area, the municipal authorities are faced with a set of difficult problems.[58] They lack the jurisdiction to control development around the 'fringe,' so the city is liable to be bled economically by the municipalities surrounding it. Private projects such as shopping centres, industrial estates, or high-class residential subdivisions, which yield more revenue to the municipality than they cost in terms of services, can easily be diverted into these fringe communities, leaving the city in a difficult financial position. To the extent that the civic authorities are attempting to impose a plan of urban development – for aesthetic, environmental, economic, or social reasons – they are liable to be frustrated by their suburban competitors. Even the extension and improvement of the urban infrastructure (including the transportation system) may be frustrated by suburban opposition, or by suburban refusal to share the expense of improvement. The city will be dependent on co-operation not only from its suburbs, but also from its more distant hinterland, since power, water-supply, and sewage and waste disposal cannot be secured in the immediate area. Thus there is a great incentive to secure for the purposes of metropolitan development a government with a wider territorial jurisdiction.

To a considerable extent, the metropolis and its hinterland have a common interest in transferring functions to a higher level of government. This may not be so when the rural areas cannot possibly expect to have urban services – as was generally the case in the nineteenth century. But when it becomes feasible to bring electricity, gas, and telephone service to farms and villages, and when access to the better schools and hospitals and other facilities of the cities becomes possible for almost everyone, then the rural areas have much to gain from a shift of functions to the federal or provincial government. The larger government can tax the densely populated areas to provide services for the sparsely populated ones and guarantee access to metropolitan facilities for everyone, regardless of place of residence. Thus the penalty of living in a rural area can be largely eliminated. The metropolitan communities must obviously bear the cost of improving services in the hinterland, but in exchange for this they get greater access to the land and resources of the remoter areas. A hydroelectric authority under provincial control, which offers relatively cheap power to the rural communities, ought to have comparatively little difficulty in acquiring land for future developments. Its moral, legal, and political authority will be greater than that of any municipal electric company. Similarly, urban access to rural land for garbage disposal, housing development, or recreational activities ought to be more easily secured by a province than by a city. The suburbs that profit from physical proximity to and political independence from the cities can also gain from provincial intervention, in the sense that plans for infrastructural development or land-use control may be more disinterested if imposed by the province rather than by a municipal authority dominated by the central city.

The belief that larger problems can only be solved by wider authorities has been reinforced by the financial obstacles to municipal action. Even when a local authority has the broadest conceivable powers of taxation, it has greater difficulty extracting revenue than a wider authority. People can shift their businesses or residences in response to differential tax rates. Such moves can have an effect on the fiscal capacity even of a national government, but clearly a local authority is more vulnerable to this sort of pressure than a wider authority. A business may be reluctant to move out of the Vancouver area altogether, but it is easy enough to shift from the city to one of its suburbs. The threat to the municipal tax base posed by this sort of action obviously encourages fiscal caution.[59] This caution is increased by the problems of municipal borrowing. Given its narrower tax base, a municipality is not as good a financial risk as a larger government and it can borrow only at a higher rate of interest. Unlike the federal government, a municipality cannot print money to cover its debts, so excessive borrowing inevitably means higher taxes. In the circumstances, it is hardly surprising that the municipalities have been reluctant to make commitments for expensive improvements to public services, except when they were persuaded that the services would be self-financing or that the improvements would increase the fiscal capacity of the municipality by enlarging the economic base of the community.

'Rates' or taxes on real property have always been the main source of municipal revenue. One of the reasons for this is that real property taxes are comparatively difficult to escape. Land and buildings cannot be moved about like money or other personal property. This makes the effective collection of taxes easier and contributes to the generally low administrative costs of taxing real property. Unfortunately, this form of taxation also seems to be inequitable, regressive, and highly inelastic. It penalizes people who keep their wealth in the form of real property; it hurts low-income earners who spend a higher proportion of their income on rents or mortgage payments; and, because rates are levied as a proportional tax and property assessments rarely keep pace with increases in property values, the growth in revenues tends to be smaller than the growth in personal incomes.[60] Since the rate is a highly visible tax (presented as it is in the form of an annual demand), the municipalities have found it difficult to keep their revenues increasing, and this has reinforced their natural fiscal caution.

Of course, caution has sometimes been forgotten by municipal governments, but the consequences were such that the maxims of prudence seemed wiser than ever. During the nineteenth century, many municipalities pushed themselves to the brink of bankruptcy (or over) in an effort to stimulate economic growth.[61] They gave subsidies to railways and manufacturing concerns, invested huge sums of money in physical improvements, and extended their services to outlying suburbs almost as rapidly as the speculative developers demanded. In many cases, private gain provided the motive for municipal expenditure. When the boom that was supposed to generate the necessary revenue collapsed, the local taxpayers were faced with a burden they could hardly carry. The movement for municipal reform at the end of the nineteenth century was intended, in part, to prevent such abuse of public power for private purposes; so fiscal prudence naturally became a basic tenet of reform.

Municipal extravagance also provided the provinces with reasons to curb municipal powers. There were already moves in the nineteenth century to put limits on municipal borrowing and to control the practice of 'bonusing' companies that agreed to move into town. The Ontario Railway and Municipal Board, established in 1906, was given a wide range of responsibilities for regulating municipal activity and had a particular duty to protect municipal solvency. This presaged the tight administrative controls on the local authorities imposed by all the provincial governments in the twentieth century.[62] Typically, the municipalities were obliged to seek provincial approval for large capital expenditures, and hence for any major public works. As zoning and planning developed, these activities were subjected not only to legislation defining municipal powers but also to requirements for provincial review and approval of municipal actions.[63] The general trend in every area of municipal activity was towards an increase in administrative duties at the price of restrictions on local initiative. These restrictions were seen as an inevitable consequence of the political unreliability and fiscal incapacity of the municipal councils.

The conditional grant gradually became the crucial instrument of central control in provincial-municipal and federal-provincial relations.[64] The provinces continued to find it useful to rely on the municipal authorities as local administrative agencies. In exchange for municipal assistance, they were prepared to allow the localities some administrative freedom, but only within the framework of provincial policies that defined the terms and conditions of service. By offering to subsidize municipal services, on condition that they met provincial requirements, the provinces were able to get the action they wanted without placing the full financial burden on the provincial treasuries. Since the consequent expansion of municipal departments met the ambitions of local administrators, and credit for the services concerned went partly to the local politicians, it was easy enough to secure municipal co-operation. However, the effect of such arrangements was to advance the idea that the municipal councils were really just administrative agencies of the provincial governments.

Until the Great Depression (indeed, almost to the end of the Second World War) the federal and provincial governments resisted the idea that they should take responsibility for matters that had long been left to private or municipal initiative. The welfare state and the planned economy were regarded as 'socialist' ideas and widely condemned by responsible politicians. Municipal autonomy in matters of social welfare and economic development was regarded as a necessary condition for freedom, and centralization was an obvious threat to it. It was only the failure of the economy in the 1930s and the success of wartime planning that convinced many people of the need for 'socialist' measures. Some of these measures might have been adopted at local initiative – in line with the aims of the bolder municipal reformers – if the collapse of the economy after 1929 had not placed most municipalities in a desperate financial position.[65] Their plight had been worsened by the efforts they made to assist in relieving the unemployed: since the ordinary charities could not cope with economic collapse and the senior governments offered only limited assistance, much of the burden inevitably fell on the municipal authorities, to whom the poor had traditionally been able to turn as a last resort. The experience of pushing themselves to the verge of bankruptcy did little to encourage the municipalities to broaden the scope of their own activities. It was natural for them to insist that the higher authorities should bear the burdens of the new welfare state.[66]

The development of the welfare state in Canada had been inhibited by regional jealousies and cultural divisions, as well as by the constitutional division of powers and the general suspicion of 'socialism.' However, national unity was great enough at the end of the Second World War to enable the federal government to extend its activities in the fields of housing and social welfare. This had a crucial effect on municipal government and politics. Unemployment insurance, old-age pensions, and hospital insurance and the later federally sponsored welfare programs relieved the municipalities of most of their responsibilities for relief. Since it was difficult, if not constitutionally impossible, for Ottawa to use municipalities as administrative agencies, much of the new welfare system developed outside the municipal framework.[67] This had the effect of excluding municipal governments from activities of central concern to the electorate, but it also allowed them to concentrate on their traditional functions in relation to urban development. Provincial legislation in the 1940s enabled the municipalities to play a more active role than ever before in promoting and regulating urban growth.[68] Federal intervention in the housing market combined with the effects of social insurance and Keynesian economic management to ensure steady urban expansion. This put the municipalities in a happier position than they had ever known, but in one that seemed to contribute to the lessening importance of local government as a forum for political activity.

THE MANAGEMENT OF URBAN GROWTH

Capital for the construction of houses, schools, and hospitals and for the improvement of the urban infrastructure had been extremely scarce during the Depression and the Second World War. The lack of urban employment in the 1930s had slowed the migration from the farms to the cities, but wartime industrial expansion had renewed the pressure on urban space. Despite fears of a post-war recession, the economy continued to expand and the problems created by the earlier lack of investment were simply intensified. Local authorities were faced with a great backlog of necessary public projects and an unsatiated demand for private housing. The priority for municipal councils, especially in the rapidly growing cities, was to ensure that the necessary construction occurred as quickly as possible. In part, this was a matter of investing public money – some of which was raised by local borrowing or taxation, but much of which was provided by the senior governments in the form of conditional grants. However, it was also a matter of stimulating private investment, since the assumption was still that commercial and industrial activity – including the construction of shopping centres, office complexes, factories, and housing subdivisions – ought to remain under private control. It would have been difficult, in any case, for the public authorities to finance such projects within the limits of normal taxation and borrowing, when there was such a demand for ordinary public works.

By the 1940s, it had come to be widely accepted that the municipal councils had a right to control the pace and form of urban development. In an expansionist period, this was partly a consequence of the need to keep public and private development in balance. In the past, municipalities had often over-extended themselves by attempting to service every new subdivision that private investors tried to construct. By using their regulatory powers, the municipal councils could ensure that new estates were opened up only as quickly as they – or the developers themselves – were able to provide services. Regulations could also be used to enhance the quality of the new developments, in terms of the standards of both professional planners and ordinary home-buyers. There was also a danger that the amenities of a neighbourhood, the quality of the environment, or indeed the standards of life within it could be threatened by private enterprise. Planning and zoning regulations were a means of enhancing and protecting the investments of home-buyers and businessmen (and hence of the developers and contractors) from the effects of unrestrained competition. Hence, they could be surprisingly well accepted by advocates of free enterprise.

Despite the extent of public investment, the growth of cities still depended on private enterprise. This put the municipal councils in a weak position in relation to private entrepreneurs. If a manufacturer found that he could not get land at the price he wanted, that the taxes he had to pay were too high, that the services he needed were unavailable, that the regulations on the use of his property increased his costs of operation, that his employees could not find suitable, easily accessible housing, or that the quality of the urban environment lowered morale, then he might well decide to locate in another city. The same was true of other types of businessmen. The developers generally responded quickly to demands for construction in a community, but they too had a certain amount of latitude with respect to the timing, scale, and location of their projects. Unfavourable municipal policies could discourage development, which in turn might lead to the diversion of commercial or industrial enterprise to other communities. In any case, the lack of development would intensify political pressures on a municipal council that was seen as an obstacle to the construction of new houses and shopping facilities or to the general expansion of the local economy. The municipalities generally took the attitude that their function was to facilitate private investment, by creating the appropriate conditions for it. This meant creating a favourable regulatory framework, as well as improving public facilities.

In adopting such policies, the local authorities were acting in the manner expected by the senior governments. Ottawa assumed that its own responsibility was to ensure the steady expansion of the Canadian economy. It became directly involved in supporting the housing market, by guaranteeing mortgages and acting as a lender of last resort.[69] This prevented the sort of blockage that had earlier inhibited suburban expansion even during periods of economic growth. The provinces were no less concerned than the federal government about removing any possible checks: this was one of their reasons for increasing conditional grants for improving public facilities in the cities. Aid of this kind to the municipal governments was more feasible than ever because of federal conditional grants to the provinces and new arrangements for sharing tax revenues, both of which had the effect of improving the financial position of the provincial governments.[70] The commitment of the provinces to the role the municipalities had adopted was reflected in legislation providing for zoning and planning.[71] The assumption on which these acts were based was that urban development would come at private initiative and that the municipal councils would play a regulatory role. Given that development was wanted, the local authorities had little alternative but to facilitate private enterprise.

This facilitative role fit in with the common conception of the appropriate functions of government. Acceptance of the welfare state and Keynesian economic management did not imply any change of heart with respect to private enterprise. The idea that government should be supportive of business remained intact. This was especially true at the local level, where municipal leaders had little responsibility for the new functions of government and could legitimately concentrate their efforts on promoting growth. By this time, the structures and practices that were advanced as ideals during the first wave of municipal reform had been widely adopted, especially in the larger cities. Business-like government was becoming the rule, and the question at issue was whether 'business' models had been misapplied. It was arguable, at least, that the federal and provincial governments provided a more appropriate model than the business corporation for municipal organization, and that many of the reforms introduced at an earlier period were reducing the effectiveness of the local authorities, even in their role as assistants to private business.

The most striking characteristic of municipal government was the fragmentation of authority. This took a number of different forms. There was a kind of internal fragmentation that appeared to have been avoided in the federal and provincial governments. In the latter authorities, the cabinet acted as a co-ordinating agency with full authority over administrative departments and effective control over the legislature. At the municipal level, no comparable agencies existed. Executive authority was sometimes vested in a board of control or board of commissioners, but the people in these bodies were not necessarily committed to common objectives and often lacked control over the municipal council. The glue of party discipline was missing. The municipal reformers, of course, had been largely responsible for giving partisanship a bad name at the local level. Moreover, the reforms they introduced – to discourage municipal councils from inadequately performing executive and administrative functions – had had the effect of creating a separation of powers on the American model, with all the attendant difficulties. To many later commentators it seemed that a more business-like government could be established if there were a fusion of powers, supported by partisan loyalties.[72]

The problems created by internal fragmentation were matched by those that arose from the division of powers between different local authorities. In any metropolitan community or region, there was likely to be a territorial division of authority among city, suburban, and rural governments. There might also be county governments although in Canada these never had authority over the cities.[73] Further complications were created by the presence of many independent or semi-independent local authorities, some of which had different boundaries than the municipalities. Among these were school boards, public utilities commissions, transit authorities, housing corporations, parks and library boards, and police commissions.[74] Since the functions of these bodies overlapped those of the municipalities, there was clearly a danger of poor co-ordination.

Many of the new generation of municipal reformers insisted on the need for consolidating local authority, so that there would be a single elected council responsible for every aspect of local administration.[75] If possible, the boundaries of the municipality would be made to correspond with those of the urban community.[76] The local council could then be expected to develop and enforce a coherent plan for physical expansion, which took account of social and environmental concerns and provided for an appropriate phasing of public and private investment. There would be no worry that the school board or a suburban council would undermine the scheme by authorizing inconsistent developments. The unified council would be able to develop a coherent plan for public expenditures taking account of city, suburban, and rural needs and paying due attention to the various functions of government. Taxation and borrowing could also be based on a unified plan, which took into consideration both the taxable capacity of the community and the concern for an equitable distribution of burdens. Public financing would no longer be undermined – and planning goals would no longer be subverted – by competition within the urban community for taxable assessment.[77]

The proposed integration of local authorities held out the promise of strengthening the political position of municipal government. So long as authority at the local level was highly fragmented, no body could speak for the local community in the way that the provincial government could speak for the province or the federal government could speak for the country. Since municipal councils were only involved in some of the activities of government, they were irrelevant to many important controversies and were often by-passed by politically active individuals and groups. This undermined the municipal claim to speak for the electorate with special democratic authority. The municipalities often failed to represent any obvious natural communities, and yet they claimed the right to make decisions that affected people far outside their boundaries. In overriding the demands of such authorities, the provincial governments could claim to be responding to the genuine needs of local communities. This usurpation of the natural political role of the municipality was a consequence of political fragmentation.

Regional or metropolitan government was supposed to provide for the political integration required – or such was the claim of reformers who pressed for consolidation in virtually every Canadian province after 1950. Metropolitan or regional authorities were established in most of the major

Canadian cities by the 1970s (and there was a parallel move in the rural areas to consolidate municipalities into larger units).[78] However, there was no apparent strengthening of municipal government in relation to the provinces. The new authorities were generally imposed on top of the existing ones, so that the metropolitan communities were no more capable than before of speaking with a single voice. Although there were some gestures towards the elimination of special-purpose bodies, most of them remained in place, so that municipal governments were no more comprehensive in function than before. From a provincial perspective, the purpose of metropolitan consolidation was not to create political rivals, but to provide for more effective administration at the local level. This involved geographical and functional integration, but not to the extent required to turn the municipalities into potent political authorities.

The hesitancy of the provinces in promoting integration was matched by resistance at the local level.[79] The autonomy enjoyed by suburban governments and special-purpose boards was greatly prized by those whose particular concerns or interests were advanced by these authorities. Local self-government, as frequently conceived, involved the dispersal of authority to parochial communities and special-interest groups. Political and administrative integration threatened to deprive these groups of their customary power and to deny them their local sovereignty. Thus the drive to consolidate could be sensibly resisted in the name of municipal autonomy, even if the ultimate effect was to prevent the municipalities from achieving a political status comparable to that of the provinces. This abnegation of political ambition had its counterpart in the conventional insistence of municipal politicians that their activities were outside partisan politics. If so, they did not have to be taken so seriously: the municipal leaders could be treated as the business-like administrators they claimed to be, which meant relegating them to an inferior political status.

Reformers decried this devaluation of municipal politics, and there were attempts from the 1960s on to mobilize partisan sentiment in an effort to invigorate municipal government.[80] These attempts did not meet with great success, because the type of invigoration envisaged had little appeal to most of those interested in local government. It still was as true as ever that partisan conflict was a threat to what the people interested in urban development regarded as responsible management. Whatever its theoretical value as a means for political mobilization, partisan conflict could only be relevant to the management of growth if that management were called into question. This was not something that existing municipal leaders, provincial politicians, or, indeed, most of the advocates of partisanship wanted to do. When it was eventually mounted, the assault on the management of growth came from a different direction.

THE NEW POLITICS OF REFORM

The Canadian municipalities presided over a great transformation in the twenty-five years after the end of the Second World War. The migration to the cities from the country was supplemented by foreign immigration, which ultimately came from every part of Europe and, in later years, from Third World countries. This had the effect of diversifying even the most homogeneous cities.[81] The increase of urban population was such that the major metropolitan areas doubled and redoubled in size. They spread geographically far beyond their original boundaries, so that central cities often were left with only a minority of the total metropolitan population. The characteristic suburban development was of single-family dwellings that were spread over huge tracts of former farm land. The cheaper land of the suburbs proved attractive to manufacturers and wholesalers who began to follow the outward migration, bringing some of their workers with them. Retailers moved to suburban shopping centres to capture the market in the subdivisions. These settlements were at such a low density that automotive transportation became virtually a necessity. Every effort was made to increase its convenience, and this had the effect of spreading things out and reinforcing the necessity for cars. Suburban life was relatively expensive – although not necessarily attractive to the rich – so that inner cities tended to be left to the immigrants and working class, except for pockets of choice location. Although the division this produced was not as pronounced (or racially marked) as it was in the United States, the effects were still important.[82]

One of the ironies of the post-war urban spread was that it separated the most prosperous suburbanites from their natural places of business. Although factories and warehouses could move to the suburbs, this was not the case for most major offices, which still required central locations. Thus the managerial and professional jobs filled by the upper middle class still tended to be located downtown. This put a considerable strain on urban transportation systems, for the lawyer or banker who lived in the suburbs had to get to his office in the city (while the factory worker, who could not afford to live in the suburbs, often had to make his way to a plant on the fringes). Serving the suburbs by public transport was extraordinarily expensive, because of the spread of low-density settlement. Thus it was only by improving arterial roads and constructing urban expressways that the demands of commuters could be met. Unfortunately, each improvement stimulated further spread and intensified use of the roads so that the problems at hand were hardly alleviated. What is more, the road improvements disrupted established urban neighbourhoods, which were not planned, like the suburbs, to provide for intensive automobile use. As houses were torn down, trees cut down, and roads widened to make room for the cars, some of the adverse effects of the post-war expansion became apparent.

These effects were intensified by efforts to redevelop the downtown areas. These areas were threatened by the loss of business to the suburbs. Developers attempted (with municipal aid) to compensate for the loss by capitalizing on the value of downtown location. This meant building new office complexes, convention centres, entertainment facilities, and shopping malls of a type that could not be supported in a suburb. Since the land concerned was already occupied, this new construction depended on demolition and redevelopment. The municipalities often aided in the acquisition of land, as well as in other ways.[83] Most of these projects were commercially successful, so that the cores of the major Canadian cities retained their economic vitality to an extent unknown in many of their American counterparts. The continuing importance of downtown employment, combined with the increasing costs of commuting, stimulated residential redevelopment in the central cities. This meant high-rise apartment construction, of a type that served the needs of both the high-income professional and the low-income clerk or stenographer. Again such construction depended on demolition. It also had the effect of multiplying residential densities in what had often been quiet downtown neighbourhoods.

High-density apartment development was not confined to the central cities, for suburban housing requirements ultimately could not be met by relying on single-family dwellings. Low-income people who worked in the suburbs needed more conveniently located housing, and this could be provided most economically in the form of apartments. The suburbs faced pressure from both the central cities and the higher authorities to permit such development, since it could not be accommodated in the central areas except at enormous cost. By the 1970s, the price of suburban land had risen to such an extent (for reasons that are fiercely debated) that low-density suburban development was becoming less feasible.[84] Affordable housing for rent or purchase increasingly took the form of an apartment or town house. At the same time, improved transportation and communications made the dispersal of office and commercial activities to the suburbs more feasible and reduced the advantages of downtown location for many businesses. A polynucleated pattern of development emerged as suburban centres grew in significance. This pattern combined with higher-density residential developments in the suburbs to reduce the gap that had opened between suburban and central-city life.

Nevertheless, it was in the central cities that the adverse effects of rapid urban growth were most apparent and where the reaction against it set in the 1960s. The demolition of houses to make way for new roads, apartment buildings, and office complexes became symbolic of the costs of expansion. Downtown tenants were particularly vulnerable, because they normally did not receive any compensation when the buildings they occupied were condemned to make way for new developments. The low-income householder was often forced into a worse or more expensive form of accommodation, and the small businessmen frequently found that it was impossible to relocate successfully. Home-owners were in a better position, but they were sometimes forced to sell at an unfavourable price because of the 'block-busting' tactics of developers. Municipalities anxious for growth sometimes assisted the developers by expropriating the necessary land, and the prices offered for expropriated property were extremely low. Even those who were not obliged to move often found the quality of neighbourhood life to have dropped. Traffic was greater, noise and street congestion increased, and the special qualities of the area (the ethnic mix, the style of life, the park-like setting) seemed no longer apparent. When people saw this happening to other neighbourhoods and then were faced with a threat to their own, they had a strong incentive to band together to protect what they had. This is exactly what happened with increasing frequency after 1965.

The new reform politics of the late 1960s and the 1970s grew out of such protest.[85] Its most remarkable feature was a questioning of the verities of traditional municipal reform. Even the latter-day advocates of metropolitan integration and partisan mobilization had continued to accept – in fact, to advance – a corporate conception of municipal government. They wanted recognition of the corporate unity of the metropolitan area. They talked of the need for corporate planning, under the aegis of a strong political executive. They wanted the functions of local government to be considered as a corporate whole, and the social, economic, physical, and financial plans for the municipality to be developed in relation to one another, and in light of a clear idea of the corporate good. This represented an advance from the idea that the municipality was merely a joint-stock company, but the corporate integration implicit in the latter conception was imported into the new view. The protest politics of the late 1960s was directed against the practices that followed from the corporate conception. Sacrificing the neighbourhood to the larger community, observing the proprieties of bureaucratic procedure, respecting the judgments of professional planners, and accepting the leadership of elected officials all seemed to lead to the 'wrong' results in terms of urban development. Thus the protesters were obliged to re-evaluate practices and structures associated with pre-reform politics.

Of particular importance was the idea that municipal politics should be rooted in the ward or neighbourhood, as it was supposed to have been in nineteenth-century cities. Neighbourhoods now were threatened by urban development, so neighbourhoods had to be organized to protect their interests. At this level people would and could be more directly involved in political activity, so that neighbourhood organizations could speak with special authority. Candidates for municipal office might come out of these organizations and be elected with their support. Accountability to the neighbourhood could then be maintained on a continuous basis. The federal or provincial parties would not be welcome as organizing agents, because they would tend to divide the neighbourhoods more than unite them. Purely civic parties, formed by the fusion of neighbourhood organizations and other sympathetic bodies, could be of greater value. The relevant partisan division for most of the new reformers was between the defenders of the neighbourhoods and neighbourhood values on the one hand, and the supporters of traditional urban development on the other. This was a division that cut across traditional party lines.[86]

The advocates of community politics were somewhat ambivalent about the role of government. On the one hand, they wanted a new sense of social concern upon the part of local authorities, to be manifested in innovative public programs. On the other hand, they were suspicious of public bureaucracies and favoured a dispersal of authority and responsibility among community organizations, co-operatives, and other voluntary agencies. This entailed a return to arrangements closer to the nineteenth-century model. Intellectual support for a move in this direction came from critics of modern bureaucratic government, who suggested that earlier beliefs in large-scale governments, comprehensive planning, and bureaucratic organization were based on mistaken assumptions about the virtues of centralization and coordination.[87] The view was that a dispersal of authority would stimulate initiative, encourage healthy competition, and make the agencies concerned more responsive to the people they were supposed to serve. Support for this view came from critics on both the right and the left politically and from the advocates of both communitarian values and intensified economic competition.

The new reform politics was, like the old, an attack on the whole style of municipal government. As such, it called every 'traditional' politician into question. What had changed, of course, was that the traditional politicians had adopted many of the practices suggested by the early reformers, so that they were defending non-partisan, business-like professionalism against a twentieth-century version of Jacksonian democracy. To them, the new populist reformers were either radical agitators or potential ward-heelers, whose particularistic demands had to be resisted in the general interest. The new reformers suspected that the traditional politicians and their civic officials were 'fronting' for development interests.[88] Non-partisanship and professionalism appeared to veil the realities of power and interest – to conceal the bias inherent in the way the system worked. The reformers' attacks were intended to expose this bias and force a polarization. It was natural to suppose that the 'élitist' principles defended by the traditional politicians would have to be overthrown along with the interests they represented.

The attacks of the reformers generated debate on the issues of urban development and citizen participation.[89] People took an interest in urban politics who had ignored it before, and at least a partial polarization of the electorate occurred in a number of major cities. The shift of opinion in favour of the reformers, and against the politicians who did not respond to the concern for protecting neighbourhoods or who refused to listen to citizen protests, had a perceptible impact on the conduct of municipal affairs. None the less, it would be difficult to say that municipal government was dramatically different in 1980 from what it had been in 1960. Most of the conditions that had led municipal councils to be supportive of urban growth and to aid the private developer were still extant. The advantages to everyone of a healthy, expanding local economy were as apparent as ever, and economic expansion still depended on physical development. The municipalities relied on the private developer for his initiative and were afraid of destroying the climate for investment. The senior governments expected the local authorities to do their part as before, and this was generally true of the local electorates, despite their concern for closer control of new developments. Thus, even when they achieved local office, the new reform politicians were obliged to adopt a moderate line.

In most cities, of course, the traditional politicians were not displaced by reformers – or, if they were, the reformers were traditionalists in disguise. Part of their secret was that the practice of patronage had not been altogether abandoned when political and administrative reforms were adopted in an earlier era. The nineteenth-century style of government and politics was overlaid by that of the early twentieth: although the former may have been disguised, it did not disappear, and it remained a source of political strength for traditional leaders. The irony was that established politicians could defend professionalism and non-partisan, business-like government partly because they could count on the kind of clientelist loyalties that early reformers had deplored. The support of a well-oiled ward or a sturdy ethnic base was the best protection against the new reformers. Failing this, the best strategy was to adopt the reformers' slogans and to accede to a few of their demands. This could usually be done with relatively little adjustment, although many established politicians were slow to realize this. Where the adjustment was made, the result was another overlaying of political styles, without a fundamental change in the character of municipal politics.

The economic crisis that began in the 1970s again brought the 'cutters' and 'boosters' to the fore in municipal politics. They could claim that the problem was no longer one of excessive growth, but of declining economic activity. The solutions they suggested were to cut municipal spending (to relieve burdens on the ratepayers) and to boost the local economy by stimulating construction and offering incentives to industry and commerce. Boosting and cutting were ever more frequently presented as complementary policies, with broad support from the business community.[90] The federal and provincial governments, themselves under enormous pressure to move in the same direction, made it difficult for the municipalities to adopt a different response. In some communities at least, this has had the effect of sharpening the cleavage at the municipal level between left and right, for the things to be sacrificed in the interests of economic growth are the gains most dear to the left: a high level of social services, controls over business investment, and high wages for workers in the public sector. The issues that had been raised by the new reformers had polarized people in new ways and created political links across barriers of class and ideology. As these issues faded and the new ones arose, those who remained committed to reform tended to align themselves with the traditional left, and so to reproduce the cleavages existing at other levels of government.[91]

In this context, the relative autonomy of municipal from provincial and federal politics may be difficult to sustain. Certainly for a traditional opposition party such as the New Democratic Party (NDP), municipal politics has become highly attractive as a means of establishing contact with the electorate. Once one party becomes involved, the others will be tempted to follow. In no Canadian city has this process gone far enough to produce an open contest at the municipal level between the major political parties. None the less, partisan concerns are quite apparent in many municipal contests, and they clearly colour municipal-provincial relations. The gap between municipal and other politics has also been closing; the techniques of campaigning pioneered at other levels – polling, television and radio advertising, telephoning voters, and so on – are being used more frequently at the municipal level. This represents a step away from 'community politics,' both as advocated by the new populist reformers and as practiced by traditional municipal politicians. The ultimate effects on the vitality of municipal politics are difficult to predict.

INTERPRETING THE PATTERN

It is not the purpose of this introduction to offer a definitive interpretation of city politics in Canada. However, one thing that emerges from this historical overview is that municipal politics traditionally has been different from federal or provincial politics – so different that many have been reluctant to consider it 'politics' at all. The idea that municipal affairs are outside politics reflects the popular belief that politics is a matter of party activity. One of the advantages of approaching the study of Canadian politics from the municipal level – an advantage that, sadly, has yet to be fully exploited – is that it forces one's attention away from the political parties and away from the legislatures they dominate to the rich field of political activity beyond. It is there that the realities of Canadian politics and government will be found. As students of urban affairs have long been aware, it is impossible to grasp those realities by a political science that sets itself apart from the study of history, geography, economics, or sociology. To understand the politics of cities is to understand those communities as wholes.

The studies that follow – of Montreal, Toronto, Ottawa, Halifax, Vancouver, Winnipeg, and Edmonton – are all 'holistic.' What is offered in each is a general account of the historical evolution and contemporary form of a major civic polity. The cities chosen for study are arguably the seven most important and influential in the country.[92] In that sense they are unrepresentative, but each is of interest in its own right, and together they form a group about which we may make some useful generalizations. For practical reasons, our authors have focused on the central municipalities of these metropolitan areas. As such, they have been obliged to leave out much of what might otherwise be regarded as a part of city politics. The activities of special-purpose bodies, suburban municipalities, metropolitan agencies, and local agencies of the provincial and federal governments are not considered in detail. To understand the larger whole of local politics is our obvious aim, but we must begin somewhere, and it seems logical to start with the agencies that were orginally supposed to be the central governments of the cities concerned.

Our authors have no political stance or methodological bias in common. Their analytic approach is eclectic, for they are more concerned to convey what is known than to demonstrate the merits of any particular theoretical approach. In their accounts, they rely on a literature that is strong in institutional description and weak in analysis of municipal political behaviour[93] and the political economy of local government.[94] No doubt, the strengths and the weaknesses of that literature show through in this book. What we all hope is to stimulate our readers to overcome the weaknesses, and in particular to begin the hard task of subjecting city politics in Canada to critical, comparative analysis. Out of such analysis is bound to come a very different conception of the Canadian political system than emerges from the standard texts that focus on the government in Ottawa.[95]

SUGGESTED FURTHER READING

Artibise, Alan F.J. and Gilbert A. Stelter ed *The Usable Urban Past: Planning and Politics in the Modern Canadian City* Toronto 1979

Banfield, Edward C. and James Q. Wilson *City Politics* Cambridge, Mass, 1963

Bellan, Ruben C. *The Evolving City* Vancouver 1971

Bish, Robert L. and Vincent Ostrom *Understanding Urban Government: Metropolitan Reform Reconsidered* Washington 1973

Bollens, John C. and Henry J. Schmandt *The Metropolis* 3rd edn New York 1975

Feldman, Lionel D. ed *Politics and Government of Urban Canada* 4th edn Toronto 1981

Fraser, Graham *Fighting Back: Urban Renewal in Trefann Court* Toronto 1972

Gertler, Len, and Ron Crowley *Changing Canadian Cities: The Next 25 Years* Toronto 1977

Hall, Peter *Urban and Regional Planning* London 1974

Higgins, Donald J.H. *Urban Canada: Its Government and Politics* Toronto 1977

Kaplan, Harold *Urban Political Systems: A Functional Analysis of Metro Toronto* New York 1967

Leo, Christopher *The Politics of Urban Development: Canadian Urban Expressway Disputes* Toronto 1977

Lorimer, James *A Citizen's Guide to City Politics* Toronto 1972

Masson, J.K. and James D. Anderson ed *Emerging Party Politics in Urban Canada* Toronto 1972

Nader, George A. *Cities of Canada* 2 vols Toronto 1975–6

Peterson, Paul E. *City Limits* Chicago 1981

Saunders, Peter *Urban Politics: A Sociological Interpretation* London 1979

Stelter, Gilbert A. and Alan F.J. Artibise ed *The Canadian City: Essays in Urban History* Toronto 1977

Weaver, John C. *Shaping the Canadian City: Essays on Urban Politics and Policy, 1890–1920* Toronto 1977

Williams, Oliver P. *Metropolitan Political Analysis* New York 1971

NOTES

1 This is a paradoxical claim, for the authors concerned have gone to great lengths to specify the institutional differences between municipal governments in Canada. Underlying this effort, however, is the assumption that municipal government and politics are essentially the same from coast to coast and that the variations are all on a common theme.

2 The best single reference is Donald J.H. Higgins *Urban Canada: Its Government and Politics* (Toronto 1977) – a book that is much more sensitive than its competitors to the politics of municipal government. On the structures and administrative processes of local government, see also T.J. Plunkett and G.M. Betts *The Management of Canadian Urban Government* (Kingston 1978), C.R. Tindal and A.N. Tindal *Local Government in Canada* (Toronto 1979), T.J. Plunkett *Urban Canada and Its Government: A Study of Municipal Organization* (Toronto 1968), and K.G. Crawford *Canadian Municipal Government* (Toronto 1954). Descriptions of the institutional structures of metropolitan Calgary, Edmonton, Halifax-Dartmouth, Hamilton-Wentworth, Montreal, Ottawa-Hull, Quebec, Toronto, Vancouver, and Winnipeg are also available in the Profile series (1974–5) issued by the now defunct federal Ministry of State for Urban Affairs. On the physical, social, and economic development of Canadian cities, see Len Gertler and Ron Crowley *Changing Canadian Cities: The Next 25 Years* (Toronto 1977), G.A. Nader *Cities of Canada* 2 vols (Toronto 1975–6), and James W. Simmons 'The Evolution of the Canadian Urban System' in A.F.J. Artibise and G.A. Stelter ed *The Usable Urban Past: Planning and Politics in the Modern Canadian City* (Toronto 1979) 9–33.

3 For an analysis of this system of local government, see Sidney and Beatrice Webb *The Development of English Local Government, 1689–1835* (London 1963), taken from their monumental study *English Local Government* 11 vols (London 1911–22). Other histories of local government in England tend to concentrate on the period since 1835, but see K.B. Smellie *A History of Local Government* 4th edn (London 1968) 9–22 for a brief summary of the English system as it existed when Canada was settled.

4 John George Bourinot *Local Government in Canada* (Baltimore 1887). On the institutions of the *ancien régime*, see Gustave Lanctot 'Le régime municipal

en Nouvelle-France' *Culture* IX (1948) 255–83 and Maurice Bordes *L'Administration provinciale et municipale en France au XVIIIe siècle* (Paris 1972).

5 S.J.R. Noel *Politics in Newfoundland* (Toronto 1971) 3–25. See also *Report of the Royal Commission on Municipal Government in Newfoundland and Labrador* (St John's 1974).

6 J.H. Aitchison 'The Municipal Corporations Act of 1849' *Canadian Historical Review* XXX (1949) 107–22. The original system in Canada was based on contemporary English practice, which gave effective control over locally appointed parish or township officers to centrally appointed county magistrates. More local autonomy eventually was granted to 'cities' and 'police towns,' the first of which were incorporated in the 1830s. The Baldwin Act made municipal self-government the rule throughout Upper Canada. See Adam Shortt, 'Municipal History, 1791–1867' in Shortt and Arthur G. Doughty ed *Canada and Its Provinces* (Toronto 1913–17) XVIII 403–52 and G.P. de T. Glazebrook 'The Origins Of Local Government' in F.H. Armstrong et al ed *Aspects of Nineteenth Century Ontario* (Toronto 1974) 36–74. On the subsequent evolution of local government in Ontario, see K.W. McKay 'Municipal History, 1867–1913' in Shortt and Doughty *Canada and Its Provinces* XVIII 455–510 and Romaine K. Ross *Local Government in Ontario* 2nd edn (Toronto 1962). In Lower Canada, Anglo-French hostilities inhibited the development of municipal institutions, but the system as established in 1855 was surprisingly similar. See Shortt and Doughty *Canada and Its Provinces* XV 285–320 and Roger Bussières *Le régime municipal de la province de Québec* (Quebec 1964).

7 Henri Pirenne *Medieval Cities: Their Origins and the Revival of Trade* (Princeton 1939) 168–212. More generally, see Max Weber *The City* (New York 1958), Lewis Mumford *The City in History* (New York 1961), and R.C. Bellan *The Evolving City* (Vancouver 1971).

8 Ernest S. Griffith *History of American City Government: The Colonial Period* (New York 1938)

9 Jon C. Teaford *The Municipal Revolution in America: The Origins of Modern Urban Government, 1650–1825* (Chicago 1975), W. Ivor Jennings 'The Municipal Revolution' in H.J. Laski et al ed *A Century of Municipal Progress, 1835–1935* (London 1935) 55–65, and Josef Redlich and F.W. Hirst *Local Government in England* 2 vols (London 1903)

10 Richard B. Splane *Social Welfare in Ontario, 1791–1893: A Study of Public Welfare Administration* (Toronto 1965) and Margaret K. Strong *Public Welfare Administration in Canada* (Chicago 1930). In the Atlantic provinces, poor relief was (as in England but not in the Canadas) a municipal responsibility: Judith Fingard 'The Relief of the Unemployed: The Poor in Saint John, Halifax, and St. John's, 1815–1860' in G.A. Stelter and A.F.J. Artibise ed *The*

Canadian City: Essays in Urban History (Toronto 1977) 341–67. See also John Taylor 'The Urban West: Public Welfare and a Theory of Urban Development' in A.R. McCormack and Ian MacPherson ed *Cities in the West* (Ottawa 1975) 286–313.

11 J. Donald Wilson et al ed *Canadian Education: A History* (Scarborough 1970)

12 S. Morley Wickett 'City Government in Canada' in Wickett ed *Municipal Government in Canada* (Toronto 1907) 10

13 On the history of local government in the Maritimes, see H.J. Whalen *The Development of Local Government in New Brunswick* (Fredericton 1963), J.M. Beck *The Evolution of Municipal Government in Nova Scotia* (Halifax 1973), and F. McKinnon *The Government of Prince Edward Island* 274–86. More generally, see Crawford *Canadian Municipal Government* 19–47, Higgins *Urban Canada* 15–44, and Tindal *Local Government in Canada* 1–18 for surveys of the development of municipal institutions in each province of Canada.

14 There is a good brief survey of the early development of American municipal institutions in George S. Blair *American Local Government* (New York 1964) 18–40. Earlier American texts offer more information: Thomas H. Reed *Municipal Government in the United States* (New York 1926), William B. Munro *The Government of American Cities* (New York 1912), John A. Fairlie *Local Government in Counties, Towns and Villages* (New York 1906), and George E. Howard *An Introduction to the Local Constitutional History of the United States* (Baltimore 1889).

15 This principle was reaffirmed by Subsection 92(8) of the British North America Act of 1867, which reserved to the provincial legislatures the exclusive right to 'make Laws in relation to ... Municipal Institutions in the Province.'

16 In England, the most forceful exponent of local sovereignty was Joshua Toulmin-Smith: see his *Local Self-Government and Centralization* (London 1851) and *The Parish* 2nd edn (London 1857). In the United States, such localism was more common. It found inspiration in the works of such men as Thomas Jefferson and institutional expression in the arrangements for 'municipal home rule' adopted in many states after 1875. However, Dillon's Rule – first articulated in 1868 and confirmed by the Supreme Court in 1907 – established the same constitutional principle as had been accepted in Britain and Canada: that the states were sovereign in relation to their municipalities. On the evolution of American thinking, see Anwar H. Syed *The Political Theory of American Local Government* (New York 1966).

17 Unless a municipality can point to some specific statutory authority for its acts (i.e. to some definite provision in provincial legislation), the courts will consider these acts illegal – *ultra vires*, or beyond the powers of the municipality. Crawford *Canadian Municipal Government* 48–54 offers a short sum-

mary of the legal situation. The standard text on the subject is Ian M. Rogers *The Law of Canadian Municipal Corporations* 2nd ed (Toronto 1971–).

18 This is implicit in the distinction between different types of municipalities: (in Ontario) townships, villages, towns, cities, counties, and (recently) regional municipalities. Each type of municipality has slightly different powers under provincial legislation: 'cities' traditionally have had the most.

19 John Garner *The Franchise and Politics in British North America, 1755–1867* (Toronto 1969)

20 'When you look closely at the functions of city government, it becomes quite apparent that almost everything city hall does is related to real estate. In fact, the real business of city government *is* property'; James Lorimer *A Citizen's Guide to City Politics* (Toronto 1972) 4.

21 On the English pattern, see Derek Fraser *Urban Politics in Victorian England: The Structure of Politics in Victorian Cities* (Leicester 1976). There is no comparable account of American local politics before 1870, but see Jerome Mushkat *Tammany: The Evolution of a Political Machine, 1789–1865* (Syracuse, NY, 1971) on New York City.

22 The best short discussion of this subject is S.J.R. Noel 'Leadership and Clientelism' in D.J. Bellamy et al ed *The Provincial Political Systems: Comparative Essays* (Toronto 1976) 197–213. See also Michael Katz *The People of Hamilton, Canada West: Family and Class in a Mid-Nineteenth Century City* (Cambridge, Mass, 1975).

23 H.G. Thorburn ed *Party Politics in Canada* 3rd edn (Scarborough 1972) 2–22

24 Various explanations have been offered for the withdrawal of the major parties from the municipal arena. See Jack K. Masson and James D. Anderson ed *Emerging Party Politics in Urban Canada* (Toronto 1972) 5–21 and 192–202 for accounts that differ in emphasis from the one offered here.

25 The politically disruptive temperance movement became powerful only in the latter part of the nineteenth century. On earlier efforts at social control, see Susan Houston 'Politics, Schools, and Social Change in Upper Canada' *Canadian Historical Review* LIII (1972) 249–71.

26 Part 2 of Bellan *The Evolving City* reviews the development of municipal functions globally. See also John A. Fairlie *Municipal Administration* (New York 1901), Asa Briggs *Victorian Cities* (London 1963), and Sam Bass Warner *The Urban Wilderness: A History of the American City* (New York 1972). No general history has been written of the development of municipal functions in Canada, but see Shortt and Doughty *Canada and Its Provinces* XV 306–15, XVIII 413–25, 431–51, 475–94; Wickett *Municipal Government in Canada*; and John Taylor ed 'Fire, Disease, and Water in the Nineteenth Century City' *Urban History Review* VIII (1979) 7–116, for some details.

27 Railways were the prime beneficiaries of municipal largesse in the nineteenth century. Jacob Spelt *Urban Development in South-Central Ontario* (Assen, Netherlands, 1955) 100–6 and Shortt and Doughty *Canada and Its Provinces* XVIII 443–51 discuss the unhappy experience of the Ontario municipalities that competed for railways in the 1850s. Similar competition occurred elsewhere: John Gilpin 'Failed Metropolis: The City of Strathcona, 1891–1912' in Alan F.J. Artibise ed *Town and City: Aspects of Western Canadian Urban Development* (Regina 1981) 259–88 offers an exemplary tale from Alberta. In the last decades of the century, efforts to attract manufacturing industry led to new forms of competition: see Tom Naylor *The History of Canadian Business* II (Toronto 1976) 130–60 and Elizabeth Bloomfield 'Municipal Bonusing of Industry: The Legislative Framework in Ontario to 1930' *Urban History Review* IX 3 (1981) 59–76.

28 The term 'ratepayers' refers to those who pay 'rates' or taxes on real estate that are levied by municipal or other local authorities: hence it is synonymous with holders of real property and not with the citizenry as a whole. Originally, of course, only ratepayers were citizens in the fullest sense. The term 'cutters' is my own invention, but 'boosters' and 'boosterism' are part of the common parlance of urban history: see, for example, Alan F.J. Artibise 'Boosterism and the Development of Prairie Cities, 1871–1913' in Artibise *Town and City* 209–35.

29 In Ontario, for instance, the universal franchise for municipal elections was established only in 1972 (although some cities had adopted it by 1959). Crawford *Canadian Municipal Government* 138–62 reviews franchise provisions as they existed in the 1950s. Higgins *Urban Canada* 245–52 provides more current information. Compare T.H. Qualter *The Election Process in Canada* (Toronto 1970) 1–40 on the development of the federal and provincial franchises.

30 There are few studies of small-town (or even small-city) politics in Canada, but some impressions may be gained from Horace Miner *St. Denis: A French Canadian Parish* (Chicago 1939), Everett C. Hughes *French Canada in Transition* (Chicago 1943), Rex A. Lucas *Minetown, Milltown, Railtown: Life in Canadian Communities of Single Industry* (Toronto 1971), Anthony Cohen *The Management of Myths: The Politics of Legitimation in a Newfoundland Community* (St John's 1975), Neville O. Matthews 'Small Town Power and Politics' in L.D. Feldman and M.D. Goldrick ed *Politics and Government of Urban Canada* 3rd edn (Toronto 1976) 156–75, and Graeme Lang 'Shopping Centres: The Case Study of Corner Brook' in James Lorimer and Carolyn MacGregor ed *After the Developers* (Toronto 1981) 46–61. See also Paul Voisey 'Boosting the Small Prairie Town, 1904–1931: An Example from South-

ern Alberta' in Artibise *Town and City* 147–76 and Gilbert A. Stelter 'Community Development in Toronto's Commercial Empire: The Industrial Towns of the Nickel Belt, 1883–1931' *Laurentian University Review* VI (1974) 3–54. On somewhat larger communities, see A.W. Rasporich 'Faction and Class in Modern Lakehead Politics' *Lakehead University Review* VII (1974) 31–65, Alan Alexander 'The Institutional and Role Perception of Local Aldermen' in Feldman and Goldrick *Politics and Government* 3rd edn 186–99, Elizabeth Bloomfield 'Economy, Necessity, Political Reality: Town Planning Efforts in Kitchener-Waterloo, 1912–1925' *Urban History Review* IX (1980) 3–48, Conrad Winn and John McMenemy 'Political Alignment in a Polarized City: Electoral Cleavages in Kitchener, Ontario' *Canadian Journal of Political Science* VI (1973) 230–42, Jack Pasternak *The Kitchener Market Fight* (Toronto 1975), and Caroline Andrew et al *Les Élites politiques, les bas-salariés et la politique du logement à Hull* (Ottawa 1976).

31 Asa Briggs 'Birmingham: The Making of a Civic Gospel' in Briggs *Victorian Cities* 184–240

32 See Derek Fraser *Power and Authority in the Victorian City* (Oxford 1979) on the 'municipalization of local government' in England between 1835 and 1888. The municipal councils in this period became the primary local authorities and were expected increasingly to act as positive governments.

33 The Fabian Society *The Fabian Municipal Programme* first series (1891) and second series (1899–1901) and *The New Heptarchy Series* (1905) give an indication of this socialist thinking. (The term 'socialist' here is used in its loosest sense.) See also Sidney and Beatrice Webb *A Constitution for the Socialist Commonwealth of Great Britain* (London 1920) and G.D.H. Cole *The Future of Local Government* (London 1921).

34 Ken Young *Local Politics and the Rise of Party: The London Municipal Society and the Conservative Intervention in Local Elections, 1894–1963* (Leicester 1975) attacks the myth that the Labour party was solely responsible for the intensification of partisan conflict. As Derek Fraser makes clear, local politics in the nineteenth century was always partisan in some degree: *Urban Politics in Victorian England*. On twentieth-century party politics in English local government, see J.G. Bulpitt *Party Politics in English Local Government* (London 1967), L.J. Sharpe ed *Voting in Cities* (London 1967), and John Gyford *Local Politics in Britain* (London 1976).

35 On the modern development of English local government, see Laski *A Century of Municipal Progress*, William A. Robson *The Development of Local Government* 3rd edn (London 1954), Smellie *A History of Local Government*, and Bryan Keith-Lucas and Peter G. Richards *A History of Local Government in the Twentieth Century* (London 1978). There are many valuable studies of

particular local government functions: for example, Derek Fraser *The Evolution of the British Welfare State: A History of Social Policy since the Industrial Revolution* (London 1973), William Ashworth *The Genesis of Modern British Town Planning* (London 1954), Peter Hall *Urban and Regional Planning* (London 1974), J.A. Critchley *A History of the Police in England and Wales, 1900–1966* (London 1967), W.H.G. Armytage *Four Hundred Years of English Education* (London 1964), J.B. Cullingworth *Housing and Local Government in England and Wales* (London 1966), and Herman Finer *Municipal Trading* (London 1941).

36 On the American movement for municipal reform, see Martin J. Schiesl *The Politics of Efficiency: Municipal Administration and Reform in America, 1800–1920* (Berkeley 1977), James Weinstein *The Corporate Ideal in the Liberal State: 1900–1918* (Boston 1968), Blaine A. Brownell and Warren E. Stickle ed *Bosses and Reformers: Urban Politics in America, 1880–1920* (Boston 1973), Paul Boyer *Urban Masses and Moral Order in America, 1880–1920* (Cambridge, Mass, 1978), and Michael H. Ebner and Eugene M. Tobin ed *The Age of Urban Reform: New Perspectives on the Progressive Era* (Port Washington, NY, 1977).

37 Martin Shefter 'The Emergence of the Political Machine: An Alternative View' in Willis Hawley et al *Theoretical Perspectives on Urban Politics* (Englewood Cliffs, NJ, 1976) 14–44. See also Alexander B. Callow jr ed *The City Boss in America: An Interpretive Reader* (New York 1976), and Bruce M. Stave ed *Urban Bosses, Machines and Progressive Reformers* (Lexington, Mass, 1972).

38 Bradley R. Price *Progressive Cities: The Commission Government Movement in America, 1901–1920* (Austin, Texas, 1977) and Richard J. Stillman II *The Rise of the City Manager* (Albuquerque, NM, 1974).

39 The American reformers were ambivalent about municipal democracy. They wanted to reduce the number of elected officials in local government and generally to insulate municipal administration from politics. Especially in the early years, some of them advocated restrictions on the franchise (which was generally wider than in Canada). In contrast, many later reformers gave support to populist proposals that would allow for direct popular legislation. Such measures were apparently acceptable because they seemed consistent with non-partisan, business-like government: they provided only a check on the abuse of power and not a means for day-to-day popular intervention in municipal affairs. See William B. Munro ed *The Initiative, Referendum and Recall* (New York 1912) for the contemporary debate.

40 Robert K. Merton *Social Theory and Social Structure* (New York 1957) 71–82 and Edward C. Banfield and James Q. Wilson *City Politics* (Cambridge, Mass,

1963) 115–27. The party machines offered support for many reforms of benefit to the lower class; see John D. Buenker *Urban Liberalism and Progressive Reform* (New York 1973).

41 Mel Scott *American City Planning since 1890* (Berkeley 1971), Roy Lubove *The Progressives and the Slums: Tenement House Reform in New York City, 1900–1917* (Pittsburgh 1962), Lubove *The Professional Altruist: The Emergence of Social Work as a Career, 1880–1930* (Cambridge, Mass, 1965), Allen F. Davis *Spearheads for Reform: The Social Settlements and the Progressive Movement, 1890–1914* (New York 1967), and Lawrence A. Cremin *The Transformation of the School: Progressivism in American Education, 1876–1957* (New York 1961)

42 On the Canadian movement, see Paul Rutherford ed *Saving the Canadian City: The First Phase 1880–1920* (Toronto 1974), John C. Weaver *Shaping the Canadian City: Essays on Urban Politics and Policy, 1880–1920* (Toronto 1977), Stelter and Artibise *The Canadian City* 368–418, Artibise and Stelter *The Usable Urban Past* 39–111, H.V. Nelles and Christopher Armstrong 'The Great Fight for Clean Government' *Urban History Review* no 2 (1976) 50–66. See also William B. Munro *American Influences on Canadian Government* (Toronto 1929). Thanks partly to the American influence, non-partisanship in municipal politics became an explicit ideological principle in Canada after 1890.

43 See Appendix, Tables 1 and 2 for historical population data.

44 On urban conditions in this period, see Terry Copp *The Anatomy of Poverty: The Condition of the Working Class in Montreal, 1897–1921* (Toronto 1974), Michael J. Piva *The Condition of the Working Class in Toronto, 1900–1921* (Ottawa 1979), Greg Kealey ed *Canada Investigates Industrialism: The Royal Commission on the Relations of Labor and Capital, 1889* (Toronto 1973), Michael S. Cross ed *The Workingman in the Nineteenth Century* (Toronto 1974), A.F.J. Artibise *Winnipeg: A Social History of Urban Growth, 1874–1914* (Montreal 1975).

45 The most detailed account of this process is in Peter G. Goheen *Victorian Toronto, 1850 to 1890: Patterns and Process of Growth* (Chicago 1970).

46 On these working-class movements, see Greg Kealey and Peter Warrian ed *Essays in Canadian Working Class History* (Toronto 1976), Greg Kealey *Toronto Workers Respond to Industrial Capitalism, 1867– 1892* (Toronto 1980), Piva *The Condition of the Working Class*, Bryan D. Palmer *A Culture in Conflict: Skilled Workers and Industrial Capitalism in Hamilton, Ontario, 1860–1914* (Montreal 1979), and David J. Bercuson *Fools and Wise Men: The Rise and Fall of the One Big Union* (Toronto 1978).

47 Christopher Armstrong and H.V. Nelles *The Revenge of the Methodist Bicycle Company: Sunday Streetcars and Municipal Reform in Toronto, 1888–1897*

(Toronto 1977) provides a delightful illustration and analysis of this. See also Desmond Morton *Mayor Howland: The Citizen's Candidate* (Toronto 1973) and more generally Richard A. Allen *The Social Passion: Religion and Social Reform in Canada, 1914–28* (Toronto 1971).

48 It should be noted that labour and socialist organizations generally supported these efforts, on the assumption that they would cleanse municipal government and give it greater capacity for positive action. See Nelles and Armstrong 'The Great Fight for Clean Government.'

49 A board of control is an executive agency composed of politicians (normally elected by the voters of the city at large). The big Ontario cities all had boards of control from the beginning of this century until recently, when they were replaced in a number of communities by executive committees – essentially boards of control elected by the municipal councillors from among themselves. Such committees are also found in Quebec. In western Canada, boards of commissioners are common. These are supposed to be purely administrative bodies and are composed largely or wholly of appointed officials; but they perform many of the same functions as a board of control. An alternative is to have a single person as chief administrative officer or city manager, reporting directly to the municipal council or indirectly through the board of control or executive committee. The permutations are explained and discussed in Plunkett *Urban Canada and Its Government* and Higgins *Urban Canada* 108–22. See also the Profile series (n 2 above).

50 The relationship between these special-purpose agencies and the municipal councils was and is quite varied. Some – such as the school boards – are directly elected and completely autonomous. Others – such as the typical library board – are appointed by the municipal council and are subject to various financial and administrative controls. See Dominic Del Guidice and Stephen M. Zacks 'The 101 Governments of Metro Toronto' in Feldman *Politics and Government of Urban Canada* 4th edn 267–76 for one attempt to classify such agencies.

51 The literature on the development of the Canadian professions is scant. See John C. Weaver 'The Modern City Realized: Toronto Civic Affairs, 1880–1915' in Artibise and Stelter *The Usable Urban Past* 39–72 on the activities and influence of some early professionals.

52 In effect, cheap public utilities were intended as a subsidy to business: John C. Weaver '"Tomorrow's Metropolis" Revisited: A Critical Assessment of Urban Reform in Canada, 1890–1920' in Stelter and Artibise *The Canadian City* 393–418. See also H.V. Nelles *The Politics of Development: Forests, Mines and Hydro-electric Power in Ontario, 1849–1941* (Toronto 1974) 215– 306.

53 Walter Van Nus 'The Fate of City Beautiful Thought in Canada 1893–1930' in Stelter and Artibise *The Canadian City* 162–85, Van Nus 'Towards the City

Efficient: The Theory and Practice of Zoning, 1919–1939' in Artibise and Stelter *The Usable Urban Past* 226–46, Peter W. Moore 'Zoning and Planning: The Toronto Experience, 1904–1970' in ibid 316–41, and Kent Gerecke 'The History of Canadian City Planning' in James Lorimer and Evelyn Ross ed *The Second City Book* (Toronto 1977) 150–61

54 John T. Saywell ed *Housing Canadians: Essays on the History of Residential Construction in Canada* Economic Council of Canada Discussion Paper No. 24 (Ottawa 1975), Shirley Spragge 'A Confluence of Interests: Housing Reform in Toronto, 1900–1920' in Artibise and Stelter *The Usable Urban Past* 247–67, and John C. Weaver 'Crises and Reform: Housing, Planning and Public Ownership' in Weaver *Shaping the Canadian City* 25–40

55 Then as now, their main source of revenue was the tax on real property; Solomon Vineberg *Provincial and Local Taxation in Canada* (New York 1912). Although there were municipal income taxes in some communities, there was neither the administrative apparatus nor the public acceptance necessary to make them a major source of revenue. In any case, the authorizing provincial acts tended to put limits on all municipal tax rates.

56 Gertler and Crowley *Changing Canadian Cities* 121–37

57 The delocalization of urbanites should not be exaggerated: there is evidence that both the immediate neighbourhood and the wider local community remain of great importance in people's lives. However, in metropolitan areas especially, community boundaries and municipal boundaries are liable to be widely divergent. See Higgins *Urban Canada* 163–92 on the problems involved in matching political to social boundaries. Compare Alan Powell ed *The City: Attacking Modern Myths* (Toronto 1972) 80–100 and Feldman *Politics and Government* 4th edn 39–86. Even when a municipality represents a distinct social community, its inhabitants still may identify with the nation or the province more strongly than with it.

58 A provincial legislature may alter municipal boundaries, but it is usually reluctant to do so in face of local opposition. Towards the end of the nineteenth century, opposition to extension of civic boundaries became more pronounced. The richer suburbs tended to insist on their own autonomy, and the poorer ones came to be regarded as financial liabilities by many city councils. Thus the pace of annexation slowed; cities were ringed by autonomous suburban municipalities; and reformers came to press for overarching metropolitan governments. For analyses of these developments in a North American context, see Jon C. Teaford *City and Suburb: The Political Fragmentation of Metropolitan America, 1850–1970* (Baltimore 1979), William K. Tabb and Larry Sawers ed *Marxism and the Metropolis* (New York 1978), and Warren Magnusson 'Metropolitan Reform in the Capitalist City' *Canadian Journal of*

Political Science XIV (1981) 557–85. Compare V.D. Lipman *Local Government Areas, 1834–1945* (Oxford 1949) on England.

59 The businesses concerned (and the politicians who represent them) have an obvious interest in exaggerating this threat, so it usually appears greater than it actually is.

60 See A.J. Robinson and James Cutt ed *Public Finance in Canada* 2nd edn (Toronto 1973) 352–85 and 'Property Tax Reform' *Canadian Public Policy* II (1976) 299–362. Richard M. Bird and Enid Slack 'The Incidence of the Property Tax in Canada: A Review of the Literature' in *Report of the Tri-Level Task Force on Public Finance* III (Ottawa 1976) Appendix A casts some doubt on traditional complaints about the property tax. Compare United Kingdom *Report of the Committee of Inquiry into Local Government Finance* Cmnd 6452 (1976). N.P. Hepworth *The Finance of Local Government* 3rd edn (London 1976) and J.A. Maxwell and J.R. Aronson *Financing State and Local Governments* 3rd edn (Washington, DC, 1977) describe British and American fiscal arrangements that are also heavily dependent on property taxes.

61 See, for example, Shortt and Doughty *Canada and Its Provinces* XVIII 445–51. This process continued after the turn of the century, especially in the Prairie West: see A.F.J. Artibise 'Patterns of Prairie Urban Development, 1871–1950' in David J. Bercuson and Phillip A. Buckner ed *Eastern and Western Perspectives* (Toronto 1981) 115–46.

62 Crawford *Canadian Municipal Government* 344–55 and Higgins *Urban Canada* 71–6 summarize the development of these controls. See also Horace L. Brittain *Local Government in Canada* (Toronto 1951) 33–44, 220–42 and Winston W. Crouch 'Administrative Supervision of Local Government: The Canadian Experience' *American Political Science Review* XLII (1949) 509–23. Compare Schuyler C. Wallace *State Administrative Supervision over Cities in the United States* (New York 1928), James W. Fesler ed *The 50 States and Their Local Governments* (New York 1967), A.K. Campbell ed *The States and the Urban Crisis* (Englewood Cliffs, NJ, 1970); Robson *The Development of Local Government*, J.A.G. Griffith *Central Departments and Local Authorities* (London 1966), and R.A.W. Rhodes *Control and Power in Central-Local Government Relations* (Farnborough, Hants, 1981).

63 For a good illustration, see Ontario Economic Council *Subject to Approval: A Review of Municipal Planning in Ontario* (Toronto 1973). Compare Gerald M. Adler *Land Planning by Administrative Regulation: The Policies of the Ontario Municipal Board* (Toronto 1971), L.D. Feldman 'Legislative Control of Municipalities in Ontario' *Canadian Public Administration* IV (1961) 294–301, and Bureau of Municipal Research (Toronto) 'Urban Development and the Ontario Municipal Board' *Civic Affairs* (1971).

64 Higgins *Urban Canada* 60–71. See also J. Stefan Dupre *Intergovernmental Finance in Ontario: A Provincial-Local Perspective* (Toronto 1968), J.A. Johnson 'Provincial-Municipal Intergovernmental Fiscal Relations' *Canadian Public Administration* XII (1969) 166–80, John R. Cameron *Provincial-Municipal Relations in the Maritime Provinces* (Fredericton 1970), Tri-Level Task Force on Public Finance *Report* (Toronto 1976), Canadian Federation of Mayors and Municipalities *Puppets on a Shoestring: The Effects on Municipal Government of Canada's System of Public Finance* (Ottawa 1976), and Kenneth Cameron ed 'Municipal Government in the Intergovernmental Maze' *Canadian Public Administration* XXIII (1980) 195–317. Compare Douglas E. Ashford ed *Financing Urban Government in the Welfare State* (London 1980).

65 H. Carl Goldenberg *Municipal Finance in Canada* (Ottawa 1939)

66 John Taylor '"Relief from Relief": The Cities' Answer to Depression Dependency' *Journal of Canadian Studies* XIV (1979) 16–23. See also Taylor in McCormack and MacPherson ed *Cities in the West* 286–313, Patricia E. Roy 'Vancouver: "Mecca of the Unemployed," 1907–1929' in Artibise *Town and City* 393–413, Harry M. Cassidy *Unemployment and Relief in Ontario, 1929–1932* (Toronto 1933), Roger E. Riendeau 'A Clash of Interests: Dependency and the Municipal Problem in the Great Depression' *Journal of Canadian Studies* XIV (1979) 50–8, and Terry Copp 'Montreal's Municipal Government and the Crisis of the 1930s' in Artibise and Stelter *The Usable Urban Past* 112–29.

67 The municipal reaction to this remains ambivalent: see *Municipal Submission to the First National Tri-Level Conference* Session 2a (31 October 1972) II G-1-66.

68 Ontario's Planning Act of 1946 – which replaced the weaker Planning and Development Act of 1937 – was the exemplary legislation for the other provinces.

69 On federal policies, see A.D. Wilson 'Canadian Housing Legislation' *Canadian Public Administration* II (1959) 214–28, Canada *Report of the Task Force on Housing and Urban Development* (Ottawa 1969), David G. Bettison *The Politics of Canadian Urban Development* (Edmonton 1975), James Lorimer *The Developers* (Toronto 1978), Albert Rose *Canadian Housing Policies, 1935–1980* (Toronto 1980), Michael Dennis and Susan Fish *Programs in Search of a Policy: Low Income Housing in Canada* (Toronto 1972), Humphrey Carver *Compassionate Landscape* (Toronto 1975), and L.B. Smith *Anatomy of a Crisis: Canadian Housing Policy in the Seventies* (Vancouver 1977).

70 Donald V. Smiley *Canada in Question: Federalism in the Eighties* 3rd edn (Toronto 1980)

71 Brittain *Local Government in Canada* 110–21, R.W.G. Bryant *Land: Private Property/Public Control* (Montreal 1972), Larry S. Bourne *Urban Systems, Strategies for Regulation: A Comparison of Policies in Britain, Sweden, Australia and Canada* (Oxford 1975), William T. Perks and Ira M. Robinson ed *Urban and Regional Planning in a Federal State: The Canadian Experience* (Stroudsberg, Pa, 1979), and Ian M. Rogers *Canadian Law of Planning and Zoning* (Toronto 1973–). The Canadian land-use planning system is nearer to the American than to the British; see Marion Clawson and Peter Hall *Planning and Urban Growth: An Anglo-American Comparison* (Baltimore 1973).

72 On the need for disciplined parties in municipal politics, see, for example, R.M. Punnett 'Party Politics and Canadian Municipal Government' *Journal of Canadian Studies* IV (1969) 46–53, James Lightbody 'The Rise of Party Politics in Canadian Local Elections' *Journal of Canadian Studies* VI (1971) 39–44, Bill Burdeyny 'Party Politics and Regional Government' in Lloyd Axworthy ed *The Future City* (Winnipeg 1971) 34–8, Stephen Clarkson *City Lib: Parties and Reform* (Toronto 1972), Committee of Review: City of Winnipeg Act *Report and Recommendations* (Winnipeg 1976) 55–67, and J.K. Masson *The Demise of Alphabet Parties: The Rise of Responsible Party Politics in Cities* University of Alberta Occasional Paper 4 (Edmonton 1976). The growing belief in partisan politics among municipal reformers in Canada stems partly from American experience; see Willis D. Hawley *Nonpartisan Elections and the Case for Party Politics* (New York 1973). The connection between this revaluation of partisanship and the continuing commitment to managerial efficiency in local government is most evident in the City of Winnipeg Act *Report* and in Plunkett and Betts *Management of Canadian Urban Government*. For the application of modern managerialist ideas to municipal government, see also Tindal *Local Government in Canada*, J.R. Nininger et al *Developments in the Management of Local Government* (Toronto 1975), Ontario Ministry of Treasury, Economics and Intergovernmental Affairs *Managers for Local Government* (Toronto 1976–7), Paul Hickey *Decision-Making Processes in Ontario's Local Governments* (Toronto 1973), and Neil Ridler 'PPB: Its Relevance to Financially Constrained Municipalities' *Canadian Public Administration* XIX (1976) 238–53. Current proposals for increasing the efficiency of municipal government are heavily influenced by British and American theory and practice. For Britain see the Maud and Bains reports: United Kingdom *Committee on the Management of Local Government* (London 1967) and *The New Local Authorities: Management and Structure* (London 1972), J.D. Stewart *Management in Local Government: A Viewpoint* (London 1971), and Tony Eddison *Local Government: Management and Corporate Planning* 2nd

edn (Bath 1975); for the United States see B.W. Rapp and F.M. Petitucci *Managing Local Government for Improved Performance: A Practical Approach* (Boulder, Col, 1977), S.P. Powers et al *Developing the Municipal Organization* (Washington, DC, 1974), and J.M. Banovetz ed *Managing the Modern City* (Washington DC, 1971).

73 In Ontario and Quebec, municipalities other than cities traditionally have been represented on county councils that are charged with the broader functions of local government. The other provinces generally have lacked a second tier of local government; Higgins *Urban Canada* 15–44. Although the Canadian form of county government has Anglo-American origins, counties in the United States and Britain are generally quite different: see John C. Bollens *American County Government* (Beverly Hills, Calif, 1969) and Peter G. Richards *The Reformed Local Government System* 2nd edn (London 1975).

74 Higgins *Urban Canada* 104–8 reviews the phenomenon of special-purpose agencies in Canada. Compare John C. Bollens *Special District Governments in the United States* (Berkeley, Calif, 1957), Robert G. Smith *Ad Hoc Governments* (Beverly Hills, Calif, 1974), and Advisory Commission on Intergovernmental Relations *The Problem of Special Districts in American Government* (Washington, DC, 1974). Analysts of American local politics commonly include the special-purpose agencies in their purview: in Canada, these agencies have been largely ignored by political scientists (except when advocating their abolition).

75 See, for example, Plunkett *Urban Canada* 59–68, Stephen Clarkson *City Lib* 15–17, Feldman *Politics and Government* 267–76. The ideal of a 'unitary' local authority is an old one: John Stuart Mill *Considerations on Representative Government* (London 1861) chap 15 gives classic expression to it. This conventional view has been criticized by the theorists of 'public choice': Robert Bish and Vincent Ostrom *Understanding Urban Government: Metropolitan Reform Reconsidered* (Washington, DC, 1973), Vincent Ostrom, Charles Tiebout, and Robert Warren 'The Organization of Government in Metropolitan Areas' *American Political Science Review* LV 831–42, Robert Bish *The Public Economy of Metropolitan Areas* (Chicago 1971), Robert Warren *Government in Metropolitan Regions: A Reappraisal of Fractionated Political Organization* (Davis, Calif, 1966), and Robert B. Hawkins *Self Government by District: Myth and Reality* (Stanford, Calif, 1976). For the counter-attack on fragmented local government, see, for example, Gary J. Miller *Cities by Contract: The Politics of Municipal Incorporation* (Cambridge, Mass, 1981).

76 Hence the demand for metropolitan or regional government: see n 78 below for Canadian efforts in this direction. Anglo-American theory and practice have again been influential: see John C. Bollens and Henry J. Schmandt *The*

Metropolis 3rd edn (New York 1975) 237–331, James F. Horan and F.T. Taylor jr *Experiments in Metropolitan Government* (New York 1977), Jack Brand *Local Government Reform in England, 1888–1974* (London 1974), and Bruce Wood *The Process of Local Government Reform* (London 1976). The trend towards geographic consolidation of local governments has been global: see Arthur B. Gunlicks ed *Local Government Reform and Reorganization: An International Perspective* (Port Washington, NY, 1981) and Donald C. Rowat ed *International Handbook on Local Government Reorganization* (Westport, Conn, 1980). Criticisms of these efforts have been developed by public-choice theorists (e.g. Bish and Ostrom *Understanding Urban Government*), Marxist political economists (Tabb and Sawers *Marxism and the Metropolis*), and others: see especially John Dearlove *The Reorganization of British Local Government: Old Orthodoxies and a Political Perspective* (Cambridge 1979) and L.J. Sharpe 'The Failure of Local Government Modernization in Britain: A Critique of Functionalism' in Feldman *Politics and Government* 4th edn 321–57.

77 See *Report of the Royal Commission on Metropolitan Toronto* (Toronto 1965) 82 for one commentary on the effects of such competition.

78 T.J. Plunkett 'Structural Reform of Local Government in Canada' in Feldman and Goldrick *Politics and Government* 3rd edn 313–32, C.R. Tindal *Structural Changes in Local Government: Government for Urban Regions* (Toronto 1977), Advisory Commission on Intergovernmental Relations *A Look to the North: Canadian Regional Experience* (Washington, DC, 1974), and Higgins *Urban Canada* 124–62. There is a wealth of information on the structure and finance of Canadian local government in the various provincial reports on structural reform: Higgins and Tindal both list the major documents.

79 Henry J. Jacek 'Central Governmental Planning *versus* Conflicting Local Elites: Regional Government in Hamilton-Wentworth' in Donald C. MacDonald ed *Government and Politics of Ontario* (Toronto 1975) 48–63 is a case study of such resistance. The American literature on the subject is large: for example, Bollens and Schmandt *The Metropolis* 313–31 and V.L. Maranda 'The Politics of Metropolitan Reform' in A.K. Campbell and R.W. Bahl ed *State and Local Government: The Political Economy of Reform* (New York 1976) 24–49.

80 See Masson and Anderson *Emerging Party Politics*, Bureau of Municipal Research (Toronto) *Parties to Change: The Introduction of Political Parties in the 1969 Toronto Municipal Election* (Toronto 1971), Stephen Clarkson *City Lib*, Feldman *Politics and Government* 4th edn 102–47, Higgins *Urban Canada* 226–58, and J.G. Joyce and H. Hossé *Civic Parties in Canada* (Montreal 1970). A distinction must be made between the federal or provincial parties on the one hand and purely local parties on the other. As Joyce and Hossé's

study makes clear, the latter have been much more common in Canada, but few of them have persisted for long and fewer still have been disciplined organizations.

81 See the Appendix for demographic data.

82 On racial issues in Canadian cities, see Donald H. Clairmont and Dennis W. Magill *Africville: The Life and Death of a Canadian Black Community* (Toronto 1974) and E.J. Dosman *Indians: The Urban Dilemma* (Toronto 1972). Harold Kaplan *Urban Political Systems: A Functional Analysis of Metro Toronto* (New York 1967) offers (among other things) an analysis of city-suburban conflict in a metropolitan area. Compare Michael N. Danielson *The Politics of Exclusion* (New York 1976) on the American situation.

83 R.W. Collier *Contemporary Cathedrals: Large Scale Developments in Canadian Cities* (Montreal 1975). See also Lorimer *The Developers*, Boyce Richardson *The Future of Canadian Cities* (Toronto 1972), Lorimer *A Citizen's Guide to City Politics* (Toronto 1972), Graham Barker et al *Highrise and Superprofits: An Analysis of the Development Industry in Canada* (Kitchener 1973), and David C. Walker *The Great Winnipeg Dream: The Re-Development of Portage and Main* (Oakville, Ont, 1979).

84 L.S. Bourne ed *The Housing Supply and Price Debate: Divergents Views and Policy Consequences* (Toronto 1977), Peter Spurr *Land and Urban Development* (Toronto 1976), J.R. Markusen and D.T. Scheffman *Speculation and Monopoly in Urban Development* (Toronto 1977), James Lorimer *The Developers*, Manitoba *Report and Recommendations of the Winnipeg Land Prices Inquiry Commission* (Winnipeg 1977), and the Federal/Provincial Task Force on the Supply and Price of Serviced Residential Land *Down to Earth* (Ottawa 1978).

85 See Christopher Leo *The Politics of Urban Development: Canadian Urban Expressway Disputes* (Toronto 1977), Higgins *Urban Canada* 108–16, Graham Fraser *Fighting Back: Urban Renewal in Trefann Court* (Toronto 1972), John Sewell *Up against City Hall* (Toronto 1972), Lorimer *A Citizen's Guide*, Vancouver Urban Research Group *Forever Deceiving You* (Vancouver 1972), J.L. Granatstein *Marlborough Marathon: One Street against a Developer* (Toronto 1971), Donna Gabeline et al *Montreal at the Crossroads* (Montreal 1975), and Stephen Schecter *The Politics of Urban Liberation* (Montreal 1978). *City Magazine* (1974–80) was an important vehicle of 'reform' opinion: various articles from it are reprinted in Lorimer and Evelyn Ross ed *The City Book* (Toronto 1976) and *The Second City Book* (Toronto 1977).

86 Masson and Anderson *Emerging Party Politics* 60–7 has a debate on the relevance of the national parties to the new politics of reform. Michael Goldrick 'The Anatomy of Urban Reform' *City Magazine* III 4 and 5 (1978) 29–39

contains one of the best analyses of the divisions among the reformers and between them and their opponents.

87 See above, n 75 and 76 for some of this literature. Among the most rigorous critics of bigness are the public-choice analysts. There has been relatively little analysis of specifically Canadian institutions from this approach, except in the work of Mark Sproule-Jones. See, for example, his *The Real World of Pollution Control* (Vancouver 1981) and *Public Choice and Federalism in Australia and Canada* (Canberra 1975). More generally, see Vincent Ostrom and Frances P. Bish ed *Comparing Urban Service Delivery Systems: Structure and Performance – Urban Affairs Annual Review* XII (Beverly Hills, Calif, 1977).

88 For such an analysis, see especially Lorimer *A Citizen's Guide*. Compare Sewell *Up against City Hall*, Donald Gutstein *Vancouver Ltd.* (Toronto 1975), Pasternak *The Kitchener Market Fight*, Walker *The Great Winnipeg Dream*, or almost any issue of *City Magazine*.

89 On citizen participation, see W.R.D. Sewell and J.T. Coppock ed *Public Participation in Planning* (New York 1977), Fraser *Fighting Back*, W. Magnusson 'Community Organization and Local Self-Government' in Feldman *Politics and Government* 4th edn 61–86, Bureau of Municipal Research (Toronto) *Citizen Participation in Metro Toronto: Climate for Co-operation?* (Toronto 1975), James A. Draper ed *Citizen Participation: Canada* (Toronto 1971), and Powell *The City* 193–244. The debate on urban development was greatly influenced by Jane Jacobs *The Death and Life of the Great American Cities* (New York 1961). See Gertler and Crowley *Changing Canadian Cities* and N.H. Lithwick *Urban Canada: Problems and Prospects* (Ottawa 1970) for other views.

90 Kenneth Newton ed *Urban Political Economy* (London 1981), Roger E. Alcaly and David Mermelstein ed *The Fiscal Crisis of American Cities* (New York 1977), and L.J. Sharpe ed *The Local Fiscal Crisis in Western Europe: Myths and Realities* (London 1981) discuss the politics of cut-backs in other countries, in relation to local government. In Canada, there has as yet been little comparable academic work.

91 See Donald Higgins 'Progressive City Politics and the Citizen Movement: A Status Report' in James Lorimer and Carolyn MacGregor ed *After the Developers* (Toronto 1981) 84–95 for one overview of the contemporary state of municipal politics in Canada.

92 In 1981, there were nine census metropolitan areas in Canada with populations of more than half a million. No other metropolitan areas approach this size, although there are six (St Catharines-Niagara, Kitchener-Waterloo, London, Halifax-Dartmouth, Windsor, and Victoria) in the 200–300,000 range. Of the nine 'big' Canadian metropoles, three are not represented in this collection: Calgary, Hamilton, and Quebec. These omissions are essentially for

reasons of space. On the politics of Calgary see A.W. Rasporich and H.C. Klassen ed *Frontier Calgary: Town, City and Region, 1875–1914* (Calgary 1975), Max L. Foran *Calgary: An Illustrated History* (Toronto 1978), David H. Breen 'Calgary: The City and the Petroleum Industry since World War Two' *Urban History Review* 2–77 (1977) 55–71, and André Bernard et al *Profile: Calgary* (Ottawa 1975). On Hamilton's politics see Michael Katz *The People of Hamilton, Canada West*, Bryan Palmer *A Culture in Conflict*, Richard Lucas 'The Conflict over Public Power in Hamilton, Ontario 1906–1914' *Ontario History* LXVIII (1976) 236–46, D.J. Middleton and D.F. Walker 'Manufacturers and Industrial Development Policy in Hamilton, 1890–1910' *Urban History Review* VIII (1980) 20–46, John C. Weaver 'From Land Assembly to Social Maturity: The Suburban Life of Westdale (Hamilton), Ontario, 1911– 1951' *Histoire sociale* XI (1978) 411–40, Henry Jacek 'Central Government Planning' in MacDonald *Government and Politics of Ontario*, André Bernard et al *Profile: Hamilton-Wentworth*, Bill Freeman and Marsha Hewitt *Their Town: The Mafia, the Media and the Party Machine* (Toronto 1979), and *Dictionary of Hamilton Biography* I (Hamilton 1981). For politics in Quebec see F.-X. Chouinard and Antonio Drolet *La Ville de Quebec, histoire municipale, 1608–1867* 2 vol (Quebec 1963–7), Jacques Godbout 'La formation de la communauté urbaine de Québec et le rôle de l'état dans la restructuration des pouvoirs locaux' *Recherches sociographiques* XII (1971) 185–205, Guy Lord et al *Les Communautés urbaines de Montréal et de Québec: Premier bilan* (Montreal 1975), André Bernard et al *Profile: Quebec* (Ottawa 1975), and Louise Quesnel-Ouellet and Gilles Bouchard 'Urban Transportation: Politics of a Policy' in Feldman *Politics and Government* 4th edn 219–45.

93 Among the studies of political behaviour are Harlan Hahn 'Ethos and Social Class: Referenda in Canadian Cities' *Polity* II (1970) 294–315, J.A. Long and B. Slemko 'The Recruitment of Local Decision-Makers in Five Canadian Cities' *Canadian Journal of Political Science* VII (1974) 550–9, Bureau of Municipal Research (Toronto) *Parties to Change*, Robert R. Gilsdorf 'Cognitive and Motivational Sources of Voter Susceptibility to Influence' *Canadian Journal of Political Science* VI (1973) 624–38, Jerry F. Hough 'Voters' Turnout and the Responsiveness of Local Government: The Case of Toronto, 1969' in Paul Fox ed *Politics: Canada* 3rd edn (Toronto 1970) 284–96, Barry J. Kay 'Voting Patterns in a Non-Partisan Council' *Canadian Journal of Political Science* IV (1971) 224–42, J.K. Masson 'Decision-Making Patterns and Floating Coalitions in an Urban City Council' *Canadian Journal of Political Science* VIII (1975) 128–37, Feldman and Goldrick *Politics and Government* 3rd edn 156–75 and 186–219, Winn and McMenemy 'Political Alignment in a Polarized City,' and Harold Kaplan *Urban Political Systems: A Functional Analysis* (New York

1967). Kaplan's book is perhaps the leading example of an attempt to apply American social science techniques to the study of Canadian local politics. His more recent book – *Reform, Planning, and City Politics: Montreal, Winnipeg, Toronto* (Toronto 1982) – is more ambitious, but less successful.

94 See n 84–8 for works on political economy, most of which are more popular than academic. Lorimer *A Citizen's Guide* is still the most stimulating of the popular works. Compare Caroline Andrew et al *L'Urbanisation : une affaire* (Ottawa 1981) and Jacques Leveillée *Développement urbain et politiques governementales urbaines dans l'agglomeration montréalaise, 1945–1977* (Montreal 1978).

95 Compare Richard Van Loon and Michael Whittington *The Canadian Political System* 3rd edn (Toronto 1981).

ANDREW SANCTON

Montreal

Jean Drapeau is undoubtedly Canada's best-known mayor. By sponsoring Expo 67 and the 1976 Olympics he has become an international personality, an accomplishment that must make him the envy of more cautious Canadian politicians. In office from 1954 to 1957 and continuously since 1960, Drapeau appears to have had an unparalleled opportunity to shape local policy-making in Canada's largest municipality. By capitalizing on its unique ethnic and linguistic composition, Drapeau has done everything in his power to establish Montreal as one of the world's most famous and cosmopolitan cities.

Not all Drapeau's favourite projects have been international extravaganzas. As a crusading crime-fighter, a firm supporter of large-scale private urban redevelopment, and as the master builder of Montreal's luxurious subway system, he has left his mark on the day-to-day life of hundreds of thousands of Montrealers. Although carefully avoiding direct involvement in federal and provincial politics, he has been assiduously courted by leaders of virtually all parties at both levels of government. On some occasions, notably during General de Gaulle's 1967 visit to Quebec, Drapeau's political constituency has extended far beyond the arbitrary boundaries of the city.

Whatever his accomplishments, Drapeau has done surprisingly little to increase the local political system's capabilities to regulate urban development or to provide new directions for municipal policies. There are two explanations for these apparent shortcomings. First, Drapeau's ideological orientations are such that he is naturally suspicious of any systematic policy of governmental intervention, even at the municipal level. Consequently he has not been especially concerned with recruiting a competent, highly educated civil service of the type that emerged at the provincial level in Quebec in the 1960s and 1970s. He has paid careful attention to such matters as the aesthetics of major downtown buildings, but otherwise he has given a virtual free reign to private developers. Second, to the extent that Drapeau has in fact attempted to increase the political authority of the city of Montreal, he has consistently been foiled by either the provincial government, neighbouring suburban municipalities, or both. At various times Drapeau has been fervently committed to extending the city's boundaries, protecting and expanding its functional jurisdiction, enlarging its financial resources, and increasing its influence in the planning of metropolitan development. In contrast to his successes in sponsoring large projects, his political accomplishments in this sphere have been negligible.

To understand fully Drapeau's remarkable career, we must first look at the unique economic and social context in which Montreal's municipal government originally evolved. This discussion is followed by a more detailed treatment of Montreal city politics since the First World War, a period characterized by long-serving French-Canadian mayors of whom Drapeau is now the most important example. The next section documents how Drapeau has fought relentlessly to bolster his municipality's population, territory, and political strength, despite its declining importance in relation to the metropolitan area as a whole. Finally, we shall look again briefly at Montreal's role in the North American economy, this time in the context of modern Quebec nationalism. Selling Montreal as the new meeting place of Europe and North America is at the heart of Drapeau's latest dream. It is a vision inspired by Montreal's early successes at the centre of the North American fur trade.

THE EVOLUTION OF URBAN GOVERNMENT

The first permanent settlement in Montreal, originally called Ville-Marie, was founded in 1642 by Paul de Chomedey, sieur de Maisonneuve, as an outpost for zealous French missionaries. Attacks from hostile Iroquois constantly threatened the survival of the settlement and ensured that its population remained low.[1] After New France became a royal colony in 1663, a regiment of French soldiers was sent to protect the settlement, and by the end of the century it was relatively secure. Despite the official French policy favouring the development of a pious, self-sufficient agricultural colony, the main feature of this period was the emergence of the fur trade as the most vital element in the economy of New France. Because of its strategic location on an island at the junction of the Ottawa and St Lawrence rivers, Montreal soon emerged as the main centre for the organization, supply, and financing of a far-flung network of French-controlled fur-trading posts. By

1750 the non-Indian population of Montreal was 8,800.[2] The settlement had become an important service centre for agriculture but its control over the North American fur trade was weakening. British encroachments in the Great Lakes area and around Hudson Bay were constantly eating away at Montreal's hinterland. The culmination of this expansion of British power in North America came in 1759 when General Wolfe captured Quebec City. In the following year Montreal fell to General Amherst.

British merchants accompanying the conquering army were quick to seize control of the fur trade from the departed French administrators. However, in order to manage it efficiently, they needed, and received, the co-operation of the French Canadians who were the middlemen and couriers between Montreal and the interior posts. The main objectives of the merchants were to defend and extend the trading pattern left to them by the French and to wrest political power from the aristocratic governors who were intent on limiting their activities.[3] Because of their frustration at failing to achieve these objectives, some of them were tempted to support the cause of the revolutionaries in the thirteen American colonies to the south. However, the majority realized that, as part of an independent United States, the economic position of Montreal would be even weaker. Following the Revolution, the British fur traders in Montreal formed themselves into the Northwest Company. For a brief period the Nor'westers did extremely well in the fur trade, and some of Montreal's oldest private fortunes can be traced back to their profits. However, despite their impressive exploration of much of what is now western Canada, the Montreal fur traders were doomed by the English surrender of vital Great Lakes trading posts to the United States in 1783 and by relentless southern and western expansion of the Hudson's Bay Company.

In 1821, when 'The Bay' absorbed the Nor'westers, Montreal's role at the centre of the North American fur trade was over. This ended the only private commercial venture in which French Canadians actively participated with British entrepreneurs.[4] Although some of these investors were ruined by the demise of the Northwest Company, many others were still prospering as a result of prior diversification. During the Napoleonic Wars the shipping of squared timber from the Ottawa Valley became particularly important. None of this new economic activity required the high-level involvement of French Canadians. This started a pattern that was to last until very recently. The French Canadians of Montreal were relegated to manual employment, small businesses, and the professions while the British occupied the major financial and entrepreneurial functions that controlled the economy of mid-nineteenth-century British North America.

From 1764 until 1833 local government in Montreal had been carried out by a panel of twenty-seven magistrates who, rotating two by two, were empowered to issue local ordinances.[5] Although the charter that incorporated Montreal was passed in 1831, it was not proclaimed until 1833, the year of the first municipal election. In 1836, at the height of the political crisis that led to armed rebellion, the charter expired and was not renewed. Rule by the magistrates was restored. In 1840, however, the governor-general of the United Province of Canada granted a new charter, and Montreal once again possessed an elected municipal council. In 1852 the charter was amended to provide for the direct election of the mayor.[6] In 1860 tenants received the vote.[7]

At the time of its original incorporation Montreal's population was 31,000.[8] From then until 1865, the city contained more people of British origin than of French.[9] This reflected three facts: Montreal's growing importance as the economic centre for all of the Province of Canada, the arrival of thousands of working-class Irish immigrants, and the continuing tendency of French Canadians to shun the city and remain on the farm. English-speaking Montrealers constituted about 60 per cent of the city council until well into the 1870s.[10] Although the position of mayor was carefully alternated between French and English, there is little doubt that the municipal government was originally an English institution. Since local self-government scarcely existed in New France,[11] there is virtually nothing in Quebec's municipal system that is inherited from the French régime.

The major preoccupation of the early city council was the water-supply. After purchasing the existing privately owned delivery system, the council constructed a new one that drew water from just above the Lachine rapids, pumped it to a reservoir on Mount Royal, and then distributed it throughout the city. This system, which was completed in 1856, is still in use today.[12] While the council did not hesitate to take over direct ownership of the water-supply, it facilitated the private ownership of street railways and the distribution systems for gas and, later, electricity. The city council gave private companies franchises that granted them exclusive control over the delivery of these services.[13] Because the council was dominated by wealthy businessmen until at least 1873,[14] it is not surprising that its members were reluctant to interfere with the private sector's control of these generally lucrative businesses. However, the granting of these franchises, and the apparently excessive profits and corruption that resulted, provided generations of populist provincial and municipal politicians with ample ammunition for their continuous attack on the greedy trusts and monopolies that provided essential services to a captive market.

Another important activity of the early city council was to subsidize or invest in railways. Such financial involvement was allowed by provincial legislation passed in 1871.[15] Municipalities throughout the province were soon competing with each other to give money to railway promoters. In Montreal the city councillors' special preoccupation was to ensure that any railway heading east via Ottawa used Montreal as its St Lawrence terminus. In 1872, after much competition among various routes and syndicates, city council granted a subsidy of $1 million to the Montreal Colonization Railway to connect east-end Montreal to Ottawa via the north shore of the Ottawa River.[16] Although the early years of the MCR were financially disastrous, the subsidy eventually bore fruit. Hugh Allan, founder of the MCR and later head of the CPR, was able to use the MCR as the Ottawa-Montreal link in the Canadian Pacific route to the West, thereby confirming Montreal's position as the transportation centre of Canada.

One of the city council's more laudable actions in this period was its decision to expropriate private property on the top of Mount Royal and to create a public park overlooking the city. Expropriation proceedings began in 1871, and, after considerable litigation initiated by the owners, the park was inaugurated in 1876. It was laid out by Frederick Law Olmsted, who also designed Central Park in New York City.[17] In 1873 the city took over the former military installations on St Helen's Island and converted the area into another public park. Finally, in 1888 a former military property in the east of the city was acquired by the council and converted into what is now Lafontaine Park.[18] Large public parks were clearly a source of great civic pride in many North American cities during the latter part of the nineteenth century. In Montreal at least, smaller neighbourhood parks were apparently seen as less essential, because few were established. However, by developing the network of major parks, the city council did preserve Montreal's main physical assets for public use. Municipal politicians from that period onwards have always been quick to point to the parks as evidence of the virtues of far-sighted planning and progressive city government.

City government in Montreal, as in other Canadian cities, has been concerned above all with promoting urban development. On occasion, however, it has been forced to turn its attention to other matters. For five years after 1841 the municipality was directly responsible for the provision of local public education. In 1846 religious sensibilities caused the Canadian legislature to establish separate and distinct Catholic and Protestant school boards, thereby removing the city council from this crucial governmental activity.[19] Despite the important presence of the Roman Catholic church and numerous charitable organizations, social welfare has been a field in which the municipality has had, in certain circumstances, no alternative but to carry a significant burden. City contributions to provide social assistance during the 1930s were a major cause of the financial default of 1940.[20] Municipal financial involvement in such assistance was finally abolished in 1960.[21] From that time on, local politicians have focused their attention and financial resources on issues relating to the physical development of the city and, to a lesser extent, to policing.

The important decisions concerning Montreal's development had, of course, been taken long before 1960 – but not by the municipal government.[22] The building of the Lachine Canal and the Victoria Bridge in the mid-nineteenth century was sponsored in one form or another by the government of the whole colony. Both projects helped establish Montreal as the hub of British North America's transportation system. They also attracted a considerable amount of manufacturing activity to the southwestern part of the island of Montreal. Crowded working-class housing accompanied this industrial development, and what remains of this housing stock causes considerable problems for Montreal's current municipal authorities. The area is depressed because many of the industries on which it once relied have now closed or moved away, leaving aged, immobile, and often unemployed workers behind them. Later in the nineteenth century, a subsidiary manufacturing area emerged on a north-south axis along Boulevard Saint-Laurent. This newer area specialized in light manufacturing, particularly clothing. This section of the city, populated mainly by new immigrants, has traditionally been a kind of buffer zone between the English-speaking west and the French-speaking east.

Much of the physical expansion of Montreal took place outside the city's boundaries. In 1845, apart from the city of Montreal, there were only nine other incorporated municipalities, all rural parishes. By 1881 there were twenty-seven. Most had the official status of village but two, Lachine and Saint-Henri, were towns.[23] Their combined population was about 52,000 while that of the city was 141,000.[24] Municipal incorporation was a relatively easy and uncontrolled process, especially after 1876 when a law was passed enabling the newly created ecclesiastical parishes in Montreal to be incorporated municipally as well.[25]

The period from 1881 to 1921 saw drastic changes in the municipal boundaries on Montreal island. Fifty-one new municipalities came into being.[26] Many survived for only a few years and existed only as part of elaborate schemes by real estate developers to pass on their excessive construction costs for elaborate roads, public buildings, and utilities to unsuspecting property owners and ultimately to the city of Montreal. The prime example of such a case was the city of Maisonneuve, which was incorporated in 1898 and annexed by Montreal in 1918.[27] E.W. Villeneuve, an ardent opponent of the annexation, described the process this way: 'The bunch of "get rich quick" artists that undertook the exploiting of Maisonneuve bought farm lands, blocked them out into city streets, had sewers built, water mains laid, permanent pavements and sidewalks installed, out of the civic treasury through miles of vacant land, with not a house erected thereon.'[28] The developers also built a lavish city hall, market, and fire station. A huge park was established on land purchased at inflated prices from provincial politicians.[29] After its annexation, Maisonneuve accounted for 5 per cent of the city of Montreal's population, 3½ per cent of its taxable property, and 16 per cent of its debt.[30]

The development of the suburban municipality of Mount Royal is an example of a case in which larger, more established capitalist interests also made considerable profits on land development, but without resorting to the kinds of methods used in Maisonneuve. The Canadian Northern Railway purchased undeveloped land on the north side of Mount Royal and then proceeded to have its new transcontinental railway approach Montreal through a tunnel under Mount Royal. The tunnel was finished in 1918, thereby opening up the northern part of the island for urban development.[31] The holdings of the Canadian Northern were contained within the town of Mount Royal, which had been incorporated in 1912. The Canadian Northern Montreal Land Company then proceeded to build a 'model city,' with carefully planned streets radiating from a convenient railroad station at the centre.

The requirement that large houses be built on large lots ensured that Mount Royal was to become almost exclusively a high-income residential suburb. This was explicitly stated in a contemporary prospectus: 'The appeal of this property will be to people of taste and discrimination, of education and refinement. The names of many prominent people are already included in our list. Fully restricted as to costs of houses and against any nuisances, no undesirable or objectionable elements will be permitted. Constant care and vigilance to preserve the high standard of citizenship is our aim.'[32]

When the Canadian Pacific Railway later opened up some vacant land in the extreme western part of the municipality, the town council developed it as a valuable industrial area and consequently greatly improved an already healthy tax base. Unlike Maisonneuve, Mount Royal has never been a serious candidate for annexation because it has always been more than capable of paying its bills.

Between 1881 and 1921 the city of Montreal annexed twenty-three suburban municipalities. The annexations added about 150,000 people to the city's population and increased its indebtedness by $28 million. Although the annexations appeared to be financially damaging to Montreal at the time, it is important to note that in 1961 85 per cent of city residents were living in areas that had been annexed between 1881 and 1921. These areas also contained 86 per cent of the property in the city, 90 per cent of the houses, and 55 per cent of the commercial establishments.[33] It is primarily because the annexations in this period were so extensive that the city of Montreal has subsequently been so dominant in the local politics of the island of Montreal and the whole metropolitan area.

The annexation period is also important for another reason. In 1881 Canadians of French ethnic origin made up only 56 per cent of the population of the city of Montreal. However, they made up 73 per cent of the population of the annexed municipalities. This fact, combined with increased in-migration of French Canadians from rural areas, helps account for the increase in the proportion of people of French ethnic origin in the city to 63 per cent by 1921. When it is realized that, because of massive immigration from Europe, the proportion of people in the city of non-French and non-British ethnic origin rose in the same period from 3 per cent to 13 per cent, the increase in the French proportion is all the more remarkable. From 1881 to 1921 the proportion of people of British ethnic origin in the city sunk to 24 per cent from 41 per cent. Only one of the annexed municipalities, Saint-Gabriel, had a British (mainly Irish) majority. Most of the British decline can be accounted for by the departure of British Montrealers to independent suburban municipalities. This period saw the incorporation of such clearly English-speaking suburbs as Baie d'urfe, Beaconsfield, Côte-Saint-Luc, Hampstead, Pointe Claire, Roxboro, and, of course, Mount Royal. In 1881 people of British ethnic origin made up only 19 per cent of the island population outside the city of Montreal. In 1921 the figure was 47 per cent.[34]

One of the most thorough chroniclers of Montreal's history has noted that the city's first major annexation, that of Hochelaga in 1883, was of special importance because it tipped the delicate French-English political balance in the city decisively towards the French.[35] A resulting hypothesis, which would be difficult to prove conclusively, is that this loss of power within the city prompted residents of British origin to accelerate their departure to the suburbs, thus further decreasing their strength in city politics. This pattern is, of course, quite consistent with the way in which members of the middle class lost political control in other North American cities and then entrenched themselves behind the boundaries of independent suburbs to escape the supposed evils of city life. In Montreal, however, because of the additional language cleavage, the temptation for stalwart members of the English-speaking middle and upper-middle classes to leave the central city was even greater.

By 1921 the patterns of municipal boundaries and linguistic segregation that exist today on the island of Montreal were clearly established. The city of Montreal had much the same boundaries as it has today and the transition to complete francophone control was almost complete. In the suburbs on the western part of the island it was already clear that, as old French farms were subdivided for residential use, the new occupants would be English. Although French suburban areas to the east and north were later to rival the population figures in the English western areas, the image of wealthy English suburbs spreading west from a French-dominated city of Montreal had become the central feature of Montreal's metropolitan development.

POLITICS IN THE CITY OF MONTREAL

Guy Bourassa considers the modern era of Montreal local politics to have begun in 1914. He points out that the main characteristics of this period has been the mobilization of the mass of voters behind powerful and popular mayors who frequently succeeded in being re-elected.[36] The first such mayor was Méděric Martin, a skilful politician who carefully exploited his working-class origins and his occupation as a cigar-maker. In 1906 he was elected both as a Montreal city councillor and as a federal MP. At the federal level he became a trusted lieutenant of Sir Wilfrid Laurier. Locally, his somewhat dubious political practices made him a target for the anglophone-dominated reform coalition of businessmen and progressives that had been battling since the mid-1890s against the growing strength of patronage-based political machines in local elections. As a result of the Cannon Commission inquiry in 1909, Martin was forced to resign his council seat. The same inquiry was instrumental in establishing a directly elected board of control that removed much important power from the mayor and council.[37] Nevertheless, Martin was re-elected as a councillor in 1912 and then led the opposition of the 'little men' against the 'vested interests.' In 1914, when it was considered the anglophones' turn to nominate a mayor, Martin violated the tradition, ran for the position himself, and defeated his chief opponent, George Washington Stevens, by 5,000 votes.[38] The tradition of alternating the mayor's position between anglophones and francophones was never revived. In 1926 Martin campaigned successfully under the slogan 'No more English mayors here.'[39]

Martin's natural constituency was based in the thousands of French-Canadian rural migrants who had recently flocked to the new jobs in Montreal's growing industries. In this respect the conflict between Martin and the Anglo-Saxon business-oriented reformers was quite similar to the conflicts going on between urban reformers and the immigrant-based machines in the large cities of the United States. One student of the reform movement in Montreal has concluded that it was less successful in Montreal than elsewhere because Martin was able to counter it by appealing to 'a growing ethnocentrism in French Canada.' This ethnocentrism, coupled with a rapidly declining participation of the English in Montreal's political life, would make future reform very difficult.[40]

Martin remained as mayor, with one two-year interruption, until 1928, during which time he presided over a thoroughly corrupt and virtually bankrupt city administration. In 1918 the provincial government, the members of which were not free of questionable involvements in the Montreal property market, virtually took over the administration of the city. They replaced the board of control with a provincially appointed five-man administrative commission, leaving Martin as little more than a figurehead. In 1921 the provincial government restored some of Martin's powers and abolished the commission. In its place the government set up an executive committee which, although composed of and elected by councillors, had substantial authority independent of both the mayor and the council.[41] The executive committee still survives as an important and unique mechanism of Montreal's municipal government. Its chairman has often wielded more political power than the mayor himself.

By the late 1920s Martin's political appeal was fading. He had clearly amassed considerable personal wealth during his period of alleged service to the working man. He was unable to establish the same personal contact with the unskilled recent immigrants to Montreal as he had developed with the semi-skilled long-time residents. In the election of 1928, Camillien Houde, a Conservative member of the provincial legislature since 1923, challenged Martin for the office of mayor and defeated him by 22,000 votes.[42]

Houde's origins were even humbler than Martin's and he gained great support from the people whom Martin once viewed as his own. Houde was mayor from 1928 to 1932, 1934 to 1936, and 1938 to 1940. During this period he did not have a firm grip on the city of Montreal, largely because of his heavy involvement in provincial politics. His political career was interrupted in 1940 when he was arrested after urging young men not to register under the National Resources Mobilization Act. He spent the next few years under military guard at Petawawa and Fredericton.

Prior to his arrest Houde had already lost most of his powers as mayor. In 1940, for the second time in his mayoralty, the provincial government had placed the city under trusteeship in an attempt to remedy its dangerous financial position. Although the period of trusteeship was to last four years, the provincial government acted quickly to give Montreal its twelfth different form of city government since 1833. The membership of the council was increased to ninety-nine. One-third were to be elected by the property-owners in eleven new wards (class A councillors), one-third by all householders voting in the same eleven wards (class B councillors), and one-third by thirteen designated public bodies such as universities, unions, chambers of commerce (class C councillors). The council was to elect a six-man executive committee that in turn elected its chairman and vice-chairman. The mayor was to continue to be elected by all householders on a city-wide basis.[43]

This system was to last, with some modifications, until 1962. Its main effect was to protect the interests of the property-owners and to bolster anglophone representation on the council. The property-owning and anglophone groups overlapped to a considerable extent. Both benefited from the creation of class A and class C councillors. The anglophones, however, gained most from class C because they controlled six of the thirteen designated organizations.[44] The Liberal provincial government that imposed this system was anxious to improve Montreal's financial reputation, and the scheme ultimately did aid in this objective, however opposed it was to usual democratic principles. Houde's successor, elected under the new system in 1940, was Adhémar Raynault, a former protegé of Premier Maurice Duplessis; Raynault had also succeeded Houde in 1936 when the city was similarly under temporary provincial supervision. Raynault was able to remain in office only for as long as Houde was interned. In 1944 Houde was released, and in the municipal elections of that year he defeated Raynault by almost 15,000 votes.[45]

In 1947 Houde became the only mayor this century to be elected by acclamation. He was re-elected for a four-year term in 1950. Although Houde's personality dominated city politics from 1944 to 1954, he accomplished little except to make peace with Premier Duplessis, who kept the provincial government out of Montreal's affairs in return for Houde's support at provincial elections.[46] During this period Montreal was noted for its obviously corrupt city government. The close relationship of the police force to criminal organization based on gambling and prostitution was the main feature of this corruption. It was first exposed in 1949 and 1950 in articles in *Le Devoir* by assistant police director Pacifique Plante.[47] Although Plante was dismissed from his position soon afterwards, he continued his battle with the support of the almost exclusively francophone Civic Action League and its offshoot, the Committee for Public Morality. In 1950 the latter group succeeded in forcing a judicial inquiry into commercialized vice in Montreal.[48] The chairman of the inquiry was Judge François Caron. Its two investigators were Plante and Jean Drapeau, a young lawyer with a strong nationalist political background whose father was a city councillor.[49] Judge Caron's report was made public in 1954. Although it implicated many prominent city politicians and policemen, Houde, who had refused to co-operate, was ignored and hence allowed to retire with a theoretically unblemished record.

The Civic Action League's candidate to succeed Houde in the election of 1954 was Drapeau. On the strength of his prominence during the Caron inquiry, Drapeau was the easy victor, although the league did not gain full control of the council. A curious feature of Drapeau's campaign was his manner of combining great praise for Houde's political career[50] with continued denunciations of the corruption over which he presided. Drapeau's admiration of Houde was an early indication that he did not fully share all the attitudes of the group that sponsored his election. Because the Civic Action League did not have a majority on council, Drapeau was in a difficult position. The most obvious example of his political weakness was the decision taken by council, supported by the provincial government, to build a massive public housing project in central Montreal. Drapeau was outspokenly opposed to such projects but there was nothing he could do to prevent it.[51]

The mayor did favour the private commercial revitalization of the downtown area, and on this subject his will prevailed. He entered into a close working relationship with William Zeckendorf, a highly successful American developer who proposed the building of a huge office complex to cover the gaping hole created by the Canadian National Railway tracks as they emerged from the Mount Royal tunnel. Drapeau helped in the assembly of the land by sponsoring the expropriation of the venerable St James Club which was perched on the edge of the CNR property. He generally smoothed the way for the realization of Zeckendorf's imaginative plans. After Place Ville Marie had been completed, Zeckendorf praised Drapeau as 'a political Hercules' and 'our practical but also visionary ally.'[52] With Drapeau's fervent support, the Zeckendorf development shifted Montreal's business centre from St James Street to Dorchester Street, launched the creation of Montreal's 'underground city,' and served as a model for subsequent developments in all of Canada's major cities.

During his first term Drapeau did little to bolster his tenuous political base. He was opposed by Duplessis, and his reputation among anglophones as a dangerous nationalist was confirmed when he replaced the Queen's picture in the mayor's office by a crucifix.[53] In the 1957 election Drapeau was defeated by Sarto Fournier, a Liberal senator who was supported by virtually all of Drapeau's enemies. Although Fournier had a 4,000-vote majority, his nebulous local party, the Greater Montreal Rally, did not win as many seats in the council as did the Civic Action League.[54] The period 1957–60 was one of political stalemate.

During these years Drapeau had no formal role in local government. The opposition to Fournier was led in the council by Pierre DesMarais, a founder of the Civic Action League and the former chairman of the executive committee. Meanwhile Drapeau made a national reputation for himself by speaking publicly about a wide variety of federal and provincial issues.[55] It appeared that his political future might lie outside Montreal. But Drapeau decided instead to re-enter municipal elections, this time as the undisputed leader of his own highly disciplined local party. As a result of some rather treacherous manoeuvring in 1960,[56] Drapeau disassociated himself from the Civic Action League, taking most of its city councillors (but not DesMarais) with him to form the new Civic party. Drapeau's action, just before the 1960 election, came too late for the league to react effectively. Drapeau easily defeated Fournier, and his Civic party followers won forty-six of the sixty-six class A and B seats.[57] In a referendum held at the same time, 74.7 per cent of the electors followed Drapeau's advice and voted to abolish the class C councillors. Not surprisingly, voters in anglophone areas of the city were generally not as willing as francophones to part with this peculiar form of representation.[58] And they did not support Drapeau any more than previously.

Drapeau's first objective after 1960 was to restructure Montreal's system of government. To this end he was helped by a provincial commission established to investigate the matter. The commission in effect recommended a parliamentary form of government with the mayor being a kind of constitutional monarch and the executive committee being the cabinet. The commission also recommended that the control of the police be transferred from the council to a police commission consisting of the mayor and two judges.[59] The new Liberal provincial government accepted many of the recommendations but not those regarding the mayor and the police commission. Under the new system, which came into effect in 1962, the mayor retained substantial authority although most of the normal administration of the city remained in the hands of the chairman of the executive committee. The executive committee consisted of the mayor and six members, including a chairman and a vice-chairman, elected by the council on the nomination of the mayor.[60] The council was composed of forty-five members, three each from fifteen electoral districts.

Drapeau and his Civic party completely dominated the municipal elections of 1962 and 1966:[61]

	Turnout (percentage)	Popular vote for Drapeau (percentage)	Council seats for Civic party
1962	42.5	87.1	42 of 45
1966	32.7	94.4	45 of 48

The 1960s were the years of Drapeau's greatest accomplishments. Operating almost completely without local opposition, Drapeau's administration attracted more massive construction projects to downtown Montreal, built the first phase of the city's long-awaited subway system, and brought Expo 67 to those magical islands on the St Lawrence that were created from thousands of loads of earth trucked from the subway tunnelling sites.

The 1960s were a time of great prosperity for the Montreal property industry. Much of the construction was fuelled by the capital of foreign investors, particularly Europeans.[62] They were obviously attracted by the hospitable political environment in Montreal and by the fact that it was achieving a growing reputation as a world city. The Drapeau administration placed few obstacles in the way of any development, big or small. A recent paper for the Economic Council of Canada[63] has documented the relative absence of planning controls during the late 1960s and the 1970s. While other cities developed elaborate official plans and mechanisms for public involvement in planning, Montreal continued to make zoning decisions on an apparently ad hoc basis. Requests for zoning changes were channelled directly to the politicians on the executive committee before even being considered by the technical experts in the city's planning and legal departments. Zoning laws were considered to be more a reflection of demands for the use of real estate in a given area than part of a system to shape and regulate such demands. The study concludes that Montreal's 'market zoning' resembles more the non-zoning system in Houston, Texas, than it does the planning procedures of any other major Canadian city. Although the Parti québécois government in Quebec has introduced extensive new legislation concerning land-use planning in the province as a whole, the legislation specifically exempts the city of Montreal.[64] In zoning matters Drapeau still carries on much as he did in the 1960s.

It was also during the 1960s that Drapeau's conception of 'disciplined democracy'[65] clearly began to emerge. Rather than building his Civic party into a participatory mechanism for ordinary citizens who shared his vision of Montreal, he maintained it as a pure 'caucus party'[66] in which only he and his council candidates were members. The candidates were chosen by Drapeau, often on the recommendation of his long-time political organizer and fund-raiser, J.H. Brien. Until the municipal electoral reforms imposed by the province in 1978, the party levied a fee of at least $1,000 on all candidates at the time of each election.[67] In other words, significant personal financial resources, preferably obtained through ownership of a small business, were a prerequisite for Civic party councillors. Even within the select group of Civic party members, Drapeau reigned supreme. The only member who ever became a true colleague of the mayor was Lucien Saulnier. As chairman of the executive committee he administered the city in an efficient manner and was occasionally successful in restraining Drapeau in his constant search for a new civic extravaganza. Saulnier left municipal politics in 1972.

Once Civic party candidates are elected to council, they find that they have neither administrative nor political responsibilities. The city provides them with little more than a common room – there are no individual offices or secretaries. The council meets only a few times a year and, when it does, the rules of procedure, as strictly interpreted by Drapeau himself, provide little opportunity for significant public debate. Except for the all-powerful executive committee, there are no standing or special committees of council – unless one counts the committee on street names and the committee to plan the annual golf tournament. In short, the role of a Civic party councillor consists of little more than aiding local residents and businessmen in their brushes with the municipal bureaucracy and in ensuring that his area of the city receives an appropriate share of whatever overall level of municipal services and expenditures Drapeau chooses to provide.

Throughout most of the 1960s Montreal newspapers and radio and television stations were constantly lauding the mayor's numerous accomplishments. They seemed quite willing to overlook the fact that Drapeau's city hall was undoubtedly the most secretive in the country. Executive committee meetings were held in private; internal city documents were rarely released to the public; and press conferences – except to announce a new project – were almost unheard of. As far as Drapeau was concerned, it seemed that the role of the journalists was to inform the people of the administration's accomplishments. To engage in any serious political reporting or analysis was to distort the direct relationship between mayor and citizen, a relationship that manifested itself at election time every four years.

The first serious opposition to the Civic party surfaced in 1970. Certain trade unions and left-wing nationalist organizations joined together at the local level to form the Front d'action politique (FRAP).[68] This movement did not nominate a candidate for mayor but attempted to win council seats in the poorer areas of francophone Montreal in order to build a base for future action. The election was scheduled for 25 October. During the final three weeks of what was the most active campaign since 1960, the city was shaken by the FLQ kidnappings of British Trade Commissioner James Cross and provincial cabinet minister Pierre Laporte. While Drapeau took the strongest position possible against the FLQ, FRAP declared its approval of the FLQ political manifesto while at the same time expressing its disapproval of its methods. During the last two weeks of the campaign, FRAP's small chances of electoral success were totally smashed by its apparent association with the FLQ. When the federal government proclaimed the War Measures Act on 16 October, a number of FRAP candidates and organizers were jailed. Although the remaining FRAP members pleaded that the elections be postponed, the provincial government refused the request. Montrealers voted as planned, with the streets and polling booths guarded by soldiers. On this occasion 51 per cent of eligible voters turned out to exercise their franchise. Many were obviously interested simply in showing their support for the existing system of government and their opposition to the FLQ. In this hostile environment, FRAP failed miserably, the Civic party won all the council's fifty-two seats, and Drapeau won 91.8 per cent of the popular vote.[69]

During the period 1970–4 there was increasing opposition to Drapeau from two main sources. Those who constituted the remnants of FRAP were anxious to build a left-wing municipal political movement devoted to attacking Drapeau's failure to provide sufficient housing and social and recreational services in the poorer sections of the city. At the same time a more middle-class movement emerged that was devoted to stopping uncontrolled high-rise development in downtown Montreal, saving the city's older buildings and neighbourhoods, and bringing about a more democratic and open municipal system of government.[70] In early 1974 these two sections of anti-Drapeau opinion came together to form the Montreal Citizens' Movement. After searching for a better-known candidate for the mayoralty, the MCM finally settled on Jacques Couture, a social worker and priest who lived and worked in the Saint-Henri district. Although Couture gained considerable exposure in the media, he was in no way considered the party's leader.

When voting took place on 10 November, Drapeau was given one of the greatest shocks of his political career. He received only 55.1 per cent of the popular vote while Couture obtained 39.1 per cent.[71] More importantly, the MCM won eighteen council seats and a small group called Democracy Montreal won another. Drapeau's Civic party delegation to the council was cut to thirty-six. The most important feature of the election was that it placed a strong opposition group in council. But the significance of the MCM was even greater because it proved that it was possible to create a reform movement in Montreal that could gain strong support from both the anglophone and francophone communities. The MCM won all three council seats in the anglophone electoral districts of Notre-Dame-de-Grâce and Côte-des Neiges, the ethnically mixed centre city district of Saint-Louis, and the francophone working-class district of Saint-Jacques.

The period 1974–6 was probably the most difficult for Drapeau in all his years as mayor. He faced a strong opposition in council for the first time since 1954–7; he no longer had Saulnier at his side; and, above all, he lost control of one of his most prized projects, the 1976 Olympic Games. The story of the Olympic fiasco need not be told here. In the context of city politics, three aspects are important. First, although Drapeau had promised a modest, self-financing Olympics, it ended up being the most extravagant ever held. Although the federal and provincial governments eventually helped pay the $1-billion deficit, municipal taxpayers will be paying a special Olympic property tax until 1997.[72] Second, because the city government was so obviously incapable of bringing the project to fruition, the provincial government, in November 1975, took over from the municipality by establishing an Olympic Installations Board. For the first time Drapeau had failed to deliver on a major project. The provincial intervention meant that after the games ended, the major installations remained in provincial ownership. Third, for the first time, there was clear evidence of substantial corruption within the administration. The most serious incident involved the chairman of the executive committee, Gérard Niding. There were disclosures that his country house had been built for him without payment by one of the major Olympic contractors.[73]

Fortunately for Drapeau, his civic opposition was unable to benefit from his difficulties. When the games took place, the mayor again emerged as a local hero. All seemed to be forgotten as Montreal was once again the focus of world attention. However, when the euphoria had died down, one would have expected the opposition to have been well placed for a renewed attack. Instead, the Montreal Citizens' Movement split apart.

The underlying problem was a fundamental difference in outlook between those who viewed the MCM as a socialist movement in an urban setting[74] and others who saw it as a political party concerned with winning local elections and hence changing the direction of municipal government. Prior to 1976 there had been frequent skirmishes between the two groups at all levels of the MCM's scrupulously democratic party machinery. However, the difficulties came to a head in late 1976 when two MCM councillors, Nick Auf der Maur and Bob Keaton, were expelled from the party for having violated MCM rules by running in the provincial election as candidates for the Democratic Alliance, a party they had founded in an attempt to capture the votes of reform-minded anglophones in Montreal. At the same time the MCM adopted a radically anti-capitalist housing policy that further discouraged the moderate electoralist wing of the party.[75] By 1977, doctrinaire socialists were clearly in control, but the new MCM was now resting on a much narrower political base.

With the election of the Parti québécois in November 1976 one might have expected the MCM to have greatly benefited from having a sympathetic government in Quebec. However, the PQ was reluctant to be too closely associated with the MCM. First, the PQ was anxious to project an image of moderation and responsibility. As the MCM swung leftward, it was clearly in conflict with this objective. Second, the PQ had a healthy respect for the political power of Drapeau. It could not afford to alienate Drapeau and risk having him play an active role against its policy of sovereignty-association. By mid-1977 it was quite obvious that Drapeau and the PQ had struck a deal: Drapeau would stay out of the sovereignty debate in return for the PQ staying aloof from Montreal's local politics.[76]

Perhaps because of its apparently cozy relationship with Drapeau, the PQ government did not launch a drastic reform of Montreal's municipal political system. It had previously flirted with the MCM idea of establishing official neighbourhood councils within the city of Montreal and had examined the idea of having the mayor elected by the council instead of by the electorate as a whole. But when the reform legislation was introduced in 1978 such drastic changes were not proposed. In two separate pieces of legislation the government made three major changes in the way in which the council was to be elected. Drapeau, although hardly an enthusiastic supporter of these changes, could quite easily adapt to all of them.

First, the legislation abolished Montreal's old multi-member wards and established a procedure whereby the permanent provincial commission for electoral boundaries would create fifty-four new municipal electoral districts, each of which would elect one councillor.[77] Second, there was to be official recognition of municipal political parties. If candidates were members of official parties, their party affiliation was to appear on the ballot. Third, the reforms provided for the public subsidization of municipal election campaigns and placed controls on overall spending. Only individual electors were to be allowed to contribute to individual candidates or local parties, and such contributions were limited to $500 a year.

As the November 1978 election approached, a new political party, the Municipal Action Group, inevitably emerged. It consisted mainly of the former moderate element within the MCM. Its candidate for mayor was Serge Joyal, the somewhat rebellious Liberal MP for Maisonneuve-Rosemont, who had been speaking out on municipal issues for a good many months. The MAG tried to establish a middle position between Drapeau's extravagant and authoritarian 'politique de grandeur' and the MCM's urban socialism – it probably had more in common with moderate urban reform groups such as Toronto's CIVAC or Vancouver's TEAM than with any of Montreal's previous local parties.

The 1978 campaign was the most keenly contested since 1960. Nevertheless, Drapeau ran primarily on his record, still appealing to the pride of Montrealers. The holding of the Olympic Games and the existence of the Olympic facilities were trotted out as laudable accomplishments. He simply asked for a mandate to continue. Meanwhile, the two opposition parties could scarcely avoid attacking each other as each tried to establish its credentials as the most obvious alternative to Drapeau. Given the political upheaval at the provincial level in 1976, it was perhaps too much to expect that Montrealers would risk further change by rejecting such a symbol of stability and authority as Drapeau. Whatever the reasons, the 1978 election was a stunning setback for both opposition parties.

With a comparatively high turnout of 53.8 per cent, Drapeau won 60.9 per cent of the vote. Joyal won 25.5 per cent and Guy Duquette of the MCM got only 12.5 per cent. In the council elections, the Civic party swept fifty-two of the fifty-four seats and it won 55.6 per cent of the popular vote. The MAG and the MCM each won only one seat with 25.8 per cent and 18.1 per cent of the vote, respectively.[78] There were only eleven other seats in which the

Civic party did not win an outright majority. For the anti-Drapeau forces, the election was a disaster.

The election marked the return of Drapeau to a position of overwhelming power within city politics. In some respects Drapeau's ascendant position seems very similar to that of his predecessors Martin and Houde. All three based their appeal on the simple but effective notion that, as individuals, they deserved support because they personified the city itself. To vote against a Martin, a Houde, or a Drapeau was somehow to vote against the city itself, or at least against the French-speaking part of the city. Further similarities are, however, hard to find. Martin and Houde established themselves in the traditional political parties before running for mayor. Drapeau, in contrast, supported the nationalist Bloc populaire in the late 1940s, but since then has avoided affiliation with parties at other levels of government. Martin and Houde played on their working-class origins and humble professions. Drapeau, in contrast, is very much the traditional French-Canadian lawyer for whom dignity and devotion to duty are the greatest virtues. Martin and Houde gleefully exploited their public position as mayor but rarely had the political will or power to bring about any kind of significant change. Drapeau makes few public appearances but, especially in the 1960s, used his position and his faithful council majority to implement one major scheme after another.

Martin and Houde were clearly part of the pre-Quiet Revolution style of Quebec politics. Their connections to political leaders at other levels were part of a complex network of traditional machine-based politics. When Houde decided not to contest the 1954 municipal elections, the older patterns could not be sustained. Drapeau's victory in 1954 was not unlike the 1960 victory of the Lesage Liberals over the decaying Union nationale. His win can be seen as the first electoral manifestation of the Quiet Revolution. Robert Burns, then a trade union organizer and later a PQ cabinet minister, described the event in these terms: 'For progressive people of all kinds, Jean Drapeau was a symbol of opposition to the Duplessis regime ... The 1954 election was Duplessis' first important defeat. And in a way, it was the first victory for the "*Revolution Tranquille.*"'[79]

Drapeau's failure in 1957 and the subsequent collapse of the Civic Action League can be understood by realizing that in Montreal in the late 1950s there were simply too many fronts on which the 'new middle class' reformers were fighting. Once Drapeau had become mayor, the agents of change in Quebec were quite content to leave Montreal's municipal government in his apparently capable hands, even though there were some who did see cause for serious misgivings. This interpretation of events explains both Drapeau's rise to power and his subsequent lack of opposition. Even now, the young, well-educated francophone Montrealers, who could be expected to be his opponents, are generally far too busy with Quebec's national question to be much concerned with municipal politics. An aroused Drapeau has been perceived as a potentially powerful political enemy, and most supporters of the Parti québécois have been quite content to ignore his foibles, if not openly to pay him homage.

It now seems virtually certain that Drapeau cannot be defeated in an election for the post of mayor of Montreal. He will likely remain as mayor for as long as he is willing and able to hold the office. The obvious question for Montreal politics is 'What happens next?' It is clear that, without its founder, the Civic party will be little more than a collection of small businessmen and other conservatives who will lack the electoral appeal resulting from Drapeau's record as both a crusading reformer and a successful visionary. Given that Quebec's national question remains unsolved and that the MCM and the MAG are still engaged in a bitter struggle,[80] it would be folly to speculate on what form the opposition to the Civic party might take. However, there can be little doubt that a strong alternative to the Civic party is already emerging.

More than any other Canadian city, the mechanisms are in place in Montreal for full-scale party politics at the local level. There is a large council, a powerful executive committee that meets in private like a cabinet; local parties are officially recognized; and there is a tradition of strong local leadership. Since 1960 the dominance of Drapeau has meant that formal institutional arrangements have been almost irrelevant. When he is gone, these institutions will be well suited to provide an environment in which competitive political parties can appeal to the electorate on the basis of varying conceptions of the city's future.

THE CITY OF MONTREAL IN ITS METROPOLITAN ENVIRONMENT

The city of Montreal is the most populous and important municipality within the metropolitan area. According to the 1981 federal census, the city's population was 980,354, while the second-largest municipality, Laval, had only 268,335. The problem for the city, however, is that its share of the metropolitan population is declining. In 1921 the city included 78 per cent of the population of the Montreal census metropolitan area; in 1981 the figure was only 35 per cent (see Table 1 in the Appendix). With every increase in the suburbs' relative share of total population, the city sees a reduction in its ability to shape the future of the metropolitan areas as a whole. This section is concerned with documenting how the city of Montreal has coped with the changing political environment caused by the growth of suburbia.

As with other major Canadian cities, the most explosive period of suburban growth came in the period immediately after the Second World War. Suburban areas around the city of Montreal were developed by a great many small independent entrepreneurs, contractors, and builders. Although land speculators played a major role in forcing up the price of land on the urban fringe,[81] they never, as in other cities, gave way to large vertically integrated development companies. The existence of about one hundred independent municipalities in the metropolitan area, virtually all of which have protected their own small builders, is often cited as an important reason for Montreal being such an exceptional case.[82] The tough competition among municipalities and suppliers of housing has undoubtedly had the beneficial effect of restraining increases in the price of housing in Montreal. However, the absence of any controls on municipal land development policies, either by the province or by a metropolitan authority, has meant that Montreal's suburban residential development has been almost completely unplanned and haphazard.

Despite much wringing of hands in the 1950s about the need for larger-scale municipal government in metropolitan Montreal, nothing much was done until Drapeau took office as mayor for the second time, in 1960.[83] With characteristic nerve, he launched a campaign to have the city of Montreal annex all the municipalities on the island of Montreal.[84] The campaign was a failure, netting only three financially shaky suburbs – Saint-Michel, Saraguay, and Rivière-des-prairies. Seemingly undaunted, Drapeau governed as if he were mayor of the whole metropolitan area. He started to build Montreal's subway system in 1961 without financial assistance from either the province or the suburbs. The original plans called for a line using the CNR tunnel to connect the municipalities of Outremont, Mount Royal, and Saint-Laurent with the central business district. However, when it was clear that these municipalities were unwilling to be annexed, the project was abandoned. Despite his original claims that the city could finance the subway itself, Drapeau persuaded the provincial government in 1965 to force those suburbs served by the city buses to help pay for its construction. As a result of Drapeau's skilful gambling, the suburbs found themselves helping to finance a subway over which they had no influence in planning.

Starting in 1962 the city of Montreal Planning Department investigated problems of urban growth in the entire metropolitan area. While the work generated interesting data and projections, it was clear that metropolitan planning could not take place without some new form of metropolitan government. Following a pattern established in the 1950s, the provincial government established a commission to study the matter. Many proposals for change were made,[85] but, once again, it seemed that nothing was going to be done. On 24 September 1969, following adverse reaction from the city to the latest plan for metropolitan government, the Union nationale provincial minister of municipal affairs announced that any action on the subject would be postponed for one year. By the end of the year, however, a new metropolitan government, the Montreal Urban Community (MUC), had come into being. This surprising turn of events had nothing to do with problems of metropolitan planning but was rather the direct result of a strike by Montreal's police force in late October. In order to finance the cost of the eventual settlement, the provincial government established a mechanism that forced suburban municipalities on the island of Montreal to subsidize the city's police costs. The MUC was that mechanism.

The establishment of the MUC was a clear victory for the city of Montreal. Regardless of the various functions that, in theory, were within its jurisdiction,[86] the MUC was primarily designed to channel suburban tax revenues directly to the city. This redistribution process was provided for by provincial law and came into effect even before the MUC decision-making institutions ever met. These institutions were themselves closely modelled on those of the city of Montreal. For example, the MUC council – comprising mayors of MUC municipalities and all city of Montreal councillors – could initiate nothing without prior approval of the executive committee, which was simply the city's seven-man executive plus five suburban representatives. Although they were forced to share police costs, the suburban mayors were able to protect themselves on other matters by employing a provision of the law that stated that, in order for a motion to be approved by the council, it required the support of at least 50 per cent of the city of Montreal's councillors and 50 per cent of the suburban mayors.

The most important structural feature of the MUC was this 'suburban veto' within the council. This procedural rule prevented Drapeau from treating suburban mayors on the MUC council in the same way as he treated troublesome opposition members on city council. He can dismiss the objections of the latter group and carry out his plans regardless of their concerns. When he attempted to ignore the suburban mayors, he found his plans at the MUC level in serious jeopardy. Although the mayors were at first reluctant to use their veto, they soon overcame their initial hesitation, especially when they realized that Drapeau had no intention of seriously negotiating with them. Once Drapeau knew that he could not effectively control the MUC, he soon lost interest. This is illustrated by the fact that Drapeau chose his trusted lieutenant, Lucien Saulnier, to be first chairman of the MUC executive committee. When Saulnier left municipal politics in 1972, Drapeau picked a much less important member of the city executive committee, Lawrence Hanigan. Finally, when Hanigan left in 1978, Drapeau was content to let the suburban mayors have a turn. When Pierre DesMarais II, mayor of Outremont, became chairman, it appeared that Drapeau was content to leave the MUC in the stalemated condition to which it had grown accustomed.

DesMarais and the suburban mayors had other ideas. Following the provincial referendum on sovereignty-association in May 1980, the PQ government agreed to suburban demands that the whole legislative framework of the MUC be reviewed. The suburbs' major objective was to obtain parity with the city on the MUC executive committee while at the same time not surrendering the suburban veto on the MUC council. The main justification for parity was that the total suburban contribution to the MUC budget was now almost equal to that of the city and that the suburban share of MUC population was continually growing and had already reached 44 per cent.

Drapeau did not co-operate with the government in its attempts to encourage an internal MUC consensus on structural reform. He steadfastly maintained that the city deserved its dominant position within the MUC and that no further changes were required. However, now that the sovereignty-association referendum was behind it, PQ ministers had no particular reason to fear the mayor of Montreal. Because suburban mayors had launched an effective lobbying campaign, and because some francophone ones had openly supported the PQ, the government was soon convinced to move towards the suburban position.

This became evident in September 1981 when Municipal Affairs Minister Jacques Léonard announced the government's proposals.[87] They did nothing to change municipal boundaries and functions and hence did little to confront the community's most pressing problems. Nevertheless, they did provide for city-suburban parity on the executive committee and, as a result, they outraged Drapeau, who claimed that the proposals reduced Quebec's metropolis to the level of a mere suburb, just one among many.[88]

Heedless of Drapeau's impressive performance at parliamentary hearings[89] and of discontent on its own back benches,[90] the government held firm. Meanwhile, the mayor counter-attacked in a quite different arena. In early 1982 the council of east-end Pointe-aux-Trembles, burdened by high taxes and debts and a low level of municipal services, expressed interest in being annexed by one of its wealthier neighbours – Anjou, Montreal East, or the city of Montreal. Only the city expressed serious interest. Within a few months, citizens of Pointe-aux-Trembles had approved the annexation and Drapeau had added 36,000 east-island residents to the city's population.[91] By this single measure Drapeau had skilfully shifted the population balance between city and suburbs within the MUC from about 56 per cent–44 per cent to 58 per cent–42 per cent.

Just as the Pointe-aux Trembles annexation was officially proclaimed, the revised structures for the MUC were being given final approval in the province's national assembly.[92] Despite the city's dominant share of MUC population, it now controls only one half of the seats on the executive, all the members of which are elected by the council. The executive comprises the chairman and vice-chairman of the council as well as the chairmen and vice-chairmen of its five new standing committees. The council, by a two-thirds vote, also chooses, from among other council members, an executive committee chairman. If no candidate receives the required number of votes after two successive council meetings, the provincial government has the authority to make the appointment itself.

In order for a motion to be approved by the executive committee, it cannot receive more than four negative votes from either city or suburban representatives. If a motion receives a majority of votes but is blocked by either city or suburban delegation, it is automatically placed on the agenda of the next meeting. If there is another such result, the matter is referred to the council where, if a two-thirds majority is obtained, it is deemed to be approved.

For approval by council, other motions now require the support of both half the total city and suburban votes. As was the case previously, each council member still has one vote for every one thousand people represented. The previous veto arrangements required the approval of at least half the city and half the suburban representatives; the new system is based only on votes. The effect of this change is to reduce dramatically the power within council of small suburban municipalities, most of which are anglophone.

Other changes served to increase the authority of the community at the expense of its associated special-purpose bodies. This was especially true in relation to policing. The Public Security Council, which previously had direct control over the MUC Police Department (established by provincial legislation in 1971), is now only one of the five new standing committees of the MUC council. Its former administrative responsibilities are taken over by the MUC executive committee, but the director of the MUC police is still named by the provincial government. The MUC Transportation Commission retains its corporate identity but loses virtually all policy-making authority to the executive committee, the council's new standing public transit committee, and the council itself.

Despite their achievements in convincing the government to implement the 1982 changes, suburban mayors will never be enthusiastic MUC supporters. The MUC remains, above all, a redistributive mechanism that forces suburban taxpayers to finance police services in areas of greatest need, notably the city of Montreal. From this suburban perspective it is most unlikely that the MUC will ever be perceived as the kind of benign provider of services so often described by provincial politicians.

Notwithstanding the continuing financial importance of policing, the MUC is now spending $1.5 billion to help clean up the St Lawrence River. Buttressed by major federal and provincial subsidies, the MUC started construction in 1974 of an integrated sewer system that will eventually connect with a new primary sewage treatment plant being built at the extreme eastern tip of the island.[93] When this system is finally completed, the practice of dumping over 500 million gallons of raw sewage a day directly into the St Lawrence will finally be over. The project can be viewed as a major MUC accomplishment, but it could easily have been built without the existence of a metropolitan government. The province is making the major decisions concerning the timing of the construction.

The MUC has suffered its greatest failures in precisely those fields in which its political authority as a metropolitan level of government was most needed – regional planning and transportation. In 1973, the MUC Planning Department, staffed largely by former city of Montreal planners, released a vague but visually appealing document called *Proposals for Urban Development*. It called for the creation of three major new suburban parks which, together with five large parks in the city of Montreal, would constitute a geographically balanced network financed by the MUC. It also proposed the establishment of two major 'satellite centres,' one based around the Fairview Shopping Centre in the western part of the island and the other around Galéries d'Anjou in the east. Intensive development – high-rise office buildings and apartments – would be encouraged within the area of the satellite centres and generally prohibited elsewhere. This would supposedly ease the pressure on the central business district, bring some order to suburban development, and facilitate the creation of new public transit networks. Other major proposals involved the integration of the subway and the commuter rail lines and a halt to the expansion of the island's expressway system.

The proposals were the subject of two separate investigations by committees of MUC councillors and, finally, in 1976, a by-law implementing the main provisions of the plan was drafted. Suburban mayors raised strong objections primarily because, except in the proposed satellite centres, the by-law involved strict limitations on the density of their future development. By this time the organization known as the Conference of Suburban Mayors of Montreal had hired a full-time staff and had become quite articulate in expressing suburban interests. The CSMM dispatched three of its members to Europe to study suburban development patterns there and then hired one of Quebec's most prestigious planning consultants to provide further advice. The mayors then announced that good planning for Montreal would involve the encouragement of higher-density development in the traditional commercial sectors of the older suburban municipalities.[94] Although the debate between the suburban mayors and the MUC planners was muddled and incomplete, at least some of the major issues were raised. Should development in Montreal be concentrated in order to maintain the economic health of the central city or should decentralization be encouraged in order to reduce transit problems and create self-sufficient suburban areas? Should shopping centres be recognized as the real foci of suburban communities around which public transit should be oriented or can they continue to serve only those who have their own cars? Should undeveloped land be put aside for major parks or is this land too valuable for that kind of use?

Unfortunately, no serious effort was made to subject these issues to intensive public debate. Drapeau showed little interest and neither did anyone else. Knowledgeable observers knew that there was little chance a meaningful by-law could ever be approved and hence there was no reason to become exercised about the various arguments being made.

By the end of 1976 it was apparent that the MUC planning by-law had quietly been dropped. Since then MUC planners have had little to do except spend a provincial subsidy of $10 million to acquire land for the metropolitan parks. Activity is now picking up, however, because the 1982 MUC legislation requires the community to adopt a development plan sometime within the next three years. Presumably the old issues will be reopened, but there is no guarantee they will be settled.

Even if the MUC does manage to draw up a plan for its own territory, further provincial involvement is inevitable. This is primarily because, although the MUC adequately covers the territory of the east-west axis of Montreal's urban development, it has virtually no control over the north-south axis. Following the construction of the St Lawrence Seaway in the late 1950s and the Champlain Bridge in the early 1960s, the south-shore area experienced a massive boom in suburban development. To the north of the MUC, on Île-Jésus, was the city of Laval. It was created in 1965 by provincial legislation that merged thirteen previously independent municipalities. By the 1970s Laval had emerged from a difficult beginning and was conducting a vigorous campaign to attract industrial and residential development. North of Laval was another band of outer suburban development, anchored in the west by the new municipality of Mirabel which, in 1969, the federal government chose as the location for Montreal's second international airport.

Ottawa's choice of Mirabel was probably the most important single decision concerning the physical development of Montreal taken by any level of government since 1945.[95] The decision was taken against the expressed wishes of the Quebec government, which wanted the airport located to the southeast of Montreal. Although the city of Montreal Planning Department was represented on the site selection task force, there were no other mechanisms for any other variety of municipal participation.[96] In choosing Mirabel, the federal government single-handedly ensured that the northern section of metropolitan Montreal would be the main focus of new industrial development and that future provincial investments in roads and public transit would also be heavily weighted towards that area.

As far as public transit was concerned, the MUC originally seemed firmly in control. It was given authority to build extensions to the subway system, to control traffic on main thoroughfares and, through the MUCTC, to operate the public transit network. By 1973 it had launched a plan for the construction of 61 new subway stations and 32 more miles of track. This would complete the original network of 28 stations and 14 miles of track.[97] However, after work was largely completed to extend the system to the new Olympic site, the provincial government announced, in May 1976, that it would not continue to subsidize the building of the extensions until it had completed a thorough study of the public transportation needs of the entire metropolitan area.[98] While the PQ government carried out the studies that the Liberals had called for, the MUC executive committee, having seen the fate of the subway extension program transferred to provincial hands, began the search for other areas in which it could improve public transit.

In early 1979 a plan was worked out to integrate the declining commuter train service on the west island with the bus and subway network of the MUCTC. In return for this and for a limited extension of the MUCTC bus service, the twelve west island municipalities in the MUC would have to start paying, for the first time, their share of the MUCTC deficits.[99] However, when the city officials calculated that the net effect of these changes would be that the MUCTC deficit would increase more than the amount of the west island contributions, Drapeau ensured that the plan was scuttled.[100] This is yet another example of how difficult it is to obtain both city and suburban support for any new policy initiative within the MUC.

Given this environment, it was inevitable that the provincial government would intervene. In late 1979 the government announced that the west island municipalities would begin to share MUCTC deficits in 1980,[101] that the province would pay all the cost of future extensions to the subway system, and that existing rail lines in the west island and elsewhere would be used to create a 'regional metro' fully integrated with the MUCTC system.[102] In financial terms this was a one-billion-dollar commitment to be spread over five years. Whether or not the plan is ever fully carried out, its announcement makes it perfectly clear that the MUC no longer has any control over the planning of public transit in the Montreal area.

The relative powerlessness of the MUC creates no problems for Drapeau. He prefers a weak metropolitan government that he can ignore rather than a powerful one in which he must seek the co-operation and consent of the suburbs. He believes that the city of Montreal is too big and too important to have to be concerned with the views of its insignificant suburban neighbours. The ideal solution is to annex them; failing that, make them pay for the city services they use but refuse to treat them as political equals. For Drapeau, the 1982 changes in the MUC legislation were an outrage precisely because they place the suburbs on an equal political footing with the city. How to respond to this unacceptable arrangement is Drapeau's next challenge in the metropolitan arena. The annexation of Pointe-aux-Trembles is perhaps a foretaste of what is to come.

THE FUTURE OF MONTREAL

Issues relating to the future of Montreal can be divided into two major categories; those that are common to virtually all major North American cities and those that are unique to Montreal because of its linguistic and ethnic make-up. Examples of the first kind of issue are pollution control, public transit, low-income housing, crime, and suburban sprawl. As in most other places, these matters have now largely passed beyond the control of the local, or even metropolitan, political system and occupy the attention of hundreds of technicians, planners, and politicians associated with the provincial government.

Provincial policy-making capability in these fields was relatively late in developing in Quebec but, during the 1970s, it grew dramatically. Since 1976 the Parti québécois government has gone further than any of its predecessors in working out an integrated urban policy. Its legislation to protect the province's diminishing farm land, its transportation plan for the Montreal area, and its attempts to co-ordinate water-supply and sewer developments in metropolitan Montreal seem to be all part of a coherent approach to the provincial control of urban development. Critics of centralization can deplore the continuing decline in the importance of local government but those concerned with the quality of the urban environment are likely to agree that the Parti québécois, in this field at least, has provided the kind of 'good government' that it so clearly promised in 1976.

Among the second variety of urban issues are those that relate to what can best be labelled 'the national question.' Here the issue is, in its most fundamental form, whether Montreal is to continue as a major centre of business for all Canada or whether it is simply to be the business capital for Quebec. If it is to be the former, it is difficult to see how Montreal can ever be as French as Toronto is English. If it is to be the latter, then Montreal still faces major economic dislocations as more head offices inevitably move away. Jane Jacobs has recently pointed to the potential advantages for Montreal of going through these dislocations and then establishing a compact, innovative economy of the type found in some of the smaller western European democracies.[103]

In terms of political parties, the main protagonists in this debate are the federal and provincial Liberal parties and the Parti québécois. The Liberals stress the need for head offices to remain in Montreal and for the burden of bilingualism to be spread more equally across the country. This policy clearly prevents those Montreal-based companies that are sensitive to federal politics (Bell Canada, Canadian Pacific, the chartered banks) from following the current trend and moving to Toronto. Seen from this perspective, such Liberal policies can scarcely be seen to be in the interests of these large corporations. Whose interests, then, do they serve? Above all, they serve the interests of middle-aged, relatively immobile anglophone executives and of the thousands of bilingual francophone professionals and managers whose successful careers in Montreal have been built on their ability to act as a link between the large corporations and the Quebec social, legal, and political environment in which they are physically located. The PQ policy, in contrast, seems more sensitive to the interests of smaller indigenous businesses and co-operatives as well as those of the vast array of public and para-public enterprises (Hydro-Quebec, SIDBEC) that have flourished since the early days of the Quiet Revolution. It is assumed, of course, that with Montreal acting as the economic hub of a sovereign Quebec, the opportunities for young, educated francophones in the management of the economy will be greatly increased.

Where does the mayor of Montreal fit in this debate? Given the limited scope of municipal authority, one might expect him not to be involved at all. Such limitations have not stopped Drapeau in the past, however, and they seem unlikely to do so now. His passionate commitment to bringing Expo 67 and the 1976 Olympic Games to Montreal give an obvious clue about his hopes for Montreal's future. It seems that he does not confine his view of Montreal to its role in either a sovereign Quebec or a federal Canada. He sees Montreal as being on the world stage, as the great cosmopolitan city of North America. While others fret about the Canadian or Quebec national identity, Drapeau brings in a William Zeckendorf to build Place Ville Marie or a Roger Taillebert to design the Olympic Stadium. His latest plans involve converting part of the city's older harbour-front area into a world film-making centre and developing Mirabel as the futuristic jet port for the entire eastern seaboard of the continent.

Jean Drapeau first became mayor of Montreal in 1954. Despite the unprecedented period of social and political change experienced in his city and province since that time, the mayor's policies and style have scarcely changed. The irony is that, while appearing so unchanging himself, Drapeau presided over a transformation in Montreal's physical environment that is almost as impressive as the social changes in Quebec as a whole. Place Ville Marie, Place des Arts, the subway system, Expo 67, and the Olympic stadium were all brought to Montreal by Drapeau. No Canadian politician at any level of government can point to such lasting monuments to his political skills. Whether any future mayor of Montreal will ever again have the political power or opportunity to operate on such a grand scale is highly doubtful. The province simply cannot afford another Jean Drapeau.

SUGGESTED FURTHER READING

Aubin, Henry *City for Sale* Montreal and Toronto 1977

Auf der Maur, Nick *The Billion-Dollar Game: Jean Drapeau and the 1976 Olympics* Toronto 1976

Bourassa, Guy 'The Political Elite of Montreal: From Aristocracy to Democracy' in L.D. Feldman and M.D. Goldrick ed *Politics and Government of Urban Canada* Toronto 1969

– *Les Relations ethniques dans la vie politique montréalaise* Document 10 de la Commission royale d'enquête sur le bilinguisme et le biculturalisme, Ottawa 1971

Cooper, John Irwin *Montreal: A Brief History* Montreal 1969

Copp, Terry *The Anatomy of Poverty: The Condition of the Working Class in Montreal 1897–1929* Toronto 1974

Divay, Gérard and Jacques Godbout *La Décentralisation en pratique: quelques expériences montréalaises, 1970–1977* Montreal 1979

Eger, A.F. *Time to Approve: Land Development Risk and Regulation in Montreal, 1966–1977* Working Paper No. 10, Regulation Reference, Economic Council of Canada, Ottawa 1980

Gabeline, Donna et al *Montreal at the Crossroads* Montreal 1975

Gauvin, Michel 'The Reformer and the Machine: Montreal Civic Politics from Raymond Préfontaine to Médéric Martin' *Journal of Canadian Studies* XIII 2 (summer 1978) 16–26

Léveillée, Jacques *Développement urbain et politiques gouvernementales urbaines dans l'agglomération montréalaise, 1945–1975* Montreal 1978

Marsan, Jean-Claude *Montreal in Evolution* trans Arnaud de Varent, Montreal 1981

McKenna, Brian and Susan Purcell *Drapeau* Toronto 1980

Milner, Henry *Politics in the New Quebec* Toronto 1978, chap 10 'New Politics in Montreal'

Sancton, Andrew *Governing the Island of Montreal: Language Differences and Metropolitan Politics* forthcoming

NOTES

1 For Montreal's early years, see Gustave Lanctot *Montreal under Maisonneuve 1642–1665* trans Alta Lind Cook (Toronto 1969).

2 Raymond Tanghe 'La population' in Esdras Minville ed *Montréal économique* (Montreal 1943) 100

3 D.G. Creighton *The Commercial Empire of the St. Lawrence* (Toronto 1937) 35

4 Ibid 154

5 John Irwin Cooper *Montreal: A Brief History* (Montreal 1969) 25

6 Ibid 26–7

7 The assessed value of the rented dwelling had to be at least $300 or have an assessed yearly rental of $30. See Province of Canada *Statutes* 1860 chap 72 sec 2.

8 Cooper *Montreal* 26

9 Richard J. Joy *Languages in Conflict* (Toronto 1975) 104

10 Guy Bourassa *Les relations ethniques dans la vie politique montréalaise* Document 10 de la Commission royale d'enquête sur le bilinguisme et le biculturalisme (Ottawa 1971) 128

11 Gustave Lanctot 'Le régime municipal en Nouvelle-France' *Culture* IX 3 (Sept 1948) 255–83

12 Cooper *Montreal* 27

13 Ibid 98–100
14 Bourassa *Les Relations ethniques* 125
15 Brian J. Young *Promoters and Politicians: The North Shore Railways in the History of Quebec* (Toronto 1978) 38
16 Ibid 49
17 J. Cléophas Lamothe *Histoire de la Corporation de la Cité de Montréal* (Montreal 1903) 51 and 103
18 Cooper *Montreal* 76
19 Province of Quebec *Report of the Royal Commission of Inquiry on Education in the Province of Quebec* (Quebec 1963) 11
20 See Terry Copp 'Montreal's Municipal Government and the Crisis of the 1930's' in A.F.J. Artibise and G.A. Stelter ed *The Usable Urban Past* (Toronto 1979) 112–29.
21 Province of Quebec *Report of the Study Committee on Public Assistance* (Quebec 1963) 36
22 For a valuable history, see Jean-Claude Marsan *Montreal in Evolution* trans Arnaud de Varent (Montreal 1981).
23 Bureau de recherche économique (Montréal) 'Tableaux schématiques de l'évolution des municipalités de la région de Montréal' mimeo 1970
24 Canada *Census of Canada, 1880–81* (Ottawa 1882) 52 and 56
25 Cooper *Montreal* 23
26 Montreal 'Tableaux schématiques'
27 For the complete story, see Paul-André Linteau *Maisonneuve ou comment des promoteurs fabriquent une ville* (Montreal 1981).
28 E.W. Villeneuve *Where Are We Going? Some Facts Concerning Our Municipal Situation* pamphlet dated 3 October 1918
29 The park later became the site of the Olympic stadium and village. Consequently it served the purposes of yet another generation of Villeneuve's 'get rich quick artists.'
30 Villeneuve *Where Are We Going?*
31 Cooper *Montreal* 129
32 *Mount Royal 'The Model City'* prospectus published by Davidson and McRae, General Agents
33 Montréal *Memoire du comité executif de la Cité de Montréal* (Montreal 1962) 8–9
34 Figures in this paragraph are derived from Canada *Census of Canada, 1880–81* I 52 and 56 and from Canada *Sixth Census of Canada, 1921* (Ottawa 1924) I 534 and 542.
35 William Henry Atherton *Montreal 1535–1914* II (Montreal 1914) 184
36 Bourassa *Les Relations ethniques* 32

37 Michael Gauvin 'The Reformer and the Machine: Montreal Civic Politics from Raymond Préfontaine to Médéric Martin' *Journal of Canadian Studies* XIII 2 (summer 1978) 20–3
38 Cooper *Montreal* 138–42
39 Quoted in Leslie Roberts *Montreal: From Mission Colony to World City* (Toronto 1969) 313
40 Michael Gauvin 'The Municipal Reform Movement in Montreal, 1886–1914' MA thesis, University of Ottawa, 1972, 153
41 Bourassa *Les Relations ethniques* 14
42 Cooper *Montreal* 163
43 Ibid 168
44 Bourassa *Les Relations ethniques* 148
45 Adhémar Raynault *Témoin d'une époque* (Montreal 1970) 145
46 Roberts *Montreal* 331–2
47 These articles were then published in a book entitled *Montréal sous la régime de la pègre* (Montreal 1950).
48 J.-Z. Léon Patenaude 'Le Comité de moralité publique et l'enquête Caron' *Le Devoir* (Montreal) 10 August 1972, 5
49 For details of Drapeau's early involvement in politics see Brian McKenna and Susan Purcell *Drapeau* (Toronto 1980) 1–94.
50 Raynault *Témoin* 188
51 McKenna and Purcell *Drapeau* 108–9
52 William Zeckendorf *Zeckendorf* (New York 1970) 167 and 196
53 J.M. McIver 'The Administration of Montreal: Past, Present, and Future' MA thesis, Carleton University, 1961, 158
54 Roberts *Montreal* 340
55 These speeches were published as *Jean Drapeau vous parle* (Montreal 1959).
56 This is described in full, from an anti-Drapeau perspective, in J.-Z. Léon Patenaude *Le Vrai Visage de Jean Drapeau* (Montreal 1962).
57 Cooper *Montreal* 192
58 Bourassa *Les Relations ethniques* 42
59 Province of Quebec, Department of Municipal Affairs *Report of the Commission to Inquire into the Administrative System of Montreal* 2 vol (Quebec 1960 and 1961)
60 Marcel Adam *La Démocratie à Montréal* (Montreal 1972) 30
61 Data taken from Montreal Municipal Archives, Municipal Election Results, 1962 and 1966
62 Henry Aubin *City for Sale* (Montreal 1977)
63 D.F. Eger *Time to Approve: Land Development Risk and Regulation in Montreal, 1966–1977* Working Paper No. 10, Regulation Reference (Ottawa 1980)

64 Québec, Assemblée nationale *Loi sur l'aménagement et l'urbanisme* (1979) 252
65 The term is Nick Auf der Maur's. See his *The Billion Dollar Game: Jean Drapeau and the 1976 Olympics* (Toronto 1976) 31.
66 See Maurice Duverger *Political Parties* trans Barbara and Robert North (New York 1963) 18.
67 McKenna, Brian and Susan Purcell *Drapeau* (Toronto 1980) 129–31
68 See Front d'action politique *Les Salariés au pouvoir* (Montreal 1970).
69 Montreal Municipal Archives, Municipal Election Results, 1970
70 See Donna Gabeline, Dane Lanken, and Gordon Pape *Montreal at the Crossroads* (Montreal 1975).
71 Montreal Municipal Archives, Municipal Election Results, 1974. In the 1976 provincial election Couture was elected as the Parti québécois member for Saint-Henri. He did not run again in 1981.
72 For a description of Olympic financing, see the *Montreal Star* 15 January 1977.
73 For details see Province of Quebec *Report of the Commission of Inquiry into the Cost of the 21st Olympiad* IV (Quebec 1980) 21–68.
74 Members of this group were prolific writers. Much of their material has appeared in the periodical *Our Generation*. See also Stephen Schecter *The Politics of Urban Liberation* (Montreal 1978) chapter 6.
75 For more details, see Henry Milner 'The M.C.M.: Back to the Drawing Board' *City Magazine* (April 1979) 37–41.
76 Terence Moore 'Drapeau and P.Q. Mend Fences' *Montreal Star* 21 May 1977
77 For a map of the boundaries, see *Le Devoir* 26 August 1978. Three more council members were added in 1982 following the annexation of Pointe-aux-Trembles. See *Le Devoir* 25 June 1982.
78 Montreal Municipal Archives, Municipal Election Results, 1978. See also Ludger Beauregard *Les Élections municipales de Montréal* Université de Montréal, Département de géographie, 1980.
79 Quoted in McKenna and Purcell *Drapeau* 102
80 In the 1982 municipal election the MCM prevailed. Its mayoralty candidate, Jean Doré, won 37 per cent of the vote while Henri-Paul Vignola of the MAG received only 15 per cent. Drapeau was re-elected with 48 per cent. Council standings were: Civic party 39, MCM 15, MAG 3. There was a 55 per cent turnout. See the *Gazette* (Montreal) 15 November 1982 and *Le Devoir* 20 November 1982.
81 Montreal Planning Department *Urbanisation: A Study of Urban Expansion in the Montreal Region* 3rd edn (Montreal 1969) 103–14
82 See, for example, A. Garacz, N. Lithwick, and L.O. Stone *The Urban Future* Research Monograph No. 5 of Urban Canada: Problems and Prospects (Ottawa 1971) 138.

83 For details concerning the weak forms of metropolitan government that were established prior to 1960, see Andrew Sancton 'The Impact of Language Differences on Metropolitan Reform in Montreal' *Canadian Public Administration* XXII 2 (summer 1979) 231–2.

84 The campaign is thoroughly described in Roger J. Bédard *La Bataille des annexions* (Montreal 1965).

85 Province of Quebec *Report of the Study Commission on Intermunicipal Problems on the Island of Montreal* (Quebec 1964)

86 For the complete list see Province of Quebec *Statutes* 1969 chap 84 sec 112–14 and 318.

87 Québéc, Ministère des Affaires municipales *Une Nouvelle Communauté: La réforme de la Communauté urbaine de Montréal* (Quebec 1981)

88 *Le Devoir* 5 January 1982

89 Québec *Journal des débats* Commissions parlementaires, Troisième session, 32e Législature, Commission permanente des affaires municipales, 3 mars 1982, no 46, B-2397-B-2436

90 See *Le Devoir* 13 May 1982.

91 *Le Devoir* 19 May, 20 May, and 25 June 1982

92 Quebec, National Assembly *Bill 46: An Act to Amend the Act respecting the Communauté urbaine de Montréal* (Quebec 1982).

93 For details see recent annual reports of the Communauté urbaine de Montréal.

94 Conférence des Maires de la Banlieue de Montréal 'Aménagement du Territoire de la Communauté urbaine de Montréal' mimeo 1976

95 For a thorough account of these decisions, see Jacques Léveillée *Développement urbain et politiques gouvernementales urbaines dans l'agglomération montréalaise, 1945–1975* (Montreal 1978).

96 Roger Gosselin and Jean-Piere Brassard *Mirabel: Site Selection Process and Decision* Case Program in Canadian Public Administration, 1977, 5

97 Montreal Urban Community *1971 Annual Report* (Montreal 1972) 37–47 and *Le Devoir* 10 August 1973

98 *Montreal Star* 20 May 1976

99 *Gazette* 30 May 1979

100 *Le Devoir* 20 June 1979

101 Ibid 21 November 1979

102 *Gazette* 18 December 1979

103 Jane Jacobs *Canadian Cities and Sovereignty Association* (Toronto 1980)

WARREN MAGNUSSON

Toronto

In the last fifteen years, municipal politics in the city of Toronto has become polarized about a set of issues related to urban development. What has been at stake, in part, has been the form and quality of life in the inner city; but it is more complicated than that, for the ultimate issue is for whom the city and its government should exist. The topics of dispute have naturally changed as the growth-pressured city of the 1960s has given way to the economically troubled metropolis of the 1980s. Underlying these changes, however, is a consistent conflict between those who want the city to continue in its traditional role as an agency of support for business and those who insist on a fundamental redirection. This conflict has been played out in a context that helps to sharpen the issues, but makes anything but a traditional response to them difficult. In some respects, this context is common to municipal politics throughout Canada, but in other respects it is peculiar to Toronto.

With less than 600,000 people, the city of Toronto includes only about a fifth of those living in the wider metropolitan area. As such, it is clearly the inner city of a great metropolis. Not only is it much smaller than the city of Montreal, but it is confronted with a far stronger metropolitan government, which has a powerful influence over the course of urban development. Like other Canadian municipalities, it is subordinated to a provincial government and confined to a relatively narrow range of functions, which it must discharge in face of a host of provincial regulations, using funds from a narrow revenue base. The most important of these functions relate to the control of land use and the development of physical services: municipal power in other fields is extremely limited. Nevertheless, as the inner city of Canada's largest metropolis – one of two of truly world scale – Toronto is faced with the concentrated pressures of national development. When growth is rapid, things explode at the centre; when it slows, the effects are felt among a population still drawn to the centre, which includes within itself the very extremes of Canadian society. The city is thus a pressure-cooker for political action and for new definitions of the urban issues that face Canadians.

In Montreal, these urban issues have been overlaid and somewhat obscured by more complex political struggles. In Toronto, they appear more sharply defined. Partly because of this (and partly because of the Torontocentric character of the Canadian media), the city's recent experience has been definitive for a generation of activists and academic observers who identify themselves with the contemporary movement for reform in municipal politics. Unfortunately, this experience has usually been considered abstractly, without any attempt to place it in its historical context. To situate it historically does not mean simply to describe the relevant events of the last thirty years, for what are of crucial importance in the present context are the structures and attitudes that have developed over a longer period. These things are explicable historically, and to explain them is essential for understanding what is given in the present context – in the problems people have, the options they face, and the solutions they seek.

This essay offers a historical perspective on the current situation in Toronto city politics. As such, it not only reviews that situation in some detail, but it provides an overview of the development of city politics and government since their beginning. To some readers, that overview will be of interest in itself. Others may wish to draw some appropriate conclusions: that there is much greater continuity in Toronto politics than most contemporary reformers like to imagine; that this continuity finds expression in a kind of conservatism contained even within movements for reform; and that this conservatism is to some extent imposed by conditions inherited from the past, which reformers cannot easily escape. To understand all this, we must begin at the beginning, in the distant reaches of the colonial past.

THE VICTORIAN CITY

Given Toronto's recent ascendancy over Montreal, it is worth remembering that the community was originally established as an economic outpost of the older city.[1] The French fur traders built a fort there in the eighteenth century, at the intersection of the 'Toronto Passage' from Georgian Bay to Lake Ontario with the main trading route between Montreal and Detroit. It was never a very important outpost for the French, but after the American Revolution the British selected it as a convenient site for the permanent capital of the new province of Upper Canada. For the first thirty years of its history, the town of York was a struggling little settlement heavily dependent on the patronage of the colonial government.[2] By the 1820s, however, the natural economic advantages of the site – on a fine harbour at the junction of overland communications in the centre of a rich agricultural district – began to have their effect, and the town developed rapidly as the main entrepôt for the expanding province. When it was incorporated in 1834, the city of Toronto had almost 9,000 inhabitants, and it was much the largest settlement west of Montreal. Even the temporary loss of its status as provincial capital in 1841 did little to impede its growth.

A key to Toronto's success was its relationship with New York.[3] The Erie Canal, which opened in 1825, provided Upper Canada with a new link to the sea, and Toronto's merchants took advantage of it to break free from their dependence on Montreal. When the Americans followed their canals with railways, ties to the south were cemented. The main problem for Toronto's businessmen in the 1850s was to make sure that the new railway system within the province had its terminus at Toronto. Despite competition from Hamilton and other centres, the Torontonians were successful, and afterwards there was no serious challenge to the city's position as the provincial metropolis. Almost automatically it became the capital of the new province of Ontario in 1867 and thus the unquestioned centre of its political, social, and economic life. As a national metropolis, it was still inferior to Montreal, but its economic hinterland was constantly expanding. The railways gave it a link to the West and to the great timber and mineral resources of northern Ontario. They also strengthened its position in relation to the rest of southern Ontario, which was already the most populous and prosperous region of the country. Toronto began to rival Montreal as a centre for banking and finance as early as the 1870s, and it became the major manufacturing centre in Ontario in the same decade. By 1901, it was a substantial city of over 200,000, ready to bid for national supremacy.[3]

There was remarkably little change in its social composition during this period. In the 1840s, less than 5 per cent of the people in Toronto could trace their origins to any other country than the United Kingdom, and about 80 per cent of the population were Protestants. Despite massive immigration during the next half-century, foreign and Catholic elements actually declined in proportion to the total.[4] Almost all the immigrants came from the British Isles. Many of them were Irish, but Protestants – not Catholics as in Boston or New York – were predominant among them: Toronto became known as the 'Belfast of the North.' Toronto's loyalism, which had been tested and reinforced by Mackenzie's rebellion of 1837,[5] was strengthened by these Irish and British immigrants. This worked to the advantage of the Tories, who had established themselves early as the dominant party in the city. The purported threats of republicanism, annexationism, Catholicism, and French resurgence (however remote they may have been) helped to unify an otherwise divided WASP majority and to buttress the position of those whose loyalty could least be questioned.

There were serious religious divisions among the Protestants, particularly between the Anglicans and the other sects (especially the Presbyterians and Methodists). There also were rivalries between the English, Irish, and Scots, so that this apparently homogeneous city was often riven by ethnic and religious conflict. Churches and churchmen played a part in political mobilization, but more important were the countless fraternal societies, which were closely connected to particular ethnic and religious communities. The most powerful of these was the Loyal Orange Order, which had its base among the Irish Protestants.[6] The fraternal societies acted as primitive welfare agencies for their members and provided crucial support for many new immigrants. The lodge brethren relied on one another for jobs and business connections. Political support was one of the things 'little' men could give to the greater in return for their patronage. Aspirant politicians could thus find in the lodges ready-made political machines. Their members could be mobilized by a judicious combination of appeals to the appropriate loyalties and promises of 'jobs for the boys.'

The political, social, and economic life of the community was structured by a complicated pattern of clientelist relations.[7] It was conceded generally that political office should be reserved for men of substance. The franchise was based on property qualifications, which were retained for municipal elections long after they were abolished provincially. Although the restrictions were gradually relaxed, they remained tight enough to exclude the ordinary workman.[8] At the bottom of the electorate economically were the jobbers, artisans, and shopkeepers, who depended on private and public patronage. Bigger businessmen looked to government for contracts and other assistance and relied on their clients to support them. Men elected to municipal office were not necessarily (or even usually) great businessmen, but if not they were effective political brokers (lodgemen, tavern keepers, jobbers) who could sustain support on the understanding that the benefits from government to business would be shared by their own dependants. Relations were structured by ethnic, religious, and fraternal loyalties. This added heat to political contests, but helped to inhibit any class-based challenge to the existing order.

The government of the city was only one of the prizes for local politicians. The lines between municipal, provincial, and (later) federal politics were not very sharply drawn, and the political parties exploited their opportunities wherever they lay. Municipal politics was as partisan as any other, but the parties were just loose coalitions that could and did break apart under pressure. In a straight party fight, the Tories could almost always win an election in Toronto, and their men usually dominated the municipal council. The Liberals – or the Reformers as they were earlier known – tried to get round this by making non-partisan appeals. On the council itself, the Tories rarely acted as a unit, for they were divided over the spoils of office. Thus there was considerable scope for alliances across party lines, and many came to think that party allegiances were, or ought to be, irrelevant to municipal politics. John Bowes, the Tory mayor of Toronto in 1853, displayed this non-partisan spirit when he joined with Francis Hincks, the Reform premier, in a little speculation in railway debentures backed by the municipal treasury.[9]

If there was an ideological split in municipal politics, it cut across party lines and set the 'boosters' against the 'cutters.' The latter were concerned about the ever-increasing expenditures on public works and related municipal activities. Since there was justified suspicion that the municipal treasury was being tapped by a variety of contractors, jobbers, and political hangers-on, the pressure for economy was bound up with the demand for honesty in government. The middle-class ratepayers' association provided important support for the cutters.[10] Its constituents paid the bulk of the taxes, but depended little on the municipal authorities for jobs or business opportunities. When the city had over-extended itself in the latest round of public works (as it did periodically), the cutters attracted a wider following. However, in times of prosperity the boosters had greater influence, since they expressed the general confidence in metropolitan expansion. Businessmen at the top of the heap and workmen at the bottom (as well as many in between) had an interest in expanding public works, since the contracts were always let to private enterprise. Service improvements were also the key to developing new urban real estate, in which many with an interest in municipal politics were speculating. Then as now, all such investments were justified to the public as helps to the local economy and improvements to the quality of urban life.

That the main function of municipal government was to provide the hard services necessary for urban life hardly anyone doubted. Unlike the English local authorities, the ones in Ontario never had a legal responsibility to provide for the poor.[11] This suited them well, as they could leave such assistance to the private charities. The city of Toronto was somewhat more generous than other cities (faced as it was with a more obvious problem), but it satisfied itself by making grants to autonomous charitable institutions, such as the House of Industry[12] and Toronto General Hospital. The only social service for which there was a strong commitment was public education, and the management of the school system was early entrusted to a board of education elected separately from the municipal council. This helped to insulate the municipal council from the religious disputes connected to education and allowed it to concentrate on its primary business of building the city.[13] The council levied rates on city properties to finance street improvements, sidewalks, and sewers and ultimately to provide the city with piped water and gas, street lighting, and tramways, all of which were necessary to the infrastructure of a nineteenth-century metropolis. The city also provided its inhabitants with police and fire protection and was concerned with various forms of regulation thought necessary for public health and security and the peaceable conduct of trade.[14] Its activities were thus designed to protect the social and economic infrastructure of the developing metropolis.

Perhaps the most controversial and expensive of the municipal activities was the letting of franchises for public services to private entrepreneurs. Great scandals were associated with the franchises for gas and water-supply (1841–72) and tramways (1861–1921) and helped to create early pressure for public ownership as a cheaper alternative.[15] However, the management of services under direct municipal control, such as policing and fire protection, never inspired much confidence and helped to convince the majority of ratepayers that private enterprise in the public services was essential for efficiency. The evidence for this was similarly scanty, but the entrepreneurs who profited from municipal franchises wielded enough influence to turn many a vote on council and gain the favour of the political brokers. Council was also involved in offering 'bonuses' (or subsidies) to industries thought necessary for the city's development. The railways, in the 1850s, were the main beneficiaries of this largesse and put a considerable strain on the municipal treasury.[16] Some of the most expensive (and disruptive) of early public works were designed to facilitate railway access to the harbour and the centre of the city: Toronto still bears the marks of these efforts, which gave its waterfront over to the railways. Later in the century, interest shifted to 'bonusing' manufacturing industries,[17] but the ostensible aim – to boost the development of the city – remained the same. The business of the municipal council was business.

THE AGE OF REFORM

Toronto's success as an economic centre necessarily brought changes in the conduct of municipal government and in the character of municipal politics.

There were 100,000 people in the city and its environs in the early 1880s, and the population quadrupled in the next thirty years. This put considerable strain on the existing administrative system. There was originally little in the way of a civil service, and the aldermen elected to council were expected to do most of the managerial work themselves. All of them were part-time officials, and few of them were interested in much beyond their own wards. As the city expanded, new seats were added to the council, and it became less effective as a decision-making body. Most of the important business was left to the council's committees, the chairmen of which became very powerful. The mayor was largely a ceremonial figure, elected by his fellow aldermen to preside over the full meetings of council and represent the city on official occasions. In the absence of party discipline, decisions depended on complicated trade-offs among the aldermen and the interests they represented. No one within the council took obvious responsibility for the good management of the city as a whole, and the aldermen generally stood on their records as ward representatives. As the business of the municipality expanded, the apparent lack of responsible central management became a cause of increasing concern.

Toronto caught the fever of American municipal reform, which began in the 1880s and started to come to fruition in the following decade.[18] Already, in 1873, the city had acquired an American-style mayor, elected at large by the ratepayers.[19] He was the first official chosen to be responsible to the electorate as a whole. Then in 1891, the size of the council was reduced from forty to twenty-five, and the old wards were scrapped in favour of six elongated 'strips' running north from the lake.[20] The new wards were designed to be heterogeneous and so to create for each alderman a constituency as diverse as the city as a whole. This was supposed to enlarge their political vision. Five years later, a board of control was established as a kind of executive committee of the council, with special powers in relation to the budget, appointments, and tenders. Since on many matters it could be overruled only by a two-thirds vote of the council, the board was extremely powerful.[21] Its independence was reinforced in 1903, when the four controllers also were made subject to election at large.[22] In principle (if not always in fact), the day-to-day management of the city passed out of the hands of the ward aldermen and into the five-man board chosen by the city as a whole.

These changes were complemented by two other developments. First, responsibility for particular public services was assigned to bodies independent of the municipal council. This had been a well-established tradition before the age of municipal reform, because it had always been clear that certain services would be badly administered if left to the aldermen. Three sorts of functions were involved: public utilities, social services, and police regulation. The latter was one of the primary functions of local government, but there was considerable suspicion about the council's ability to act impartially. Thus, control of the police was given to an independent commission in 1859, as later were the regulatory functions of liquor licensing and public health.[23] With respect to social services, council was anxious to maintain its relationship at arm's length, in order to minimize its own financial responsibility. The many charitable institutions that emerged towards the end of the nineteenth century and at the beginning of the twentieth – refuges, asylums, reformatories, orphanages, special schools, hospitals, children's aid societies, settlement houses, housing societies, and so on – remained autonomous, even if they looked to the municipality for assistance.[24] Autonomous management by those most interested was supposed to enhance efficiency and encourage (financial) self-reliance. Similar considerations applied to the public utilities, which could in principle operate as self-supporting businesses within a framework of municipal regulation. The Victorian preference was to franchise private companies for this purpose, but there was growing sentiment towards the end of the nineteenth century in favour of public ownership. Thus, the city ended up providing water (1872), electricity (1905), and transit (1921) services.[25] The preference for independent management remained, however, and these utilities were placed under the control of separate commissions (appointed by the council).[26] The effects of such arrangements were to reduce considerably the range of business under the direct control of the municipal council and so to lighten the administrative burden. Nevertheless, the municipality remained the only local authority with powers of taxation, so it was an important funding agency. It was also at the centre of the local authority system, in that it set policies and made appointments in relation to the other agencies and was a centre of initiative for new activities.

Crucial for the maintenance of its position was the second development associated with municipal reform: the emergence of a professional bureaucracy. The existing system of civic administration was strongly criticized in a report commissioned from New York's Bureau of Municipal Research in 1913.[27] This led to the appointment of a powerful new commissioner of finance three years later. He became one of a set of officials, including the commissioner of works (1912), the city auditor (1908), and the medical officer of health (1883), who enjoyed a new sort of autonomy and status in relation to the council.[28] Although the merit system was not fully established until after the Second World War,[29] the municipal service attained much of the character of a professional bureaucracy long before then. Thus, from the viewpoint of municipal reform, the city of Toronto was near to achieving what it needed for efficient, honest, and responsible government: a small political executive accountable to the electorate at large, but made sensitive to ward concerns by the council; a professional civil service, selected on merit and organized on sound administrative principles; and a rational division of authority among functional agencies, controlled by those with the appropriate interests and expertise.

The fears of the upper and middle classes about democratization played an important part in these changes. There was continuing pressure for widening the franchise, especially after universal suffrage for men was introduced in provincial elections in 1888.[30] This pressure was resisted with some success, but the introduction of the secret ballot in 1876[31] made it more difficult to exercise control over those who did have the right to vote. The conditions for social and political control were in any case changing as a result of urban and industrial development. The railways and tramways made it possible for people to move away from the centres of commerce and industry. Thus the rich and the not-so-rich were able to segregate themselves more effectively from the poor. People could also sort themselves on an ethnic or religious basis.[32] Toronto finally began to receive significant foreign immigration just before the turn of the century, and the new arrivals tended to concentrate in a few small neighbourhoods.[33] This immigration was connected to the development of the factory system, which produced another sort of distance between workers and employers. Unions emerged and threatened to monopolize working-class loyalties.[34] They were rivalled by more traditional organizations, but control of the latter by the upper and upper-middle classes had become more difficult because of social and physical distancing.

The structural reforms introduced were intended to make the municipality less vulnerable to inappropriate influences from 'below.' The labour unions supported many of these reforms, because they seemed to work against the traditional political machines controlled by the Liberals and Tories.[35] However, the movement for municipal reform was dominated by businessmen and associated intellectuals.[36] In its earliest form, it was bound up with the campaigns for temperance and moral regeneration. W.H. Howland, who swept from nowhere into the mayoralty in 1886, was its most prominent standard-bearer.[37] He and his followers had considerable success in tightening control over drink and other forms of 'degeneracy' (such as selling newspapers on Sundays) and so solidified the city's reputation as 'Toronto the Good.'[38] Their efforts had widespread support, especially among Methodists and other non-Anglican Protestants, who had become an increasingly important element both in the population as a whole and in the socio-economic élite.[39] None the less, the linkage of municipal reform to moral reform alienated potential supporters, and people interested in business efficiency had to detach themselves from the moralizers to get the changes they wanted.[40]

Of course, the prohibitionist emphasis of the movement for reform was connected to concerns about poverty and its political effects. As the movement matured, more attention was given to concrete remedial measures. The most important of these related to public health, in its broadest sense. Toronto at the turn of the century was by no means a healthy place to live: indeed, by standard measures such as infant mortality it was worse than London or New York.[41] Its water was often contaminated, and its milk and foodstuffs adulterated. Measures for controlling the spread of disease were primitive at best. It was not until ca 1910 that a serious effort to come to terms with these problems began, chiefly under the influence of the medical officer of health.[42] The water was chlorinated, sewage disposal was improved, milk supplies were controlled, and free vaccination programs were begun. As a result of such efforts, the Department of Public Health gradually became involved in various welfare programs. Some of these grew out of a concern for the health of children, which led to home visits by nurses in the department's employ. This in turn brought pressure from the nurses concerned for action on the problem of housing: unsanitary accommodation was obviously a source of disease. The city responded by tightening enforcement of building regulations, condemning various houses as unfit, and requiring improvements (especially indoor plumbing) in others. In a classic pattern, this tended to reduce the stock and raise the rents of housing for the poor.[43] The city came under pressure, as a consequence, to meet the shortfall by sponsoring some form of social housing. It managed to deflect this pressure only by lending its support to the Toronto Housing Company and the Toronto Housing Commission, which built a few low-cost houses in 1913 and 1920 respectively.[44] Neither of these civic-sponsored organizations lasted long or had much effect on the housing market, but their emergence reflected pervasive demands for positive action on social problems.

Similar pressures forced the municipality to take a greater interest in poor relief. It had gradually been increasing its assistance to the charities, but they were incapable of handling the problems of relief during periods of high unemployment. The city was obliged to accept the fact that the municipality was the place of last resort for the destitute, and it responded by making emergency grants for relief through the appropriate charities.[45] It also sponsored free employment agencies and stepped up its own works programs to make more jobs available.[46] As its financial liabilities became greater, it became more concerned about the administrative inadequacies of the charities it supported. This led to the formation of a Social Service Commission in 1912, to advise the council on its own funding activities and to help co-ordinate the work of the voluntary agencies. The former responsibilities were transferred to the new Social Welfare Division of the Public Health Department in 1921.[47] The establishment of this unit finally confirmed the fact that municipal involvement in welfare was permanent. Its increasingly professional officers not only administered relief (and paid out the mothers' allowances and old-age pensions introduced by the senior governments), but also involved themselves in various forms of casework.

Important as these developments were, it should not be imagined that municipal reformers were interested in turning the city into a miniature welfare state. On the contrary, most of them insisted that the municipal role in social services had to be strictly limited, if the city was not to be stretched beyond its fiscal capacity. The commonly accepted idea was that the city was essentially a joint-stock company belonging to the ratepayers who contributed to its funds.[48] These funds were to be used to enhance the value of property in the city, improve amenities for its residents, and stimulate local business. The burden of other activities, it was suggested, should not fall on the local ratepayer, but be borne by the general taxpayer. This did not mean that the city would be inactive. Quite the reverse: it had much to do to improve the system of transportation, make public utilities (such as water and electricity) readily available, remove threats to health and safety, and generally to enhance the quality of urban life.[49] The financial and administrative burdens of these basic activities were quite sufficient to tax the reformed city government. There was great pressure upon it before and after the First World War to extend its efforts in these directions. The municipalization of electric utilities and public transit were two of the important consequences of this. Another was the emergence of a new concern for planning the development of the city.

Planning meant different things to different people, but it generally had a physical emphasis. It was concerned with rationalizing land use in order to improve the efficiency of transportation, beautify the centre of the city, and enhance the quality of the environment in residential neighbourhoods. The general hope was that private and public agencies could work together for these purposes without being obliged by legislation. With this end in mind, a series of advisory plans were produced in Toronto from 1909 onwards.[50] However, none of these plans had much effect, because they involved a level of public expenditure unacceptable to the ratepayers. What did prove effective and acceptable (to those with political influence) was the system of restrictive zoning that the city had begun to develop under authority obtained from the province between 1904 and 1927.[51] This system was essentially designed to protect established residential neighbourhoods from unwanted intrusions, in the form of industry or high-density low-income housing. Council responded assiduously to the demands of home-owners for by-law restrictions on these forms of land use and thus gave legal protection to some city residents against the unwanted effects of urban development.

These forms of planning and zoning were acceptable to business because they left ample room for entrepreneurial manoeuvre. Nevertheless, there was a continuing tension in municipal politics between the business interest in expansion and the ratepayer-consumer interest in public economy, environmental quality, and service to civic residents. This tension was apparent within and between people of the same class and within and between the different elements of the municipal council. One expression of this tension was the debate over extending city boundaries (and services) to developing suburbs. The boosters who favoured expansion had considerable success in getting the council to agree to such extensions during the real estate booms of the 1880s and the early 1900s.[52] However, the cost to the city of servicing these suburbs was so great that it stimulated an economizing reaction (always made more severe by the inevitable collapse of the boom). The fact that such a reaction set in in 1912, before the city had completed the absorption of its pre-war suburbs, was to have profound effects on the future of municipal politics.[53]

THE DEVELOPMENT OF THE METROPOLIS

The Great Depression was less devastating for Toronto than for such cities as Winnipeg and Montreal. Toronto was not as dependent as they were on the Prairie wheat economy, which almost collapsed during the 1930s. The city benefited from its position as the centre of the Canadian mining industry – a position it had established after 1903, when the great mineral deposits of northern Ontario were opened up.[54] Gold mining especially remained profitable during the Depression and buttressed the position of Toronto's financial institutions. As Montreal suffered, Toronto surpassed it as a financial centre and so established a base from which it could expand when prosperity returned.[55] Manufacturing in southern Ontario, which was centred on Toronto, had long been better developed and more diversified than in Quebec.[56] Of particular importance was heavy industry, which had located originally in the area because of access to cheap energy and mineral resources. Other industry was dependent both on the products of the heavy industrial sector and on the markets of southern Ontario, so that it was drawn to locate in the same region. As Toronto developed as a financial and administrative centre, the comparative advantages of an Ontario location increased. This was especially true for American enterprises looking to expand into Canada from their bases immediately south of the Great Lakes.[57]

During the Depression itself, of course, there was little expansion going on. The city of Toronto was faced with the same, if less severe, problems as other municipalities in Canada, as thousands defaulted on their property taxes and thousands more demanded unemployment relief. Despite its reluctance, it was ultimately obliged to assume the main responsibility for relief and to create a separate Department of Public Welfare for this purpose.[58] The federal and provincial governments stepped in to provide the bulk of the money for municipal relief, but the cities (which attracted more than their share of the unemployed) still were faced with a large escalation of costs at a time when their ability to collect taxes was decreasing. Fortunately for the city of Toronto, it could rely on revenues from downtown business. This was not the case for its suburbs (where well over 100,000 people were living even before the Depression). Almost all these fringe municipalities became virtually bankrupt and passed under provincial control.[59] In a way, this vindicated the city's earlier decision not to expand its boundaries, but the province's intervention foreshadowed a new system of metropolitan government, which would seriously diminish the city's role.

Traditionally, the city had enjoyed considerable autonomy in relation to the province. Before 1930, nearly 99 per cent of its revenues were its own,[60] so it was not subject to much financial pressure from the provincial government. The province lacked the administrative apparatus to keep the city in check even if it had wanted to. Although it retained the legislative authority to determine what the city could and could not do, it tended to extend the city's powers in response to pressures from the municipal council and other local politicians.[61] Thus the initiative in provincial-municipal relations remained with the city. However, beginning in the 1880s the province started to take a more consistent interest in business it had previously left to the municipalities.[62] This was partly because of local reluctance to deal with problems of public health, education, and social welfare, and partly because of municipal incompetence and extravagance in dealings with the railways and other utility companies. There was not much legitimate concern about

Toronto in either respect, since the city was as sound financially and as competent and progressive administratively as the province itself. Nevertheless, it got caught in a web of controls that applied to the other municipalities.

The most powerful agency of provincial control was the Ontario Railway and Municipal Board, which was established in 1906 to regulate railways and local utilities and to control the issuing of municipal debentures.[63] It was also given appeal jurisdiction in relation to municipal assessments and allowed to regulate the subdivision of land on the fringes of cities. In 1921, its powers in relation to land use were extended to include the approval of restrictive zoning by-laws. When municipalities began defaulting on their debentures in the early 1930s, they were put under the direct supervision of the board. In 1934, a provincial Department of Municipal Affairs was organized with a reconstituted Ontario Municipal Board (OMB) as one of its agencies. The existing system of controls was tightened, so that all municipalities, including Toronto, had to get provincial approval for their capital spending plans, public utilities policies, and zoning activities.[64] Later, between 1937 and 1944, the province took exclusive control of the taxation of income and corporate profits, both of which had been (minor) sources of municipal revenue. In return, it began providing small, unconditional subsidies to the municipalities and in 1945 started a great expansion of its conditional grants for municipal services.[65] As a result, Toronto came at last to depend on provincial funding. To an increasing extent, it also became an administrative agency of the province, as it organized services in accordance with the conditions attached to provincial grants.

The realignment of financial and administrative responsibilities that occurred in the 1930s and 1940s tended to confirm the city in its role as a business agent for local property-owners. This role had been threatened by the overwhelming burden of relief expenditures during the Depression; but a consensus soon emerged in favour of transferring responsibility for such matters to the senior governments. They alone had the legislative authority and powers of taxation necessary for the wider regulation of the economy and the effective development of social services. In Toronto as elsewhere, municipal leaders preferred to withdraw from the field except as agents of the senior governments and to confine their attention to activities that could be financed from taxes on property.[66] These activities related to the services, regulations, and facilities necessary for urban life. In the expansionist mood of the 1940s (and the subsequent decades) the hope was to develop an infrastructure for rapid metropolitan expansion. The difficulties of the 1930s had left Toronto and other cities with a great backlog of investments to be made, and municipal leaders were generally determined to protect their revenues for this purpose.

For half a century business leaders in Toronto had feared a serious challenge from the labour movement and its socialist allies, but it never really emerged. There were various reasons for this. Despite considerable growth in union membership, only a minor fraction of the work-force ever became organized.[67] Toronto's manufacturing sector contained a high proportion of small, marginally profitable firms, which relied on cheap immigrant (often female) labour. These firms were difficult for the unions to organize. At the other end of the scale, by virtue of Toronto's emergence as a financial and administrative centre, its labour force contained a high proportion of white-collar workers who were equally difficult to unionize. Although the structure of the society was changing, at mid-century clientelist relationships were still of major importance. Thus the fraternal societies and the traditional political parties maintained their strength. It was particularly difficult for the labour organizations to challenge the traditional pattern of municipal politics, because the franchise was still so restrictive that many unionists were excluded from voting. During the Depression even fewer could vote, because they had been forced on welfare or had lost their homes for tax arrears. Those who remained in the electorate had a great incentive to vote conservatively, since any rise in municipal expenditures could lead to a disastrous increase in property taxes.

As a result, the municipal political system in Toronto survived even the Depression without much disturbance. The most dramatic challenge came from Jimmy Simpson, a long-time unionist and socialist who was elected mayor in 1935.[68] His policies were not very radical, since his main concern was to provide more generous relief for the unemployed and higher wages for municipal workers. Nevertheless, this brought him into conflict with the provincial government and threatened the interests of the ratepayers, who turned him out of office a year later. His successor was a maverick Tory named Sam McBride: the sort of populist, anti-establishment figure who came to power in many Canadian cities in this period, when people were suspicious of traditional politicians but unwilling to commit themselves to more radical alternatives.[69] McBride's tenure was brief, and it had equally little impact on the character of municipal politics in the city. In the early 1940s, there was another brief flurry of excitement when both the Communists and the CCF (which was then at the height of its national popularity) mounted strong campaigns.[70] This challenge was effectively repelled. Socialists and unionists continued to run for municipal council after the mid-1940s, but generally as independent, non-partisan candidates. The CCF formally abandoned municipal politics. It thus imitated the strategy earlier adopted by the Liberals, who could see no advantage in testing their partisan strength against the dominant Conservatives. By this time, non-partisanship was widely accepted as a principle of municipal politics, and it was not easy for anyone to challenge it.[71]

When the Conservatives returned to power provincially in 1943, they and their counterparts on the Toronto city council were prepared to take a more active role than ever in promoting economic development. The city had been a main beneficiary of the industrial expansion engendered by the Second World War, and there was hope that with public support the boom would continue after the end of hostilities. The city's new permanent Planning Board, which had been established in 1942, issued a master plan for the development of the metropolis.[72] It entailed massive infrastructural investments, and it also confirmed what everyone could already tell – that most of the new housing and much of the new industry would have to be located in the suburbs. This put the problem of metropolitan government on the city's political agenda. Since the early 1920s, the province had been pressing the city to accept some financial responsibility for the development of services in the suburbs it refused to annex. The city resisted this pressure and managed to defeat any plan for establishing a metropolitan service district.[73] The prospect of massive growth in the suburbs in the 1940s finally changed its attitude, for there were justifiable fears that the suburban councils could not cope with the financial and administrative burdens involved and that the development of the whole area would be held back as a result. Only the city and the province had the resources to cope with the problems of metropolitan expansion, and the city preferred to keep control for itself.

These imperialistic designs were ultimately defeated by the province, acting on behalf of the suburbs. After several major studies of the matter, the city had finally applied to the OMB in 1950 for authority to annex all the municipalities surrounding it. This application was denied in favour of a plan that preserved all the existing municipalities and established an overarching metropolitan government.[74] As constituted by provincial legislation in 1953, the new Metropolitan Toronto Council was formed of a dozen representatives from the city and a dozen from its suburbs. Its first chairman was appointed by the province for a one-year term, but subsequently he was to be elected annually by Metro Council itself. In a sense, the new authority was simply to be a joint agency of the municipalities concerned, but it turned out to be much more than that. Especially under the leadership of its original chairman, Frederick Gardiner (1953–61), Metro came to displace the city as the leading municipal authority in the area.[75]

From the beginning, it was obvious that Metro's major responsibility was to facilitate suburban expansion. The city's financial resources were made available for this purpose. Municipal borrowing was centralized under Metro control, to make it possible for the suburbs to raise money on the city's credit rating. Metro's own services were financed from the rates levied by the area municipalities. This meant that it could tap the resources of the city's central business district to finance services in the suburbs. Its crucial powers were to build arterial roads and lay sewer and water-mains. It also took control of the city's public transit system, with the understanding that services would be extended to the suburbs. The other major suburban need – school construction – was met by the Metropolitan School Board, which had been constituted at the same time and given similar power to tap city resources for suburban purposes.[76] The Metropolitan Planning Board was given overall responsibility for land-use planning on the fringes of the metropolitan area, as well as within its constituent municipalities.[77] Thus the metropolitan authorities were expected to act as a kind of senior government intermediate between the province and the municipalities.

Metro's growth as a government was held partly in check by the municipal representatives who constituted Metro Council and were concerned about preserving a measure of local autonomy. This localist influence was offset by the Metro chairman, who emerged as a figure of exceptional power. Gardiner came to the office with unusual advantages. Not only was he an experienced municipal politician, but he was a confidant of the provincial premier and a force to be reckoned with in the Conservative party.[78] He was also an extraordinarily skilful politician, who knew well how to appease his opponents and bully and cajole his supporters into line. Fortunately for him, the other members of Metro Council devoted little time to metropolitan affairs: their service on the wider body was an incident of local office, and their prospects of re-election depended mostly on what they did on their own municipal councils. Thus Gardiner and his senior administrators were left with the policy initiative. They got widespread support for what they did, since they were acting on the general commitment to support metropolitan expansion. So long as the parochial concerns of each municipality were respected, the local politicians were content to let Metro take the lead.

The most significant opposition to Gardiner and Metro came from the city of Toronto, which had most to lose as a political unit from the development of a strong metropolitan government. Toronto city council continued to press for full amalgamation of the area municipalities – i.e. for the dissolution of the metropolitan government and incorporation of the suburbs into the city.[79] This became a less and less likely prospect as Metro established itself as a separate government and the suburbs gained in population and financial strength. The city supported the growth of Metro at its own expense only because it regarded every transfer of services to the wider authority as a step towards full amalgamation. Thus it gave up control of its police to Metro in 1957 and backed a number of other measures for the unification of services.[80] In response to pressures from the city, the province appointed a royal commission to review the whole system of metropolitan government in 1963–5.[81] To Toronto's disappointment, the commission opposed complete amalgamation and recommended measures to strengthen the suburban municipalities. In 1966, the province consolidated the suburbs into five boroughs, which ranged in population from about 100,000 to 500,000. The idea was to create municipalities that could operate on a par with the city within the metropolitan system. Metro was also strengthened by a new accretion of powers, and its council was enlarged to give greater representation to the suburbs.[82] The result was to diminish even further the city's role in metropolitan government.

While the metropolis as a whole had doubled in population (from 1 million to 2 million) between the early 1940s and the early 1960s, the city had remained static at about 650,000. So long as its boundaries remained fixed, it was bound to be reduced to the status of an inner-city municipality within a wider metropolitan unit. Although city politicians resisted this outcome, they adapted themselves pragmatically to their role. One consequence of this was their lobbying on Metro Council for the special interests of the inner city – most notably the shift of funds from expressway construction to public transit and the opening of the suburbs to public housing.[83] With respect to the overall development of the metropolis, the city's main concern was to protect itself from decline, since outward dispersal threatened to weaken the centre. Thus, the city council began in the 1950s to rezone land for high-rise development and to give whatever encouragement it could to potential investors.[84] In itself, this support for development was far from new, but it occurred within a context that ultimately produced enormous pressure for restraint. This was to give the politics of the 1960s and after its distinctive character.

THE TRANSFORMATION OF THE INNER CITY

The city was transformed during the post-war boom.[85] At the beginning of the Second World War, its population was still almost 80 per cent British in origin and overwhelmingly Protestant. Thirty years later, the WASPS were in a clear minority. The Roman Catholic church became the largest in the city, and almost 40 per cent of local residents had a mother tongue other than English. In most of the west end and parts of the east, recent immigrants had become the dominant element in the population.[86] This gave the city a social character that distinguished it not only from its former self, but also from the surrounding suburbs.[87] The old industrial districts near the centre of the city remained a major source of employment for new immigrants, and ethnic enclaves developed in the surrounding neighbourhoods.[88] In terms of its housing stock and its commercial and industrial space, the city afforded facilities that were older, more densely packed, and potentially cheaper than anything in the suburbs (especially when transportation costs were taken into account). Thus it held on to the people and businesses that could not afford to join in the movement to the suburbs.

The city might have become impoverished if the central business district had not profited as much as it did from metropolitan expansion. There was a strong and continuing demand for central office space, which in turn created a demand for high-class residential and commercial space in the centre. Massive office and apartment complexes were developed to meet these demands, and there were complementary moves to renovate older downtown neighbourhoods for middle-class life.[89] For prosperous professionals and business people, the immigrant element in the city's population added to its metropolitan ambiance: so too did the artists and intellectuals attracted to what was emerging as the centre of English-Canadian culture and communications. Thus, for both social and economic reasons, the city remained an attractive locale for the upper crust of the metropolitan community. Despite worries, Toronto never was seriously threatened by the sort of racial conflict that devalued the inner areas of American cities, and it was one of the continental leaders in downtown renovation and redevelopment.

Each level of government played its part in these changes. Ottawa, of course, was responsible for organizing the reception of successive waves of immigrants – first from northern, then from southern Europe, and finally from various parts of the Third World. As the developing national metropolis, Toronto was the conduit and destination for much of this immigration.[90] It was also the centre of the economic revival being engineered by the federal government. American capital was being attracted to Canada to extract resources for export to the United States and to develop an array of factories and services for the domestic Canadian market. With its convenient location and traditional ties to the United States, Toronto was the natural headquarters for these ventures.[91] However, the development of the economy, locally and nationally, depended on infrastructural modernization. This involved the switch to a road-based transportation system and the spread of business operations across the suburbs and into the satellite towns of the metropolis. The provincial and municipal governments – and in Toronto the metropolitan authorities – provided the necessary infrastructural support, but it was the federal government that sustained the effective demand for expanding production. Through the Central Housing and Mortgage Corporation (CMHC), it also produced and sustained a mass market for suburban housing, which made the development of the suburbs more profitable and helped to justify massive public investments there.[92]

In a sense, the city of Toronto was a spectator in the development that transformed the metropolis, since it had little control over what happened in the suburbs. However, the municipal council did what it could to create a favourable climate for investment in the central city. Toronto was a leader in the development of municipal planning, which was conceived as (among other things) a guide and support for private investment.[93] The Planning Department, established as early as 1930, and the Planning Board, formed in 1942, were responsible for producing the city's first official plan, which was adopted by council in 1950. More important for day-to-day land-use control was the comprehensive zoning by-law, which finally came into effect in 1954, after almost twenty years of preparation. It was a consolidation of existing land-use restrictions, supposedly also reflecting the principles of the official plan. The zoning by-law was intended to protect existing property investments (especially home-owner investments in middle-class neighbourhoods), while locating areas suitable for redevelopment. The city's own infrastructural investments (such as the country's first subway system, completed just as the transit system was taken over by Metro in 1954) were supposed to be guided by the policies implicit in both the plan and the zoning by-law. It was hoped that private investors would be attracted by a situation in which they could plan securely, count on the services they needed, and get zoning protection for the investments they made.

As it happened, investors often wanted permission to build in ways or places not allowed by existing regulations. The city council generally obliged them, by 'spot-rezoning' to permit the proposed development.[94] This reflected its anxiety to make planning and zoning work for development (although it weakened the rationale for the whole system). The city also attempted to act as a developer on its own, but in ways complementary to private enterprise. Its transportation investments and other infrastructural improvements were of course of this sort, but so too were its 'slum-clearance' projects. The first of these – the first in the country – was Regent Park (North), initiated in 1947.[95] It involved the clearance and redevelopment for public housing of a large portion of Cabbagetown, one of the main slums identified in a 1934 report on the city's housing conditions. Federal money for public housing, which became available in 1944, made such investment attractive, and the city eventually committed itself to the largest program of public housing and urban renewal in the country. This commitment was justified as a means of preventing the social and economic deterioration of the inner city, and hence for preserving a favourable climate for private investment.

What was not yet clear in the 1950s was that policies of this kind were bound to generate strong political opposition. In the mid-1950s, the city's planners identified a number of other impoverished neighbourhoods and set in motion studies that would lead to redevelopment. Several of these projects were carried to completion over the next fifteen years, but each succeeding scheme generated more opposition.[96] It became clear that the poor did not want to be expropriated and removed to make way for new developments, on the chance that they would be included some years hence in the public housing constructed. They were seldom consulted about the plans concerned and were paid extremely low prices for the properties they lost. The federal, provincial, and even the Metropolitan authorities responded more quickly than the city to the signs of discontent and began pressuring it in the early 1960s to make its policies more sensitive.[97] Once the city started to open its planning to participation (as it did in 1962), the opposition it encountered actually increased. Demands for more participation led to further openings in the process, which in turn led to more complaints and more demands for more participation. As a result, the city's program for slum-clearance and redevelopment became completely bogged down by the late 1960s.

Toronto's difficulties in this field had a great influence on the federal government, which decided then to shut off its support for 'urban renewal' (the current euphemism for slum-clearance).[98] Ottawa itself had had a part in generating the difficulties, since it had started in the mid-1960s to finance community organizers to help the poor help themselves.[99] In Toronto, the poor helped themselves to protection from the city's developers. The federally paid organizers were not the only ones in the field: others were sponsored by churches or even by the city. However, they all tended to stimulate community organizations that put increased demands on the city and placed obstacles in the way of unilateral action. On the whole, this was the effect the organizers sought, since they wanted to redress the balance in the pressure-group system, which worked in favour of people with money and skills.[100] It seems doubtful whether the balance actually shifted, for the mobilization (such as it was) coincided with the mobilization of middle- and upper-class consumers. The latter had a more profound effect on civic politics.

Middle- and upper-class neighbourhoods had come to be threatened by private and public developers. The former were responsible for the wave of apartment construction that began in Toronto in the mid-1950s (earlier than elsewhere in the country) and for the high-rise commercial redevelopment in the core that started about ten years later.[101] Apartment-building (facilitated by spot-rezoning) had a profound and (from the local residents' viewpoint) deleterious effect on residential neighbourhoods. Opposition to such projects stimulated the formation or revival of ratepayers' and residents' groups, which became increasingly militant in face of a city council insensitive to their concerns.[102] In 1968, a Confederation of Residents' and Ratepayers' Associations (CORRA) was established as a co-ordinating agency; it not only linked the middle-class organizations with one another, but brought them into contact with community groups being formed in poorer neighbourhoods. The result was a network of opponents to the existing council. Equally important as an oppositional agency was SSSOCCC: the Stop Spadina, Save Our City, Coordinating Committee.[103] It had been formed to oppose the Spadina Expressway, which had been planned by Metro to penetrate the core of the city from the northwest. The potential disruptiveness of this project (which had generally been criticized by city council, but not opposed with the vigour or unanimity desired) was sufficient to mobilize a mass opposition that overlapped with the one contained within CORRA.

As the opposition to civic policies coalesced, it found expression in a new ideology – or ideologies – of urban reform.[104] In part, this involved a new urban conservatism. The city and Metro were both accused of adopting policies that would lead to the ultimate destruction of the inner city. Their aim was ostensibly to support the central business district, by opening up access from the suburbs, but the influx of commuters meant more traffic congestion, noise, and pollution. All this made the inner city less habitable, drove more people out to the suburbs, and created more demand for commuter access. Providing such access for commuters relying on automobiles meant widening roads and building expressways: these projects themselves had a deleterious effect on downtown neighbourhoods. Construction of downtown apartments of course was intended to make it easier for people to live near work, but the buildings constructed were out of scale with the surrounding neighbourhoods and generated their own traffic pressures. In any case, the haphazard development permitted by council was disruptive to community life, visually ugly, and potentially inefficient. It also resulted in the destruction of many sound, and sometimes historic buildings, so that it seemed to threaten both the heritage and the aesthetic quality of the city. This was particularly the case in and around the central business district, where the past was rapidly being obliterated. As conservatives, the new reformers were keen to have as much of the old city preserved as possible – not only the historic centre, but the established residential and even commercial and industrial areas surrounding it.

However, there was also a radical thrust to this critique. In part, this involved opposition to big business. The development company – which constructed whole suburbs or satellite towns, built gigantic shopping or office complexes, and littered the city with high-rise apartments – was a post-war phenomenon, both cause and effect of the explosive development of Canadian cities. From among the opponents of the new urban form came the suggestion that the development industry had effectively captured the agencies that were supposed to regulate it.[105] The most immediate of these agencies were the city councils. In Toronto, criticism of council for selling out to the developers was particularly sharp and strong, and it gave a radical populist tone to an opposition that otherwise appealed to conservative values. The other side of this criticism was, of course, the suggestion that council was particularly insensitive to the concerns of the inner-city poor. To a limited extent these concerns overlapped with those of the middle-class urban conservatives, so there was potential for a broadly based popular movement.

One of the 'radical' demands that all opponents of the council could agree to was that it should be opened up for wider citizen participation.[106] The turn-of-the-century reforms in Toronto's municipal structure made it difficult for the opposition to have an immediate impact. The city government had been insulated from unwanted pressures from below, by redrawing ward boundaries on the strip system, creating a plural executive elected at large, and establishing a strong professional civil service. The creation of a second-tier metropolitan authority, one step removed from the electors, provided further insulation; so too did a restrictive municipal franchise. The aim of the earlier reformers had been to make the municipal government into an efficient, business-like agency, above parochial and partisan pressures. Now it was suggested that they had made it an agency of business, alienated even from middle-class ratepayers. The new reformers demanded a repoliticization, which would make the municipality sensitive to a wider range of concerns. One step in this direction was taken in 1958, when the city finally offered the franchise to all its adult residents (except foreigners).[107] The impact of this change was reduced by low participation among the newly enfranchised.[108] Of more immediate effect was council's decision in the late 1960s to abandon the board of control in favour of an executive committee (with similar powers) elected by council from among the aldermen. To replace the controllers' seats, it was decided to increase the number of wards in the city from nine to eleven, with, as usual, two aldermen to be elected from each. To council's surprise, the OMB responded to pressure from the new reformers and forced it to abandon the strip-ward system when it redrew the boundaries, and eleven new 'block' wards were created for the 1969 elections.[109] This gave the opposition, with its roots in the community associations, a marvellous opportunity.

The minority political parties also saw a chance of exploiting the situation. As ever, the Conservatives dominated the city and suburban councils, but not as a formally organized party.[110] The Liberals had not, as a party, contested their position within living memory, although individual Liberals had had some success.[111] There was a persistent hope among them that something might happen to shatter the Tory hegemony in the city and ultimately in the province at large. In 1963, a Liberal – Phil Givens – had succeeded to the mayoralty when the Conservative incumbent died. Briefly, it appeared that the Liberals might make some gains, as Givens identified himself as Toronto's answer to Montreal's dynamic Jean Drapeau. The booster spirit worked in his favour in the 1964 elections, but he went down to defeat two years later in a contest with William Dennison, a conservative New Democrat and long-time city councillor, who had powerful support from the organized labour movement.[112] Givens's failure convinced a portion of the local Liberal party that a more systematic approach to municipal politics was needed, one in which the party presented itself as an organized force with a coherent program and did not depend on a single man to win its laurels.[113]

Similar thinking was apparent in the New Democratic Party, which was locked in a seemingly endless battle with the Liberals to establish itself as the logical alternative to the provincial Conservatives. Both parties saw in the reorganization of the ward system and the abolition of the board of control the chance for a major political upheaval. Since the rationale for abolishing the board was to end the bickering between it and the council and create the conditions for coherent policy-making, it seemed logical to suppose that Torontonians might be ready for disciplined party government. On this assumption, the Liberals and the NDP entered the 1969 campaign. Unfortunately for them, both were too badly divided to take good advantage of their opportunities. The New Democrats were faced with a mayor of their own party who refused to take part in a partisan campaign.[114] They had to concentrate their efforts on aldermanic contests. The Liberals at least were able to offer a candidate for mayor, but they failed to get a prominent person to run. Liberal incumbents were as reluctant as Mayor Dennison to accept the risks or the discipline of a party campaign, and there was an obvious division between them and other Liberals flirting with the new reformism. In the end, neither party was able to convince the electorate that it was prepared to form a government, and neither was able to win more than a handful of seats on council.[115]

The real victory in the elections was won by the new, non-partisan opposition associated with CORRA and SSSOCCC. This was not apparent on the surface, for the mayor and majority of the council's 'old guard' were re-elected. The new reformers were represented by a handful of inexperienced aldermen, who found themselves in constant opposition to the council majority. Ultimately this worked to their advantage, for the reformers were able to present themselves as the logical alternative to the governing group. Party labels soon proved irrelevant, as reformers elected as Liberals or New Democrats coalesced with sympathetic independents on council.[116] To a remarkable extent, these opposition aldermen were able to impose on the council's debates their own definition of the issues and to force the governing group into a reactionary stance. In part, this was a reflection of the ability of the persons concerned: they were bright, modish professionals of the sort who were reinhabiting the inner city, and they knew how to win debates against the parochial politicians they confronted. They also knew how to make news for the media, by creating dramatic confrontations that publicized their concerns. The residents' associations and other groups associated with the reform movement coalesced sufficiently to establish a loose city-wide organization for the 1972 elections and to nominate strong reform candidates for a majority of the aldermanic seats.[117] When Dennison announced his retirement, one of the moderate reformers already on council, David Crombie, announced that he would run for the mayoralty. In face of the new forces of reform (which included many of their activists), the political parties withdrew from the field, and the elections shaped up as a simple contest between the reformers and the old guard. To the dismay of the council's traditionalists, the reformers emerged triumphant, and it seemed to many that a new age of municipal politics had begun.

URBAN CONSERVATISM AND POPULIST RADICALISM

It was perhaps symbolic that Toronto's new reform mayor was a Progressive Conservative. The movement that brought him and the other reformers to office was, despite its radical populist overtones, remarkably conservative in origins and political disposition. Crombie originally represented one of the prosperous wards in the north end of the city. Like many of his constituents, he was reacting against the council's insensitivity to the concerns of city residents, and he promised in his campaign 'protection of neighbourhoods, common sense about the automobile and concern for the style of development.'[118] The Conservative government he supported at Queen's Park had signalled a move in the same direction when it put an end in 1971 to Metro's plans for further expressway development in the city of Toronto.[119] This was a popular gesture politically. Crombie represented a new Conservative sensibility, more attuned to the need for restraint in urban government, but no less committed to private property and private enterprise. What he promised implicitly was to find a way of assuring continued development without the disruption and dislocation that had been associated with it for the past fifteen years.

To an extent, this meant a return to normality in Toronto politics, for the council had traditionally been conservative in its development strategy. The city had not, like some in Canada, bankrupted itself by over-extending suburban services or making inordinately expensive concessions to the railways or other businesses. It had early offered zoning protection to residential neighbourhoods, and it had committed itself to planned development before other Canadian cities. The council's obsession with promoting development in the 1960s was something of an aberration in its lack of restraint (although, of course, this was not the first time in the city's history that the boosters had taken control). It was partly an effect of concerns about inner-city decay, stimulated by the American experience and consequent upon the rapid development of the suburbs. As it happened, however, the redevelopment of central Toronto hardly needed a boost from the council to proceed very rapidly. The local economy had intrinsic strength, which drew people into the centre. There was little to be gained and much to be lost from relaxing controls on the redevelopment occurring, for the quality of life (and business) in the inner city could easily deteriorate if the fabric of the community were rent asunder. Conservatives such as Crombie were determined to prevent this, and to restore the cautious 'good government' the city had normally enjoyed.

This did not mean that the new policies adopted by council during Crombie's mayoralty (1972–8) were easily accepted by business. Since they involved new restrictions on private enterprise and important extensions of public activity, they generated much opposition. None the less, Crombie and his allies were able to move forward with broad support from their conservative constituency; he himself never faced a serious electoral challenge until he left municipal politics. Perhaps the boldest policy adopted was a 'hold' on large-scale downtown development imposed in 1973.[120] This was to allow time for reformulating the 1969 official plan – a highly permissive updating of the 1950 plan, which was clearly out of tune with the new council's objectives. New projects continued to receive approval on an individual basis, but council was able to impose conditions on them that reflected its new attitude. The city was challenged by an array of developers before the OMB for its 'arbitrary' action, and it had to relax its controls.[121] By that time, however, a new central area plan was virtually ready. As adopted by council early in 1976, it committed the city to a more conservative development strategy, 'including the deconcentration of office employment, the retention of low-rise neighbourhoods within the Central Area, the expansion of the residential function of the Central Area emphasizing housing suitable for families with children in appropriate areas ... and housing for households without school age children in the form of mixed-use buildings in the Central Core, the conservation of buildings of historic or architectural value or interest, the avoidance of unacceptable levels of congestion on the transportation system, and a substantial increase in the availability of parks and recreational space for both those who live and those who work in the Central Core.'[122]

The central area plan was supposed to give permanent effect to the policies the reformers had been advocating. It too was modified in face of legal challenges, and critics claimed that it was much less stringent than appeared on the surface.[123] None the less, it reflected the shift in policy Crombie and his allies were seeking. Supportive of this shift were the changes they introduced in the process of land-use planning. These were designed to allow for greater citizen participation, especially at the neighbourhood level.[124] Ironically, the new procedures so reduced frustration – and absorbed so much energy – that the citizens' groups demanding them soon encountered a drop in participation in their own activities. This weakened the reform movement at its base.[125] However, the detailed plans developed under the city's aegis increasingly reflected the reformers' concerns for the preservation of existing buildings and established neighbourhoods, the restriction of traffic flows, the improvement of local amenities, and the encouragement of renovation, rehabilitation and low-rise in-fill construction. The latter fit in with the new housing policy adopted by the city in 1973.[126] The council was generally opposed to massive single-use projects, be they public or private, residential or commercial. It also questioned the segregation of people relying on public assistance. Thus its policy was to encourage the location of assisted tenants in existing buildings, to expand the supply of non-profit housing for people of low to moderate incomes, and to ensure the integration of new developments into existing neighbourhoods. There were related pressures to include commercial facilities in residential developments and vice versa, on the understanding that this would contribute to neighbourhood self-sufficiency.

These changes in policy in the city of Toronto coincided with shifts at the federal and provincial levels. The 1973 amendments to the National Housing Act combined with similar legislation in Ontario to make the city's new initiatives feasible, especially with respect to non-profit housing.[127] An interchange of ideas and political pressures was occurring, as it had when Toronto's original commitments to slum-clearance and public housing had run into trouble. The city was able to move in the direction it sought because the senior governments accepted the need for reorientation. Immediate opposition to the city's policies came from Metro Council, which remained under the control of suburban politicians anxious for continued rapid development. From their perspective, the reform politicians were protecting the inner city from changes necessary for metropolitan expansion and hence were attacking the interests of the metropolis as a whole. Under the leadership of the suburban Conservative Paul Godfrey – who became its fourth chairman in 1973 – Metro Council continued its support for expressway construction and downtown redevelopment.[128] The inner-city reformers might well have been forced to accept such policies if it had not been for the protection of the provincial government, which was concerned about its own rather precarious political base in the city.[129]

On the city council itself, Crombie and his allies faced stronger criticism from the reformers on his left than from the remnants of the 'old guard' on his right. The reform majority that theoretically took control in 1972 soon split between moderates and more militant reformers, and the latter drifted into an oppositional role.[130] Crombie was determined to govern from the centre, with broad support from left and right. This involved him in compromise unacceptable to the militants. The most prominent of the latter was Alderman John Sewell, a former organizer in a community threatened by urban renewal and a representative since 1969 of the traditionally working-class area east of the city centre. Sewell declared it his aim to polarize the council between those who were genuinely committed to reform and those who were not.[131] This involved exposing the compromises implicit in Crombie's policies and revealing the limits of urban conservatism as an approach to the problems of the poor and the ordinary wage-earners. Sewell attacked concessions to private developers and pressed for an extension of public controls. His ultimate message was that the process of urban development should not be governed by the pursuit of private profit and that it should instead become subject to popular control and initiative. As such he expressed the populist radicalism contained within the movement for reform.

There were others on council who voiced similar criticisms. After the 1974 elections (which little altered the council's political composition), Crombie's critics on the left established a Reform Caucus to concert their efforts.[132] Thanks partly to personality conflicts, it lasted only for a couple of years as a formal organization, but the reformers (as they called themselves) remained a distinct group on council and in the public mind. Their strength gradually increased during the 1970s: by 1980, they could claim nine of the twenty-three seats on council. Perhaps the most significant aspect of the group's evolution was its increasing identification with the NDP. All but one of the reformers elected in 1980 ran with official party endorsement. This was a reflection of the party's quiet but successful re-entry into municipal politics, which began in the mid-1970s.[133] The split between the urban conservatives and the more militant reformers generally coincided with the partisan division between Liberals and Conservatives on the one hand and New Democrats on the other. This in turn coincided (though not so clearly) with the division between middle-class and working-class areas of the city. After Dennison retired, it was easier for the NDP to identify itself with the cause of reform, which (as articulated by the militants on council) had an increasingly socialist orientation. Those who rejected this socialist direction tended to identify with Crombie and so to distance themselves from the reform movement. This meant that the majority of people still associated with the movement also were supporters of the NDP.

Despite this, there were serious obstacles to NDP control of the reform movement. Many reformers remained convinced that too close an identification with the party would harm their cause. Some of the voters they were attempting to attract refused for various reasons to support the NDP. The party, in any case, had not been closely associated with the original movement, and there were suspicions that its influence might actually be conservative, since it was linked to unions concerned about restrictions on construction. Many reformers wanted to create their own party, and there were various efforts in this direction.[134] Ultimately, however, these attempts came to little, partly because the NDP was unwilling to withdraw from the field, and partly because the local community organizations that had generated the original movement for reform were determined to retain their political independence. Interpretations of 'reform' within these organizations varied from neighbourhood to neighbourhood, as did the concerns of the people involved; so it was difficult to establish an acceptable city-wide platform.[135]

The other main obstacle to the coalescence of the reform movement was John Sewell, a determinedly independent politician who remained the most prominent and effective spokesman for reform in the city. He made some effort to build a reform party around himself, but he was unsuccessful,[136] and when, inevitably, he presented himself as a candidate for mayor on Crombie's retirement in 1978, it was as an independent reformer.[137] As ever, the issues he defined were his own, and other reformers had to relate themselves to the positions he adopted. These positions were in some respects radical, but in others conservative. He continued to be a strong critic of the land-development industry and recommended, for example, that land held by speculators in the suburbs be expropriated and made available for housing.[138] However, his attitude towards private property and private business was far from socialistic. He perceived himself as a defender of the home-owner and the small businessman against the big companies that threatened to take over the city. What Sewell wanted was to protect people's communities and ensure them control over their own homes and enterprises. He regarded the extension of community services and facilities as a necessary complement to individual enterprise and not as a negation of it. Thus his radicalism was that of a populist and not of a socialist. This set him apart from some of the other militant reformers, who saw their mission in socialist terms.

Sewell's combination of radicalism and conservatism was expressive of the ambivalence of the original movement for reform. Despite having criticized Crombie repeatedly, he presented himself effectively as the mayor's logical successor – the man needed to carry the newly established civic policies to fruition.[139] As a progressive urban conservative, he got surprising electoral support in the prosperous north-end neighbourhoods where Crombie had had his base.[140] This was combined with support (especially in the east end and centre) that he had won with his populist radicalism. The result was a clear victory for him in a race with two prominent candidates who had failed to identify themselves effectively with the cause of reform. Significantly, when Sewell assumed office as mayor, he declared his intention to work with all the council, as Crombie had done, rather than aligning himself simply with the reform bloc.

Nevertheless, Sewell's tenure as mayor (1978–80) was highly controversial, partly because of his personal style and partly because of his efforts to raise a new set of reform issues, now that the old ones had been 'put to bed.' These were arguably the vital urban issues in Canada for the 1980s – which looked to be a decade of economic stagnation and growing social conflict. In Toronto, the influx of immigrants from outside Europe had given the city a substantial non-white population, and for the first time the racial tensions felt before in American and European cities had become apparent in Toronto. The inner city had also become a haven for people not easily accepted in suburban society – the large gay community was the most obvious example.[141] Purely social tensions were being exacerbated by the continuing economic slump. The general recession in the country's economic activity coincided with a relative decline in Toronto's position. The city continued to lose businesses and people to the suburbs, as it had done for decades, but, more important, the metropolis as a whole had ceased to grow very rapidly. This reflected the shift of economic activity to Alberta and British Columbia. For the city it meant that the stimulative effects of rapid development would no longer be felt so strongly in the central business district. Growth would be slower and easier to regulate, but the prosperity on which the reformers had counted was no longer assured.

Sewell and some of the other reformers responded to the economic challenge by attempting to articulate a new strategy for boosting the local economy. Sewell's own strategy was set within the framework of Jane Jacobs's theory of economic development, which suggested that the city was a natural generator of economic activity.[142] To protect its cheap industrial and commercial space and to aid its indigenous entrepreneurs would ensure its continued prosperity. According to this theory, the main threat was from the multinational corporations, which would reform the city for their own purposes and destroy its vitality. Thus, from Sewell's perspective, defence of the city and support for its entrepreneurs were the crucial means for ensuring its continued prosperity – boosterism had to be assimilated to urban conservatism. However, it was difficult to develop a convincing program on this basis, since the city could hardly alter the logic of capitalist development that worked in favour of the big companies. As a result, Sewell's ideas never gained the breadth of support they required.

More support and certainly more media attention were given to the efforts by Sewell and other reformers to address the complaints of inner-city minorities, especially about discriminatory treatment at the hands of the police. Sewell was particularly bold in his demands for police reform, and his criticisms generated a strong conservative reaction.[143] This reaction, however, was in large part a suburban one, since the Metropolitan Police Department was and is suburban-dominated at every level. The issue of policing was one of many that brought city reformers into conflict with the suburban conservatives who dominated Metro Council and, indeed, the provincial government. Sewell and his allies represented a constituency sensitive to issues that had hardly been brought to the surface in the suburbs or in the province as a whole. The reformers had to address these issues from a position of great institutional weakness, since the power to deal with them lay mainly with the senior governments, Metro Council, or independent agencies, such as the Police Commission. This weakness was more obvious with respect to the issues of the 1980s than to those of the 1960s, for the former were not so closely related to the process of physical development that the city traditionally had been allowed to manage.

The controversies generated by the second (Robarts) royal commission on the metropolitan system of government were indicative of the city's sense of impotence. Unlike on previous occasions, there were strong demands from within the city for the decentralization of power.[144] The reformers were naturally most vocal about this. When the commission reported in 1977, it acknowledged the decentralist case, but made practical proposals for strengthening Metro.[145] Metro Council would have become a directly elected body and have received more powers from the province, if not from the constituent municipalities. The city was saved from this only because the province ultimately was unwilling to do anything that might have threatened its own hegemony.[146] From a provincial perspective, there was much to be said for keeping Metro and the city in a competitive balance, to weaken them both. Although Metro was potentially the stronger authority, it lacked the legitimacy conferred by direct elections, and the political resurgence of the city combined with the development of strong suburban councils to put a check on it. This check was not one the province was anxious to remove, even though Metro Council was generally sympathetic politically.

Thus the city remained in the position it had been in since the 1950s – as an inner-city authority with significant powers of control over development but limited ability to pursue social and economic policies of a broader compass. Sewell and the other reformers continued to test the limits upon the city, but with mixed success. In the 1980 elections, Sewell lost the mayoralty in a close contest with Arthur Eggleton, a Liberal with strong support from the business community.[147] Eggleton's claim, in effect, was that he had a more realistic sense of the limits of possible reform – and the necessary conservative image and connections to get things done. Indeed, he proved successful enough as mayor to prevent any challenge from the left in the elections of 1982. In his 1980 campaign Eggleton refused to take issue with Sewell on matters of substance. The reformers had succeeded in shifting the centre of political gravity in the preceding ten years, so that a conservative candidate had to identify himself with the heritage of reform.

The year 1980 did not mark any serious decline in the electoral fortunes of the reformers. The balance of power on council remained essentially the same as before, with the forces of the left and the right roughly equal and enough 'moderates' in the centre to shift the balance either way. The most significant change was that the reformers had become more clearly identified with the traditional left – and hence with the labour movement and the NDP. Organizational and financial support from the NDP had become increasingly important for reform candidates, and they were generally more open about their identification with the party. Most of the conservative community groups in middle-class neighbourhoods had fallen away from the reform movement, and the community groups that remained attached to it were bound up with issues such as day care and tenants' rights and had more of a working-class base. This pattern reflected the way in which the issues that had agitated the middle-class reformers – the issues of urban conservatism – had been settled in the 1970s. The settlement was partly the result of the new policies adopted by council and partly the result of the economic decline that had reduced development pressures. That same decline had given rise to new issues related to public spending, social services, and the rights of the disadvantaged; the resulting disagreements produced a division between left and right similar to the one in provincial politics.

REFORM AND CONSTRAINT

The emergent pattern of politics in Toronto marks a break from the nonpartisan tradition that has been dominant in the city for nearly a century. However, it would be a delusion to think that such a change could be as decisive as some of the others that have occurred in the city's long political history. The most important developments were the ones that defined the city's role institutionally. Many of these occurred in the nineteenth century: the creation of the municipality as an organization representative of the ratepayers; its commitment to providing the hard services necessary for urban growth; and its exclusion from most of the social services. In the twentieth century, the city was bureaucratized, professionalized, and to some extent insulated from partisan and parochial pressures. The provincial government assumed responsibility for most services beyond the traditional municipal ambit and bound the city into its administrative system. The city's geographical boundaries were also set, and a metropolitan government was created to perform many of the historic municipal functions for the city and its suburbs together. The effect of these developments was to entrench the municipality in its traditional role as a manager of urban growth. Other changes – such as the extension of the municipal franchise, the growing acceptance of government planning and the welfare state, and the spread of community organizations – affected the way this role was performed, but they were insufficient in themselves to transform the municipality into something different.

As Marx put it, 'The tradition of all the dead generations weighs like a nightmare on the brain of the living.'[148] This tradition is encountered as much in the ideas of reformers as in the institutions and circumstances they confront. As an earlier generation of municipal reformers defined its objectives in terms of business efficiency, so the present one originally defined itself in terms of urban conservatism. In both cases, the traditional role of the municipality was confirmed. The more militant reformers have sensed these limits on their thinking and action, but have had difficulty developing a strategy for transcendence. Whether the present generation of reformers will be any more successful than their predecessors in this respect is a moot point. Perhaps the likeliest outcome is that struggles for reform will be contained within the ideological and institutional limits implicit in the traditional municipal role. Open partisanship will not of itself affect this outcome, since the major parties (including the NDP) are committed to the arrangements that fix the municipality in this position.

This is not to suggest that the constraints of the situation make significant change at the municipal level impossible. On the contrary, as Toronto's history illustrates, municipal politics and government are in continual transformation within the boundaries set, and those limits themselves are constantly being tested. Toronto's character as the inner city of a great metropolis creates unusual pressures on municipal government. The very weakness of the city in relation to the province and Metro has been a stimulus to innovation, and because of that weakness the province has been more tolerant of innovative action than it might otherwise have been. These conditions will continue, and there is every reason to expect that the city's reform politicians will be at the forefront of efforts to extend the scope of municipal government. However, if past experience is any guide, the changes they secure will be far from revolutionary.

SUGGESTED FURTHER READING

Armstrong, Christopher and H.V. Nelles *The Revenge of the Methodist Bicycle Company: Sunday Streetcars and Municipal Reform in Toronto, 1888–1897* Toronto 1977

Artibise, Alan F.J. and Gilbert A. Stelter *The Usable Urban Past: Planning and Politics in the Modern Canadian City* Toronto 1979

Baine, Richard P. and A. Lynn McMurray *Toronto: An Urban Study* rev ed Toronto 1977

Caulfield, Jon *The Tiny Perfect Mayor: David Crombie and Toronto's Reform Aldermen* Toronto 1974

Clarkson, Stephen *City Lib: Parties and Reform* Toronto 1972

Colton, Timothy J. *Big Daddy: Frederick G. Gardiner and the Building of Metropolitan Toronto* Toronto 1980

Fraser, Graham *Fighting Back: Urban Renewal in Trefann Court* Toronto 1972

Goheen, Peter G. *Victorian Toronto, 1850 to 1890: Patterns and Process of Growth* Chicago 1970

Goldrick, Michael 'The Anatomy of Urban Reform in Toronto' *City Magazine* III 4 and 5 (1978) 29–39

Glazebrook, G.P. *The Story of Toronto* Toronto 1971

Hough, Jerry F. 'Voters' Turnout and the Responsiveness of Local Government: The Case of Toronto' in Paul Fox ed *Politics: Canada* 3rd ed (Toronto 1970) 284–96

Journal of Canadian Studies XIV 1 (1979) 35–58

Kaplan, Harold *Urban Political Systems: A Functional Analysis of Metro Toronto* New York 1967

Kay, Barry J. 'Urban Decision-Making and the Legislative Environment: Toronto Council Re-examined' *Canadian Journal of Political Science* XV (1982) 553–73

Kealey, Gregory S. *Toronto Workers Respond to Industrial Capitalism 1867–1892* Toronto 1980

Lorimer, James *A Citizen's Guide to City Politics* Toronto 1972

– *The Real World of City Politics* Toronto 1970

Masters, Donald C. *The Rise of Toronto, 1850–1890* Toronto 1947

Middleton, Jesse E. *The Municipality of Toronto: A History* 3 vols Toronto 1923

Piva, Michael J. *The Condition of the Working Class in Toronto, 1900–1921* Ottawa 1979

Report of the Royal Commission on Government in Metropolitan Toronto Toronto 1977

Rose, Albert *Governing Metropolitan Toronto: A Social and Political Analysis, 1953–1971* Berkeley, Calif, 1972

Sewell, John *Up against City Hall* Toronto 1972
Spelt, Jacob *Toronto* Toronto 1973
Weaver, John C. *Shaping the Canadian City: Essays on Urban Politics and Policy 1890–1920* Toronto 1977

NOTES

1 G.P. Glazebrook *The Story of Toronto* (Toronto 1971) surveys the city's development. On its early history see P.J. Robinson *Toronto during the French Regime* (Toronto 1933), Edith G. Firth ed *The Town of York, 1793–1834* 2 vols (Toronto 1962, 1966), and J.E. Middleton *The Municipality of Toronto: A History* 3 vols (Toronto 1923).

2 The town was originally governed by provincially appointed magistrates; see Glazebrook *Story of Toronto* 23–30.

3 On the economic history of the city see F.H. Armstrong 'Metropolitanism and Toronto Re-examined, 1825–1850' in G.A. Stelter and A.F.J. Artibise ed *The Canadian City: Essays in Urban History* (Toronto 1977) 37–50, D.C. Masters *The Rise of Toronto, 1850–1890* (Toronto 1947), Peter G. Goheen *Victorian Toronto, 1850 to 1890: Patterns and Process of Growth* (Chicago 1970), Jacob Spelt *Urban Development in South-Central Ontario* (Toronto 1972), and Jacob Spelt *Toronto* (Toronto 1973).

4 For data on the changing social composition of the city, see Middleton *Municipality of Toronto* I 225, 234 and Goheen *Victorian Toronto* 51, 71.

5 Ironically, Mackenzie was Toronto's first mayor: F.H. Armstrong 'William Lyon Mackenzie, First Mayor of Toronto: A Study of a Critic in Power' *Canadian Historical Review* XLVIII (1967) 309–31, P. Romney 'William Lyon Mackenzie as Mayor of Toronto' *Canadian Historical Review* LVI (1975) 416–36.

6 About two-thirds of Toronto's mayors to 1923 were Orangemen; Middleton *Municipality of Toronto* II 788. Cf Gregory S. Kealey 'The Orange Order in Toronto: Religious Riot and the Working Class' in Kealey and Peter Warrian ed *Essays in Canadian Working Class History* (Toronto 1976) 13–34 and Hereward Senior 'Orangeism in Ontario Politics, 1872–1896' in Donald Swainson ed *Oliver Mowat's Ontario* (Toronto 1972) 136–53.

7 On the concept of clientelism, see S.J.R. Noel 'Leadership and Clientelism' in David J. Bellamy et al ed *The Provincial Political Systems* (Toronto 1976) 197–213. Cf Magnusson's introduction to this book, above.

8 John Garner *The Franchise and Politics in British North America, 1755–1867* (Toronto 1969) 114–16. In 1838, when the city's population was about 10,000, only about 370 votes were cast in the municipal elections; Middleton *Municipality of Toronto* I 204.

9 William G. Ormsby 'Sir Francis Hincks' in J.M.S. Careless ed *The Pre-Confederation Premiers* (Toronto 1980) 177–84, Middleton *Municipality of Toronto* I 250–1
10 Middleton *Municipality of Toronto* I 244–57
11 Richard B. Splane *Social Welfare in Ontario, 1791–1893* (Toronto 1965)
12 Stephen A. Speisman 'Munificent Parsons and Municipal Parsimony: Voluntary vs. Public Poor Relief in Nineteenth Century Toronto' *Ontario History* LXV (1973) 33–49
13 Michael B. Katz and Paul Mattingley ed *Education and Social Change: Themes from Ontario's Past* (New York 1975)
14 Armstrong 'Metropolitanism and Toronto,' Glazebrook *Story of Toronto* 58–9, 67–9, Middleton *Municipality of Toronto* I passim
15 E. Jones and D. McCalla 'Toronto Waterworks, 1840–77: Continuity and Change in Nineteenth Century Toronto Politics' *Canadian Historical Review* LX (1979) 300–23 and Christopher Armstrong and H.V. Nelles *The Revenge of the Methodist Bicycle Company: Sunday Streetcars and Municipal Reform in Toronto, 1888–1897* (Toronto 1977)
16 Middleton *Municipality of Toronto* I 243–72. See also William A. White 'A Cautious Elite: Toronto's Reluctant Entrance into the Railway Mania of the 1850s' *Urban History Review* X 1 (1981) 31–8.
17 K.W. McKay 'Municipal History, 1867–1913' in Shortt and Doughty *Canada and Its Provinces* XVIII 493–4, S. Morley Wickett 'The Municipal Government of Toronto' in Wickett ed *Municipal Government in Canada* (Toronto 1907) 54–5, and Elizabeth Bloomfield 'Municipal Bonusing of Industry: The Legislative Framework in Ontario to 1930' *Urban History Review* IX 3 (February 1981) 59–76
18 Stephen Spencer 'The Good Queen of Hogs: Toronto, 1850–1914' *Urban History Review* 1–75 (June 1975) 38–42, H.V. Nelles and Christopher Armstrong 'The Great Fight for Clean Government' *Urban History Review* 2–76 (October 1976) 50–66, John C. Weaver 'The Modern City Realized: Toronto Civic Affairs, 1880–1915' in A.F.J. Artibise and G.A. Stelter ed *The Usable Urban Past: Planning and Politics in the Modern Canadian City* (Toronto 1979) 39–72, John C. Weaver *Shaping the Canadian City: Essays on Urban Politics and Policy, 1890–1920* (Toronto 1977), Desmond Morton *Mayor Howland: The Citizens' Candidate* (Toronto 1973), Armstrong and Nelles *Revenge of the Methodist Bicycle Company*. More generally, see Paul Rutherford ed *Saving the Canadian City: The First Phase, 1880–1920* (Toronto 1974) and Stelter and Artibise *The Canadian City* 368–418.
19 The Liberals were behind this measure for reform, which they hoped would shake the Tory hegemony. They had once before (1859–66) secured popular

election, and this brought them the mayoralty briefly; Middleton *Municipality of Toronto* I 250–69.

20 Dennis Carter-Edwards 'Toronto in the 1890's: A Decade of Challenge and Response' MA thesis, University of British Columbia, 1973, 54–113

21 Armstrong and Nelles *Methodist Bicycle Company* 129–43 and Weaver *Shaping the Canadian City* 41–54

22 Weaver 'Modern City Realized' 49–50

23 Middleton *Municipality of Toronto* I 268, 304–5, 320, Mary Powell 'Provincial Control of Local Activity: The Case of Public Health in Ontario' paper delivered at the CPSA Annual Meeting 1981, Glazebrook *Story of Toronto* 127, 146–7

24 Speisman 'Munificent Parsons and Municipal Parsimony,' Glazebrook *Story of Toronto* 147–9, 154–9, and Middleton *Municipality of Toronto* I 304–20, 535–52

25 Middleton *Municipality of Toronto* I 228–36, 300–2, 357, 363–73, E. Jones and D. McCalla 'Toronto Waterworks,' H.V. Nelles *The Politics of Development: Forests, Mines and Hydro-Electric Power in Ontario, 1849–1941* (Toronto 1974) 215–306, M.J. Doucet 'Mass Transit and the Failure of Private Ownership: The Case of Toronto' *Urban History Review* 3–77 (February 1978) 3–33, Donald F. Davis 'Mass Transit and Private Ownership: An Alternative Perspective on the Case of Toronto' *Urban History Review* 3–78 (February 1979) 60–98

26 The Harbour and Exhibition commissions also operated as independent agencies; Middleton *Municipality of Toronto* I 312–13, 413–67.

27 City of Toronto *Report on a Survey of the Treasury, Assessment, Works, Fire and Property Departments* prepared for the Civic Survey Committee

28 Weaver 'The Modern City Realized' 55–9 and Glazebrook *Story of Toronto* 226–8

29 Horace L. Brittain *Local Government in Canada* (Toronto 1951) 89–91 and Kenneth G. Crawford *Canadian Municipal Government* (Toronto 1954) 185–6

30 F.F. Schindeler *Responsible Government in Ontario* (Toronto 1969) 73–4, McKay 'Municipal History' 464–6, 474–5, and Garner *The Franchise and Politics* 114–16

31 John Garner 'The Ballot in the British North American Colonies' in J.H. Aitchison ed *The Political Process in Canada* (Toronto 1963) 17–35

32 Goheen *Victorian Toronto* provides a careful analysis of residential 'sorting' in late-nineteenth-century Toronto.

33 Weaver 'The Modern City Realized' 40–9, and Michael J. Piva *The Condition of the Working Class in Toronto, 1900–1921* (Ottawa 1979) 9–14

34 Gregory S. Kealey *Toronto Workers Respond to Industrial Capitalism, 1867–1892* (Toronto 1980), Piva *The Condition of the Working Class*, and Piva 'Workers and Tories: The Collapse of the Conservative Party in Urban Ontario, 1908–1919' *Urban History Review* 3–76 (February 1977) 23–39

35 Armstrong and Nelles *Methodist Bicycle Company* 130–2
36 Ibid and Weaver *Shaping the Canadian City*
37 Morton *Mayor Howland*
38 C.S. Clark *Of Toronto the Good* (Montreal 1898)
39 Armstrong and Nelles *Methodist Bicycle Company*, Masters *The Rise of Toronto*, and Goheen *Victorian Toronto*
40 Cf Weaver 'The Modern City Realized' 39–40.
41 Piva *Condition of the Working Class in Toronto* 113
42 Paul Adolphus Bator 'The Struggle to Raise the Lower Classes: Public Health Reform and the Problem of Poverty in Toronto, 1910 to 1921' *Journal of Canadian Studies* XIV (1979) 43–9 and Piva *Condition of the Working Class* 113–41. For the earlier efforts see Heather A. MacDougall 'The Genesis of Public Health Reform in Toronto, 1869–1890' *Urban History Review* X 3 (February 1982) 1–9.
43 Piva *Condition of the Working Class* 125–38 and Weaver *Shaping the Canadian City* 25–32
44 H. Shostack 'Business and Reform: The Lost History of the Toronto Housing Company' *City Magazine* III (September 1978) 24–31 and Shirley Spragge 'A Confluence of Interests: Housing Reform in Toronto, 1900–1920' in Artibise and Stelter *The Usable Urban Past* 247–67
45 James Pitsula 'The Emergence of Social Work in Toronto' *Journal of Canadian Studies* XIV (1979) 35–42
46 Piva *Condition of the Working Class* 72–82
47 Ibid 73–80 and Bator 'The Struggle to Raise the Lower Classes' 47–8
48 Weaver 'The Modern City Realized' 51–9
49 Weaver *Shaping the Canadian City*
50 Walter Van Nus 'The Fate of City Beautiful Thought in Canada, 1893–1930' in Stelter and Artibise *The Canadian City* 162–85, Van Nus 'Towards the City Efficient: The Theory and Practice of Zoning, 1919–1939' in Artibise and Stelter *The Usable Urban Past* 226–46, Weaver *Shaping the Canadian City* 32–7, Spelt *Toronto* 90–4, Glazebrook *Story of Toronto* 223–6, John Dakin 'Historical Instrument for Considering Toronto Planning' *Papers on Planning and Design* Department of Urban and Regional Planning, University of Toronto, no 16 (August 1978)
51 Peter W. Moore 'Zoning and Planning: The Toronto Experience, 1904–1970' in Artibise and Stelter *The Usable Urban Past* 316–41
52 Glazebrook *Story of Toronto* 114, 137, 211
53 Middleton *Municipality of Toronto* I 371
54 Spelt *Urban Development in South-Central Ontario* 170–226 and George A. Nader *Cities of Canada* II (Toronto 1976) 199–203
55 Spelt *Toronto* 71–7

56 Maurice Yeates *Main Street: Windsor to Quebec City* (Toronto 1975) and Spelt *Urban Development in South-Central Ontario*
57 Nader *Cities of Canada* II 205 and Spelt *Toronto* 60–2
58 Roger E. Riendeau 'A Clash of Interests: Dependency and the Municipal Problem in the Great Depression' *Journal of Canadian Studies* XIV (1979) 50–8 and Harry M. Cassidy *Unemployment and Relief in Ontario, 1929–32* (Toronto 1932)
59 Riendeau 'A Clash of Interests' 50. See also H. Carl Goldenberg *Municipal Finance in Canada* (Ottawa 1939).
60 Civic Advisory Council of Toronto *Municipal Finance* (Toronto 1950) 16–23, 174. On the early system of taxation see McKay 'Municipal History' 467–75, and Solomon Wineberg *Provincial and Local Taxation in Canada* (New York 1912).
61 Wickett *Municipal Government in Canada* 8, 12–14
62 Kenneth G. Crawford 'The Independence of Municipal Councils in Ontario' *Canadian Journal of Economics and Political Science* VI (1940) 543–54, Brittain *Local Government in Canada* 230–2, and Romaine K. Ross *Local Government in Ontario* (Toronto 1949) 87–99
63 Wickett *Municipal Government in Canada* 344–8, McKay 'Municipal History' 483, and Brittain *Local Government in Canada* 225–32
64 Bureau of Municipal Research (Toronto) 'Urban Development and the Ontario Municipal Board' *Civic Affairs* (winter 1971) and Ontario Economic Council *Subject to Approval: A Review of Municipal Planning in Ontario* (Toronto 1973) 3, 15–19
65 J. Stefan Dupré *Intergovernmental Finance in Ontario: A Provincial-Local Perspective* (Toronto 1967)
66 John Taylor '"Relief from Relief": The Cities' Answer to Depression Dependency' *Journal of Canadian Studies* XIV 1 (1979) 16–23
67 Piva *Condition of the Working Class* 147
68 Riendeau 'A Clash of Interests' 57, 'Jimmy Simpson' in J.E. Middleton and W.S. Downs ed *National Encyclopedia of Canadian Biography* (Toronto 1935) 365–72, and Gerald Caplan *The Dilemma of Canadian Socialism: The CCF in Ontario* (Toronto 1973) 70–1, 81. On a similar development in the suburbs, see Patricia V. Schulz *The East York Workers' Association: A Response to the Great Depression* (Toronto 1975).
69 'Sam McBride' in Middleton and Downs *National Encyclopedia* 152–8. More generally, see John Taylor 'Mayors à la Mancha: An Aspect of Depression Leadership in Canadian Cities' *Urban History Review* IX 3 (1981) 3–14.
70 Caplan *Dilemma of Canadian Socialism* 118–20 and James Lorimer *A Citizen's Guide to City Politics* (Toronto 1972) 124–6
71 J.D. Anderson 'Nonpartisan Urban Politics in Canadian Cities' in J.K. Masson and Anderson ed *Emerging Party Politics in Urban Canada* (Toronto 1972) 3–21

72 City Planning Board of Toronto *The Master Plan for the City of Toronto and Environs* (Toronto 1943)
73 Timothy J. Colton *Big Daddy: Frederick G. Gardiner and the Building of Metropolitan Toronto* (Toronto 1980) 52–9
74 Ontario Municipal Board *Decisions and Recommendations of the Board* (20 January 1953) (Cumming Report)
75 Colton *Big Daddy*, Harold Kaplan *Urban Political Systems: A Functional Analysis of Metro Toronto* (New York 1967), and Albert Rose *Governing Metropolitan Toronto: A Social and Political Analysis, 1953–1971* (Berkeley, Calif, 1972)
76 W.J. McCordic 'Urban Education: An Experiment in Two-Tiered Administration' in L.D. Feldman and M.D. Goldrick ed *Politics and Government of Urban Canada* 2nd ed (Toronto 1972) 86–98 and T.R. Williams 'Some Facts and Fantasies Concerning Local Autonomy in the Metropolitan Toronto School System' in Feldman ed *Politics and Government of Urban Canada* 4th ed (Toronto 1981) 277–90
77 Rose *Governing Metropolitan Toronto* 38–40, 45–64
78 Colton *Big Daddy* 27–39, 63–73, 123–32
79 Rose *Governing Metropolitan Toronto* 102–3, Kaplan *Urban Political Systems* 113–14, 256–7, and Glazebrook *Story of Toronto* 241–2
80 Kaplan *Urban Political Systems* 114–16, Rose *Governing Metropolitan Toronto* 36–7, and Colton *Big Daddy* 84–5
81 *Report of the Royal Commission on Metropolitan Toronto* (Goldenberg) (Toronto 1965)
82 Rose *Governing Metropolitan Toronto* 105–23
83 Kaplan *Urban Political Systems* 137–42, 170, 178–9 and Colton *Big Daddy* 166–8
84 Moore 'Zoning and Planning' 335 and Colton *Big Daddy* 156
85 On the social and economic development of the post-war city see Nader *Cities of Canada* II 190–243, Spelt *Toronto*, and Richard P. Baine and A. Lynn McMurray *Toronto: An Urban Study* rev ed (Toronto 1977). More generally see Len Gertler and Ron Crowley *Changing Canadian Cities: The Next 25 Years* (Toronto 1977).
86 Baine and McMurray *Toronto* 67–8
87 Metropolitan Toronto Planning Board *Metropolitan Toronto Key Facts* (Toronto 1970)
88 Spelt *Toronto* 104–10, 131–3
89 Spelt *Toronto* 118–54 and Nader *Cities of Canada* II 210–17, 233–40
90 Gertler and Crowley *Changing Canadian Cities* 72
91 Spelt *Toronto* 60–2, Nader *Cities of Canada* II 205, Gertler and Crowley *Changing Canadian Cities* 127–31, 154–9, and Michael Ray and Roger Roberge

'The Pattern of Post-War Urban Growth: Multinationals as City and Regional Planners' in James Lorimer and Caroline MacGregor ed *After the Developers* (Toronto 1981) 14–24

92 James Lorimer *The Developers* (Toronto 1978), David G. Bettison *The Politics of Canadian Urban Development* 81–40, and Albert Rose *Canadian Housing Policies, 1935–1980* (Toronto 1980)

93 Moore 'Zoning and Planning,' Spelt *Toronto* 90–4, Glazebrook *Story of Toronto* 223–6, and Rose *Governing Metropolitan Toronto* 40–5

94 Moore 'Zoning and Planning' 332–4

95 Albert Rose *Regent Park: A Study in Slum Clearance* (Toronto 1958)

96 Rose *Governing Metropolitan Toronto* 50–3, 63–4 and Graham Fraser *Fighting Back: Urban Renewal in Trefann Court* (Toronto 1972) 56–73

97 Fraser *Fighting Back* 5–8, 146–8. Cf Ontario Department of Municipal Affairs 'The Three R's of Citizen Participation: A Guide for Municipal Urban Renewal Administrators' (1969).

98 Fraser *Fighting Back* 150–7. See also *Report of the Task Force on Housing and Urban Development* (Ottawa 1969).

99 Margaret Daly *The Revolution Game: The Short, Unhappy Life of the Company of Young Canadians* (Toronto 1970) and Martin Loney 'A Political Economy of Citizen Participation' in Leo Panitch ed *The Canadian State* (Toronto 1977) 446–72

100 For the views of various organizers, see Fraser *Fighting Back*, John Sewell *Up against City Hall* (Toronto 1972), Donald R. Keating *The Power to Make It Happen* (Toronto 1975), and Marjaleena Repo 'The fallacy of "community control"' and 'Organising "the poor" – against the working class' in John Cowley et al ed *Community or Class Struggle?* (London 1977) 47–90.

101 Lorimer *The Developers*, Spelt *Toronto* 118–25, Metropolitan Toronto Planning Board *Metropolitan Toronto Key Facts* (Toronto 1970) tables 17, 23, Peter Spurr *Land and Urban Development: A Preliminary Study* (Toronto 1976) 98–128, and Nader *Cities of Canada* II 233–40

102 Bureau of Municipal Research (Toronto) 'Neighbourhood Participation in Local Government: A Study of the City of Toronto' *Civic Affairs* (Toronto 1970), Maureen Quigley *Democracy Is Us: Citizen Participation in Development in the City of Toronto* (Toronto 1971), Jack Granatstein *Marlborough Marathon: One Street against a Developer* (Toronto 1971), Fraser *Fighting Back*, Sewell *Up against City Hall*, and Keating *The Power to Make It Happen*

103 On the Spadina controversy, see Colton *Big Daddy* 62–3, 171–3, Rose *Governing Metropolitan Toronto* 134–44, Christopher Leo *The Politics of Urban Development: Canadian Urban Expressway Disputes* (Toronto 1977), and David and Nadine Nowlan *The Bad Trip: The Untold Story of the Spa-*

dina Expressway (Toronto 1970). Cf Juri Pill *Planning and Politics: The Metro Toronto Transportation Plan Reviews* (Cambridge, Mass, 1979).

104 The best expression of this ideology is in the works of James Lorimer: *The Real World of City Politics* (Toronto 1970), *Working People: Life in a Downtown City Neighbourhood* (Toronto 1971), *A Citizen's Guide to City Politics*, and *The Developers*; see also *City Magazine* (1976–9), Lorimer and Evelyn Ross ed *The City Book* (Toronto 1977) and *The Second City Book* (Toronto 1977), and Lorimer and MacGregor *After the Developers*. Cf Susan Fish 'Winning the Battle and Losing the War to Improve Municipal Policy Making' in Feldman *Politics and Government of Urban Canada* 90–101, Alan Powell ed *The City: Attacking Modern Myths* (Toronto 1972), and Granatstein *Marlborough Marathon*.

105 Lorimer *A Citizen's Guide* and Sewell *Up against City Hall*

106 Fish 'Winning the Battle and Losing the War,' Sewell *Up against City Hall*, Stephen Clarkson 'Private Politics, Citizen Politics, and the Public' in Powell *The City* 225–33, James Draper ed *Citizen Participation: Canada* (Toronto 1971), Frances Frisken and H.P. Homenuck ed *Citizen Participation: Views and Alternatives* (Toronto 1972), and Bureau of Municipal Research (Toronto) 'Citizen Participation in Metro Toronto: Climate for Cooperation?' *Civic Affairs* (Toronto 1975)

107 Provincial legislation that year authorized Ontario municipalities to adopt a universal franchise, given ratepayer approval in a referendum. There had been a gradual widening of the municipal electorate after the turn of the century, because the property qualifications for voting were not adjusted to take account of inflation. Spouses of ratepayers were eventually enfranchised, but other non-householders remained excluded until 1958. They constituted a substantial minority of the adult population.

108 Jerry F. Hough 'Voters' Turnout and the Responsiveness of Local Government: The Case of Toronto' in Paul Fox ed *Politics Canada* 3rd ed (Toronto 1970) 284–96 and Stephen Clarkson 'Barriers to Entry of Parties into Toronto's Civic Politics' *Canadian Journal of Political Science* IV (1971) 206–23. According to the official records at the Municipal Reference Library in Toronto 'ratepayer' turn-out was about 50 per cent higher than that of the new 'resident' electors after 1958.

109 Lorimer *The Real World of City Politics* 37–52 and Fraser *Fighting Back* 161–6

110 Bureau of Municipal Research (Toronto) 'The Metro Politician: A Profile' *Civic Affairs* (Toronto 1963). See also Nathan Phillips *Mayor of All the People* (Toronto 1967) for a Tory mayor's view of his own career.

111 The mercurial Allan Lamport was one example: Kaplan *Urban Political Systems* 137–42, Colton *Big Daddy* 166–8.

112 *Globe and Mail* (Toronto) 10 November–2 December 1966
113 Stephen Clarkson *City Lib: Parties and Reform* (Toronto 1972)
114 'The Tragic Career of William Dennison' in Lorimer *A Citizen's Guide* 124–6. Alignments in the 1966–9 council are analysed in Barry J. Kay 'Voting Patterns in a Non-Partisan Legislature: A Study of Toronto City Council' *Canadian Journal of Political Science* IV (1971) 224–42.
115 A third, purely municipal organization (CIVAC) endorsed candidates as well in both the 1966 and 1969 elections, but it had little more success. Its chairman was the future mayor David Crombie; Peter Silcox ed *Parties to Change: The Introduction of Political Parties in the 1969 Municipal Election* (Toronto 1971) and Masson and Anderson *Emerging Party Politics* 45–67, 158–81.
116 Kay 'A Model of Non-Partisan Legislative Bargaining and the Impact of Toronto Council's Partisanization, 1967–1972' paper presented to the CPSA Annual Meeting 1974, John Sewell, David Crombie, William Kilbourn, and Karl Jaffary *Inside City Hall* (Toronto 1971) 22–9, 66, Lorimer *A Citizen's Guide* 119, and John Sewell 'The Voting Record: 1971' *City Hall* II 8 (27 January 1972) 59–61
117 Jon Caulfield *The Tiny Perfect Mayor: David Crombie and Toronto's Reform Aldermen* (Toronto 1974) 1–18
118 Ibid 21
119 'Provincial Control over Municipalities: The Case of the Spadina Expressway' in Feldman and Goldrick *Politics and Government of Urban Canada* 2nd edn 197–211
120 Caulfield *Tiny Perfect Mayor* 95–112
121 'The Ontario Municipal Board Decision on the City of Toronto's 45 foot By-Law, The City of Toronto's Appeal and the Statement of the Hon. W. Darcy McKeough' in Feldman and Goldrick *Politics and Government of Urban Canada* 3rd edn 235–54. See also E.P. Fowler and David White 'Big City Downtowns: The Non-Impact of Zoning' in Thomas Dye and Virginia Gary ed *Determinants of Public Policy* (Lexington, Mass, 1979).
122 City of Toronto Planning and Development Department *Part 1 Official Plan: Office Consolidation* (November 1979) 3
123 John Sewell 'Did Toronto Fall Short in Its Plan for Downtown?' *Globe* 7 September 1976, 7. The plan did not finally come into effect until 31 January 1979 because of delays in provincial approval.
124 More radical measures to decentralize services and stimulate participation, such as proposed in *Report of the Neighbourhood Services Work Group* (April 1976), were rejected by council. Cf Caulfield *Tiny Perfect Mayor* 131–2.
125 Caulfield *Tiny Perfect Mayor* 126–7
126 Housing Work Group *Living Room: An Approach to Home Banking and*

Land Banking for the City of Toronto (Toronto 1973), Caulfield *Tiny Perfect Mayor* 51–72, and Rose *Canadian Housing Policies* 125–9

127 Rose *Canadian Housing Policies*

128 Caulfield *Tiny Perfect Mayor* 73–94

129 The most important provincial gesture was to block the Spadina Expressway.

130 The best analysis of this is in Michael Goldrick 'The Anatomy of Urban Reform in Toronto' *City Magazine* III 4 and 5 (May–June 1978) 29–39. See also Caulfield *Tiny Perfect Mayor* 12–14, 127–8, 138–42, 150–61, Barry Kay and P.H. Wichern 'Legislative Decision-Making in Two Canadian Cities: Toronto and Winnipeg Compared' paper presented to the CPSA Annual Meeting 1979, and Barry Kay 'Urban Decision-Making and the Legislative Environment: Toronto Council Re-examined' *Canadian Journal of Political Science* XV (1982) 553–73.

131 Sewell *Up against City Hall*

132 Goldrick 'Anatomy of Urban Reform' 37–9

133 Henry Mietkiewicz 'Party Politics Regaining Role after 10 years' *Star* 6 November 1978, A 12

134 The most important product of these efforts was Reform Metro, which endorsed numerous candidates in the late 1970s: 'New reform movement woos suburban supporters' *Star* 25 November 1975, Rosemarie Boyle 'Reform Metro: Much Strategy, Few Candidates' *Globe* 3 April 1978, and Mietkiewicz 'Party Politics.'

135 Middle-class community organizations often supported 'moderate' or conservative candidates for council.

136 According to Sewell, he modelled himself, in this respect, on René Lévesque.

137 Crombie's own popularity was such that he faced no serious opposition in the 1974 and 1976 mayoralty elections.

138 *Globe* 18 May 1977 and 2 and 30 November 1978 and *Star* 21 June 1978. Cf Sewell's articles on the suburbs in Lorimer and Ross *The Second City Book* 10–47.

139 *Globe* 16 June 1978. Crombie himself seems to have accepted this view.

140 Harvey Shepherd 'Sewell's Northern Drive Provides Key to Victory' *Globe* 14 November 1978, 9. See also Bill Freeman 'John Sewell and the New Urban Reformers Come to Power' *Our Generation* XIII (1979) 7–17.

141 The city also contained a high proportion of the metropolitan élite.

142 John Sewell 'Industrial Strategy for City Hall' in Lorimer and MacGregor *After the Developers* 25–9, Jane Jacobs *The Economy of Cities* (New York 1969), and *Globe and Mail* (23 January and 4 February 1980). Cf City of

Toronto Planning and Development Department *A Selective Economic Development Strategy for the City of Toronto: Policy and Program Proposals* (January 1980). Tax reform seemed an essential tool if the city were to encourage the forms of economic development it wanted. Sewell pressed hard for it on these and other grounds. See City of Toronto and Toronto Board of Education *Report of the Joint Committee on Property Tax Reform* (1980). Some suburban politicians condemned the scheme as 'socialistic' (*Globe* 13 October 1979) and the province resisted it for similar reasons ('Sewell Tax Reform Plan Unacceptable to Miller' *Globe* 6 December 1979), but also to protect its own jurisdiction.

143 *Star* 18 September–30 October 1979

144 See the briefs from the Ontario NDP (June 1975) and the Confederation of Residents and Ratepayers Associations (July 1975) to the (Robarts) Royal Commission on Metropolitan Toronto.

145 *Report of the Royal Commission on Metropolitan Toronto* 2 vols (1977)

146 Ontario *Government Statement on the Review of Local Government in the Municipality of Metropolitan Toronto* (Toronto 4 May 1978), 'Liberals, NDP vow to block changes in Metro' *Star* 4 May 1978, 'Cabinet Rejects Direct Election of Metro Council' *Star* 8 April 1980, A 3

147 *Globe* 11 November 1980. See also Leo Casey 'Toronto the Bad: The Gays, the NDP and the Civic Election' *This Magazine* XV (February–March 1981) 4–7.

148 David McLellan ed *Karl Marx: Selected Writings* (Oxford 1977) 300

CAROLINE ANDREW

Ottawa-Hull

Ottawa-Hull is Canada's most unusual metropolitan community. Unlike any other Canadian metropolis it spans a provincial boundary, and its linguistic diversity is matched only by Montreal's. Both facts are connected to the presence of the federal government. Its impact on municipal politics has been felt in two quite different ways. First, through the National Capital Commission (NCC), it has been active in traditional areas of municipal concern, especially in parks and park planning. Second, as the region's most important employer it has profoundly affected both the class composition of the population as a whole and the territorial distribution of the two major language groups.

Visitors and residents alike see ample evidence of the federal presence in local planning. The Rideau Canal (with skating in winter), the green belt, Gatineau Park, and the numerous green spaces throughout the region are the most conspicuous examples. In addition the federal government is involved in transportation, sewage, housing, and renovation – in fact in almost every area of municipal responsibility.

The NCC, established in its present form in 1958, covers 4,662 square kilometres, of which almost 60 per cent is in Ontario. In 1976 its population was 715,110, with 73 per cent in Ontario. On each side of the river there is a regional government with boundaries corresponding fairly closely to those of the NCC. Both the Regional Municipality of Ottawa-Carleton (RMOC) and the Communauté régionale de l'Outaouais (CRO) were established by their respective provincial governments to help check the expanding influence of the NCC. Ottawa-Carleton is made up of eleven municipalities, of which the largest by far is Ottawa. Indeed, the second in size, Nepean, has only 28 per cent as many people as Ottawa. The smallest municipality is wealthy Rockcliffe Park, home of federal politicians and diplomats, whose politically

TABLE 1
Employment in Ottawa-Hull 1976–9

	Ontario portion	Quebec portion	National Capital Region
Labour force (1976 Canadian census)	258,160	82,000	340,160
Federal employment (NCC survey 1976)	95,607	7,099	102,706
Federal employment (NCC survey 1979)	84,129	18,851	102,980

SOURCE: National Capital Commission *Annual Report 1979–80* 28

aware representatives have so far been successful in maintaining an independent existence. In Quebec, the regional government consists of six municipalities. The most important of these is Hull, but the most populous is Gatineau, east of Hull.

Multiple municipal jurisdictions within one urban area are, of course, common in Canada, but the Ottawa-Hull area is exceptional. The role of Ottawa-Hull as federal capital ensures fragmented, multi-levelled competition between intervening governments. Conflicts between the Quebec government and Hull, Ottawa-Carleton and Ottawa, the NCC and Quebec and Ontario all ensure that local politics becomes intergovernmental relations.

Table 1 demonstrates the significance for Ottawa-Hull of federal employment. In 1976 it represented 30 per cent of the total labour force. As the region's dominant employer, the federal government creates a heavily middle-class population. Consequently, the politics of Ottawa is middle-class. This manifests itself principally in terms of a 'consumption orientation'[1] towards municipal government, in which citizens look at local government primarily in terms of the services it will provide to residential neighbourhoods and to residents of the city as a whole. They expect 'collective consumption expenditures' (such as on parks, public transportation, and social housing) to be given priority. Others see municipal government principally in terms of its role in material production – as a means of support for economic development, and hence for the maximization of profits.

The expression of consumption and production interests represents the most apparent and visible municipal political cleavage. However, from a more theoretical point of view, there is no fundamental contradiction between the two. Consumption expenditures are often supportive of production, and production cannot go on without a work-force that is housed and provided access to the place of employment. There are, however, very important differences within the consumption and the production perspectives that relate to the particular social groups being served. Being concerned about providing housing for the working class is not the same thing as being concerned with housing the affluent middle class, yet both are related to consumption interests. Similarly, creating jobs for female, single-parent heads of families has not the same social impact as concern for the profitability of the commercial sector. However, these differences have not been highly visible and municipal politics has been played out largely in terms of the difference between the consumption interests and the production interests.

Although both interests are expressed in Ottawa city politics, the consumption interest has been particularly strong. This is linked to the dominance of federal employment and to the heavily middle-class composition of the population. Federal employment has meant that people have not thought of municipal government as having a role related to furthering employment or production, an attitude reinforced by the secure nature and relatively high salaries in the federal government. Of course, the city has not always had this middle-class character: the massive expansion of the federal civil service dates only from the Second World War. Furthermore, although Ottawa has been a civil-service town for most of the twentieth century, the transformation of Hull from an industrial town to a civil-service centre was only completed during the 1970s. Thus, the character of local politics has been and is different in Hull.

The federal presence has also been crucial in terms of the balance between the anglophone and francophone populations, one of the most important political cleavages of the region (see Table 2). In 1857 the government of the Province of Canada decided to situate the Parliament Buildings in Ottawa's Upper Town, thereby giving an economic base to the Upper Town's Anglo-Protestant community; this decision decisively tilted the local political balance towards the anglophone population.[2] This was then reinforced in the early twentieth century by the introduction of the merit principle within the civil service which, because of the respective education systems, further favoured the anglophone population. Recent attempts of the federal government to create a bilingual and bicultural national capital have called into question the extremely limited nature of municipal services provided to the French-language population by the city of Ottawa. Having been responsible for destroying the local political balance between francophones and anglophones, the federal presence is now behind the return to greater francophone influence. The increasing number of federal government jobs located in Hull – 10,000 were transferred there from Ottawa

TABLE 2
Population by mother tongue 1976

	Ontario portion (percentage)	Quebec portion (percentage)	National Capital Region (percentage)
English	70.4	16.2	56.1
French	19.1	78.9	34.9
Others	10.5	4.9	9.0

SOURCE: 1976 Canadian census as cited in NCC *Annual Report 1979–80* 28

between 1976 and 1979 (see Table 1) – is bound to influence the linguistic balance in the region.

As the central purpose of this book is to facilitate the comparison of government structures, public policies, and political cultures within the major urban areas in Canada, the principal focus of this article will be on the largest urban unit of the region, the city of Ottawa. At the same time, the nature of the region leads us to consider the municipalities in Quebec, as they are both suburbs of Ottawa and independent urban centres belonging to their own urban (and provincial) system.

FROM LUMBER TOWN TO CAPITAL

There were established communities on both sides of the Ottawa River when Bytown (on the Ontario side) was selected as the national capital in 1857. Modern settlement began on the Quebec side in 1800 when Philemon Wright set up a sawmill in what is now Hull. This first development was a consequence of the timber trade that was opening up the Ottawa Valley. The growing importance of the lumber industry was the prime influence on development in the area. Not only were sawmills established in the region, but the industry depended on the movement of supplies and lumber. This increased the importance of trading centres. 'Bytown came into being because it was to be, in its earliest years, a fundamental, necessary part of the operation of the imperial trade route of the St. Lawrence River Valley.'[3] Ottawa's importance as a trading centre was a consequence not only of the timber trade, but also of servicing its agricultural hinterland. Settlement of the outlying region had begun with the land grants given after the War of 1812 to soldiers wishing to settle in Canada. The servicing of this population was one of the factors that permitted Ottawa's growth rapidly to outdistance

Hull's.[4] Military factors were also crucial. After the hostilities of the War of 1812, it was felt important to assure a secure transportation route from Montreal to Kingston not in close proximity to the American border. The settlement of Ottawa began in 1826 with the building of the Rideau Canal under Colonel John By.

By the middle of the nineteenth century, the Ottawa-Hull area had changed from a commercial to an industrial centre. The opening up of American markets, along with technological changes, led to the establishment of large mills producing both lumber and wood by-products. The period of ascendancy of this industry lasted from ca 1870–1900, and during this period 'Ottawa-Hull ranked as the foremost lumber centre of Canada.'[5] By the end of the First World War, however, Ottawa was no longer an important industrial centre. On the Ontario side of the river, the reign of the lumber barons had come to an end, and the reign of the civil servants had begun. This same process took longer in Hull; there the federal public service became clearly dominant by the 1970s. From commerce to industry to government was the dominant pattern in the evolution of the region's economic base.

This pattern of development explains the historic divisions in Ottawa – conflicts that marked profoundly the local politics of the nineteenth century.[6] The city was divided, both physically and economically, into a number of rival élites. The commercial and mercantile interests, centred on Rideau Street in Lower Town (to the east of the Parliament Buildings), were made up of both French and English, fairly equally balanced. The lumber barons and the industrial interests linked to the sawmills and the manufacturing of wood by-products were located to the west of the Parliament Buildings, on flat land near the Ottawa River. For the most part this group was American and tended to remain aloof from the other groups. The Anglo-Protestant professional élite of Upper Town had existed since the beginnings of Bytown; but only with the choice of Ottawa as the capital and the locating of the Parliament Buildings in Upper Town was it able to rival the others. The coming of the national government gave it an economic base: by providing office space and clerical and professional services to the government, it grew in power.

These élites differed not only in economic interests but also in geographical location and racial and ethnic composition. The military in the early years had retained control over what is now Parliament Hill and this created a real physical barrier between Upper Town and Lower Town. This physical separation added to the social and ethnic distance between the two communities. This same distance existed in relation to the industrial interests. Thus, fragmentation of the élites was built into the early patterns of development in Ottawa. The existence of strong groups in the Ottawa Valley whose actions influenced the development of Ottawa further fragmented the city's political direction. The politics of this early period was marked by sharp conflicts among the élites and by their inability to coalesce around a single strategy of development.

The result of these conflicts was that Ottawa never developed metropolitan stature or an economy that could dominate the surrounding area. The élite disagreements were played out on a public scene that involved a broader participation. Religious, national, and political differences within the community magnified the disagreements into strong conflicts. The early Irish-French fights in the lumber trade,[7] the riots of 1843 and 1846 between Catholics and Orangemen,[8] and the Stoney Monday riot of 1849[9] indicate the rough-and-tumble nature of nineteenth-century politics in Ottawa.

What was local government doing that could be fought over? In the very early period the main activities of local government in Ottawa were commercial.[10] Decisions related to public markets were of great importance in the 1850s, during the first few years of the council. Decisions on the site for a market were vociferously debated and always led to recorded votes. Rivalry between Upper Town and Lower Town was clear and the compromise decided upon by the council in 1848 was to set up two markets.[11] The council sought also to regulate trade. In 1848, for example, it adopted by-laws relating generally to market regulations and, more specifically, to the weight and quality of bread, defining the duties of the Inspector of Weights and Measures and licensing a variety of trades, including carters for drawing water, cabmen, and calèche drivers. The market areas played an important role in the spatial control of trade and commerce: it was only in 1888 that the city council passed a by-law permitting fresh meat to be sold in certain areas outside the market.

By this time the control of trade and commerce was no longer the central focus of city politics. As Ottawa changed from a commercial to an industrial centre with the growth of the sawmills, so local government changed the major thrust of its policies. In 1878 the council discussed a system of bonuses for manufacturing companies interested in setting up in Ottawa. Some bonuses were given but this kind of direct assistance was infrequent. Local councillors seem to have felt that the major functions of government were to provide the basic infrastructure (roads, sidewalks, sewers) for the economy and to develop civic amenities. By the end of the nineteenth century these activities had become central. Slowly the council was moving into new areas of activity.

In 1868 discussions began on the possibility of the city's taking over responsibility for Major's Hill Park (near the Parliament Buildings), and ten years later the council passed a by-law respecting its maintenance and care. By the early twentieth century a public library also had been established in Ottawa. Municipal involvement in social welfare was slower to start. The first gesture was to make payments to the railways for sending paupers back where they came from, but by the 1870s the council was also providing some grants to charities.[12]

By the First World War the basis had been laid for the modern activities of the Ottawa city governments. From an early concern with regulating trade and commerce, the city shifted its attention to the development of the physical infrastructure and gradually expanded the range of civic amenities. This evolution should be understood in relation to changing socio-economic realities. Once Ottawa evolved from a commercial to an industrial centre, the commercial élite no longer controlled the municipal agenda, and facilities necessary for industry received greater attention. However, by the beginning of the twentieth century the federal government was coming to dominate Ottawa's economy, and the municipal government became more and more concerned with providing services to residents, rather than with assisting industry and commerce. The consumption orientation grew in importance as Ottawa increasingly became a government town.

Political change did not follow automatically from socio-economic shifts. Ottawa's municipal politics continued to be dominated by business long after the federal government became the major employer in the city. Ottawa's local politics were in strong contrast with the situation in Hull, where the evolution from industrial to government centre occurred much later. In the early twentieth century Hull was still totally dominated, both economically and politically, by industrial interests. For this reason the scope of municipal activity expanded less rapidly – the basic infrastructural services were provided, but little else. From the 1920s on industrial development was in a slow decline and this was not offset, as was the case in Ottawa, by the presence of the federal government. Municipal government lacked the economic base for a major expansion of consumer services.

The federal government not only strengthened Ottawa's economic base and altered the character of its population, but it became directly involved in the provision of civic amenities. In 1899 the Ottawa Improvement Commission was set up with the magnificent budget of $60,000 per year. The commission involved itself in projects aimed at beautifying the city and improving road transportation. The federal government began to plan for the capital with the publication, in 1903, of the Todd Report and, in 1913, of the Holt Report. In 1927 the commission was renamed the Federal District Commission and was restructured to include the Quebec side of the region in its activities. This early federal government concern was fragmentary but the areas of intervention – transportation, parks, and planning – anticipated the major areas of federal activity today.

POST-WAR GROWTH

At the end of the Second World War Ottawa was on the threshold of a period of enormous growth. This was so for all major urban centres in Canada, but the very rapid expansion of the federal civil service,[13] along with major annexations of suburban municipalities, made growth especially great in Ottawa. Between 1921 and 1941 the population of the city of Ottawa had increased only from 107,843 to 154,951, but in the next twenty years the absolute increase was more than twice as large, raising the population of the city alone to 268,206 and of the metropolitan area to 344,214.[14]

The structure of the city also changed as the suburbs expanded. The number of individual homes in Ottawa almost tripled in the period 1945–60.[15] This development was based on universal use of the private car and this, in turn, transformed the transportation system. The changes were symbolized by the opening of Ottawa's first major urban expressway, the Queensway, in 1957.

Suburban development was also evident in Hull. However, the new residential areas were in large part built for federal civil servants working in Ottawa. Almost no industrial expansion occurred; the major changes in land use between 1945 and 1965 were an increase in residential space and in land used for roads (and a decrease in agricultural land).[16] The municipal government approved subdivision plans, supplied services, and began lobbying the federal government to increase its contribution to the development of the Quebec side of the Ottawa River. Municipal élites argued that if the federal government was to be the dominant influence in the area, it should stimulate economic development. Rather than being exclusively interested in expanding park holdings in Quebec, it should, they suggested, at least locate some of its buildings in Hull.[17]

In the city of Ottawa itself, federal government expansion and the resulting suburban residential development scarcely needed to be encouraged. As the mayor declared in his inaugural address in 1958, 'Ottawa's continuing growth goes hand and hand with its increasing stature as the Capital city.'[18] The accepted role for the Ottawa council was to support expansion: subdivision approvals came up at every council meeting in 1958 and were almost invariably accepted. However, there were some doubters, including Charlotte Whitton, Ottawa's best-known municipal politician. She was mayor from 1952 to 1958 and from 1960 to 1964, and her battles with city officials, politicians, and developers[19] were legion. Whitton dominated media attention, both in the region and across the country, but did not always – or even usually – win her battles.[20] She brought to the mayor's office a strong belief in a limited role for government and an equally strong view that large private economic interests ought not to be allowed to dominate public decisions. Despite this, civic policy reflected an acceptance of the large development companies and (somewhat reluctantly) of a positive role for local government in supporting and facilitating private development.[21] Although Whitton's views were shared by certain parts of the population, the majority of the electorate favoured rapid residential expansion and municipal encouragement of this trend. Municipal policy was oriented to growth in the residential sector.

In the post-war period, the influence of the federal government was felt everywhere. In 1958 the main federal agency changed its name to the National Capital Commission (NCC) and substantially increased its budget. It reinforced the suburbanization of Ottawa, through the construction of parkways and particularly through the decentralization of federal government office buildings. And, although the intention of the green belt was to contain urban sprawl, residential development simply jumped the green belt.[22] Thus government policy at all levels acted to support and reinforce private market trends towards low-density residential development. The federal influence has been exercised primarily through its own land holdings. The NCC's power to expropriate land was confirmed by the Supreme Court in 1966,[23] but in recent years the federal government has relied more on the purchase of land and less on expropriation. 'Federal land is very strategically placed around the Capital ... The witholding of approval for encroachments proposed by municipal or provincial bodies is a powerful weapon and although it has been used sparingly, it gives the federal government a considerable say in new developments.'[24]

The last twenty years have provided further proof of the dependence of Ottawa on the federal government. In the 1960s the region continued to expand at a rapid rate, thanks to the growth of the federal civil service. In the 1970s the civil service did not increase substantially and the federal government went ahead with plans for the relocation of office buildings in Hull. As a result, the region grew slowly during the 1970s, and the city of Ottawa not at all.[25] The major hope of the city now lies with the continued growth of the high technology industry: 'An infectious boom-town atmosphere is gripping Ottawa these days – the kind that has not been felt here since Queen Victoria chose the city as Canada's capital more than 100 years ago. Ottawa is no longer a slightly sleepy, one-industry town. Red tape is being smothered in computer tape; bureaucrats are watching anxiously as engineers move in next door; traffic on the Queensway is flowing both ways in rush hour. High technology – a whole series of new business made possible by computerization and miniaturized electronics – has come to town.'[28]

Whatever happens, federal government policies will be vital, since government support for research has been crucial to the high technology industry. Federal influence over Ottawa's growth will remain high, either directly or indirectly. In socio-economic terms employment in the high technology sector is fairly similar to federal government employment, and the development of this sector is not likely to alter to any significant degree the class composition of the Ottawa population.

PROBLEMS IN THE CENTRAL CITY

Despite the recent lack of overall growth, there have been important changes in the socio-spatial organization of the city, which have generated new political issues. Municipal politics and policies continue to evolve as socio-economic realities change. The city core and the inner-city residential neighbourhoods have been most affected. As a study of the central area makes clear, the major factor in these changes is the demand for office space, both public and private: 'The Ottawa central area has changed considerably since the early 1960's. This dynamic evolution is closely linked to the city's economic base. The major catalyst is the strengthening of the city's administrative function which, in turn, is related to the post-war growth of the tertiary sector in advanced economies.'[27]

The rapid development of the privately owned office building sector in the 1960s can be explained in terms of the federal government's public works policies. Until 1960 the federal government had primarily used its own buildings, but after 1960 it began leasing space in private buildings on a large scale.[28] By the end of the 1960s, 60–70 per cent of the new office space in central Ottawa was being leased for government activities.[29] This boom in the private office market came to a temporary end in the mid-1970s when the federal government began moving out of a number of previously leased buildings to relocate in Hull.

The other major change in the downtown core is the increasing height of buildings.[30] During the 1960s the municipal government gradually weakened the height control it had previously exerted and gave in to the private developers who wanted increased heights for increased profits. Robert Campeau defied city policy and went ahead with plans to build a complex, Place de Ville, higher than allowable. The reaction of the city was to change its policy and reduce the area of the downtown core covered by the height restrictions. The original point of these restrictions had been to highlight Parliament Hill as the focus of the central core, but the modifications to this policy have permitted extensive high-rise development in the central core.

Not surprisingly, these transformations have led to declining residential land use within the central core. This in turn has led to pressure on the adjacent residential areas, the inner-city neighbourhoods. These neighbourhoods have undergone the greatest pressures for change, with the most dramatic social consequences. Besides the pressures for non-residential uses of land, and for high-rise development, these neighbourhoods are under strong pressures leading to their social transformation. Middle-class families and individuals have been moving into these areas, dramatically reducing the stock of low- and moderate-priced rental accommodation.

The city of Ottawa has documented this reduction in great detail for the period 1974–8, in which the inner-city neighbourhoods lost a total of 1,873 low-rental units.[31] Units were lost through demolition, severances,[32] conversions of rooming houses, rehabilitation of units for luxury rental – in other words, through white-painting and gentrification. Private market trends are clearly towards the elimination of the low- and moderate-income population from the centre city: almost all (530 of 555) the new low rental units in the period 1974–8 came from the non-profit, co-operative, and public-housing sectors of the housing market.[33]

The characteristics of the inner-city neighbourhoods have therefore changed markedly over the past twenty years. Multiple-unit dwellings have become predominant. An important increase in the number of non-family households has occurred, particularly in the centre city. Demands for the use of inner-city neighbourhoods by the affluent, in both new high-rise apartments and in renovated houses, have created pressures on the residents of these areas. Most of these trends are not specific to Ottawa, but here again the dominance of federal government employment produces a unique situation. The high percentage of non-family households (mostly one person living alone) and the high percentage of renters are related to the large number of affluent, young, mobile civil servants. As Table 5 in the Appendix indicates, Ottawa has one of the highest combinations of renters and non-family households of any large metropolitan area in Canada.

THE PATTERN OF CONTEMPORARY POLITICS

The basic character and major issues of recent Ottawa politics emerge from these socio-demographic changes. This is illustrated by the neighbourhood planning experience that began in Ottawa in the early 1970s. The city wished to review its 1964 zoning regulations, most particularly in the core area, and decided that individual neighbourhood studies should form one part of this review. The city therefore decided to do neighbourhood plans for the inner-city neighbourhoods, and in all cases the planning process included participation by the citizens. The basic pattern was to form a committee composed of all those people wishing to be involved, and usually this committee formed subcommittees responsible for different sectors of the plan (transportation, recreation, land use, commercial, etc). The committees worked closely with city officials during the preparation of the plan, though not always harmoniously. Most of the plans went beyond traditional planning areas to include schemes related to a broad range of social needs identified through the planning process.

The neighbourhood planning efforts were instrumental in organizing and channelling consumption interests in municipal politics. The 1960s and particularly the 1970s witnessed an important increase in the organization and articulation of consumption interests, largely as a result of the creation of neighbourhood-based citizen groups. Their overall number is hard to estimate: one study put it at between 45 and 65 in 1972,[34] and in 1979 a list of community groups listed 217 associations.[35] The neighbourhood planning process served also as an initiation ground for municipal politicians. Through citizen groups, particularly those involved in neighbourhood plans, a whole generation of municipal politicians has attained office. These politicians have tended to be active in the representation of consumption interests, to be concerned with the preservation of residential communities, and to favour public transportation, social housing, better social services (notably day care), and better recreational facilities.

This has produced major changes in the make-up of the council. After the 1978 elections a clear majority of the council represented consumption rather than production interests; in the 1970–2 council less than one-third of council represented consumption interest.[36] The 1980–2 council was somewhat more divided than its predecessor but consumption interests were clearly important. Ottawa politics in the 1970s was in large measure concerned with residential or consumption interests. The elected representatives tended to be sympathetic to such interests, to listen to their points of view, and to allocate city resources to the development of these groups.

Nevertheless, production interests are still important in Ottawa politics. The Board of Trade and the Commercial and Industrial Development Corporation of Ottawa-Carleton continue to be important pressure groups. Indeed the example of the Rideau Centre redevelopment scheme[37] suggests that business interests still wield considerable influence at city hall. The municipal government's initial reluctance to agree to this massive redevelopment scheme in downtown Ottawa changed to acceptance, and even enthusiasm, because of the economic slump and the business pressure brought to bear on government. Business interests pushed for the development of a convention centre in order to stimulate the building industry and the tourist industry and to counter the possibility of tourist dollars being diverted to Hull, if Hull's convention centre were to be alone in the region.[38] The municipal council accepted the project despite protests from a variety of citizen groups and individual citizens who argued that it would harm the market area, do nothing to encourage residential development in the city core, harm nearby residential communities, and, in general, diminish the quality of life in Ottawa.

Differences exist within both the consumption and the production perspectives. Again, neighbourhood planning illustrates these differences. The early neighbourhood plans recommended increased density by means of in-fill housing projects and tended to be sympathetic to social housing, whereas most of the later plans are more exclusively directed towards the preservation of single-family, low-density residential communities. Despite this recent tendency, the Ottawa council has maintained a commitment to an interventionist role in social housing. The City of Ottawa Non-Profit Housing Corporation (CONPHC) was set up in the 1970s and took over responsibility for the existing portfolio of limited-dividend housing. It has played an active role in providing housing for low- and moderate-income residents and in offering support to co-operative and private non-profit groups. The municipal political will in the housing field has been strong, but activity has been hampered to some extent by reaction from some neighbourhood groups, by the hesitation of the provincial government, and, since 1980, by some of the new municipal councillors.

The political novelty of the 1970s in Ottawa was the organized articulation of consumption interests. During the mid-1970s the consumption orientation became the new orthodoxy, but by the early 1980s there was some swing back to the production viewpoint. Although there are some clear differences between these two points of view, conflict is not always apparent or highly visible. This is in part because of the prevalence of the nonpolitical view of local politics that tends to play down the importance of philosophical or ideological bases to political action at the local level. In addition, the opposition between consumption and production cuts across traditional political divisions and therefore makes these divisions less easily identifiable and less visible (this is particularly true of those with Liberal affiliations who range across the entire municipal political spectrum). Finally, as there is no fundamental contradiction between consumption and production points of view, disagreement in emphasis or in priorities can exist without involving a clear-cut opposition.

For these reasons political debate was not very sharp during the 1970s, and the tone of most of the political campaigns was subdued. An analysis of the 1980 elections concluded that the campaign had not given rise to a discussion of the real issues of urban planning and that the question of personalities and leadership had taken the place of genuine debate over issues.[39] This same conclusion could easily have been reached for all the recent municipal elections, despite the fact that the 1978, 1980, and 1982 elections offered a choice between the consistent victor, Marion Dewar, clearly identified with consumption interests, and rivals Pat Nicol and Darrell Kent, who were identified with production interests. Notwithstanding the contrast between Dewar and Nicol in 1978 and 1980, there was little difference in their platforms, in the issues they emphasized, and in their promises. Dewar emphasized her concern for the economic prosperity of the city whereas Nicol underlined her support for social programs.

In recent elections the tradition has been for the city to organize election meetings in each of the wards of the city and, in addition, for a variety of special-interest groups to hold all-candidate meetings. Attendance and interest vary widely, and, as in politics at all levels, media attention is often more important than real performance. A good deal of importance is given to door-to-door canvassing by candidates and their organizers. Voter turn-out recently has been low, and there has been a general trend towards decreasing participation: 63.9 per cent in 1960, 58.2 per cent in 1962, 57.2 per cent in 1964, 45.0 per cent in 1966, 38.2 per cent in 1969, 32.2 per cent in 1972, 36.3 per cent in 1974, 30.1 per cent in 1976, 41.6 per cent in 1978, 38.5 per cent in 1980, and 46.8 per cent in 1982.[40] There seem to be both a lack of interest in muncipal issues and municipal government and difficulties in voting on a rational basis, given the absence of party affiliation, totally inadequate media coverage, and the small likelihood of knowing the candidates. Both influences are clearly at work and each affects the other.

Despite the relatively low level of interest, Ottawa elections do bring out salient political cleavages. The most recent elections have been described as contests between New Democrats and Conservatives. This description contains an element of truth. Many of the candidates representing consumption interests are allied to the New Democratic Party and several of the production-oriented councillors, particularly the more recently elected, have links to Ontario's ruling Conservative party. Ethno-linguistic cleavages also play some role in Ottawa politics, particularly within the two wards where the francophone population is most concentrated. These cleavages may be more salient in the future. The federal government's concern about bilingualism and biculturalism in the region has generated some spin-off at the local level. Ottawa has taken a few timid steps towards better services for the francophone population, but pressures for further action may well increase. Relations between the two linguistic communities have been eased by the existence of separate municipalities. However, there have been proposals for annexing the francophone suburb of Vanier to Ottawa, and this would make politically more acute the question of levels of services for the two linguistic groups.

ORGANIZATIONAL CHANGES

The structure of Ottawa's municipal government has also been changing. The board of control was abolished in 1980, after long debate and the Ottawa council is now composed of fifteen aldermen elected by wards, plus the mayor elected at large. The board had been created in 1908 to act as the executive arm of the council and was composed of four controllers elected at large. It examined all proposals going before council, prepared the budget, and nominated senior administrative personnel. Its proposals could be defeated by a simple majority of council but expenditures not previously approved by it needed a two-thirds majority.[41] This system led to conflict between the board and council members. By the 1970s this conflict became more and more apparent. Consumption-oriented politicians first emerged on the ward level and found themselves in conflict with the city-wide elected (and more business-dominated) members of the board of control. In addition, members of this new generation of elected representatives tended to put more time into their role as councillors and therefore to be more conscious of their limited role in relation to the controllers. By their background and education, the more activist aldermen were more interested in questions of general policy than in looking after ward sidewalks and were therefore interested in shaping these general policies.

The increasing importance of intergovernmental relations also meant that the costs of deadlock were seen more clearly: if the council was not able to agree on policy relating to provincial-municipal or to federal-municipal questions, its chances of being able to influence the senior governments were severely reduced. With executive power so dominant at both provincial and federal levels, pressure built up for a more unified political direction at the municipal level. The abolition of the board of control was debated at length. Those who were against abolition tended to argue either that its existence increased the number of points of contact between citizens and elected representatives or that the group favouring its abolition were dangerously 'left-wing' and wanted control of city hall. Those favouring abolition wanted more control by the council as a whole or by individual aldermen and the possibility of a more unified political direction and/or less duplication of debates. These differences in objectives led to disagreement about what system should replace the board of control, and, after much debate there is now a Committee on Administration, Policy and Priorities rather than an executive committee. This committee does not deal with items coming through other committees and has not played an active role in budget presentation. Despite expectations that it would play a co-ordinating role, this has not been the case. Little pressure exists to change this role but it seems likely that such pressure may increase.

The debate over the board of control can be seen as an attempt on the part of the new generation of activist and largely consumption-oriented politicians to gain control of Ottawa's local government. During the same period there were also efforts to restructure the administration so as to make the bureaucracy more responsible to the council. These reforms had the objectives of improving co-ordination within the civic bureaucracy and increasing its efficiency, but there was also a concern to ensure that municipal activity reflected council's decisions. The traditional structure of civic administration created problems for the efficient co-ordination and control of the bureaucracy. A large number of separate departments existed, each of which reported directly to the board of control or to a council committee. As new activities were taken on, new departments were created and only very slowly were outdated departments abolished. Finally, in the 1970s, a major reorganization took place, with a substantial reduction in number of departments through the creation of departments of Community Development and Physical Environment. A Committee of Department Heads under a chief commissioner was set up to provide for administrative coordination. The council's committee system was also reorganized to correspond to the new departmental structure, in the hope of increasing political control.

While some moves have been taken to strengthen political control over the administration, a number of factors exist that militate against this control. The fact that the council members are elected on an individual basis, with only informal alliances on specific questions, makes political control that much more difficult. In addition, the mayor has very few powers and cannot exercise strong executive direction. The greater access of the mayor to the media coupled with the prestige of the office does mean that the mayor's political agenda gets a greater airing, but this does not ensure that specific measures will be adopted. The elected representatives have very little staff and little time for the kind of investigation of city activities that would be even a first step towards being in a position to control these activities. In 1982 there was not even one assistant for each elected representative – even the mayor had only two personal assistants.

The demand for better control over the civic administration has been related to a concern about public participation. This concern is obviously not specific to Ottawa, but Ottawa has been particularly active in meeting it. In part this is a result of having elected representatives who, in being committed to the representation of consumption interests, wanted to encourage citizens to take an active role in local politics. In terms of education, familiarity with government procedures, and belief in its own political efficacy, Ottawa's civil service population is strongly predisposed to active involvement in public affairs. Moves towards greater citizen involvement have been motivated by a number of objectives (sometimes harmonious, sometimes conflicting): that people should be better informed about government actions, that they should be consulted about future (or present) activities, that they should participate in decision-making, and that they should have control over their lives. A great number of individual decisions have been taken that relate to these concerns: notification of zoning changes to tenants as well as property-owners, publication of a handbook on civic structures and activities, initiation of grants to community groups, employment of community animators to work with these groups, establishment of a freedom of information policy, and better advertisement of city activities in both city and community newspapers. Moreover, the problem has been studied by an incredibly large number of committees, working groups, public meetings, and consultants.[42] Citizen participation or at least better information to citizens is now seen as a legitimate, and largely accepted, part of the policy process, although the specific mechanisms for integrating it in the civic administration have not been fully developed.

EXTERNAL RELATIONS

The Ottawa council has been very active in lobbying for better provincial funding of its social programs. This has not always been easy because of the nature of relations between Ottawa and Queen's Park. In the 1970s, the council was often in disagreement with the Ontario government, and relations were generally strained. The Ottawa council wanted to expand social services and consumption-oriented expenditures at a time when the Ontario government was attempting to cut back expenditure on social service programs. The Conservative government saw the council as being 'NDP-dominated,' and this partisan dimension meant that the provincial government was all the more likely to refuse Ottawa's requests. One of the strategies used by the city to gain provincial approval has been that of trying to act with other municipalities. For that reason Ottawa has worked actively within the Ontario Municipal Association (OMA).

The city council has also had to contend with a conservative regional government, which has the main financial and administrative responsibility for social services. The Regional Municipality of Ottawa-Carleton (RMOC), created in 1969 from sixteen municipalities (since reduced to eleven), was made responsible for water-supply and distribution, sewage collection and treatment, the design and maintenance of regional roads, overall planning, debt financing, and the provision of social services.[43] RMOC has since acquired responsibility for public transportation plus some responsibility in housing matters and in the provision of day care. The council of RMOC is composed of thirty-one people, including the entire Ottawa council (sixteen) plus representatives from the other municipal councils. In theory, Ottawa has a majority on the council, but more often than not some of the suburban Ottawa representatives vote with the rural municipalities. The chairman is elected by the regional council and, although the person may be either from within the council or from outside, so far they have been chosen from within the regional council.

The urban-rural or, perhaps more accurately, the Ottawa–non-Ottawa split within the regional council has been clearly illustrated by recent debates over housing and day care. Elected representatives from the townships tend not to be sympathetic to spending in these areas and feel that these expenditures help only the city of Ottawa. Ottawa representatives argue that the needs are engendered on a region-wide basis and that the arguments of equity indicate that costs be borne on a regional basis. The result is in housing a very weak and ambiguous role and in day care an excessively complicated funding formula that leads to municipal responsibility.

In other areas of activity, the regional municipality has been less hampered by the Ottawa–non-Ottawa conflict. Public transportation has increased its percentage of overall ridership by such improvements as bus lanes, monthly bus passes, teletranspo (dial-a-bus), and a proposed system of transit ways (roads designed uniquely as express bus ways to serve the suburban areas of the region).[44] The region's Social Services Department has also been active, and Ottawa-Carleton has been willing to put more of its own money into social services than most other Ontario municipalities.[45] Inner-city politicians have been able to convince or outweigh their more rural colleagues, at least to a greater extent than elsewhere in the province.

The 'structure, organization and operations'[46] of local government in the region were the subject of a review commission in the mid-1970s. The major recommendations of the resulting Mayo report were the strengthening of regional government by transferring a number of municipal responsibilities to the regional level and direct election of the regional councillors. The provincial government accepted some of the recommendations relating to changing municipal boundaries but did not accept any of the major recommendations relating to structures. Regional councillors continue therefore to be elected on a municipal basis. The problems raised in the Mayo report of 'accountability to, and access by, the public'[47] continue to exist, and, as the report states, 'It is extremely difficult for electors to hold councillors accountable for their decisions at the Regional level if they are on the Regional Council by virtue of their positions on the area councils.'[48] As regional responsibilities increase, this problem is accentuated. Regional responsibilities are considerable, but their visibility is extremely limited. Nevertheless, it appears unlikely that any major changes will be made. The political unpopularity of regional government is such that the Ontario authorities are hesitant to increase their powers or visibility. At the same time, for administrative reasons, the province finds it useful to maintain regional structures in one form or other.

The existence of RMOC and of the Outaouais Regional Community on the Quebec side of the river has influenced federal-local relations in the region. As the NCC's 1979–80 annual report indicates, the existence of two regional governments has reduced the NCC's direct role in the overall planning of the region:

> In the late 1960's the local government structure was drastically altered when the two provinces created regional governments with strong planning mandates. These two regional governments ... have prepared Official Plans which reflect local aspirations for the development of their cities and towns. The local municipalities have prepared their own plans in conformity with the policies adopted at the regional level. This has permitted the NCC to redirect its effort towards the federal elements of the Capital; the lack of local planning resources which had forced Greber to produce an overall plan for the Capital in all its aspects has been filled by the regional governments. The development of the NCR (National Capital Region) must now proceed

on a co-operative basis, with each level of government responsible for planning those aspects of regional development which are within its jurisdiction.[49]

This new federal policy direction is also influenced by the desire of the federal government to cut expenditures. To respect regional priorities means less direct federal intervention and fewer federal dollars for the capital region, in clear contrast with the policies of the 1970s, when the NCC was heavily involved in planning for the region. The NCC produced a plan, *Tomorrow's Capital*, in 1974, which argued for strengthening the northwest-southeast axis of development (Aylmer to Orleans) in contradiction to the existing development trends that are northeast-southwest (Gatineau to Kanata). The NCC's explicit justification was in terms of recentring the region on the Parliament Buildings, but the plan was also designed to strengthen the anglophone sector of Quebec and the francophone sector of Ontario and therefore to cut against the correspondence between the political and ethno-linguistic boundaries. The plan has not been followed through, and as the quotation indicates, the NCC has accepted the priorities of the regional governments.

It would not be accurate, however, to suggest that the federal government's influence on the development of the region has disappeared. The NCC has been the chief mover behind the Rideau Centre project. On the Quebec side of the river, the federal government has played an even more important role in the past ten years. At a 1967 federal-provincial conference Prime Minister Pearson obtained agreement that the capital of Canada was to be Ottawa-Hull. In 1969 the federal government announced its intention to expropriate land in the centre of Hull in order to construct office buildings. The reasons behind this decision were numerous: a desire to counteract the independence movement in Quebec by integrating western Quebec into the federal capital region, a desire to recentralize federal buildings close to the Parliament Buildings, and pressure from Hull élites to distribute federal expenditures more equally in the capital region.[50] The Quebec government also decided to expropriate land in downtown Hull for a complex to include Quebec government offices, a convention centre, and a shopping mall. These actions have transformed the centre of Hull into a sector for office buildings, principally those of the federal government. Industrial employment has declined and government employment increased. If Hull was an industrial centre far longer than Ottawa, it was certainly no longer one by the end of the 1970s.

Hull council strongly supported the federal intervention. Anxious to bring development and to share in Ottawa's prosperity, the municipal leaders had pressured the federal government throughout the 1960s to increase its expenditures on the Quebec side of the river. The kind of political evolution that we described for Ottawa in the 1970s was only just beginning in Hull in the late 1970s. Most of the municipal politicians represented 'production' interests, with real estate and commerce predominant. The one important exception was Mayor Michel Légère, elected in the summer of 1981 on a platform of municipal change and citizen participation. During the period of urban renewal in the late 1960s, citizen groups had been active and had had some success in improving the terms of expropriation. Despite an unsuccessful attempt by citizens' groups to present a group of candidates in the municipal elections of 1974,[51] the consumption perspective has been little represented in terms of elected positions. It will be interesting to see whether the Hull council will follow the trend towards greater representation of consumption interests.

The activities of the federal government in Hull during the 1970s increased the integration of the Quebec community into the Ottawa metropolitan region and eliminated the major economic differences between Ottawa and Hull. Greater political similarity between the two communities may be the ultimate result.

CONCLUSION

The underlying theme of this article has been the importance of the division between consumption and production interests in the politics and government of the Ottawa-Hull region. Questions relating to collective consumption expenditures have been central to local politics, and political divisions fall between those wishing greater local involvement in areas relating to consumption expenditures and those wishing fewer consumption expenditures or more local expenditures designed to directly support economic development.

As Ottawa evolved from a commercial through an industrial to a civil service town, a growing concern developed for the provision of civic amenities, and as the provision of amenities became more and more important, local government became increasingly associated with collective consumption expenditures and with the representation of consumption interests. This perspective has been clearly present in Ottawa and, in the recent past, it has strongly marked the policies and politics of the region. Will this situation change in the present climate of cut-backs and government restraints? There will probably be slight modifications, but it seems unlikely that the basic pattern of local politics in the region will change.

SUGGESTED FURTHER READING

Andrew, C., A. Blais, and R. Des Rosiers *Les Elites politiques, les bas-salariés et la politique de logement à Hull* Ottawa 1976

Andrew, C., S. Bordeleau, and A. Guimont *l'Urbanisation : une affaire* Ottawa 1981

Brault, L. *Hull, 1800–1950* Ottawa 1950

– *Ottawa Old and New* Ottawa 1946

Deachman, H., and J. Woolfrey 'Les Terrasses de la Chaudière' *Our Generation* 14-3 (winter 1981) 7–34

Eggleston, W. *The Queen's Choice* Ottawa 1961

Fullerton, D. *The Capital of Canada: How Should It Be Governed?* Ottawa 1974

Mayo, H.B. *Report of the Ottawa-Carleton Review Commission* Ottawa 1976

Newton, Michael *Lower Town Ottawa 1826–1854* Ottawa 1979

Rowat, D.C. 'Ottawa' in D.C. Rowat *The Government of Federal Capitals* Toronto 1973

– *Urban Politics in Ottawa-Carleton: Research Essays* Ottawa 1974

Taylor, J. 'Ottawa as Metropolis' paper presented to the Annual Meeting of the Canadian Historical Association, Saskatoon 1979

– 'Fire, Disease and Water in Ottawa: An Introduction' *Urban History Review* 8-1 (June 1979) 7–37

Wesche, R., and M. Kugler-Gagnon *Ottawa-Hull: Spatial Perspectives and Planning* Ottawa 1978

NOTES

1 This distinction between consumption and production interests has been in part inspired by the work of Manuel Castells and others on the importance of collective consumption issues to municipal politics. See Manuel Castells *La Question urbaine* (Paris 1972), *Crise du logement et mouvements sociaux urbains* (Paris 1978), and *Monopolville* (Paris 1974).

2 My thanks to John Taylor for this interpretation. See John Taylor 'Ottawa as Metropolis' paper presented to the Canadian Historical Association, Saskatoon 1979

3 Michael Newton *Lower Town Ottawa 1826–1854* (Ottawa 1979) 1

4 Even by the late 1830s Ottawa's population was greater than that of Hull. See George A. Nader *Cities of Canada* II (Toronto 1976) 165.

5 Peter Gillis 'Ottawa and Hull 1870–1930: A Description and Analysis of Their Industrial Structure' in Rolf Wesche and Marianne Kugler-Gagnon *Ottawa-Hull: Spatial Perspectives and Planning* (Ottawa 1978) 14

6 Taylor 'Ottawa as Metropolis'
7 Michael Cross 'The Shiners' War: Social Violence in the Ottawa Valley in the 1830's' *Canadian Historical Review* LIV (1973) 1–26
8 Newton *Lower Town* 279–80
9 Newton *Lower Town* chap 15 and Michael Cross 'Stoney Monday, 1849: The Rebellion Losses Bill Riots in Bytown' *Ontario History* LXIII (1971) 177–90
10 This discussion of municipal activities is based on secondary sources and on the analysis of the council minutes for one year in every ten over the period 1848–1978. All decisions of the council were noted.
11 Newton *Lower Town* chap 12. The Upper Town market was never very prosperous and it ceased to be used, whereas the Lower Town market flourishes to this day.
12 This policy underlines the importance of the private associations in the field of social welfare. Municipal activity has often consisted more in the support of private initiatives than in the direct provision of services.
13 In 1951 there were 30,069 federal government employees in the National Capital Region. In 1961 there were 46,095 and, in 1971, 65,928. However, this refers only to employees of departments and departmental corporations as designated in schedules A and B of the Financial Administration Act; Douglas Fullerton *The Capital of Canada: How Should It Be Governed?* (Ottawa 1974).
14 Ibid 23
15 Wilfrid Eggleston *The Queen's Choice* (Ottawa 1961) 214
16 Pierre Houde 'Hull et l'avenir de l'ouest du Québec' PHD thesis, Université de Strasbourg, 1970, 165
17 See C. Andrew, A. Blais, and R. Des Rosiers *Les Élites politiques, les bas salariés et la politique du logement à Hull* (Ottawa 1976).
18 Inaugural address, 6 January 1958, minutes of the council of the city of Ottawa
19 Particularly with Robert Campeau, whose international development interests had their origin in Ottawa
20 Unfortunately for students of municipal politics, most of what has been written about Whitton touches her earlier social work career as director of the Children's Aid Bureau. There has yet to be a really thorough account of her career as mayor, and this analysis is therefore subject to revision.
21 A number of possible explanations can be suggested: Whitton's inability to obtain the support of the majority of council, the difficulty of translating council votes into executive action, the public's strong support for development, and the determination of the developers to get what they wanted from governments.

22 The green belt was one of the principal recommendations of the Gréber report submitted to the federal government in 1950. The other major proposals, most of which have been implemented, were for the relocation of the railway station away from the city centre, the extension of Gatineau Park, and the construction of a parkway system of roads.
23 *Harold Munro* v *National Capital Commission*, judgment of Supreme Court of Canada 28 June 1966
24 Fullerton *The Capital of Canada* 17–18
25 Ron Kellestine and Barry Nabatian *Demographic and Housing Changes in Ottawa-Carleton* Report by Urban Policy and Research Division, Community Development Department, City of Ottawa 1979, 5
26 Ottawa *Citizen* 'Boom Grips Region' 24 March 1981
27 Joanne Sabourin 'The Evolution of the Ottawa Central Area' in Rolf Wesche and Marianne Kugler-Gagnon *Ottawa-Hull: Spatial Perspectives and Planning* (Ottawa 1978) 53
28 Fullerton's description of this change is as follows: 'In 1963 there was growing government reluctance to grant the DPW the construction funds it needed to meet burgeoning demands, and a new policy of leasing office space from speculative builders was adopted'; *The Capital of Canada* 45.
29 Sabourin 'Evolution' 59. This figure was taken from a 1969 study by Larry Smith and Co Inc, *Downtown Demand Study: Ottawa and Hull*, prepared for the National Capital Commission.
30 This question is discussed by Sabourin 'Evolution' 59–60 and by Helen Deachman and Joy Woolfrey 'Les Terrasses de la Chaudière *Our Generatin* 14-3 (winter 1981) 7–34.
31 *Instability and Tenant Displacement within the Inner City Rental Market* Report of Community Development Department, Ottawa 1979
32 Severances have been a major cause of the loss of low-rental housing because they have been used by people wishing to convert rental accommodation into single-family ownership. Typically, severances are sought for a row of rental houses and these are then sold separately.
33 *Instability* 12
34 Nils Larsson 'Political Participation at the Municipal Level' in D.C. Rowat ed *Urban Politics in Ottawa-Carleton: Research Essays* (Ottawa 1974) 93
35 City of Ottawa *Community Catalogue Master Contact List of Community Groups in Ottawa-Carleton* n.d.
36 Harvey Goldberg 'The Property Industry at City Hall: The Case of the City of Ottawa' in Rowat *Urban Politics* 126. The study of the 1970–2 council identified 9 of the 27 as clearly working in the property industry, 5 as having other business occupations, 4 as having other professional occupations, and 9 as

civil servants. Reclassifying this list in terms of consumption and production orientation, the 4 professionals largely represented consumption interests. The civil servant category is more mixed; a supervisor of public works represents production interests whereas a teacher is more probably consumption oriented. On the basis of the information provided, 3 of the 9 civil servants can possibly be considered consumption oriented, which brings a total of about 7 out of 27.

37 The Rideau Centre redevelopment plan covers a large part of downtown Ottawa and involves the construction of a hotel, department store, and boutiques. See C. Andrew 'Ottawa: Progressives in Power' in James Lorimer and C. MacGregor *After the Developers* (Toronto 1981).

38 Andrew 'Ottawa'

39 Monique Desrochers, Hélène Dion, Annick Le Hénaff, and Robert Parenteau 'Les élections municipales à Ottawa' *Le Droit* 25 and 26 November 1981

40 For the elections 1960–72, the figures come from Owen Thomas 'Voter Turnout at the Municipal Level' in Rowat *Urban Politics* 69. For the more recent elections, the figures are from the city clerk's office.

41 A. Bernard, J. Léveillée, and G. Lord *Profile: Ottawa-Hull* (Ottawa 1974)

42 Since 1972 there have been at least seven reports on information and participation, by the Citizens' Information Committee (1972), by the Community Liaison Committee (1975), by the Participation Advisory Group (PAC): phase I (1978–9) and phase II (1979–80), *Getting Our Act Together* (GOAT – a consultant's report stemming out of a 1980 workshop), by the Committee on Information (1980–1), and a current study by a consultant to do a preliminary study with a view to designing a plan for implementation. It is clear that the majority of the reforms implemented by council, and the majority of the recommendations presented to council, relate far more to better informing citizens than to ensuring greater participation from citizens.

43 H.B. Mayo *Report of the Ottawa-Carleton Review Commission* (Ottawa 1976) 9

44 Public transportation is the responsibility of a separate agency, OC Transpo, which reports to regional council. There have been numerous recommendations to bring OC Transpo directly under regional control, but this has not yet occurred.

45 Mayo *Report* 165

46 Ibid xi

47 Ibid 112

48 Ibid

49 National Capital Commission *Annual Report 1979–80* (Ottawa 1980) 10

50 See C. Andrew, A. Blais, and R. Des Rosiers *Les Élites politiques*, for a description of the federal intervention in Hull.

51 See C. Andrew, S. Bordeleau, and A. Guimont *L'Urbanisation : une affaire* (Ottawa 1981) for an analysis of these groups.

DAVID M. CAMERON and PETER AUCOIN

Halifax

INTRODUCTION

City politics in Halifax can be described as the politics of accommodation. The accommodative nature of the political process is founded upon a lengthy history in which military, commercial, and then institutional interests have dominated and shaped both the city and the province of which it is the capital. Religious and racial divisions have been pronounced, but the antagonisms often bred by such divisions have seldom been violent or lasting. Accommodations suited to one time have been allowed to atrophy in another.

No doubt a major factor explaining the remarkably peaceful character of Halifax politics has been the relatively slow pace of growth and change. When change has been rapid, as with the influx of service personnel in war or the urban development of the 1960s and 1970s, the city has had some difficulty adjusting. The story of Halifax is thus a story of both change and continuity. The change has been gradual; the continuity is revealing of a rich political culture. Both derive from the very origins of the city and its role in provincial and colonial affairs.

HISTORICAL BACKGROUND

Founded primarily for British imperial strategic purposes in 1749, Halifax's fortunes as a military centre have ebbed and flowed, as a locally popular Parks Canada documentary film puts it, with 'the tides of [military] history.' Wars and threats of war have brought a certain kind, and a certain measure, of prosperity to this naval port. Peace has traditionally brought an end, if not a 'bust,' to these 'booms,' but the military presence has never lapsed entirely.

The 'defence establishment' has been, and continues to be, a very significant component in the city's economy.[1]

During its initial decades, Halifax lived under 'a kind of perpetual martial law imposed by the succession of military governors and their obedient councils.'[2] By the end of the eighteenth century, the influence of the defence establishment had declined significantly, and the early years of the nineteenth century witnessed the emergence in the colony of a council – a 'family compact,' comprising the financial and merchant élite of Halifax – which dominated the politics of both city and province. This family compact formed a virtual coalition with the military leadership that was not broken until the advent of responsible government at the provincial level in 1848.[3] What began as a military command gave way to a military-commercial coalition, to be followed by a governmental-commercial régime which, in its turn, was overtaken by party government. During this evolutionary process, the politics of Halifax came gradually to be separated from the politics of Nova Scotia.

Throughout its first century, Halifax experienced the demand for local government so prominent in the southern parts of British North America, primarily as a result of significant immigration from the New England colonies. Indeed, almost half the population of Halifax two decades after its founding was 'American,' and Boston was a principal source of both supplies and political ideas. The British military presence, supported by British colonial policy, however, was dedicated to the Virginia, rather than the New England, model of local self-government. As a consequence, efforts to have Halifax incorporated languished before the colonial establishment. The New England influence was substantially weakened following the American Revolution and the War of 1812, and the continuing demand for local government came to derive from a different source.

This demand became fused with the demand for what was to become known as 'responsible government.' The fusion occurred precisely because one of the principal irritants to would-be reformers of the colony's council was its exclusive power to appoint the 'clique of magistrates' that governed Halifax's local affairs. The attacks of Joseph Howe's newspaper on these magistrates provoked the famous libel case of 1835 in which Howe successfully defended himself in the name of freedom of the press.[4] In 1841, Halifax was incorporated by an experimental coalition council that included Howe and was backed on this issue by 'reform' members from Halifax in the provincial assembly. The act of incorporation was given an additional measure of 'liberalization' by the Reform (or Liberal) government that assumed power after the establishment of responsible government in 1848.

The establishment of responsible government constituted a victory for those who sought to diminish the power of Halifax in provincial politics. The council that had been able to control local government was itself controlled by families in Halifax. 'Of fifty-one councillors appointed between 1760 and 1830, only six can be said to have been resident outside the environs of the capital, and none of them gave anything like regular attendance.'[5] With the executive council no longer a self-perpetuating family compact of Halifax notables but, instead, a cabinet responsible to the elected assembly, party government meant the advent of a legislature and cabinet increasingly dominated by rural representatives and interests. By the time of Confederation, Halifax contained 15 per cent of the provincial population but elected only 8 per cent of the representatives in the assembly. The place of Halifax in the provincial scheme of things was bound to diminish in a governmental system in which the executive power was responsible to an area-based, elected assembly. Thus J.M. Beck could write in 1957: 'In determining basic policy any evidence that Halifax has been singled out for special favours is difficult to find.'[6] Indeed, he says: 'Only infrequently have there been allegations either that Halifax is suffering from discriminatory treatment or that it is being favoured over the rest of the province.'[7] Since 1967, however, Halifax (including its metropolitan environs) has begun to reassert its position in provincial politics, a fact reflected in an increased number of seats and especially an increased representation in the cabinet (almost half the present cabinet is from metropolitan Halifax).

While responsible government had its effects on the position of Halifax in provincial politics, Confederation had its effects on the socio-economic order of what, in the 1860s, was a prosperous city. Although Confederation and the national economic policy on which it was predicated may not have been the only, or even the major, cause, the founding of the Dominion of Canada did coincide with the end (or at least the beginning of the end) of a half-century of significant economic development and growth for Halifax.[8] The two decades following Confederation – against which Howe and a good portion of the Halifax mercantile class fought – were a time when the capital investments on which the great shipbuilding, shipping, and related activities depended were either withdrawn or reduced. The withdrawal of capital was significant irrespective of whether that capital originated within or outside Nova Scotia. This decline in prosperity placed Halifax and Nova Scotia in a backwater position relative to central Canada and, later, western Canada. The defence establishment (and, to a lesser extent, its status as capital city) helped to support Halifax through the first half of this century, but it is only recently that the city has clearly established itself as a major centre in Atlantic Canada with its bureaucratic, educational, scientific, financial, and commercial services. Apart from its port facilities, most of its industrial developments have occurred in its metropolitan environs (in Dartmouth or Halifax County).

The economic decline of Halifax in the latter part of the nineteenth century resulted in the city being bypassed by the population growth of Canada. The great waves of immigrants merely passed through Halifax en route westward. As a consequence, the socio-economic order of the city was virtually static. Its political structures and processes were also firmly established. With a transient military population, this small city was populated by a relatively diverse mix of ethnic and religious communities. Collectively, they had developed a political culture that was traditional and even conservative in its adherence to community and deference to established rights.[9] At the same time, it was a culture both receptive to sentiments of popular government and tolerant of minority privileges.

At the time of Confederation, Halifax was one of Canada's principal cities. Montreal, with well over 100,000 people, stood in a class by itself. It was followed, in terms of size, by Quebec and Toronto, each with 60,000, and Saint John, New Brunswick, with 41,000. Halifax was the sixth largest city, boasting a population of some 30,000. Hamilton and Ottawa followed, with populations of 27,000 and 24,000, respectively, and no other city had as many as 20,000 people.

In the space of a century, Halifax dropped from sixth to sixteenth in order of population among Canadian cities, as a result of much more rapid urban growth, first in central and then in western Canada. Halifax grew steadily, but other cities grew faster. By 1961, the population had reached 93,000, and Halifax stood fifteenth in order of size. A major annexation occurred in 1969, pushing the 1971 census population to 122,000. Even with that, it dropped to sixteenth place.

To include the complete metropolitan area increases the relative standing of Halifax somewhat but still reveals a relative decline over time. The population of the Halifax census metropolitan area increased by 126 per cent between 1941 and 1971, from 99,000 to 223,000. At the same time, however, it dropped from ninth to fourteenth place among metropolitan areas in Canada.

The many Halifax communities represent class structures that are inextricably interwoven with ethnic and religious dimensions, yielding significant political consequences. Religion and religious cleavages were, for much of Halifax's history, the most significant. Roman Catholics won concessions and rights at an early stage in the history of Halifax, in part because some

Catholics were members of the community's upper classes and in part because the non-Catholic population was so heterogeneous. The Church of England was the most prominent perhaps, but immigration from England and New England had resulted in a heterogeneity in the religious affiliations of all classes, including the upper echelons. This same immigration (and the settlement of those who came as military) produced a similar diversity in ethnic communities, again with a cross-cutting of class structures.

The separate, but related, diversities produced by these developments were important for the kind of socio-economic order that was established. Most notable perhaps was the accommodation of the cleavage between Catholic and Protestant, especially in the establishment and maintenance of a 'dual' school system in which Catholics enjoyed de facto separate schools within the public school system. Significantly, this system of separate schools was not legislated and, therefore, not accorded constitution protection under the British North America Act. Perhaps because of that, it gave rise to none of the bitterness characteristic of the separate school issue in some other provinces. Catholics were not a minority demanding rights from the majority. Rather, two majorities simply agreed that one school board, supported by a single municipal tax levy (with provincial support, of course), would operate parallel schools – in each neighbourhood, one public school was identified as Catholic and the other as 'public' or non-sectarian.

Also, there developed a system of representation whereby certain offices, such as that of mayor, alternated between Catholics and non-Catholics by way of a series of informal but explicit 'gentlemen's agreements.' Such arrangements, as these two major examples indicate, encompassed questions of both policy and structure.

While these understandings were never without their detractors, they were developed and maintained for generations with the very minimum of dissent. Their symbolic and real implications were acknowledged, and efforts were made to treat them as not only convenient but desirable. In order to give greater effect to them – or at least the more important of them – political leaders in Halifax gave them a status as 'constitutional conventions,' which raised them above the arenas of political debate. (Others might wish to suggest that such religious issues were 'submerged' or 'swept aside.') Even when events and the times brought them to an end, efforts were made to find other ways to express continuing concerns, such as the teaching of religion in the public schools, that developed as the 'dual' school arrangements faded into history.

Both of these conventions, over schools and mayors, were abandoned with remarkably little pain and almost no regret. The dual school system was weakened in the 1969 annexation, which added large suburban populations to the city. The residents of this area, formerly part of the County of Halifax, which physically surrounds the cities of Halifax and Dartmouth, had not experienced a dual system and, in the end, made it quite clear they did not wish to develop one. As a result, Halifax came to have a dual system in its core and an integrated system in its suburbs. Very shortly, however, the central city's dual system was faced with declining enrolment and the economic necessity of school closings. This presented the residents of urban neighbourhoods with an interesting choice: would they preserve the dual system by sending children to more distant schools or preserve the neighbourhood school by integrating the 'separate' elements? The latter has been the dominant choice and, as a result, the number of identifiably Catholic schools is every year declining.

The tradition of alternating Catholic and Protestant mayors passed away at approximately the same time. The tradition was first challenged in 1966 when Charles Vaughan, the incumbent (and Catholic) mayor, sought reelection for a second consecutive term and was defeated by Allan O'Brien, a Protestant. While the 1966 election did maintain the effect of alternating mayors, for the first time a Catholic and a Protestant had contested an election. The 'gentleman's agreement' had thus been violated, although the electors maintained its effect. Even that was abandoned in 1968 when O'Brien won reelection against another Protestant. As Vaison and Aucoin have observed: 'A Catholic would not now occupy the highest civic position in Halifax alternatively with a non-Catholic.'[10]

The demise of these conventions did not mark the end of accommodative politics, which continues to find expression in other aspects of the governing of Halifax. Three of these require special attention: the politics of planning and development, the political and administrative structures of city government, and the relationship of the city as a governmental unit to the governmental units with which it interacts at the municipal and provincial levels. These three are lenses through which one can consider the most significant aspects of city politics in Halifax.

PLANNING AND DEVELOPMENT

The political culture of Halifax appeared increasingly antiquated in the period following the Second World War, as the city (and much of the province and region) were largely excluded from the economic development and resultant prosperity of central and western Canada. The war itself had, of course, brought a temporary burst of activity to this naval port. That activity had not been without its difficulties, as a housing crisis and occasional sailor's misbehaviour testified. Yet, despite even a mini-riot, the war was clearly temporary and, with the cessation of hostilities, the city seemed determined to settle down to quieter ways. Under Robert Stanfield (premier 1956–67), the provincial government flirted with state-supported industrial projects, and for a time this venture seemed to promise real, and sometimes spectacular, success. Almost none of this industrial development occurred in Halifax, however, and the severe structural impediments to growth and development in the province adversely affected the city.

Urban growth and development did eventually come. The tradition of a dominant government-commercial class had produced a resident pool of capital and several 'business families' with personal control of some of that capital and access to the financial institutions that controlled more. This wealth eventually responded to the same forces stimulating economic activity elsewhere. An indigenous development boom began in the 1960s and transformed radically the physical structure of the city. The first, and largest, development project was Scotia Square, a massive residential, office, and commercial complex located on redeveloped land in the downtown core, financed by local businessmen. The first phase opened in 1969. Other phases and other projects were to follow in rapid succession.

As noted earlier, the economic decline of Halifax occurred with the withdrawal of investment capital in the 1860s. A century of stagnation – with spurts of growth artificially fuelled by war – was being overcome in the 1960s as entrepreneurs, many of them Nova Scotians, began investing once again in the city's future. Much of this investment was residential and commercial, rather than industrial, confirming Halifax's role in the economic and political life of the province and region.

In the 1960s and 1970s, a new group of Canadians joined the city's population. Perhaps as a result of its military origins and its economic stagnation, Halifax had developed into a community both orderly and genteel. A number of academic, professional, and artistic people now came to Halifax because it was not a 'boom town.' These new arrivals were to play an important role in the rebirth of activist civic politics in the 1970s.

Activist politics received a significant stimulus in the 1970 experiment called Encounter on Urban Environment. The Stanfield government had created an advisory panel consisting of leading business and professional people and chaired by the president of Nova Scotia Light and Power Company, A.R. Harrington. Known as Voluntary Economic Planning ('Economic' was subsequently dropped from the title), the agency was to assist in the preparation of long-range plans for economic development. To this was added a cabinet committee on planning and programs, with its own secretariat headed by Leonard Poetschke (both the committee and the secretariat were abolished by the successor Liberal government of Gerald Regan). Poetschke and Harrington combined in 1969 to propose a unique urban forum, at once challenging Haligonians to consider their collective future and pointing out shortcomings and lost opportunities from their past.

The idea was novel and radical. A group of twelve outside experts would spend one week in Halifax, meeting principally with representatives of interest groups and government during the day and participating in a 'town hall' meeting each evening. The event would be the subject of massive media coverage and was designed deliberately to challenge 'the deep and persistent psychological climate that gripped Halifax and the Maritimes, a climate of passivity bred of a long history of defeat, a climate that shied away from change because of past experience which suggested things could grow still worse.'[11]

The encounter took place in late February 1970. It was a dramatic event, evoking strong, and often angry, participation by a surprisingly large number of people. Each evening for a week, hundreds of Haligonians showed up at a hotel ballroom – and thousands more watched on television at home – while twelve strangers[12] took turns berating the city's lack of imagination and enterprise and complimenting its gracious life-style (at least that of the well-to-do). To the surprise of many, and the delight of the organizers, Haligonians did not merely come and listen. They responded and they participated.

The result was an emotional outpouring. There was a sense that something new and exciting was happening – what exactly eluded, and still eludes, definition. Perhaps the official historian of the event put it best: 'A community was coming awake.'[13] Certainly there was a pervasive sense of pride – pride in the city's heritage, in its tolerance, and – perhaps the critical change – in its future. One of the 'experts' saw the event as a vehicle for getting together that 'led to a dialogue and debate around issues. The debate led to an understanding and to some concern. I think it is quite possible that the concern will lead to action.'[14]

It would be an exaggeration to credit the encounter with responsibility for any specific change. The seeds of change were already planted in Halifax society, as indigenous development and provincial efforts at planning were demonstrating. The encounter did, however, show to ordinary people something of the power that can attach to citizen action that has both purpose and persistence. In this it subtly changed the political culture of the city.

Urban development and citizen participation were changed significantly by the province's Planning Act of 1969.[15] It required serious land-use planning for the first time by municipalities. Within the context of provincial policies and regional guidelines (prepared by the province), municipalities were to prepare and approve municipal development plans. It also established the Planning Appeal Board, a quasi-judicial tribunal with the power to veto zoning changes or development approvals judged, on appeal, to conflict with a municipal plan or, in the absence of a plan, with the best interests of the municipality. This body was to play a significant role in determining the shape of future growth in Halifax.

The planning process began in earnest when the Municipal Development Plan Committee was established. This body, comprising all ten aldermen plus nine appointed citizens, took on a real sense of purpose and direction in 1975 when the mayor, Edmund Morris, assumed the chair. After much discussion, public meetings and debate, the city adopted a Statement of Objectives and Policies in 1976. The full Municipal Development Plan, with more detailed specifications, was adopted by council in March 1978 and approved by the minister of municipal affairs in August.[16] More than one major building project has been rejected – sometimes by the Planning Appeal Board following appeal by a citizen – because it would violate that plan.

The ascendency of planning did not come easily, however. Early skirmishes pitted concerned citizens against the wrecker's hammer in a successful attempt to preserve several historic but decrepit waterfront buildings slated for demolition to make way, in part, for an expressway. In the end, the expressway was abandoned and the buildings restored by a local developer into a pleasant complex of shops and offices known as Historic Properties. Another battle eventually resulted in the adoption of municipal legislation, subsequently incorporated into the city plan, to prevent buildings from encroaching on designated 'view planes' – vistas of the harbour from the vantage point of Citadel Hill, the historic defence establishment and site of the famous town clock.[17]

Two issues appear to capture most completely the character of urban politics in Halifax as it is revealed in issues of planning and development. The first of these concerned a large-scale, private development proposed for Quinpool Road and the organization of opposition to it. The second involved the creation of an intergovernmental Waterfront Development Corporation and its efforts to stimulate redevelopment with public funds.

The Quinpool Road controversy confronted the emergent municipal planning process with the two ingredients of a classic urban conflict – a developer's plans for high-density building and citizen pressure for the preservation of residential neighbourhoods. The result of the conflict in the case of Quinpool Road had a profound influence on the future of Halifax city politics.[18]

The site of the controversy was a 14.5-acre parcel of land on the north side of Quinpool Road, a major east-west thoroughfare. The three lots had been owned by Catholic orders. In September 1972, a developer, Ralph Medjuck, and his firm, Centennial Properties Ltd, proposed to build an integrated complex consisting of three thirty-storey apartment buildings, a seventeen-storey office tower, a nine-storey hotel, a three-level commercial mall, and a service station and parking facility for 2,300 cars. It was, indeed, a massive development for an area that was largely residential with small commercial facilities limited to either side of Quinpool Road itself.

The matter started simply enough. City council greeted the proposal enthusiastically, while residents in the area appeared favourably disposed to the project. The first sign of difficulty came in November when the city manager advised council to insist on a predominantly residential development. He also raised questions about the impact of the proposed project on traffic patterns and volume. Halifax was only at the earliest stages in its comprehensive planning effort, but a perceived conflict with emerging planning principles underlay the city manager's objections.

Council's response demonstrated the traditional weakness of municipal plans. Rather than insisting that proposed developments conform to the plan, it requested staff to adjust the plan to accommodate the development project. This was done, a public meeting was arranged in which arguments were advanced both for and against the project, and, in January 1973, the developer indicated his willingness to modify and reduce the scale of the project. On this basis, council approved the project in principle by a vote of eight to two.

The revised proposal was submitted in April 1973. There would be four twenty-storey apartment towers, interconnected housing, a nine-storey office building, a hotel, and retail, commercial, and parking facilities. Council gave final approval by the same eight-to-two majority on 17 May 1973. In June, a small, essentially volunteer, environmental protection group, Ecology Action Centre, filed notice it intended to appeal the 17 May decision to the Planning Appeal Board. In September, the board dismissed the appeal.

Opposition to the Quinpool Road proposal was very slowly beginning to crystallize. The opposition was aimed at supporting planning and opposing the development ethos. Specifically, it sought to protect a residential neighbourhood and limit traffic congestion. In the fall of 1973, a petition of area residents yielded 1,100 signatures, and resident associations became active in each of the two wards straddling this section of Quinpool Road. A further appeal of the 17 May decision of council was launched in the Supreme Court of Nova Scotia, to be heard in the spring.

A group of architecture students at the Nova Scotia Technical College produced an alternative design for development. Labelled QRII, this design involved mainly low-rise housing to be built on a non-profit basis taking advantage of all available government housing subsidies and support programs. QRII was a fascinating example of citizen initiative and provided a positive alternative, but it remained a 'fringe' proposal and never attracted governmental or institutional sponsorship.

Opposition to 'Quinpool Road' attracted increasing participation from 'establishment' groups. The school board opposed the scheme on the grounds that traffic would create problems with two high schools nearby. The Downtown Merchants Association and some churches also voiced objections. Protesters marched on city hall, and council finally agreed to hold a further public meeting on 10 April 1974. Over 500 people attended this meeting, which ended 'with most people angry over Council's indignant attitude towards what they regarded as legitimate concerns.'[19] In May the Supreme Court dismissed the appeal against council's decision of a year earlier.

A new alternative to the developer's proposal emerged: the land might be expropriated and developed by a public agency. City council also showed the first modest signs of reconsidering its earlier position when it agreed to explore the idea of expropriation with provincial representatives. The provincial cabinet rejected this idea, however, and on 24 May 1974, the city issued a development permit to Centennial Properties. In November 1974, Centennial Properties announced it could no longer afford to proceed with the project and offered to sell the land to the city for $8 million. The city purchased the whole tract for $5.3 million.

Citizen opposition had succeeded in blocking the project, and the euphoria of the opponents was easily and often compared to the decision in Toronto to abandon the Spadina Expressway. It was one thing to block a private developer; it was quite another to develop a public alternative. In September 1975, city council, conscious of its own incompetence in real estate development and wary of continuing interest charges on such a major expenditure, finally issued a call for development proposals for a portion of the land and continued to press the province to purchase the rest (intended as the site of a school for the visually handicapped). Not a single response was received, and a second call was issued in December, allowing higher density.

One development proposal was submitted in response to the second call, submitted by a local consortium consisting of a construction company, an architectural firm, and a non-profit housing association. Over the next months, the province withdrew its interest in any of the land, the non-profit housing group withdrew from the consortium, and the whole enterprise appeared on the verge of collapse. Further proposals were submitted by the remaining members of the consortium in December 1976, both of which involved an indirect subsidy from the city while exceeding the city's guidelines on density. The city staff responded in January 1977 with a proposal to develop the land publicly through a municipal housing corporation. Council rejected that idea and, in committee of the whole, voted by the slimmest of margins (the mayor casting the deciding vote) to accept one of the consortium's two proposals. At this stage, the drama became truly bizarre as the regular council meeting a week later voted six to four to reject the proposal and issue a new call for proposals. Just as citizen groups were preparing to do battle once again in support of a non-profit, residential development, the consortium offered better financial terms, and council approved the project. The mayor cast the deciding vote once again on 24 March 1977. Four and one-half years had elapsed, and there was still no development.

This time, the project did proceed, however, and Quinpool Centre now stands as the uncertain symbol of citizen opposition to private development. The original proposal was blocked, to be replaced eventually by a project which, while smaller and less dense, embodied few of the positive objectives advanced by the opponents (low-cost housing, community services, preservation of neighbourhood). Yet one cannot diminish the importance or the implications of 'Quinpool Road.' The Municipal Development Plan adopted a year later codified much that its opponents had fought for. Haligonians had come to terms with planning and development and, while rejecting radical solutions involving direct government enterprise, probably accepted a commitment to planning that will make it very unlikely that another 'Quinpool Road' will emerge in the near future.

This victory for planned development is also seen dramatically in the case of the Waterfront Development Corporation. The idea of direct government involvement in development projects, rejected by city council in the case of Quinpool Road, was adopted for the city by the federal and provincial governments in their project to redevelop the waterfront.

The federal government had, for some time, through the Department of Regional Economic Expansion and also, for a brief period, through the Ministry of State for Urban Affairs been involved in stimulating the development of infrastructure facilities in Halifax as the major 'pole' of future economic growth for the province. As a new multi-million-dollar water system reached the final stages of construction, the attention of federal and provincial planners turned to inner-city improvements that would permit effective use to be made of the new water-supply. This led to the decision to embark on a major redevelopment of the waterfront area of downtown

Halifax and, in order not to favour only one side of the harbour, also of its sister city, Dartmouth. The instrument chosen to promote this redevelopment was an intergovernmental (federal and provincial) crown corporation, the Waterfront Development Corporation (WDC).

The WDC was established in the spring of 1976 with substantial funding assured for five years. (The first year had expired by the time the corporation was established). After a slow start, the assured funding was subsequently extended until 1982, but was not increased.

The corporation set about to develop conceptual plans for revitalized harbour fronts for the twin cities. It invested heavily in the installation of modern, underground services and in the modernization of ferry facilities. It also embarked on a program of land assembly, to capture the key development levers with which to control future activity. A concerted effort at beautification witnessed new street and sidewalk surfaces, new lighting, and, most spectacular, a pedestrian boardwalk that actually does return the harbour to the view of the casual pedestrian. In all, the efforts of the WDC have added to those of the private sector (Scotia Square, Historic Properties, new hotels and restaurants, and a mini-Toronto-style complex of bank towers) and the provincial government (a new maritime museum, the Metro Centre sport and entertainment complex, and a promised convention centre) to ensure a vibrant future for downtown Halifax. And while there have been some indications of public displeasure,[20] the whole enterprise has proceeded from the relative quiet of the corporate boardroom.

The one significant failure of the WDC confirms once again the power of citizens to block development when their persistence exceeds the authority of the developer. The centrepiece of the redevelopment of the Halifax waterfront was to be Chebucto Square, an open area permitting access to the harbour for pleasure boats and integrated with ferry and bus terminals and the pedestrian boardwalk. Development of this square required the relocation of The Fisherman's Market, a privately owned wholesale and retail operation. The owner, Fred Green, adamantly refused all offers by the WDC to purchase his property (he was offered alternate accommodation only a short distance away in what was envisioned as a Boston-style market area), and the WDC proceeded with construction of other elements of its proposed square, pending agreement with Green. Thousands of people responded to Green's call for help (at his store and through newspaper ads) and signed petitions urging that his market be left intact. Buoyed by this overwhelming support, Green refused to budge and, in 1981, the WDC conceded defeat and announced it would come up with a new design that would not require the demolition of Green's market.

The WDC has been a very successful agent of planned change and redevelopment in the core of Halifax. Its success, however, has come without any direct participation by the city of Halifax itself. There has been considerable co-operation among staff and liaison between corporation and council. As well, the city has a large measure of control, since the WDC is obliged to proceed in conformity with the Municipal Development Plan and related by-laws. Yet the WDC remains a federal-provincial agency and a product of the federal government's objective of regional economic development. Successful and popular as it is, one can but wonder whether the priorities that would have emerged from the structures of city government itself would have led to quite this program.

POLITICAL AND ADMINISTRATIVE STRUCTURES

As the discussion of planning and development has implicitly demonstrated, the political and administrative structures of city government in Halifax no longer represent the traditional religious accommodation. The city's political culture finds its modern expression, accordingly, in the ways by which other kinds of interests are represented in these structures. Three related aspects of these structures need to be considered.

1 The non-partisan style of civic politics is not unique to Halifax or Nova Scotia, but in a city and province so entrenched in a partisan approach to political life, it is surprising that partisanship has been so muted. The form of government in Halifax does not require or encourage party politics. Yet partisanship often seems only barely beneath the surface. The campaign organizations of individual candidates often look (and are) partisan in composition, and factions on council often appear to be partisan groupings. However, partisanship seldom constitutes the major determinant of public policy or, especially for the mayoralty, electoral success.

The reason is quite simple. Non-partisanship operates in the interests of the dominant political parties. Herein is revealed yet another feature of the accommodative nature of city politics in Halifax. Parties are an important feature of city politics but, by long-standing convention, party labels are not identified. This arrangement has enabled politicians with clear partisan affiliations to be elected to municipal offices at times not otherwise auspicious for their parties in either the provincial or federal arenas. More significantly, it has allowed politicians to be elected on platforms that would be either too reformist or too parochial for the two major political parties.[21] This latter result has produced a more accurate representation of the values and interests extant in the Halifax political community than could ever be achieved by party government. The evolution of planning and development issues provides illustrations of this outcome.

2 Halifax has a council-manager system of government, established in 1951. The resultant separation of politics and administration helps to keep religious and partisan interests out of the management of civic affairs. Such a structure, by virtue of its non-political management process, will support established rights and the prevailing socio-economic order and is clearly not unrelated to the city's political culture and its deferential attitude to governmental authority.

The council, including the mayor and aldermen, relates to the administrative branch primarily through the city manager, who is responsible for the administration of 'the day-to-day business affairs of all departments of the City.'[22] He is to 'prepare and compile the annual budget and submit it to Council and be responsible for its administration after adoption.'[23] His authority is both explicit and far-reaching in relation to the budget. For example, he is to 'make recommendations to the Council respecting any proposed expenditure for any purpose in excess of one thousand dollars and respecting any contract involving any such expenditures, and the Council shall not make any such expenditure or enter into any such contract for the same until a recommendation from the City Manager in respect thereof has been received, but the Council shall not be bound to adopt such recommendation.'[24] The powers of the city manager are considerable and derive from the city charter and by way of instructions from council, the policies and decisions of which he is to implement. The mayor and aldermen are to establish policy and scrutinize the implementation of policy, but the manager gives effect to such implementation and makes recommendations to council as to policy formulation.

This division of powers is a clear expression of a political culture that seeks to impose 'good government' through an orderly and accountable system of administration. This system was established neither in response to a 'particular crisis' nor as a consequence of a 'long history of maladministration.'[25] Rather, it was adopted some years after it was first proposed and in response to increased administrative demands placed on city government following the Second World War, when all levels of government became 'big business' (or more properly 'big government'). Since its adoption, the size of council has been altered, the council's committee system has been changed, and the mayor's position has become full-time. The basic structure of the council-manager system has, however, remained the same throughout.

The council-manager system, as Plunkett puts it, 'retains some of the features of the council-committee system. The powers granted to the city manager are not, in some respects, as broad as in some other city manager-operated cities.'[26] Council committees interact on a regular basis with the heads of city departments directly and concern themselves with a great host of details that could be considered to belong to the realm of administration. The capacity of the city manager to act as a buffer between council and its administrative departments is thus minimized, if not removed altogether.

In the fire and police departments the powers of the city manager are restricted to financial matters because 'the day-to-day business affairs of the police force and fire department shall be administered in accordance with the policies and plans approved by the Council, by the respective heads of each department but subject, nevertheless, to *the management and supervision* of the Committee on Safety.'[27] The council's committee on safety, together with the fire and police chiefs, operates in effect as a collective city manager for the purposes of the police and fire departments and their functions. Traditions – including the politics of recruitment, administrative politics, the uniqueness of the functions performed, and hesitation to devolve too much power on the city manager – have kept these two organizations at arm's length from the city manager. They have also remained at arm's length from council itself. The committee on safety has had great difficulty in performing its roles in respect to 'management and supervision'; it is closer to a committee of a legislature with all the attendant limitations.

While the city manager has authority to appoint, promote, suspend, and dismiss city employees, he does not have such authority in respect to the heads of city departments. He recommends appointments to these positions, but council has rejected certain key recommendations over the past three decades.

The limitations on the city manager's powers have permitted considerable political control over civic administration and have enhanced the accountability of council and the mayor. Some have argued that even this system has not afforded sufficient political control; others, including the incumbent city manager, would like to see the senior administrative position strengthened. The willingness to tolerate this tension illustrates again the accommodative tradition.

3 There is a series of boards, commissions, and committees outside the regular administrative structure of the council-manager system. When setting up the position of city manager, council decided to retain these non-departmental organizations, notwithstanding the theory and history of the council-manager system.[28] Various boards and commissions control the city's public schools, the waterworks, the library, the major park, the port,

two athletic centres, industrial development, tourism promotion, and some aspects of recreation.

This system has enabled council, primarily through the appointment of its own members (as well as through *ex officio* positions in the case of the mayor), to be involved with these functions without having to go through the city manager, who has virtually no authority over these quasi-independent bodies. There are obvious problems of control and accountability in such a system – only some members of council sit on the governing boards, and reporting mechanisms are often inadequate. Such a separation of powers serves further to diffuse authority and responsibility.

At the same time, however, these bodies also enable council to promote a greater degree of public participation in public affairs than would otherwise be the case. The appointment of citizens to these bodies also provides elected officials with a form of patronage – but does not guarantee a high degree of representativeness. Appointments to these bodies have encompassed only small segments of the citizenry, but have served to restrict the administrative powers of the city manager and the civic bureaucracy.

These three aspects of city government have helped to distribute power in ways that maintain and further promote the accommodative political culture of the city. Demands for citizen participation seem muted following the pressures of the 1970s. Increasing the number of women on the city's various boards, commissions, and committees is currently the most controversial issue relating to citizen participation. Another tension involves the relationship of council to the city manager on the one hand and the authority of the city manager in regard to these quasi-autonomous bodies on the other. There are no signs of any radical alteration in the basic principle of dividing authority between politicians and the administration. The same type of gradualism and accommodation may be seen in the ways Halifax has dealt with other governments and, particularly, with the challenge of metropolitan consolidation.

HALIFAX AND METROPOLITAN GOVERNMENT

The city of Halifax contains a shrinking portion of the population of the census metropolitan area. At the same time, it is by far the largest municipal unit, and this fact both colours and constrains any suggestions of metropolitan government. Boundary revisions have occurred, but any proposals for outright metropolitan government have thus far been stillborn.

Neither the pattern of urban growth nor its political accommodation is unique to Halifax, but the distinctive features of each do reveal something of the nature of city politics.

The original city of Halifax is located on a peninsula, the relatively small isthmus of which served for many decades as a natural, as well as a political, boundary. The deep harbour and immense basin meant that Dartmouth developed not merely as a residential or suburban offshoot of Halifax but as a community with its own blend of interests and its own political culture. Indeed, the physical limits on the size of Halifax, coupled with the geography of the area's transportation system, caused Dartmouth, not Halifax, to become the location for most of the limited industrial growth in the post-war period.

Yet, despite natural barriers and political boundaries, the population of Halifax did spill over into the neighbouring county of Halifax.[29] Much growth has simply followed the classic pattern of urban encroachment on formerly rural lands, usually not planned, seldom controlled, often resulting in excessive future servicing costs, and sometimes showing the worst features of 'strip development.' Expanding towns and villages in the vicinity move to meet the outward encroachment of the city itself.

As a result of this growth, the metropolitan area is now an almost continuous urban system wrapped around the two sides of the harbour, meeting at the head of the Bedford Basin. It comprises four municipalities: Halifax, Halifax County, Dartmouth, and Bedford, which was incorporated as a town in 1980. The county of Halifax is not one community but a huge area containing numerous pockets of population, some quite large and many having more in common with the central metropolis than with each other or the county of which they are part.

Although the Halifax area has never seriously flirted with metropolitan government, two principal means of handling metropolitan growth have been adopted: the physical expansion of the cities of Halifax and Dartmouth, and the creation of inter-municipal, or metropolitan, special-purpose bodies designed to provide specific services.

As early as the 1940s, proposals were made for the amalgamation of Halifax, Dartmouth, and the contiguous portions of Halifax County.[30] In 1961, Dartmouth annexed portions of the county, increasing its territory by nine times and adding 90 per cent to its population. In 1969, Halifax annexed the mainland area immediately adjacent to the peninsula, nearly quadrupling its area and increasing its population by a third. Following the development of a new water-supply system, Halifax applied in 1981 to annex parts of the county that had been reserved for the city's former water-supply. In December 1982 a decision awarded some of the area to the city.

The 1969 annexation raised two significant problems for the enlarged city. First, the city faced a considerable challenge in reconciling very different, and unequal, levels of service. Voluntary fire protection gave way to a professional fire department in the annexed area, and city water and sewer services replaced wells and septic tanks at considerable cost and great controversy. Second, the city had to decide whether to extend the historic dual school system to the annexed area. The debate was long and heated, if not bitter. The decision was ultimately against 'separate' schools.

As discussed earlier, this decision occurred on the very eve of the demise of the century-old accommodation on the peninsula. With declining enrolments, the double system was simply uneconomical. But would consolidation of the Catholic and non-Catholic schools occur along religious or neighbourhood lines? The choice was made with little controversy. The integrated system adopted in the newly annexed area served as a model for the new system on the peninsula. Like the election alternately of Catholic and non-Catholic mayors, the old arrangement had served its purpose and evaporated so quickly as almost to belie the power of the long-standing accommodation.

Annexation certainly did not end discussion of amalgamation. In the early 1970s, the province's flirtation with planning, augmented no doubt by the euphoria of the Encounter on Urban Development, yielded two studies, both of which recommended forms of metropolitan government.

The Metropolitan Area Planning Committee (later to be succeeded by a more formal body – the Metropolitan Area Planning Commission, or MAPC2, established under the Planning Act of 1969) commissioned a study by T.J. Plunkett Associates which recommended a two-tier form of government following somewhat the model of Metropolitan Toronto.[31] This proposal elicited no local or provincial enthusiasm, and a second report was requested. Plunkett's next proposal – intended to be an interim arrangement – called for the creation of Halifax-Dartmouth Regional Community, which would implement federal and provincial plans for economic development. But no problems required the creation of a metropolitan government, and there was no organized pressure in favour of such a system, and so nothing materialized from Plunkett's reports.

The establishment of a new commission served as a ready explanation for inaction. In 1971, the Liberal provincial government established a royal commission under economist John Graham to examine virtually all aspects of education, public services, and provincial-municipal relations.[32] The Graham commission came to a familiar conclusion: 'We view Halifax, Dartmouth and their urbanizing fringes as one metropolitan city.'[33] Along with equally far-reaching recommendations for municipal reform throughout the province, the Graham commission proposed complete amalgamation into a 'metropolitan county,' a single-tier structure encompassing not only the urbanized areas of the two cities and the county, but also a large area of the county deemed eligible for future urban growth.[34] There was no evident public support for so significant a change, and no action was taken on any of the amalgamation proposals.

However, a new example of Halifax's accommodative political culture was emerging in the late 1970s. Ever since the decision to build a bridge linking Halifax and Dartmouth (the resultant Angus L. Macdonald Bridge was opened in 1955) the two cities have been joined in an increasingly integrated urban system. If political union was unacceptable, regional co-operation was essential. Indeed, the Macdonald Bridge itself came under the authority of the Halifax-Dartmouth Bridge Commission. Other regional bodies existed as well, most notably the Metropolitan Area Planning Committee (later Commission), the Port of Halifax, and the Regional Authority of Halifax, Dartmouth and the County of Halifax, established initially to operate a regional jail.

The regional authority has been transformed into what may be the foundation for a true metropolitan government. Now restructured and renamed (it is now 'metropolitan' rather than 'regional') the authority operates a regional transit system (through the Metropolitan Transit Commission), a regional sanitary land-fill operation, and the original jail. It remains a regional special-purpose body, but it provides a handy mechanism through which specific services might, one by one, be shifted to a regional level. Would it then be so difficult to recognize a fait accompli and transform a regional authority into a metropolitan government? Such a development is pure speculation. What is not speculation, however, is the likelihood that Halifax will come to terms with the metropolitan problem as it has with others – gradually and by means of accommodation. Those characteristics continue to be the hallmarks of city politics in Halifax.

CONCLUSION

One cannot presume Halifax will always continue to be what it has been. The political culture seems strong enough to weather most challenges, but its conservative nature may leave the city vulnerable to external pressures for significant change. Change in the past has tended to be gradual or temporary. It is possible that economic growth and development derived from the exploitation of offshore resources, for example, will trigger a radical transformation of the city and its politics. Should this happen, Halifax will probably develop political traditions akin to other Canadian cities more familiar with rapid economic change. One can only speculate on the future. This essay has explored some of the contemporary and past events and issues in Halifax and, in so doing, has revealed something of the political culture and values that have taken shape over two and one-third centuries. One suspects that that record may influence future developments as well.

SUGGESTED FURTHER READINGS

Beck, J. Murray *The Evolution of Municipal Government in Nova Scotia: 1749–1973* a study prepared for the Nova Scotia Royal Commission on Education, Public Services and Provincial-Municipal Relations, 1973

DeBard, August A. jr 'Council-Manager Government in Halifax' *Canadian Public Administration* III 1 (March 1960) 76–81

Halifax Commission on City Government *Report on the Structure and Processes of Halifax City Government* Halifax 1982

Pacey, Elizabeth *The Battle of Citadel Hill* Hartsport, NS, 1979

Raddall, Thomas H. *Halifax: Warden of the North* rev ed, Toronto 1971

Reynolds, Dave 'Halifax: Spitting into the Wind on Quinpool Road' in James Lorimer and Evelyn Ross ed *The City Book* Toronto 1976

Vaison, Robert and Peter Aucoin 'Class and Voting in Recent Halifax Mayoralty Elections' in L.D. Feldman and M.D. Goldrick ed *Politics and Government of Urban Canada* 3rd edn Toronto 1976

NOTES

1 See, for instance, A.M. Sinclair *The Economic Base of the Halifax Metropolitan Area* (Halifax 1961).

2 Thomas H. Raddall *Halifax: Warden of the North* rev edn (Toronto 1971) 70

3 See J. Murray Beck *The Evolution of Municipal Government in Nova Scotia: 1749–1973* Study prepared for the Nova Scotia Royal Commission on Education, Public Services and Provincial-Municipal Relations, 1973, 12–24. Also see J. Murray Beck 'Ups and Downs of Halifax Influence in Nova Scotia Government, 1749–1981' Paper presented to the Royal Society of Canada, Halifax, June 1981.

4 See Beck *Evolution* 12–13.

5 J. Murray Beck *The Government of Nova Scotia* (Toronto 1957) 22

6 Beck 'Ups and Downs' 16

7 Ibid 15

8 See Raddall *Halifax: Warden of the North*.

9 Halifax shares this conservatism with the Maritimes generally. As Bellamy has observed: 'The Maritimes constitute a focal point for tradition and con-

servatism in the Canadian political culture as a whole.' See David J. Bellamy 'The Atlantic Provinces' in Bellamy et al ed *The Provincial Political Systems* (Toronto 1976) 10.

10 See Robert Vaison and Peter Aucoin 'Class and Voting in Recent Halifax Mayoralty Elections' in L.D. Feldman and M.D. Goldrick ed *Politics and Government of Urban Canada* 3rd edn (Toronto 1976) 202–4.

11 Ken O. Hartnett *Encounter on Urban Environment: Historian's Report* (Halifax 1970) 5

12 The twelve 'strangers,' or experts, were Dr Scott Greer, Department of Sociology, Northwestern University, Chicago; Dr C.A. Gunn, Department of Recreation and Parks, Texas A&M University; Dr Benjamin Higgins, Centre for Economic Development and Planning, University of Montreal; David Kirkbride, vice-president, Canadian Industries Ltd, Montreal; Edward Logue, president and chief executive officer, New York State Urban Development Corp; Dennis McDermott, Canadian director, United Auto Workers; Dr Martin Rein, Centre for Environmental Studies, London, England; T.J. Scanlon, School of Journalism, Carleton University, Ottawa; Dr Frank Steggert, Georgia State University; Dr K.W. Studnicki-Gizbert, York University, Toronto; Dr Wilbur Thompson, Department of Economics, Wayne State University, Detroit; Rev Lucius Walker jr, executive director, Interreligious Foundation for Community Organization, New York.

13 Hartnett *Encounter* 25

14 Ibid 59

15 Province of Nova Scotia *Statutes of Nova Scotia* 1969 chap 16

16 A summary document containing the essential provisions of the plan was published in tabloid form as *Municipal Development Plan for the City of Halifax, 1978.*

17 See Elizabeth Pacey *The Battle of Citadel Hill* (Hantsport, NS, 1979).

18 This account of the Quinpool Road controversy is based largely on E. Grant MacDonald 'Housing Case Study: Quinpool Road, Halifax, Nova Scotia,' prepared in 1977 for the Institute of Local Government at Queen's University, Kingston, Ontario. See also Dave Reynolds 'Halifax: Spitting into the Wind on Quinpool Road' in James Lorimer and Evelyn Ross ed *The City Book* (Toronto 1976) 171–82.

19 MacDonald 'Housing Case Study' 16

20 A public forum was organized in 1977 to focus public attention on waterfront development and the WDC, but it went largely unnoticed by other than committed activists. See 'Focus on the Waterfront' mimeographed, 1977.

21 See Vaison and Aucoin 'Class and Voting.'

22 Halifax City Charter section 159, 1 a

23 Ibid 1 c
24 Ibid 1 m
25 August A. DeBard jr 'Council-Manager Government in Halifax' *Canadian Public Administration* III 1 (March 1960) 76
26 Thomas J. Plunkett *Urban Canada and Its Government: A Study of Municipal Organization* (Toronto 1968) 138
27 Halifax City Charter section 159, 3 (emphasis added)
28 Plunkett *Urban Canada and Its Government* 138
29 Like cities in a number of other provinces, Halifax and Dartmouth are not politically or administratively a part of the county within which they are physically situated.
30 See R.G. Speller *The Halifax Metropolitan Area* (Halifax 1948) and Donald Rowat *The Canadian Municipal System* (Toronto 1969).
31 T.J. Plunkett Associates Ltd *Regional Organization for the Halifax-Dartmouth Metropolitan Area* (Halifax 1970)
32 Nova Scotia, Royal Commission on Education, Public Services and Provincial-Municipal Relations *Report* (Halifax 1974)
33 Ibid II chap 5, 117
34 The reorganization scheme would have created eleven counties as the only municipalities in the province. Three of these – Halifax, Cape Breton, and Pictou – would have been designated metropolitan counties.

DONALD GUTSTEIN

Vancouver

INTRODUCTION

For almost a century local politics in Vancouver has been dominated by business interests. The city was in effect created by the Canadian Pacific Railway; the CPR selected it in 1884 as the west coast terminus for the transcontinental railway and ended up owning much of the land in the new city, paying most of the taxes, and providing most of the jobs. In the early years most citizens agreed that what was good for the CPR was good for Vancouver. During the twentieth century the CPR's influence waned, but city government continued to be strongly affected by business. With more than half the city's revenues deriving from the property tax, and many members of council engaged in real estate activity, the city fathers were particularly concerned about land development. They accepted the business view that the functions of municipal government were to ensure orderly physical growth and provide services to real property: both would enhance land values. This consensus survived early booms and busts, the Great Depression, and the post-war years. It has been seriously challenged only since the late 1960s.

There have been three periods in the city's political history. During its first fifty years (1886–1936), Vancouver was growing in area and population, and civic attention centred on the provision of basic services. This was an era of council-committee government, with aldermen elected from wards. The second phase began during the Great Depression. By this time the city had reached its present boundaries, and population growth was confined largely to the surrounding suburbs.[1] In 1936, an attempt by the Co-operative Commonwealth Federation (CCF) to bring openly partisan politics into local affairs was thwarted by the abolition of the ward system and the formation of the Non-Partisan Association. The NPA ran slates of candidates for the council, the school board, and the park board and dominated the city's affairs with a single-minded dedication to physical development for over thirty years. A modified council-commission system of government was adopted in 1956, better to achieve the goals of physical development.

In the late 1960s, concerns about the direction of the city's development and quality of life became part of the political debate, and a new phase in city politics began. This was marked by the formation of new political parties to challenge the NPA. Since 1968, local politics has become increasingly partisan, with three groups contesting elections: the NPA on the right, the Electors' Action Movement (TEAM) in the centre, and the Committee of Progressive Electors (COPE) on the left. To understand how this situation developed requires some further analysis of the early phases of Vancouver's history.

TERMINAL CITY: 1886–1936

The city's rise to prominence began when the CPR decided to extend the statutory terminal of the transcontinental railway from Port Moody, at the head of Burrard Inlet, to Granville, twelve miles west. This move allowed the CPR to gain access to Granville's superior harbour and control over most of the land surrounding the terminal. Until then, Granville, or Gastown as it was popularly known, was a small logging community of 300 centred on the Hastings sawmill. It was economically and politically subservient to both New Westminster (population 3,000), thirteen miles southeast on the Fraser River, and Victoria (population 8,000), a mature commercial city and the provincial capital. Overnight the town's fortunes changed. The trickle of migrants turned into a flood as the 'mob,' including Vancouver's first two mayors, arrived to participate in the ensuing economic boom. By 1892, when the world-wide depression hit, Granville (or Vancouver as it was now known) had reached a population of 13,000. By the beginning of the First World War, the city had outstripped New Westminster and Victoria to emerge as the province's major industrial and financial centre.[2]

Two years after the CPR chose the site, the city of Vancouver was incorporated by CPR and Hastings mill officials, with the assistance of local real estate agents and merchants. The railway acted as a magnet for people planning to make their fortunes from the real estate boom, and the first civic election was bitterly fought by old and new elements. One mayoral candidate, Richard Alexander, the Hastings mill manager, had been a Granville resident since 1870 and was closely connected to the British-dominated ruling clique in Victoria. His opponent, Malcolm Maclean, was a real estate speculator who had arrived in Vancouver in January 1886. Maclean's partner and brother-in-law was Arthur W. Ross, a federal MP from Manitoba, better known in Parliament as the 'member from CPR.'[3] Maclean appealed to the working men as he attacked Alexander, the largest employer of Oriental labour in the province. The results were close and, by all accounts, crooked, but the new residents were triumphant. Maclean was elected mayor and CPR land surveyor Lauchlin Hamilton led the aldermanic polls.[4]

The new city's streets were laid out by Hamilton in his role as surveyor for the CPR. He named them after company dignitaries (including himself). Even the name Vancouver had been chosen by CPR general manager William Van Horne and later ratified by the provincial legislature. The company was also the city's major landholder, thanks to a grant of 6,275 acres around the terminus, which it had received from the province for extending the railway from Port Moody. This was supplemented by another 175 acres from private owners who benefitted from the coming of the railway. The CPR holdings included much of the present city, and in the early years CPR officials represented the area (now known as the west end) on city council.[5]

In May 1887 the first train arrived and, less than one month later, the first ship docked at the CPR wharf. This was the beginning of the all-British route to the Orient, and it symbolized Vancouver's importance in CPR plans. Not only was the city to be the provincial distribution centre for the coastal logging and fishing camps and for the mining camps of the interior, but it was also to be the trans-shipment point for Pacific trade. The CPR became the largest employer in the city, pumping considerable money into the economy through construction projects and the operation and maintenance of the railway. It also convinced its corporate allies, including the Bank of Montreal, to locate in Vancouver rather than in Victoria, although the latter was larger and more established financially. This helped secure Vancouver's position as Canada's Pacific metropolis.

The city's economy was based on the CPR, sawmilling and real estate speculation, but industry was also needed. City council, backed by the board of trade, advertised the city's virtues around the world and encouraged industry through 'bonusing' and other incentives. Some schemes were costly failures, but others, such as the BC Sugar Refinery, were successful and became part of the city's industrial base. Promoter Benjamin T. Rogers, an American with the backing of CPR officials, asked for and received a bonus of $30,000 to purchase the site, a fifteen-year tax exemption, and free water for ten years. In exchange he agreed to use only white labour.

By the turn of the century the city had become the provincial centre for fishing and lumber. Promoters built new railways to the interior, eastern Canada, and the northwest United States. In 1913 the Dominion government created the Vancouver Harbour Commission, formalizing the city's role as a major distribution centre. The Panama Canal was opened in 1914, and a start was made on a grain elevator at the same time, although it was not until the 1920s that the grain trade became important. During the 1930s the city's transportation role was extended by the development of a municipal airport. These changes lessened Vancouver's dependence on the CPR (and reduced the company's overwhelming influence on municipal affairs).

The city's economy was still vulnerable to the periodic depressions and recessions that swept the continent and so was caught up in a cycle of boom and bust. Each recession ushered in a period of plunging real estate values, unemployment, population losses, declining tax revenues (but debt obligations that did not decrease), soaring relief costs, and cut-backs in city staff and services. During the booms land values soared, population sky-rocketed, construction activity reached a frenzied pace, and the city reeled under the attempt to keep up with demands for services. The greatest boom occurred in the decade before the First World War, when real estate values increased six-fold and the population quadrupled. The greatest bust, of course, was the Great Depression.[6]

Politics in the new city was straightforward. The voting population was overwhelmingly male, property-owning, English-speaking, and Protestant: the large Chinese population, of course, did not have the franchise.[7] Most elected officials believed in growth and progress and the continuing increase in property values. The role of council, they believed, was to provide services in the rapidly growing centre. There was a meshing of public and private interests unmatched in the city's history. Three of the first six mayors and many aldermen were involved in real estate, and many were partners in the syndicates that built and operated the utilities.[8]

Within the general consensus there was controversy over the location of specific services and the allocation of funds. The CPR initiated the city's pattern of growth by building its station, offices, wharf, a 100-room hotel, and an opera-house to the west of the existing Granville town site and was able to control the pace of development and to capture most of the profits (since it owned the land). CPR general superintendent Harry Abbott was in the vanguard of the city's élite who built large frame-houses on sixty-six-foot lots in the west end on the cliffs overlooking Burrard Inlet, known as 'Blue Blood Alley.' Opposing the CPR was a syndicate of Victoria businessmen led by wholesaler David Oppenheimer (who became Vancouver's second mayor and the first president of the board of trade) that purchased 1,460 acres from the Hastings mill east of Granville. The land was subdivided into twenty-five-foot lots, and modest frame-houses were built and sold on the instalment plan to working men and mechanics from the mill and wharves. Within a few years of the city's birth, a pattern of growth was established that was to prevail virtually to the present – the working class on the east side, the middle class on the west side.

Both business factions vied for public investment. The CPR convinced its friends in Ottawa to dedicate as a park the 1,000-acre naval reserve on the western tip of the downtown peninsula and to build the Dominion post office next to the west end. The Oppenheimer group persuaded the citizens to build a public market close to the syndicate's lands.[9] But in spite of this competition, most aldermen agreed that the city's future was tied to the prosperity of the railway. Council offered the CPR seventy-five acres within the city and a twenty-year tax exemption for its shops and railway-yards. This initiative was strongly endorsed by the voters.

The overriding problem for the early city council was inadequate revenue to meet all the demands for services. The province provided grants for building roads and schools and land for a cemetery. Local improvement assessments, property taxes, and debentures were to provide revenues for sewers, streets, fire halls, a city hall, and the city wharves. However, the major utilities – though potentially profitable – required large capital investments and had to be left to private enterprise. The most important of the companies to emerge from the early struggles for utility franchises was the Vancouver Electric Railway and Light Co. It was taken over by British interests during the depression of the 1890s (after the civic electors of Vancouver had refused to take financial responsibility for it). The new organization – BC Electric – soon gained control over virtually every electrical utility in the lower mainland and on Vancouver Island and emerged as a powerful force in municipal and provincial politics.[10]

During the pre-war boom years population spilled into areas surrounding the city. This growth was facilitated by the electric railways. A major new line connected Vancouver to New Westminster, and there was soon a strip of development along the right-of-way. In 1892 the large new municipality of South Vancouver was formed between the city and the Fraser River. Over the next fifteen years most of the development in South Vancouver occurred on the east side, where British immigrants from a strong labour-union background built single-family houses on small lots. The west side of the municipality, in contrast, was settled by prosperous citizens who built large mansions on the bluffs overlooking the inlet.

In 1908 the CPR decided to start a new élite development in South Vancouver to replace the ageing west end. Named Shaughnessy Heights, it was a planned subdivision with broad crescents, luxurious landscaping, and one-acre lots. Before work started, the CPR ensured that Shaughnessy would not be overruled by the working-class majority of South Vancouver by petitioning the provincial government for a new municipality, Point Grey, which was carved out of the west side of South Vancouver. Over the next twenty years, CPR officials and other business leaders moved into Shaughnessy, and the rest of Point Grey was occupied by businessmen and professionals, particularly after 1922, when the University of British Columbia was established at Point Grey. As in the city itself, the CPR played an important role in the affairs of the municipality: by 1920 the railway company paid one-third of total municipal taxes.[11]

The depression of the war years hit South Vancouver hard. By 1918 the municipality was bankrupt and placed under the administration of a provincial commissioner. With the coming of better times during the 1920s, South Vancouver was restored to self-government, but still faced difficult financial circumstances. Point Grey was more solvent; none the less in 1927 it voted, along with South Vancouver, to join the city. On 1 January 1929, Vancouver became the third largest city in Canada with a population of 250,000 and an area of 44.8 square miles. The two former suburbs added their numbers respectively to the middle-class west side and working-class east side of the city.

This was the last major extension of the city's boundaries. Vancouver was soon ringed by autonomous suburban municipalities, in the familiar North American pattern. In several cases suburban independence was reinforced by physical barriers. Burrard Inlet and the two arms of the Fraser River made north-south traffic especially difficult. The suburbs were also protected by the early formation of a series of metropolitan special-purpose agencies – the Vancouver and District Joint Sewerage and Drainage Board (1914), the Greater Vancouver Water District (1926), and the Metropolitan Board of Health (1936). These agencies met many of the demands for area-wide services and so, while establishing a pattern of intermunicipal co-operation, reduced pressure for full amalgamation of city and suburbs.

In the city itself, there were early pressures to control the adverse effects of rapid physical development. Council's response was indicative of the interests it served. It used its fire and health regulations to protect certain neighbourhoods from such unwanted developments as apartment buildings and Chinese laundries. Other neighbourhoods were protected by restrictive covenants imposed by the original private developer.[12] Such covenants, however, were not as effective as 'municipal planning.' Point Grey's situation was exemplary. A quality environment had been established at the beginning, with wide streets and ample landscaping. In 1922 the Point Grey municipal council adopted one of the country's first zoning by-laws, which allowed nothing but single-family houses outside a narrow commercial strip. Businessmen in the city saw the value of such intervention as a means of controlling development and stabilizing land values.

The Vancouver Board of Trade, Associated Property Owners (APO – an organization of the largest interests), and other real estate and planning groups lobbied the provincial government for a town planning act, which was enacted in 1925. The following year city council set up a town planning commission, and one of its first actions was to retain American planner Harland Bartholomew to prepare a master plan and zoning by-law for the city. City officials recognized the importance of the APO: all drafts of the zoning by-law were sent to the APO before they were submitted to council. The APO argued successfully against measures that might have an adverse reaction on property assessments and hence on tax revenues. It was particularly effective in the west end, where property owners had been lobbying to have some areas zoned for apartment buildings. This demand was incorporated into the zoning by-law, which was adopted by council in 1928 and guided Vancouver's development for the next twenty-five years.[13]

The new system of land-use control became effective at about the time the city annexed its southern suburbs. These annexations were also the occasion for a major change in ward boundaries, which ultimately led to the abolition of the ward system itself. Under pressure from Point Grey, twelve new, single-alderman wards were created, with the intention of undercutting the old ward loyalties in Vancouver. The new divisions were artificial and unpopular. In 1935 the provincial government obliged the city to hold a plebiscite on the ward system. Abolition was supported by reform-minded business groups (including the board of trade and the real estate interests) and by the CCF, which had contested the 1933 provincial election (and won three east-side Vancouver seats) and the 1934 civic election (not winning any wards but doing reasonably well in some). The party reasoned that if all CCF votes could be grouped together in an at-large election, its electoral chances would be greatly enhanced. Only 20 per cent of the electors voted in the plebiscite, but the result was a clear two-thirds majority in favour of abolition; in a second vote 80 per cent supported the reduction of council from twelve to eight aldermen.

Overseeing the shift from ward to at-large elections was Gerry McGeer, Vancouver's seventeenth and twenty-third mayor and the city's most colourful politician.[14] He was, in succession, Liberal MLA, mayor, MP, senator, and mayor again. McGeer rose to prominence as provincial counsel during the freight-rate wrangles with Ottawa during the 1920s. During the Depression he attacked the 'eastern racketeer financiers' who, he claimed, were single-handedly causing the Depression. He sprinkled his 'social credit' money theories with a heavy dose of fundamentalist religion, two themes that appealed to the Depression-weary Vancouver voters. In 1934 he turned his fiery oratory on the holders of municipal bonds, arguing that they should accept a lower rate of interest, and swept into office with the largest majority in the city's history. His most significant achievement was the construction of the long-awaited city hall (which had been debated since 1910), financed by low-interest 'baby bonds,' in denominations small enough to be affordable to the average citizen. He appealed to the working people of the city, yet he had married a Spencer, of Vancouver's foremost merchant family: McGeer's brothers-in-law were Vancouver's business leaders. He was of a political type the city had known before and would know again.

THE NON-PARTISAN CITY: 1936–68

A new era in civic politics was inaugurated in 1936 with the first at-large election. With heavy east-side support, the CCF captured three of the eight council seats.[15] Business leaders became concerned. Provincial Liberals and Conservatives, the board of trade, the service organizations, the CPR, and BC Electric held discussions during 1937. The result was the formation of the Non-Partisan Association (NPA), which successfully ran a slate of candidates in the 1937 election. The CCF was reduced to one, the popular Helena Gutteridge, Vancouver's first woman alderman.[16] In 1938 the provincial CCF leader, Dr Lyle Telford, won one term as mayor because of his personal popularity, but the CCF was spent as a municipal force. Within a few short years the NPA tightened its grip on the council, the school board, and the park board and did not relinquish control until the 1970s.

The NPA had been formed 'to oppose the introduction of party politics into Vancouver's civic administration,' even though most members were Conservatives or Liberals.[17] Local government, it was argued, should be nonpartisan, and elections should be held at large, so that elected officials would represent neither party nor geographic constituency, thus avoiding the evils of patronage, sectionalism, and graft. The alderman's decisions, the argument continued, should be based on his judgment and 'conscience,' in the interests of the whole city. It was a corporate model of civic government, with council, as the board of directors, representing the ratepayers. The function of council was to provide services in a financially sound, efficient manner. The main activity for the 'party' was to find the best candidates for civic office – usually successful businessmen. Most interest groups were suspect, but business groups, particularly the board of trade and the real estate organizations, were not.

NPA leaders were drawn from Vancouver's social and business élite. They were owners and managers of large and small corporations. Many were members of the Vancouver Club, the preserve of the privileged. They served on the boards of the hospitals, the university, and the civic and cultural organizations. As we might expect, the NPA was well financed, the main backers being the CPR, BC Electric, the department stores, and other corporations. A.T.R. Campbell, a senior partner in one of Vancouver's leading corporate law firms, was for many years a key figure and NPA president. In 1946 he helped organize the Downtown Business Association, which became a leading voice for downtown interests. He also helped form the Downtown Parking Corporation, which built publicly financed parking garages to serve the downtown area. Campbell was a director of the Vancouver Art Gallery, the Board of Trade, and the Pacific National Exhibition (PNE). His law firm did the legal work for the PNE and major corporations such as MacMillan Bloedel and the Bank of Commerce.

As in many American cities, at-large non-partisan elections had the effect of discouraging political participation: 'By removing the party label, this reform often took away one clue a voter had to a candidate's policy orientation. Second, by removing ... [the] party's role in city politics, this reform took away the best mobilizing force for informing and involving the electorate. Third, in placing the responsibility for discovering a candidate's merits squarely on the individual citizen, it greatly raised the time and information costs of participation.'[18] In Vancouver there was a gradual but definite decline in the vote on the east side, inhabited mainly by working-class residents. After 1945 turn-out was 10 to 20 per cent lower than the west-side, middle-class voters. Further, west siders tended to vote the NPA slate (almost exclusively of west-side residents), while east siders voted more randomly.[19] Both factors ensured that the west side – especially the old municipality of Point Grey – controlled council.

The NPA-dominated city emerged from the Second World War little changed physically from the late 1920s, and yet the war years had been a boom period. The Boeing Aircraft Plant in Richmond, the Vancouver shipyards, and the shipping industry made major contributions to the war effort. Economic development continued after the war as a result of port and industrial expansion. Population surged, and returning veterans and European immigrants strained the city's housing resources. Between 1941 and

1951, Greater Vancouver's population jumped by 40 per cent. An enormous pent-up demand for housing was released, and increased automobile use created problems of congestion in the inner city and sprawl in the suburbs.

At first the city captured some of the new growth. Office demand was met from the stock of half-empty older buildings, and later by the construction of new and larger ones. Housing subdivisions were built on city and CPR land in the southern parts of the city; three-storey frame apartment buildings were erected in the inner areas (particularly the west end). However, most development was occurring outside the city. After the war the provincial government developed the province by building roads and bridges, opening up vast tracts of easily serviced farm land. Hedging their bets, the major department stores were locating in new shopping centres instead of expanding their downtown facilities. By the late 1950s stagnation had set in. Within the city, expansion of office space ground to a halt and the retail sector suffered a decline.

The NPA had come to realize that Vancouver would need a more professional administration to deal with the problems and opportunities of the post-war years. The city had operated under a council-committee system in which the standing committees were both policy and administrative bodies. By the mid-1950s a cumbersome system had evolved that made efficient government virtually impossible.[20] More than seventy bodies were required to do the city's business. There was little co-ordination. The NPA had no coherent policies and its elected members did not have a caucus; they were part-time aldermen kept busy running from meeting to meeting. At the administrative level, a general-purposes committee of the four senior officials advised council, but exerted little overall control. That government did not grind to a halt was a tribute to their talents.

In 1952 a planning department was set up to replace the old voluntary town planning commission (which became an advisory body freed from technical and administrative concerns). A technical planning board of eleven senior officials whose departments dealt with physical development was established and soon came to exert a significant influence on the course of the city's development.[21] Growing pressure for change led to a new city charter in 1953.[22] In 1955, a study by the Chicago-based Public Administration Service recommended a change to a city-manager form of government. It recommended that council's executive and administrative powers be delegated to the manager, who would review departmental budget requests, ensure that a balanced program was presented to council, and appoint department heads. Council would retain ultimate control through its powers to select and terminate the manager, to veto the budget and five-year capital plans, and to adopt regulations that defined the manager's administrative limits. Most council committees would be eliminated and others reduced in importance. Some aldermen opposed the plan, fearing that too much power would be centralized in one office (and that they themselves would lose power). After much wrangling, a compromise was reached in which the powers of the manager would be held by a three-person board of administration composed of two council-appointed commissioners and the mayor.[23]

The board was created in 1956. When Tom Alsbury was elected mayor in 1959 on an anti-NPA slate, the NPA-dominated council voted to remove him from the board, which continued with two commissioners until 1973. Once the board had been established, power tended to drift away from the elected council and into the hands of the commissioners. There were two factors involved. By the early 1960s, the NPA had entered a period of decline (which was to culminate in its loss of power in 1972).[24] It continued to win elections but seemed to have forgotten why it contested them, beyond the desire to keep 'politics' out of city hall. Its candidates were older, less energetic, and more closely connected to real estate interests – many were property, insurance, and real estate agents.

One of the commissioners, Gerald Sutton Brown, an English planner who had helped set up the planning department, came to be the most powerful person at city hall, his power verging on the absolute. No departmental reports would go to council without his approval. Often he would reject reports, sending them back for rewriting. He routed council decisions to the departments he favoured. He could bypass the 'people concerns' of the planning department by sending a council resolution to the engineering department instead. He could hire and fire the department heads, the people he sat with on the technical planning board. He prepared the annual budget and five-year capital plans for council, and his recommendations on departmental allocations were powerful bureaucratic weapons. He, or his colleague, dealt with outside boards and commissions, and he was the channel between them and city staff. He kept close tabs on major development proposals through his old planning connections. A developer with big plans would go first to Sutton Brown and second to the mayor.

During the two decades that followed the war, the basic goal of the NPA and the administration was the promotion of physical growth and development. This was to be achieved through a series of interrelated activities: downtown revitalization by public and private initiatives, higher-density development in residential areas, publicly funded urban renewal to promote industry, and a system of freeways to tie all parts of the city together. When the post-war building boom came to a halt in the mid-1950s, the pressure for action from downtown property owners became intense. The Downtown Redevelopment Advisory Board (DRAB) was established to recommend sites for renewal. One of its members, accountant-businessman Bill Rathie, ran successfully for mayor in 1962 on the slogan 'Let's get Vancouver moving.' The campaign to revitalize the downtown then moved into high gear.

Under Rathie's guidance, council hired American economic consultants who proposed building a system of freeways, encouraging apartment construction near the city centre (to provide shoppers and a pool of labour), and assembling land for commercial development with public funds and turning the land over to private interests for redevelopment.[25] These proposals were enthusiastically endorsed by Rathie, council, and DRAB, but a debate developed over the location of the new commercial centre. Once again there was a struggle between east- and west-side property owners. The consultants and the city planning department favoured an eastern site but the final decision hinged on the plans of the T. Eaton Co for a new department store. Eventually Eaton's chose a westerly site, so that the redevelopment would occur on the adjacent block. Critics claimed that the site was the poorest available and would cost too much to acquire, but the city was already committed. Council haggled with potential development groups for several more years until a deal was negotiated. The deal could be consummated only after a civic plebiscite and the passage of a provincial statute granting the city the power to expropriate the site. It involved a sizeable subsidy for the developers – CEMP Investments (the Bronfman family), the Toronto-Dominion Bank, and Eaton's. By the time construction commenced in 1969, downtown Vancouver was once again in the midst of a building boom and high-rise towers were sprouting on all sides of the development site, so that the subsidy seemed superfluous.[26]

The city's urban renewal record was also mixed. Studies were undertaken after the war, but the 1954 amendments to the National Housing Act (NHA) were needed to make renewal feasible. Thereafter, the federal government would pay for the necessary studies and assume 50 per cent of costs for land acquisition and clearing. In 1957 the city outlined a twenty-year plan designating four inner-city areas for comprehensive redevelopment. In the Strathcona neighbourhood, two projects displaced 3,000 people and cleared sixty acres between 1960 and 1967 to provide land for industry and public housing.[27] Further NHA amendments in 1964 allowed municipalities to share with the federal government the costs of roads and services in renewal areas. These prompted an even more extensive redevelopment plan for Strathcona, including a freeway that would slice through the community's southern edge. On this occasion, the Strathcona residents were better prepared to resist the city's demolition efforts.

In 1968 the Strathcona Property Owners' and Tenants' Association (SPOTA) was formed as a community protection society and lobbied intensively and effectively to halt the project. In August 1969, the federal government decided not to make funds available for Strathcona unless residents were involved in the planning process, and a Strathcona working committee was established. The committee was composed of government officials and SPOTA members and was one of the first instances in Canada of citizens sharing this kind of decision-making with government. The rehabilitation project, which was launched in 1972, became the model for other programs across the country. The rehabilitation plan did not expropriate any homes; it stressed repairs and renovation, protected small businesses, and avoided the wholesale destruction that characterized the earlier projects; and transformed Strathcona into one of the most stable, well-kept, desirable communities in the city.

More typical was the city's effort to stimulate private residential development by permitting increased densities. Once again attention was focused on the west end.[28] During the building boom of the 1950s, property owners in the west end had convinced the council to 'up-zone' the area, and in 1956 the planning department introduced a high-density zoning schedule solely for the west end. The result was the pattern of twenty-to-thirty-storey towers that dominate the landscape today. The planners gradually became aware of the negative impact of such high-density zoning and, in 1963, recommended that densities be cut by one-third. But the 'higher-density' lobby persuaded council to reject the planners' proposals. It was not until 1973 that a local planning program did 'down-zone' the west end to curtail excessive growth.

The key element in the physical redevelopment of the city was a system of freeways. In 1947 Bartholomew had updated his 1929 plan for the city to accommodate increased automobile use and to add a new type of street then coming into vogue in the United States, the freeway.[29] In 1959, city officials, led by commissioner Sutton Brown, completed a comprehensive freeway plan, and this became the basis for transportation planning during the 1960s. The plan assumed that the automobile would continue to be the primary transportation mode in the lower mainland and that some freeways would be in place by 1980. With those assumptions, the only public transit that made sense was a network of express buses using the freeways.

The provincial government balked at the excessive costs of the plan, so the city adapted its schemes to attract federal funding. A third crossing of Burrard Inlet (paralleling the clogged Lions' Gate Bridge) became part of the plan because the inlet was a federal waterway and Ottawa would contribute to the cost of the crossing. Ottawa would also participate in the financing of the east-west freeway where it sliced through the Strathcona urban renewal area. In 1965, another element was added – a waterfront freeway that would connect the third crossing with the east-west freeway. The CPR had agreed to donate some of its waterfront lands for the right-of-way. This surprising largesse became understandable when the CPR revealed its plans for a mammoth development, known as Project 200. The freeways were seen to be vital to the scheme's economic viability.[30]

Another piece in the puzzle was added in 1964 when ratepayers were asked to authorize council to spend $10 million to replace the structurally unsound Georgia Viaduct. The voters assumed this meant merely constructing a new viaduct, and they approved the by-law. They did not know that the viaduct was part of a freeway plan; they did not know that Vancouver had a freeway plan. (The 1959 plan had been used as the basis for transportation planning but it had never been officially adopted by council). It was not until 1 June 1967 that the *Vancouver Transportation Study* was presented to Council.[31] The study put all the pieces together for the first time, and it stunned Vancouver residents, sparking the strongest public protest in the city's history. The 'great freeway debate' of late 1967 led to the withdrawal of the plan and the formation of new political parties to challenge the NPA's vision of the city.

By then the grand design for the city created by the senior administrators of the technical planning board and the NPA council was unravelling. The 'recipients' of urban renewal were fighting back. The west end had become a symbol of overcrowding and big development interests. Downtown was congested, and magnificent views were blocked by mushrooming towers. Other inner-city neighbourhoods were being overrun by developers. The city was becoming polarized, as tenants and single-family home-owners lined up against landlords and developers. Even residents of more stable middle-class neighbourhoods, who were traditional NPA supporters, were unhappy with the insensitivity of the planners to community concerns.

Policies that had been effective in the 1950s no longer worked because the city had undergone some dramatic changes. Earlier, industry had been the basis of the economy – particularly the port-related functions of shipping and ship-building, sawmilling and wholesaling. Port activity remained important during the 1960s, but the city was being transformed into a national centre for service and administration that was overseeing the export of British Columbia's natural resources. This meant a larger professional and managerial class, better educated and highly mobile. The blue-collar work-force declined, but there was an increase in the populations of the elderly, the poor, and ethnic groups.[32] This changing population was creating new demands on government, and the traditional business-NPA partnership was losing touch with the needs of the citizenry. The development sought by the NPA undermined its political base and created the conditions for competitive parties.

THE CHALLENGE TO BUSINESS DOMINANCE

Business ascendancy in Vancouver politics has received its most effective challenge since 1968, but that challenge has by no means been fully effective. In 1972, TEAM (the Electors' Action Movement) won a stunning victory: many felt the civic millennium had arrived. However, TEAM was a coalition of reformers and more conservative business interests. It was racked by internal division and fell apart within four years. In 1980, a more serious challenge from the left occurred, as a man overtly identified with the NDP won the mayoralty, and the Committee of Progressive Electors (COPE) – a party more closely tied to trade unions and the working class – made an electoral breakthrough. COPE did not win a majority of seats on council, however, and the votes of the remaining TEAM aldermen were required for reform measures. This put a brake on radical action that might have threatened business interests. Those interests were well protected, in any case, by the Social Credit government of the province.

However deeply business interests may have been affected, the thirty-year hegemony of the NPA came to an end in the early 1970s. Tom Campbell, the city's most colourful mayor since Gerry McGeer, was an east-ender who made good as a lawyer and developer. He came to symbolize everything that was going wrong with the city. He developed large apartment buildings – visible evidence to many that city hall was in the hands of the developers – and he was a poor administrator, insensitive to people's needs and contemptuous of public participation. Campbell was elected mayor in 1966, in a campaign against the NPA incumbent, Bill Rathie. Significantly, one of his pledges was to get a better deal from the developers of the new downtown commercial centre. He soon made amends with the NPA and ran in 1968 and 1970 with its endorsement, using hippie-bashing law-and-order campaigns that appealed to the older, less-educated working-class voters as well as the NPA's traditional middle-class supporters. Campbell's greatest moment came on 15 March 1972, towards the end of his third term. During a public meeting on the proposed third crossing of the Burrard Inlet he complained that the crossing was in danger of being sabotaged by 'Maoists, communists, pinkos, left-wingers and hamburgers.'[33]

By then, the NPA had already alienated many of its supporters. The CPR's attempt to build a regional shopping centre in the middle of a west-side single-family neighbourhood infuriated the residents and led to a successful five-year battle to scale down the project. This issue was disastrous for the NPA, since the area consistently had the highest voter turnout in the city and usually presented the NPA with one of its largest blocks of votes. NPA supporters were also alienated by two massive waterfront developments that would have caused enormous congestion and blocked important views. The CPR's Project 200 scheme was bad enough, but even more distressing was a series of development proposals for the block of waterfront land adjacent to Stanley Park. For Vancouverites, Stanley Park is sacred, and the ranks of several 'city beautiful' organizations were swelled with outraged middle-class citizens. And, of course, the continuing threat of freeways acted as a force to mobilize middle-class opposition.[34]

Some of the city's efforts to overcome possible opposition to its policies seemed rather to stimulate it. For instance, on the initiative of the board of administration, council had established the Department of Social Planning in 1968, which was to work with councils of local residents and community workers in the city's twenty-two neighbourhoods to establish social development programs. Many of these local area councils were set up, but in some cases worked too well, becoming foci for community opposition to the plans that the city and the developers were making for their areas. Social workers and planners attached to the local councils provided crucial assistance in helping citizen groups to organize. This ran counter to the bureaucratic vision that the local councils should deal with technical problems and not become political. Several years later council abandoned the local area approach and dismantled the city's community development unit, but some of the area councils continued to flourish. With no ward system, but with growing dissatisfaction in many parts of the city, and with an NPA machine still capable of electing the majority on council, some area councils became vehicles for local political expression.[35]

Sporadic challenges to the NPA's domination had emerged over the years.[36] In 1967, socialist lawyer Harry Rankin was elected to council after ten unsuccessful attempts at school board and council. Rankin became the council's conscience and one of the city's most popular aldermen. In 1968, during Campbell's first term, TEAM and COPE were formed. TEAM was a grouping of academics, younger professionals, and business people. They were mainly Liberals, but included a scattering of unionists and New Democrats. Initially TEAM tried to recruit Rankin; he refused to join it and with the help of the Vancouver and District Labour Council formed COPE, a union-based, working-class party that, none the less, had a large professional membership.

Exactly what interests TEAM represented inspired conflicting interpretations among local political observers.[37] With some justification, COPE claimed that TEAM was a younger version of the NPA. In some ways, though, TEAM was different. It tried to be a year-round organization controlled by the membership and based on policy. Once in power the elected TEAM members did not necessarily follow party policy (but in this respect it was like any party that achieves electoral success); however, they did caucus to develop strategy and tactics. In contrast, the NPA was active only at election time, when its candidates were selected by a secret nominating committee. NPA aldermen did not caucus and did not, as a group, have any declared policies, voting according to their 'consciences.' COPE, like TEAM, exhibited qualities of a party, but was not tested in office for twelve years, because only one member, Rankin, was elected. COPE's major policy concerns were to shift the tax burden from home-owners to industry and to encourage massive public housing programs, rapid transit, and 'civic democracy' (public participation and a full ward system). TEAM favoured public consultation, a partial ward system, a moderated rate of growth, and a more 'liveable' city. The NPA continued to support the system of at-large elections and held the view that civic government should provide services to property and accommodate private development initiatives. Thus the three parties represented different parts of the political spectrum: the NPA on the right (with far right and moderate factions), TEAM in the middle (with conservative and reform factions), and COPE on the left.[38]

The new era in civic politics really began in 1968, when all three parties ran candidates. Because of the peculiarities of the election system, the full impact of this politicization was not felt for several years. All parties in Vancouver face a situation that combines a long ballot with a short campaign, resulting in what has been described as a 'minimal information election.'[39] Each candidate runs city-wide, and each voter has as many votes as there are seats to be filled: one for mayor, ten for alderman, nine for school trustee, and seven for park commissioner. With all three parties running full slates, with other slate-making bodies arising from time to time, and with many independents running as well, the voter is faced with a formidable task. His difficulty is magnified by the traditional shortness of the campaign – usually less than six weeks. In the circumstances, many voters rely on name recognition or vote for the whole slate of candidates presented by a party. Incumbents have a decided advantage, and it is rare for more than one of them to be defeated. Candidates who appeal to the working class also face the problem that turn-out in the middle-class west side is much higher than in the east: no one can get elected without substantial west-side support.

Because of these barriers to change, TEAM elected only two aldermen, one park commissioner, and three school trustees in 1968. COPE elected one alderman. In 1970 all incumbents were re-elected, although one NPA alderman had switched to TEAM. The New Democratic Party had joined the political sweepstakes that year when the Vancouver area council of the party ran a partial slate of candidates with COPE. In theory the area council represented the provincial ridings within the city of Vancouver; in fact, it was dominated by elements to the left of the moderates who ran the provincial party (some of whom had joined TEAM). There were also New Democrats in COPE. The area council's goal was to run candidates who would present a socialist program to the voters, hoping to challenge (but ultimately reinforcing) the belief that the NDP could never win under its own name.[40] The NDP ran partial slates with COPE in 1970 and 1974 and a full slate in 1972, faring poorly each time and facing harsh criticism from the party leadership. Several years later the area council was disbanded.

TEAM's landmark victory in 1972 ended thirty-five years of NPA control. Art Phillips was elected mayor and his coat-tails carried in eight TEAM aldermen (TEAM also won control of the school and park boards). Several factors were involved in this victory. When Tom Campbell decided not to run again, the NPA made a disastrous choice for its mayoral candidate, a choice that demonstrated just how out of touch it had become. Bill Street was a developer's lawyer and lobbyist as well as the NPA's chief fund-raiser. He had served a two-year term as alderman in the early 1960s, presumably to learn city hall's ways and so better to serve his clients. When these facts were revealed in a series of ruinous newspaper articles,[41] Street withdrew from the race, leaving the NPA in utter confusion. Another factor was an expensive advertising campaign mounted by Phillips's forces. A series of 'soft-sell' TV ads commenced eight months before election day to ensure the candidate's name was known to the voters. The ads were run long before Phillips was nominated by his party, making his eventual selection a foregone conclusion.

Underlying the specific causes of the spectacular 1972 election results was the NPA's inability to hold the loyalty of its traditional constituents – downtown business interests and middle-class west-side voters. They still remained in favour of growth and progress, but they felt that development should take place in an orderly fashion, so that investment plans could be made in a more stable environment. They saw the NPA's support eroding, and they feared a socialist victory (the NDP's provincial election victory in August 1972 had stunned them). The time for change had arrived, and the vehicle for change was TEAM.

TEAM's most significant change was to restructure the bureaucracy, dismissing Sutton Brown and reappointing the remaining commissioner as city manager, but denying him many of the executive powers associated with the position.[42] Executive functions were apportioned out among the mayor, chairmen of the standing committees of council, the city manager, and the individual department heads (particularly the director of finance, who received the board of administration's significant financial powers). The mayor's role took on new importance: the job became full-time, the salary was increased, and an executive assistant was appointed. Nevertheless, mayoral leadership still depends on informal persuasion since, under the city's charter, the powers attached to the mayor's office are few. In fact the mayor was unable to be a strong leader. Even his power to make appointments to committees was and is limited by the need for council's ratification. In recent years the mayor has often been an initiator of projects. He maintains day-to-day contacts with the senior administrators, and he has the highest profile in the media; but he has only one vote on council. Much depends, therefore, on party loyalties. As long as the mayor has a voting majority, council functions smoothly (this was to occur in 1973–4 and 1979–80), but when the mayor is in the minority, council seems almost directionless (1977–8 and 1981–2).

TEAM's reforms also gave committees of council more prominence. The committees became the conduit for recommendations to council, although they were not given control over departments. The make-up of the committees over the years has come to reflect the political composition of the council as a whole, so there is a high chance that committee recommendations will be accepted. Of course, when there is no majority on council, the committees may be paralysed. In this situation, the administrative staff tends to fill the policy void and so regain some of the influence it had under Sutton Brown.

TEAM also initiated modest moves to open up city hall. Meetings were held in the evenings to allow working people to attend, and council initiated an open-door policy on delegation requests. There was a significant reduction in the number of closed meetings, and the council minutes were improved (votes were recorded for the first time). One innovation required a potential developer to erect a notice board on his property when he was applying for a permit for rezoning or development.

TEAM's greatest achievement was the transformation of the south side of False Creek from a decaying industrial area into a successful mixed-use residential and recreational development housing 3,000 people.[43] False Creek separates the downtown peninsula from the inner-city residential areas. For eighty years the area south of it had been owned by the CPR and leased to industries that would generate traffic for the railway. During the 1960s the CPR decided to move its freight operations out of the congested downtown, and the future of the False Creek lands became a political issue. The NPA wanted the lands to remain industrial, a vision that was challenged by TEAM. When TEAM took control in 1972 it moved quickly to begin its residential development. TEAM also made major changes in the development process by passing flexible zoning by-laws in the downtown and other parts of the city and setting up a board of senior bureaucrats – the Development Permit Board, which was assisted by an advisory panel of representatives from the development industry – to adjudicate in public on applications for development permits.

TEAM's record on other issues was mixed. Many controversies that had led to the formation of the party in 1968 had been resolved by the time it came to power. Freeways were dead, and rapid transit was in the planning stages. Urban renewal had been transformed into rehabilitation. Major schemes, such as Project 200 and Arbutus Village, were moribund or scaled down. TEAM became racked by a growing split between its conservative and reform factions. The conservatives, led by Phillips (and later Jack Volrich), saw the need for changes so that the development process could work more smoothly and thus avoid citizen opposition. The reformers, led by aldermen Mike Harcourt and Darlene Marzari, wanted to make the city more liveable, particularly for the lower-income and disadvantaged populations.

Two issues illustrated the split. One important TEAM initiative was the establishment of area planning programs in inner-city residential areas feeling the squeeze from redevelopment – this was partially a response to the growth of the local area councils and their political muscle. Many of these programs worked because they were fuelled financially by the federal government's Neighbourhood Improvement Program, which provided money if local residents were involved in deciding how it should be spent. But the programs were really controlled by the conservative majority on council and the city planners, and no real decision-making power was ever delegated to the neighbourhood committees. Simultaneously, council killed the community development program of the United Community Services, which had provided independent professional help to citizen groups. Council was able to pass locally endorsed plans and zoning by-laws, but in the process the rich structure of citizen groups in the city was dismantled.[44]

TEAM's ambiguous attitude towards citizen participation also was demonstrated by the way it handled the issue of a ward system. As an opposition party, TEAM had supported a partial ward system, with some aldermen elected at large and some in wards. This position had been devised as a compromise to keep both conservative and reform factions satisfied. After the 1972 election, the TEAM membership voted to support a full ward system (although with significant minority support for both partial and at-large options). TEAM had promised to hold a plebiscite and initiated a series of meetings on governmental reform in preparation for the vote. Different aldermen from TEAM supported each of the three options. The public was confused, and the media played an important role in raising fears about the alleged corruption that was supposed to occur under a ward system. The question put to the voters was confusing. Only 20 per cent of the voters cast their ballots, and 12 per cent of the votes cast were spoiled. But 59 per cent rejected the ward system and TEAM let the issue drop from its priorities.[45]

The precariousness of TEAM's grip on power was obvious in 1974. Three incumbents did not run, and their seats were captured by a rejuvenated NPA.[46] During 1975 and 1976 TEAM drifted further to the right, losing interest in issues such as the ward system and public housing. This caused TEAM's most left-wing alderman, Darlene Marzari, to resign and sit out her term as an independent. Phillips did not run in 1976, and the TEAM mayoral nomination was won by conservative alderman Jack Volrich (a Liberal-Social Crediter) after a bitter contest with moderate Mike Harcourt (a New Democrat). Harcourt quit TEAM after losing, taking the remaining New Democrats with him.[47] The party was reduced to a minority position on the 1977–8 council, and there was a growing split between Volrich (who had won the mayoral race) and the other TEAM aldermen. Volrich sided increasingly with the NPA. Just before the 1978 election he quit TEAM and ran for mayor with NPA endorsement. The NPA re-emerged as the most powerful party on council; TEAM was reduced to one seat and lost all its positions on the school and park boards; COPE continued to elect its one alderman; and Harcourt and Marzari were elected as independents.[48]

Once again the right wing had taken control, and it hastened to return to the direction of the 1960s, emphasizing physical development and reducing services to people. The Volrich-led council promoted a curious blend of fiscal conservatism and lavish spending on mega-projects: a provincially sponsored trade and convention centre on the waterfront and a 60,000 seat football-baseball stadium; and in 1980 it gave unflagging support for another major provincial initiative, a 200-acre redevelopment on the north side of False Creek. This, too, was CPR land that was sold to the province for what may be the largest redevelopment project in the city's history.

The NPA's return to power was short-lived. In 1980 Volrich was challenged for the mayoralty by Harcourt, his former opponent in TEAM. Harcourt ran as an independent with NDP backing (having run for the NDP in 1975 and 1979 provincial elections). Harcourt ran a classic NDP campaign, relying on a cadre of volunteers who telephoned NDP members and others on election day to get out the vote. An estimated 10,000 new voters, virtually all tenants, had been added to the voters' list as a result of a second voter enumeration by the city. For the first time the election was held not on Wednesday but on Saturday, a day when tenants and working people are more likely to vote. Harcourt's campaign featured tenants' rights, a full ward system, neighbourhood protection, affordable housing, and a 'liveable city,' while Volrich emphasized the job-creating big-ticket projects and fiscal restraint. The result was a surprising Harcourt win and an even more surprising breakthrough by COPE (which had run a joint campaign with Harcourt): the party elected three aldermen, two park commissioners, and five school trustees (a majority). While the NPA still held the most seats on council (five), COPE had become the city's second party. TEAM was able to capture two seats on council, but was shut out on the other boards.

The 1980 election saw an increase in the cost of running for office in Vancouver. Running city-wide is always expensive, and this is an important factor in the strength of the party system. Independent candidates are at a disadvantage because few can afford to run city-wide campaigns (and rarely have a reasonable chance of winning unless they have already held office for one of the parties). They do not receive the media attention that is lavished on the major mayoral candidates and their parties. Traditionally the NPA raised its money from the large corporations such as the CPR and BC Electric. These sources dried up as the party declined in the late 1960s and the 1970s, and the NPA accumulated large deficits. The party has since regained ground and ended the 1980 election with a surplus of $20,000. To compete with the NPA, the other parties must now raise over $100,000 for a full-scale campaign. They rely heavily on the candidates themselves, as well as friendly professionals. TEAM also receives funds from corporations, while COPE is supported by the Vancouver and District Labour Council and some trade union locals.

For the NPA the main effect of electoral competition has been an organizational transformation. It has become much more of a party machine, nominating its candidates far in advance of the election, using a full-time campaign organizer, acquiring membership lists from Social Credit and Progressive Conservative associations, relying heavily on television advertising, and even formulating policies, to differentiate itself from COPE and TEAM. The NPA's veneer of non-partisanship has worn exceedingly thin.

The left's success in the 1980 elections posed the most serious challenge yet to business dominance in Vancouver politics. However, the left still lacked a majority on council. COPE plus Mayor Harcourt produced only four votes: the two votes of the TEAM aldermen were neded for reform measures.

TEAM's conservative roots showed through as one or both of the TEAM aldermen frequently sided with the NPA.[49] The 1981–2 council was fractious and bitterly divided, and every issue became clothed in political rhetoric as the parties strove to put distance among themselves. Because of the mayor's minority position, many of his initiatives floundered. He made little headway on the issues that brought him to office, such as affordable housing. Even on issues such as the ward system where the mayor could command a majority – TEAM now supported a full ward system – he accomplished little. There were two reasons for this: the traditional fragmentation of local political power and the increasing interventionism of the provincial government.

LIMITS ON THE CITY

In Vancouver, as in almost every Canadian metropolis, there is a plethora of committees, boards, and commissions that dilutes council's power and effectiveness. Some, such as the committees on the Arts and on the Disabled, the Heritage Advisory Committee, and the City Planning Commission, are appointed by council, which provides staff and operating funds. Others, such as the Public Library and Civic Theatres boards, are appointed by council, but have their own staffs, policies, and administrative functions. Vancouver's unique elected seven-member Board of Parks and Recreation, established in 1890, sets its own priorities and runs its own operations, but receives the bulk of its funding from council. This has not stopped the board from opposing council on issues that affect the allocation of land for parks. The school board, of course, is also directly elected and depends on council only for the collection of the taxes it levies, so that council receives the blame when school taxes go up. Thus a large portion of municipal business is beyond council's direct control.

It has been argued that school boards were separately constituted to avoid the taint of politics.[50] If so, this aim has not been achieved in Vancouver. The nine school trustees, ten aldermen, and seven park commissioners are all elected at the same time and are nominated by the same political parties. The school and park boards are important elements in the local political system, since they often serve as stepping-stones to successful careers on council. In 1981–2, four of the ten aldermen had such previous service.

Perhaps because the school and park boards are integrated into the local political system, they have not caused as many difficulties for council as the board of the PNE, ten of the sixteen members of which are appointed by the provincial government (the other members are five city aldermen and one park commissioner). The PNE board administers a 172-acre site in an east-end neighbourhood, the location of football, hockey, and soccer games, rock concerts, and an annual two-week exhibition in August. The city owns the land, but the province controls policy through its appointees. Noise pollution, congestion, and massive parking problems have plagued local residents for years, but the board, with its mandate focused narrowly on the financial operations of the PNE, has been unwilling and unable to resolve these difficulties. There have been demands that control of the site be turned over to the city.

Recent Vancouver mayors have had a difficult time with regional concerns as well. In 1965 the province was divided into twenty-eight regional districts, ostensibly to provide government services more efficiently. Most regional districts cover large stretches of sparsely inhabited territory, but two, the Greater Vancouver and the Capital (Victoria) regional districts, encompass the major urbanized centres of the province. Regional districts are not regional governments. Board members are appointed by the participating municipal councils, not elected by the voters.[51] The districts do not have any taxing powers and receive their revenues as levies from the municipalities and grants from the province. They were conceived as functional, not political units. The functions they perform are not enshrined in legislation but depend on approval by two-thirds of the municipalities (although some functions, such as hospital capital financing and planning, were directly imposed on the regional districts). The responsibilities of the Greater Vancouver Regional District (GVRD) include hospital and regional planning, water-supply and distribution, disposal of solid waste, air pollution control, regional parks, capital financing, transportation, housing, and labour relations.

Regional politics is affected by the tradition of local independence and an increasing alignment of local politicians with the two major provincial parties. Various inner city–suburban conflicts and competition for investment within the region further complicate matters. With such a divided regional board and a lack of electoral accountability, the GVRD has yet to establish itself with the voters, and regional politics remains largely incomprehensible to them.

One of the GVRD's major initiatives was the preparation of a Liveable Region Program in 1975, which proposed a network of town centres separated by open space and connected by rapid transit to provide a balance of jobs and housing and thus counter the trend to a concentration of office jobs in the city of Vancouver and housing in the suburbs.[52] However, this plan was upset in 1977, when the federal government proposed to consolidate all its Vancouver-area operations in a major office structure to be located in the downtown core. This federal proposal was supported by Mayor Volrich and the majority (NPA and TEAM) of aldermen, who argued that the city could not afford to lose the development to the suburbs. A slump in 1978–9 and a deferral of the building project postponed the issue, but by late 1981 the federal government indicated it would proceed with the project regardless of the wishes of the city and GVRD. The controversies it has generated reflect the differences between the city and the region as a whole; but it is even more significant that the final initiative in the matter rests with one of the senior governments.

The federal government has participated in local politics in many other ways, acting through a myriad of departments and crown corporations, such as the Post Office and the CBC. (These two organizations built major, block-large structures away from the established downtown core). Most important has been the National Harbours Board (NHB), which was set up in 1936 to administer federal ports. Port autonomy has been a perennial issue ever since. It was the NHB that ultimately killed the third crossing for Burrard Inlet in 1972. In the early 1970s, the city planned to transform its inner waterfront from industrial to urban uses, but could not proceed without Ottawa's approval. When the NHB built a container terminal on the waterfront, the city had little planning input, but the truck traffic generated by the terminal has had an explosive impact on the city's traffic patterns. Canada Mortgage and Housing Corporation (CMHC) has here, as in other Canadian cities, been a prime participant in the local housing market. CMHC has also played a key role as a developer in transforming Granville Island in the False Creek basin from heavy industrial uses into a highly successful recreational, commercial, and cultural centre adjacent to the city's False Creek project.[53]

Federal and regional initiative pale into insignificance compared to the crucial influence exerted by the provincial government on local politics. Strained relations between the two levels of government seem to exist regardless of which parties are in power and reflect a long-standing provincial jealousy over Vancouver's economic success and a suspicion of its political machines. During the 1960s, provincial power was epitomized by Premier W.A.C. Bennett's threat to build a fifty-five-storey provincial office tower (the tallest building in the city was then under thirty storeys). Yet Vancouver has a unique status in the province. It has its own charter, while every other municipality is governed by the Municipal Act. Amendments to the charter normally proceed on the initiative of the city, as a private bill, although the city often has difficulty in convincing the legislature to pass the amendments. While the province has rarely intervened in the city's internal affairs, on occasion it has amended the charter without the city's approval.[54]

The province affects the city in many ways. It is a major source of city revenues through unconditional grants and grants in lieu of taxes.[55] The province is also responsible for social welfare and ambulance services (taking these over from municipalities during the 1970s), contributes to hospital and school financing, and administers rent controls and agricultural land reserves. When the Social Credit party returned to office in December 1975, it began to intervene more directly in local affairs. For example, in 1978, the minister of municipal affairs required all municipalities (including Vancouver) to transfer a substantial portion of their accumulated surpluses (moneys put away for a 'rainy day') into the next year's revenue accounts. There were howls of protest from the municipalities, but no recourse was available.

The Social Credit government barely survived the 1979 election, winning a majority of only five seats in the fifty-seven-seat legislature. The ten Vancouver city seats began to look much more important (the Socreds had won six, the NDP four). An election promise had already been made for a fanciful trade and convention centre on the Vancouver waterfront. After the election the government intervened in the proposal for the baseball-football stadium then being touted for the PNE. A provincially appointed commission decided that the stadium should be located in the downtown area, and, in early 1980, the government announced plans for the redevelopment of the 200 acres on the north side of False Creek. It was to be the largest urban redevelopment in the city's history, and yet the city had no advance warning of the provincial plans, which included the 60,000-seat stadium, seven million square feet of office space (the entire downtown core contained only sixteen million square feet), and 12,000 housing units. A crown corporation, BC Place Ltd, was set up to develop the project, and this provincial company has forged ahead, ignoring the concerns of residents in the surrounding neighbourhoods and fighting the city every step of the way. The province also decided unilaterally to hold a major transportation exhibition – Expo 86 – on the BC Place lands, to celebrate the city's centennial in 1986.[56]

Recent transportation initiatives by the province also have affected the city. In 1980 the province decided to construct a new automobile crossing of the Fraser River, to serve the southern suburbs, even though the municipalities (including Vancouver) that will take the brunt of the increased traffic opposed the project. Most municipalities had been planning for rapid transit since freeways faded from the scene in the early 1970s. In 1976 the GVRD board agreed on a transit system that would connect the regional town centres with downtown Vancouver as part of the Liveable Region Program. Two years later, the GVRD's transportation responsibilities were undercut by the province, which established another crown corporation, the Urban Transit Authority (UTA), to be responsible for transit in general and to plan a regional rapid transit system. The UTA ignored the GVRD's proposed layout and developed its own and in 1981 commenced work on the Ontario-designed (but untried) Advanced Light Rapid Transit system that will connect downtown Vancouver to the eastern and southern suburbs and further add to the pressures for downtown development.[57]

In a province where politics is strongly polarized, the election of an NDP mayor in Vancouver was bound to exacerbate relations between the city and the Social Credit government. The Social Credit party has aligned itself increasingly with the NPA (two NPA aldermen had run for the Socreds provincially, and a senior Vancouver-area Socred cabinet minister is a former NPA park commissioner) and against the COPE-NDP group on council. This alignment was most clearly evidenced in the continuing saga of the ward system question. A second plebiscite in 1978 had resulted in a slim 51.7-per-cent majority in favour of a ward system, but the NPA-dominated council was opposed to the ward system. Eventually the council established a commission on governmental reform to investigate the issue. The commission, which was led by a retired judge who had been an unsuccessful Socred candidate in the 1960s, recommended a partial system, which was rejected by both sides. The 1980 election produced a council with a pro-ward majority (the polls that Harcourt won in 1980 were the same polls that voted in favour of a ward system in 1978), and, in 1981, the mayor, TEAM, and COPE voted to ask the legislature to amend the charter to allow ward elections. Naturally, the NPA opposed the motion and lobbied in the legislature against it. The result was a straight party vote – the Socred majority opposed, the NDP in favour. The following year council again tried to have the charter amended. This time the minister of municipal affairs intervened and announced he would allow ward elections only after another plebiscite – he would determine the plebiscite wording, and the pro-ward vote would have to be 60 per cent – and a government-appointed commission would determine the ward boundaries. Such conditions would minimize the threat to the NPA of electoral reform.[58]

The power of the provincial government is such that the city is bound to be limited in its ability to control its own development. At the same time, council is recognized to be an important enough prize to make it worthwhile for the provincial parties to intervene (however covertly) in municipal affairs; at the least they want to deny control or success to their opponents. The relative autonomy of municipal politics in Vancouver is seriously threatened by this. The city appears to be dividing on the lines established by the provincial parties, and local issues are becoming part of the wider political conflict in the province. This means that the challenge to business dominance of the city's affairs is unlikely to be resolved at the municipal level.

SUGGESTED FURTHER READING

Davis, Chuck ed *The Vancouver Book* Vancouver 1976

Gutstein, Donald *Vancouver Ltd* Toronto 1975

– 'The Developers' TEAM: Vancouver's Reform Party in Power' *City Magazine* I 2 (December–January 1975) 13–28

Hardwick, Walter *Vancouver* Don Mills, Ontario, 1974

Miller, Fern 'Vancouver Civic Political Parties' *BC Studies* XXV (spring 1975) 3–31

Morley, Alan *Vancouver from Milltown to Metropolis* Vancouver 1974

Persky, Stan *The House that Jack Built* Vancouver 1980

Roy, Patricia *Vancouver: An Illustrated History* Toronto 1980

Tennant, Paul 'Vancouver Civic Politics 1929–1980' *BC Studies* XLVI (summer 1980) 3–27

Vancouver City Planning Department *Quarterly Review* beginning with I 1 (January 1974)

– *Understanding Vancouver* II Vancouver 1979

NOTES

1 In 1931 the city's population was 73.7 per cent of Greater Vancouver; by 1981 it was down to 32.7 per cent. See Patricia Roy *Vancouver: An Illustrated History* (Toronto 1980) 168–71 for statistical tables.

2 Vancouver passed the 100,000 mark in 1910 when Victoria's population was only 31,660. For Vancouver's early history see Roy *Vancouver* 11–128, Chuck Davis ed *The Vancouver Book* (Vancouver 1976) 23–5, 28, 69–70, Robert A.J. McDonald 'Business Leaders in Early Vancouver 1886–1914' PHD thesis, University of British Columbia, 1977, and Alan Morley *Vancouver from Milltown to Metropolis* (Vancouver 1974).

3 Pierre Berton *The Last Spike* (Toronto 1971) 273–4, 284, 430

4 Roy *Vancouver* 16 and Davis *Vancouver* 25–6

5 For the location of the CPR land grant see Norbert MacDonald 'The Canadian Pacific Railway and Vancouver's Development to 1900' *BC Studies* XXXV (fall 1977) 10; for the land deal, Davis *Vancouver* 69, Roy *Vancouver* 12–14, MacDonald 'CPR' 3–35; for the importance of the CPR see Donald Gutstein *Vancouver Ltd* (Toronto 1975) 11–18.

6 See Norbert MacDonald 'A Critical Growth Cycle for Vancouver 1900–14' *BC Studies* XVII (spring 1973) 26–42 for this important boom period and his valuable chart 'Value of building permits in Vancouver 1902–36' on 31; see Gutstein *Vancouver* 63 for the booms and busts and Davis *Vancouver* 30–1 for the Great Depression in Vancouver.

7 From the beginning, women had the franchise if they met the property qualifications.

8 J.W. Horne was one example. He arrived in the city in 1885, one of the 'mob,' having made his fortune in Manitoba land speculation, and soon became the largest holder of real estate in Vancouver (after the CPR). He was an alderman, MLA, chairman of the park board, and, for a time, he controlled the Vancouver Electric Railway and Light Co. See McDonald 'Business Leaders' for the twenty-one members of the business élite of the 1890s.

9 A.W. Ross argued that council should ask the Dominion government to dedicate the 1000-acre naval reserve for park purposes, and Alderman Hamilton moved the resolution in council. Another east-west struggle occurred in 1899 for the location of Vancouver's Carnegie Library; east-enders won the plebiscite, and the library was built on the east side in 1902.

10 For the story of the proliferation of utility franchises and their eventual consolidation see Davis *Vancouver* 327, Roy *Vancouver* 36, 38–9, and Morley *Vancouver* 128–31.

11 See Davis *Vancouver* 104–6, 102–3, 112–13 for profiles of South Vancouver, Shaughnessy, and Point Grey. See Walter Hardwick *Vancouver* (Don Mills, Ontario, 1974) 105–8 for the contrasts between east and west side, also Roy *Vancouver* 68, 70.

12 John C. Weaver 'The Property Industry and Land Use Controls: The Vancouver Experience' *Plan Canada* XIX 3, 4 (September–December 1979) 211–25 for pre-by-law methods of land-use control. Also see Roy *Vancouver* 70, 72, 106, 108, 110.

13 Harland Bartholomew & Associates *A Plan for the City of Vancouver* (Vancouver 1929)

14 Davis *Vancouver* 193–4 and Roy *Vancouver* 110–16

15 In the December 1936 election all eight council seats were contested. The four candidates who polled the most votes won two-year terms, and the second four candidates, one-year terms. Thereafter, each year one-half the council was elected for two-year terms. All three council positions won by the CCF in 1936 were for one year.

16 Civic office was open to women if they met the considerable property qualifications. The first woman to hold public office in Vancouver had been elected to the school board in 1912.

17 *Vancouver News Herald* 15 November 1937. This discussion is based on Paul Tennant 'Vancouver Civic Politics 1929–80' *BC Studies* XLVI (summer 1980) 7–9. For an analysis of the NPA's success see Fern Miller 'Vancouver Civic Political Parties' *BC Studies* XXV (spring 1975) 13–15. See also Roy *Vancouver* 154.
18 Peter A. Lupsha 'The Politics of Urban Change' *Current History* (December 1968) 330, quoted in Hardwick *Vancouver* 30
19 Tennant 'Vancouver' 9
20 It was one of the 'most complex committee systems of any legislative body in the world,' according to Public Administration Service *Report on an Administrative Survey of the Municipal Government, City of Vancouver, BC* (Chicago 1955) 3.
21 Harold Spence-Sales and John Bland *Report upon the Establishment of a Planning Department in the City of Vancouver* (Vancouver 1951) and G.F. Fountain 'Zoning Administration in Vancouver' *Plan Canada* II 3 (1961) 115–21
22 British Columbia *Statutes* 1953 chap 55
23 The board of administration is similar to the council-commission system in western cities such as Edmonton, Calgary, and Saskatoon. See Donald Higgins *Urban Canada: Its Government and Politics* (Toronto 1977) 112–14, 119–22 and Thomas J. Plunkett *Urban Canada and Its Government* (Toronto 1968) 143–8.
24 Miller 'Vancouver' 22–5
25 Larry Smith & Co *An Economic Analysis for Central Business District Redevelopment* (Seattle, Washington, 1963)
26 James Lorimer *The Developers* (Toronto 1978) 174–7; also Roy *Vancouver* 147–8 and Gutstein *Vancouver* 68–71
27 Vancouver City Planning Department *Vancouver Redevelopment Study* (Vancouver 1957). Strathcona had been zoned industrial in 1931 but had remained virtually residential. See Roy *Vancouver* 144–6, Gutstein *Vancouver* 157–61, James Lowden 'A Case Study of Community Rehabilitation: The Strathcona Rehabilitation Project' *Plan Canada* XIII 2 (August 1973) 136–40.
28 George Gray et al 'Patterns of Neighbourhood Change – The West End of Vancouver' Department of Anthropology and Sociology, University of British Columbia, May 1976, 38–71, Gutstein *Vancouver* 98–102
29 Vancouver Town Planning Commission *The Major Street Plan* prepared under the direction of Harland Bartholomew & Associates (St Louis 1947) 5: 'A new type of street has been evolved in the major highway system, namely the Vancouver-New Westminster Express Highway or freeway.' For the history of freeway planning in Vancouver, see V. Setty Pendakur *Cities, Citizens, and Freeways* (Vancouver 1972); see also Gutstein *Vancouver* 154–7, 162–6.

30 Robert Collier *Contemporary Cathedrals* (Montreal 1975) 67–80
31 Parsons Brinkerhoff Quade & Douglas Inc *Vancouver Transportation Study* (Vancouver 1967)
32 Vancouver City Planning Department *Vancouver's Changing Population* (Vancouver 1964) Table 5; also Vancouver City Planning Department *Understanding Vancouver* II (Vancouver 1979) 34–44
33 James Lorimer *A Citizen's Guide to City Politics* (Toronto 1972) 100–1; also Roy *Vancouver* 154. Mayor Campbell explained that a hamburger was 'a person without a university degree.'
34 See Hardwick *Vancouver* 32–3 for an account of the controversy surrounding the Arbutus shopping centre project and Collier *Cathedrals* 48–67 for the Coal Harbour scheme next to Stanley Park.
35 For the official view, see Maurice Egan 'Social Planning in Vancouver' *Plan Canada* XVII 2 (June 1977) 118–26; for the view of community participants, Margaret Mitchell and Cathy Goldney *Don't Rest in Peace, Organize* (Vancouver 1975).
36 Roy *Vancouver* 156, Tennant 'Vancouver' 7, and Miller 'Vancouver' 5–7
37 See Tennant 'Vancouver' 13–18, for an insider's view of the party and his concept that the TEAM aldermen were the 'cream of the cream,' but for an opposing view see James Lorimer 'Canada's Urban Experts: Smoking out the Liberals' *City Magazine* I 1 (October 1974) 21–2 and Donald Gutstein 'The Developers' TEAM: Vancouver's Reform Party in Power' *City Magazine* I 2 (December 1974) 13–28.
38 Robert Easton and Paul Tennant 'Vancouver Civic Party Leadership: Backgrounds, Attitudes, and Non-Civic Party Affiliations' *BC Studies* II (summer 1969) 19–29; see also Stan Persky *The House that Jack Built* (Vancouver 1980) 203–10 for an admittedly biased view of the parties.
39 Jacques Benjamin and Peter Hopkins 'Media Coverage of the 1976 Vancouver Civic Election' Department of Political Science, Simon Fraser University, 1977, 2
40 In 1966 Bob Williams, an alderman who became an NDP MLA, set up the Citizens for the Improvement of Vancouver, an NDP-backed group that ran, unsuccessfully, a partial slate in the civic election.
41 See Allan Fotheringham's columns in the Vancouver *Sun* in the period leading up to the December election, e.g. 'Who Is Bill Street?' (20 May 1972).
42 Vancouver City Manager *Role of the City Manager's Office* (Vancouver 1980)
43 Ruth Rodger *Creating a Liveable Inner City Community: Vancouver's Experience* (Vancouver 1976)
44 Editors of City Magazine 'Neighbourhood Improvement: What It Means in Calgary, Vancouver and Toronto' *City Magazine* I 5–6 (August–September 1975) 18–21. Another experiment in government-sponsored citizen participa-

tion was the community resource boards established in 1974 by the provincial NDP government. See Vaughan Lyon 'Making Government Democratic: Learning from Our Failures' *City Magazine Annual 1981* 114–18.

45 For the history of the ward system, see Linda Hossie 'Vancouver Politics' *Canadian Forum* (December–January 1981) 22–3, 43.

46 The 1974 election was memorable because of the mayoral candidacy of Mr Peanut with his peanut-shell torso, top hat, cane, and white spats, who tap-danced his way through the campaign saying nary a word, yet collecting 2,685 votes. See John Mitchell and Vincent Trasov *The Rise and Fall of the Peanut Party* (Vancouver 1976).

47 Harcourt ran successfully as an independent aldermanic candidate. See Donald Gutstein 'Plotting by Numbers' *City Magazine* II 5 (November 1976) 6–7 and Persky *House* 21–5.

48 Joan Andersen 'Back to the Sixties' *City Magazine* IV 2 (April 1979) 8–9 and Persky *House* 31–44, 91–100

49 Judy Lindsay 'TEAM Work Necessary for COPE' *Vancouver Sun* 31 July 1981, Jan O'Brien 'A Year of Ebb and Flow for Harcourt' *Province* 13 December 1981, F1

50 Higgins *Urban Canada* 106–7

51 Andre Bernard, Jacques Léveillée, and Guy Lord *Profile: Vancouver* (Ottawa 1975) 3–41, Vancouver City Planning Department *Understanding Vancouver* II 27–32, Paul Tennant and David Zirnhelt 'Metropolitan Government in Vancouver' *Canadian Public Administration* XVI 1 (1973) 124–38.

52 Greater Vancouver Regional District *The Liveable Region 1976/1986* (Vancouver 1975) and GVRD Planning Department *The Liveable Region from the 70s to the 80s* (Vancouver 1980)

53 Adele Freedman 'Former Swamp now Painted and Peopled' Toronto *Globe and Mail* 6 December 1980, 17

54 One example occurred in 1904 when the powers of the city police committee were transferred to a provincially appointed commission. In 1935 the province required the city to hold a plebiscite on the abolition of the ward system even though the council wanted no plebiscite. In 1970 the legislature refused any of the city's charter amendment requests including one to give non-property-owners the right to vote on money by-laws. However, for the view that 'in most cases amendments proposed by the City Council have been accepted by the Legislature,' see Tennant 'Vancouver' 4–5.

55 See recent financial statements and annual reports prepared by the city of Vancouver.

56 Donald Gutstein 'BC Place' *Architects Forum* II 2 (1982) 6–10. See also the continuing series in the Vancouver *Sun*, particularly, Mike Harcourt 'Needed: A Good Neighbour' 30 November 1981, 5.

57 Vancouver City Planning Department 'The ALRT system' *Quarterly Review* IX 2 (April 1982) 3–5 and Vancouver City Manager *Summary Report on the City of Vancouver Role in Implementing Rapid Transit* (1981)

58 Hossie 'Vancouver Politics,' Vancouver City Planning Department *Wards for Vancouver* (1982), Linda Hossie 'Hope Dies for November Ward Elections' Vancouver *Sun* 6 May 1982, 5, and Vancouver Governmental Review Commission *Report* (the Eckardt report) (1979). In the municipal elections on 20 November 1982 Vancouver voters once again approved the ward system. This time pro-ward forces won the plebiscite with 56.9 per cent of the vote. In the same election Harcourt was returned as mayor; COPE won four council seats, the NPA three, TEAM two, and independents one. With his own vote, the support of the COPE aldermen, and the support of one favourable independent, Harcourt should be in effective control of the 1983–4 council.

MATTHEW J. KIERNAN and DAVID C. WALKER

Winnipeg

Students of Canadian local government have tended to regard Winnipeg as a city characterized since 1919 by class-polarized municipal politics and as one that underwent (in 1971) the most radical structural reforms yet attempted in Canada. We will seek to demonstrate that *both* of these images are spurious, particularly the latter. We will argue that, even before the 1970s, class conflict had ceased to be the central unifying motif of Winnipeg city politics and that, partly as a result, the institutional 'reforms' of 1971 were extremely modest. Radical reform of the organizational superstructures of local government has never really been attempted. Before we consider the Winnipeg 'reform' experience, let us examine the milieu that both created the initial impetus for reform and severely limited it.

THE CONTEXT FOR REFORM

Both the form and content of Winnipeg's local politics have been determined by the interaction between two countervailing conceptions of local government, which have coexisted in an uneasy and constantly shifting equilibrium since the beginning of this century. The city's considerable ethnic diversity and working-class consciousness have found expression in an attempt to politicize local government, by transforming it into a forum for class-inspired debate over local issues. In contrast, the city's business community has tried to defuse potential class conflict by depoliticizing local government and portraying it as a disinterested mechanism for the delivery of a few allegedly non-controversial services. The balance between these two interpretations has shifted over time. Whenever Winnipeg's system of local government has been restructured by the provincial government, the 'reforms' have tended to crystallize and ossify the existing balance between the two competing conceptions. For example, the introduction in 1960 of a metropolitan system by Duff Roblin's Progressive Conservative government essentially represented the triumph of the apolitical view, while the 'Unicity' reforms of 1971 were based on the considerably more 'political' understanding of local government by the governing New Democratic Party. (Whatever its superiority to the metropolitan system in this regard, Unicity was an extremely timorous illustration of the 'political' approach.)

The dynamic interaction between these two conceptions has, since the late 1950s, occurred against the backdrop of two predominant trends that have greatly influenced its outcome. The first is the decline in the political relevance of ethnic and class conflict in Winnipeg; the second is the loss of the city's former dominance in the western Canadian economy. Let us briefly examine each of these contextual factors in turn.

The Diminishing Relevance of Ethnic and Class Conflict

When the Winnipeg-based Manitoba establishment first closed ranks on labour in 1919 during the General Strike, it precipitated the formation of alliances along ethnic and class lines. As the strike expanded, civil authority (most notably the police force) was mobilized against the workers. A general committee was struck to co-ordinate this effort and to reinforce the impression of widespread middle-class support for the economic and political élite. According to most historians, this coalition of business and professional interests has persisted for nearly sixty-five years and continues to constitute the foundation of conservative politics in Winnipeg.[1] At the local level, Winnipeg's establishment has consistently resisted the emergence of overt municipal political parties, preferring instead to advance its interests through a series of putatively non-partisan coalitions, of which the Independent Citizens' Election Committee (ICEC) is the current incarnation.

Winnipeg's main rival political coalition can similarly trace its lineage back to 1919, to those supporting the strikers. These included the union leadership, the embryonic leadership of the European migrant groups, and, later, the city's intellectual community. This alliance was geographically separated, by the rivers and by the central-city commercial zone, from the more conservative, new suburbs extending southward and westward. Winnipeg's famous north end still symbolizes and encompasses ethnicity, working-class life-styles, new migrant groups, left-wing politics, and a strong intellectual life. These older neighbourhoods – an ethnic mosaic of Ukrainians, Germans, Poles, Icelanders, Hungarians, Italians, Franco-Manitobans, Asians, Indians, and Métis – form the political base of what is now the NDP.

While this ethnic diversity continues to characterize Winnipeg's demographic composition,[2] the significance of ethnic and class conflict has declined drastically since the Second World War. The causes of its decreasing political significance have ranged from gradual integration of Winnipeg's ethnic communities to the failure of socialist electoral politics in Canada. Most importantly, the business and professional community has eviscerated local politics through its dogmatic insistence that local government is inherently non-partisan and apolitical. Its principal vehicle has been the ICEC. The group fields a centrally approved slate of candidates, caucuses before council meetings, and has monopolized key committee appointments and yet persists in denying its party status. It thus evades the necessity of campaigning on or adhering to an explicit, coherent platform. More seriously, it perpetuates the anti-political ideology of local government. Despite its lack of overt policies (or indeed perhaps because of it), the ICEC and its precursors formed the majority at city hall from 1919 until 1980.

The twenty-three-year tenure (1954–77) of Mayor Stephen Juba reinforced the depoliticizing effects of the ICEC and symbolized the declining importance of class politics in Winnipeg. While Juba's national reputation was acquired primarily through a series of flamboyant publicity stunts, his true political genius lay in his ability to forge an unlikely coalition between the ethnic, working-class communities and the establishment. His appeal to ethnic voters lay in his careful cultivation of his image as the perennial defender of 'the little guy.' However, his ostensible iconoclasm camouflaged an extremely conservative outlook on social and economic issues, and for this reason he retained the support, if not the admiration, of the city's business élite. Its members may have considered him eccentric and even irrational, but ultimately he was one of them: he was a pro-development entrepreneur. This eclecticism enabled him to bridge and overcome the schism that had characterized Winnipeg politics since the General Strike. During his mayoralty, any residual class content in local politics became completely obscured by Juba's overwhelming and bi-partisan popular support.

The triumph of non-partisanship circumscribed the potential radicalism of the various reforms that were attempted. The decline of class politics made it impossible for the provincial government to implement any changes that had an obvious class bias. When ostensibly major reforms were undertaken in 1960 and 1971, no serious attempt was made to achieve a shift in the balance of class forces. While the limits on reform depended on the political philosophy of the provincial government of the day, the reforms of 1960 and 1971 were not as fundamental a departure from the status quo as was claimed by their proponents.

If the declining political relevance of class conflict limited reform, that it occurred at all owes much to the decline in the city's economic dominance in the region and the responses this elicited from provincial governments.

Winnipeg's Decline as an Economic Power

The health of Manitoba's economy has always been inextricably linked to that of its capital city, and the latter is, therefore, one of the central preoccupations of the provincial government. By 1971 (the year Unicity was introduced), the city accounted for over 65 per cent of the province's labour force, 70 per cent of its personal income, 80 per cent of its industrial production, 62 per cent of its retail sales, fully 95 per cent of its wholesale sales, and nearly 70 per cent of total provincial tax revenue.[3] In the 1950s, substantial migration to the city resulted in a significant redistribution of seats, and ever since Winnipeg has supplied a majority of the provincial legislature. (Twenty-nine of the fifty-seven members represent ridings in Winnipeg, and its population should entitle it to more.) Consequently, the provincial government is sensitive, both economically and politically, to any significant fluctuations in Winnipeg's economy.

Unfortunately, in the recent past nearly all of those fluctuations have been negative. Winnipeg has been experiencing a slow but inexorable economic decline which can be traced back to the opening of the Panama Canal in 1914. That event made it cheaper to ship goods between eastern and western markets without using rail links through Winnipeg and thereby began the erosion of Winnipeg's traditional position as 'the gateway to the west' and the dominant economic power in the region. Subsequent improvements in transportation, including the widespread use of air travel, further de-emphasized the importance of Winnipeg's formerly strategic location and accelerated the deterioration of its economy.[4] A recent and exhaustive analysis of Winnipeg's economy documents the gravity and persistence of this decline. The city's rate of employment growth has, since 1961, been the lowest of the eleven major Canadian cities examined.[5] Its labour force participation rate ranked ninth of the eleven.[6] The average income from employment was substantially lower than in any other major Canadian city.[7] The study confirmed that Winnipeg's manufacturing, transport, communications, utilities, finance, insurance, and real estate sectors have all suffered serious decline since the late 1950s.[8]

It was clear that Winnipeg's sluggish economic performance demanded some response from the provincial government. It became politically imperative to respond with such modest weapons as lay within the provincial arsenal, among which was reform of Winnipeg's government. As early as 1952, provincial studies had begun highlighting the connection between the city's economic decline and the fragmented nature of its government.[9] That structure was the object of repeated investigation by both the province and the city. In 1958 Manitoba elected its first urban-based, activist provincial government.[10] Although Duff Roblin's Conservatives had not made reform in Winnipeg a central campaign issue, they were under considerable pressure to remove structural impediments to the growth of the city's economy. Roblin's choice of a metropolitan system was influenced by the predispositions of his party, but the fact that a response was required reflected the economic decline of the city and a nearly universal consensus that *something* had to be done. For Roblin, economic efficiency was paramount. 'Metro' was, accordingly, highly centralized and therefore arguably more 'efficient,' but inevitably lacked grass-roots political sensitivity.

A decade later, in the face of similar pressures for economic revitalization from Winnipeg's business community, NDP Premier Ed Schreyer was to propose a very different solution – Unicity. The Unicity structure was to a certain extent the product of the decentralist, participatory political philosophy of the NDP. However, this general orientation found only attenuated expression, again because of the need to create an effective, centralized force for economic development at city hall. Both premiers responded to the political pressures created by economic decline in a manner mediated by their respective political ideas.

In summary, then, the socio-political context for institutional reform in Winnipeg has been characterized by two outstanding features. The deterioration of the local economy stimulated demands for provincial action, but the absence of explicit class politics limited the range of possible reforms. The relationship between institutional reform and its socio-political environment is dialectical rather than linear. While that environment helps to determine the nature of the reforms, the reforms themselves redefine both political expectations and the likelihood of their being fulfilled. In Winnipeg, the consistent catalyst has been the conflict between the political and the anti-political conceptions of urban government. Winnipeg's local politics has been less a struggle between left and right than a more subtle and fundamental struggle between those who believe that such terms have some meaning in local government and those who do not. Though that tension may not have provided the initial impetus for institutional reform, it was arguably the largest single factor shaping its results. A critical analysis of reform in Winnipeg reveals the overwhelming importance of this central conflict and suggests a closely related truth: the most important processes of urban politics have little to do with the formal organizational superstructures of local government but have their genesis instead in the internal dynamic of the city's political and ideological substructure.[11] It is at this level that significant political developments, if they are to materialize at all, can be expected to occur.

EARLY PRETENCES AT INSTITUTIONAL REFORM

From its incorporation in 1873 until 1960, Winnipeg developed without any overall coherence to its local government structure. Like most other Canadian cities, it expanded geographically through a series of annexations and boundary extensions. At the same time, however, a number of contiguous but autonomous suburban municipalities had grown up around it as former rural municipalities urbanized and became incorporated. By the late 1950s, there were twelve autonomous municipalities in the Winnipeg region. Bickering among them had frustrated both general, area-wide planning and the provision of a regional infrastructure to service a rapidly growing suburban population.

The first major institutional response was the creation of a two-tiered, metropolitan government in 1960. Its principal objectives were the traditional ones of rationalizing delivery of services and improving the efficiency and economic viability of the local government system. The provincial cabinet, having perceived the problem to be primarily one of maximizing the efficiency and rationality of local government, accordingly believed its solution to lie within those same technocratic ideals. In order to overcome the problems of planning and development under the previous system, the new regional government was to be the undisputed area-wide planning authority. Although its new planning powers were defective in several important respects,[12] Metro was able to plan and complete roads, bridges, parks, and other public works at an impressive rate. Given the circumscribed expectations of its creators, the experiment must be counted at least a qualified success.

However, the 'reform' seems far more noteworthy for what it did not accomplish than for what it did. In no sense were the structural modifications directed towards the political dimensions of local government. The government scrupulously ignored the socio-economic disparities among the region's municipalities and the unsatisfactory political linkages between the local governments and their electorates.[13] Metro was thus typical of nearly every local government 'reform' undertaken in Canada: in leaving the political aspects of governance untouched, it remained squarely within the antipolitical tradition that has dominated thinking on local government.

In the introduction to this book, we saw that adherents of that tradition sought to rid local government of the allegedly dangerous consequences of partisan politics. The municipal mandate was construed in such a way that neither the need nor the practicability of political debate was recognized. Banfield and Wilson have summarized this conception as follows: 'In this view, the government of a city differs from other governments, or should differ from them, in that it exists solely for the sake of the service function. Cleaning streets and collecting garbage ought to be no more controversial and, therefore, no more political than selling groceries. There will be politics in City government (according to this view) only if it is injected from the outside.'[14] The structural properties of the Metro system were entirely consonant with this interpretation. There was no need to provide structures that facilitated political debate, either within Metro council or between the council and its constituents. Accordingly, the design of the Metro system sacrificed political sensitivity altogether in the interests of 'rational,' 'efficient' decision-making. Metro council was headed by an appointed rather than an elected individual, thus insulating him from any direct accountability to the electorate. The council consisted of ten members, ideal for efficient decision-making but, with a ratio of over 50,000 citizens to each councillor, scarcely a recipe for sensitive representation. Moreover, even this deliberately weak politicization was further eroded by the blurred lines of accountability within a two-tier government. It was difficult to discern which level was responsible for which functions and to assign responsibility accordingly. In addition, some important urban planning functions were discharged entirely by appointed boards.[15]

In short, the system represented the epitome of the anti-political tradition. Its structure was consciously designed to prevent a truly political role for either the council or the public and scrupulously minimized the linkages between the two groups. It was an entirely logical extension of the political ideas of its creators. The Roblin administration, though more activist and interventionist than its later Conservative descendants, was ultimately conservative. Its constituency was essentially the same coalition of business and professional interests that has sustained the electoral fortunes of the ICEC and its precursors. Accordingly, both Roblin and the ICEC's predecessors emphatically avoided any arrangement that might politicize local government, fearing the potential threat this might pose to the status quo. Both groups successfully camouflaged their subservience to business interests as simply the civic-minded advocacy of prudent, efficient administration.

With the election of a left-of-centre NDP provincial government in 1969, these manifestly inadequate arrangements became, ostensibly, one of the principal targets for reform. The new government had other important aspirations, including the abolition of municipal tax disparities and the creation of an aggressive new set of planning powers.[16] But, judging from its published statements and the private observations of key ministers and their advisers, the principal objective of the experiment was the creation of a novel type of local political relationship.[17] Unfortunately, the legislation that emerged from cabinet debate fell considerably short of the extravagant hopes of its early proponents.

UNICITY: THE ILLUSION OF STRUCTURAL REFORM

Previous structural reforms of Canadian local government, including Metro Winnipeg, had failed utterly to strengthen its embryonic political role and capability. It has become conventional to posit Winnipeg's Unicity as the exception to this general indictment.[18] Certainly the rhetoric surrounding the introduction of the legislation indicated a radical transformation of urban politics. The government's chief adviser, Meyer Brownstone, had stated his intention to create an entirely new kind of urban polity: 'A second assumption is that the politically (participatory) aspects are highly unsatisfactory at present, and that any re-organized form will need to include a meaningful attack on this problem. That is, as part of the proposed new single city structure, it will be necessary to design an effective, acceptable political decentralization providing for involvement of citizens on a scale and intensity which exceeds by far that which is in existence at present ... Traditionally [opportunities for political participation] have involved elements such as electoral procedure, galleries for the public, and Council's hearing of briefs. What is assumed here has more to do with community organization, animation, control and advocacy.'[19] This same concern is strongly reflected in the government's white paper:

> In order to avoid the kind of unresponsive government experienced by citizens in large cities ... it is necessary to devise some new and different structures, ideas and techniques. It follows logically that devising a new system of local government must involve, in addition to the necessary political and administrative structures, the creation of more direct and satisfactory avenues of access from the citizen to his elected representative ... It bears stressing again that, underlying the proposals which follow are two firm convictions: (1) that citizen participation and involvement with local government needs to be greatly increased and intensified; and (2) that, in a democracy, the elected representative must always be responsive to, and as accountable to the people he represents as is humanly possible ... We believe that it is possible to

create, at the local level, the sort of climate in which citizen interest, participation, and active involvement can, and will, flourish ... We believe, in short, that it is possible to devise, at the community level, a framework within which the local citizen cannot merely perceive clearly the issues affecting him, but can act forcefully and effectively in his own self-interest.[20]

Later, in legislative debate, the government reiterated its commitment: 'This legislation is first and foremost a total and absolute and unqualified commitment to real democracy at the local level. It is a categorical commitment to the belief that if you make it possible for people to determine how their own community shall be run, that they will do it very well indeed, and with this legislation, we hope to provide a framework to make it possible that this happens.'[21] The rhetorical flourishes indicated not only a pious faith in the efficacy of structural reform, but also a commitment to use such reform to reconstitute, decentralize, and politicize a system previously predicated on efficiency rather than political responsiveness.

Indeed, a superficial examination of the new structure would suggest that radical reform had taken place. Twelve lower-tier and one upper-tier local governments had been replaced by a single, area-wide council. That council was large by Canadian standards, with fifty seats, to permit the expression of a full range of political opinion in a parliamentary-style forum and to reduce the ratio of constituents to councillors. To increase accountability, a number of previously arm's-length, appointed special-purpose bodies (including the notorious Zoning Board of Adjustment) were abolished and their functions absorbed into the new council. This large council was subdivided into specialized standing committees with responsibility for the environment, finance, works and operations, and, later, recreation and social services. Each of these committees reported back to council through what amounted to a municipal cabinet – the executive policy committee. The standing committee structure was mirrored within the civic administration by a board of commissioners, with each appointed commissioner reporting to a corresponding functional standing committee. This method of linking political and administrative actors, unique in Canadian local government, was an attempt to counterbalance the new decentralized political process by a centralized civic bureaucracy under the leadership of a unified board of commissioners.

The chief elements of the decentralized political process were to be the community committees and the residents' advisory groups. The former were sub-regional groupings of between three and five councillors from adjacent wards, who met regularly to consider and make recommendations on local neighbourhood issues. The residents' advisory groups (RAGS) were one of the most innovative and celebrated aspects of the structure. There was to be a RAG attached to each community committee, composed of interested citizens and selected from among their number. Their mandate was to 'advise and assist the members of the Community Committee ... as to the performance of their functions under this Act.'[22] The RAGS are the only municipal groups of organized, non-elected participants ever given legal status in Canada.

The innovations and rhetorical fanfare created a climate of expectancy among local academic commentators.[23] Cabinet ministers sought to interpret their election as a triumph of the left over an establishmentarian Tory government and to portray their civic legislation as a thorough assault on class privilege in Winnipeg.[24] While the former claim has some validity, the latter must be treated with extreme scepticism, because unification was being vigorously promoted by such arch-conservative business groups as the chamber of commerce and the Downtown Business Association, as well as by Mayor Juba himself.[25] The business community clearly considered a centralized, cohesive political unit in the metropolitan region to be an essential prerequisite for arresting its economic decline. Several cabinet members had similar concerns, and they challenged those ministers who favoured a more decentralized, participatory local polity. The legislation was a synthesis, more heavily weighted in the direction of centralization and economic efficiency than of decentralization.

Moreover, the new government's 'attack' on socio-economic disparity within the metropolitan region ultimately proved oblique and attenuated. A more uniform basis of property tax assessment was established, which meant that uniform rates of local taxation now obtained universally. However, as Lightbody has demonstrated, these marginal gains in revenue were more than offset by the perpetuation of inequities in expenditure. The NDP's reformist zeal did not extend far enough for it to address the equalization of expenditures and services. Having moved haltingly towards revenue equalization, the government left the disbursement of those revenues to what was sure to be a conservative, suburban-dominated ICEC council. The government's reticence appears to have stemmed from a rather naïve faith in the efficacy of its structural reforms and a philosophical disinclination further to erode the autonomy of local government decision-making. It thereby lost a rare opportunity to redistribute urban opportunities and, indirectly, wealth and income.[26] Close analysis of the expenditures of the new councils reveals that unification changed very little: the practice of systematic discrimination against the poorer municipalities has continued unabated.[27]

Among the most conspicuous victims have been the low-income residents of the contemporary inner city. Of course it is by no means clear whether any institutional reform, however radical, could ensure significant redistribution, but this must remain a moot point. Unfortunately, the feeble tax equalization provisions, and the bankruptcy of the reforms as a whole, have been obscured by the government's rhetoric and by the uncritical responses of popular and academic commentators.[28]

Several structural flaws severely compromised the system's ability to politicize local government. First, the consultants had planned that the mayor would be selected by the members of council. In such an embryonic parliamentary system, the mayor would have to enjoy the confidence of a majority of councillors and in turn be accountable to them. Groups would campaign on explicit policy platforms, with the leader of the majority group becoming mayor. Instead, the legislation provided for direct election of the mayor. This provision represented a compromise within the provincial cabinet. One group stressed the advantages of a parliamentary-style system and noted its incompatibility with an at-large mayoralty. The other group regarded the direct election of the mayor as an antidote to the excessive parochialism of a system of fifty small wards.

Mayor Juba, who recognized that his chances of re-election were much greater under the at-large system, lobbied intensively. His considerable popularity and his leverage with the cabinet tipped the scales in favour of direct election. This departure from the white paper proposals removed the linchpin of the structure. The direct line of responsibility between the mayor and council so essential to coherent policy-making was lost. The government virtually precluded the emergence of two of the most crucial elements of a politicized structure: a mayor who could provide the leadership made possible by the support of council and a clear choice of programs defined through a party system. The consultants who had devised the original system observed: 'The consequences of this amendment were disastrous for the possibility of developing a form of responsible parliamentary government at the city level.'[29]

Second, the white paper had made extravagant references to local, grassroots democracy whereby citizens could make decisions themselves on local issues. Two instruments were to have been used in a more decentralized process: the community committees and the RAGS. Yet their powers were more apparent than real. The community committees had no powers of substance. One of their few responsibilities under the legislation had been to 'supervise employees in the delivery of all services which, until the coming into force of this Act, were administered by the area municipalities.'[30] Many advocates of decentralization interpreted this to mean that committees could hire and fire staff and thus directly influence program delivery. In 1972 the government amended the act: 'Nothing in this Act shall be deemed to authorize a Community Committee to hire, suspend, or dismiss, or to exercise ultimate administrative control over the employees of the City.'[31]

Even in the area of their greatest potential influence, land-use planning, the committees were accorded no powers of final decision. They were to conduct public hearings on planning and zoning matters that were ultimately decided by the council. Even the committees' power to permit minor exceptions to zoning by-laws was attenuated by the right to appeal their decisions to a more senior subcommittee of council.[32] The only power belonging to the committees is their ability to allocate an extremely modest (25¢ per capita) block grant from council to neighbourhood cultural and recreational groups. In short, the community committee structure provided little more than the pretence of decentralization.

The RAGS attached to them were more impotent still. Their status as advisory bodies to powerless committees was a far cry from the participatory nirvana heralded in the white paper. The act gave the RAGS no responsibilities to discharge, and the government gave them neither the finances nor staff necessary for them to make an informed contribution to the community committee's deliberations.

The absence of a meaningful devolution of power to the community committees and RAGS was not an oversight or the product of clumsy legislative draftsmanship. The provisions represented an uneasy but calculated compromise between contending factions within the provincial cabinet. Two questions were involved: how much power should the community committees have, and how much of this could safely be further devolved to the RAGS? On the one side were the committed amalgamationists such as Sidney Green, who opposed granting substantial powers to the committees on the grounds that this would replicate the two-tiered situation under Metro. In contrast, ministers such as Saul Miller and Al Mackling, who represented suburban ridings, saw the committees as the only bulwark against the erosion of the communities' cultural identities. The cabinet was similarly divided on the extent to which participatory democracy should be pursued through the instrument of the RAGS. The strongest advocate of the participatory approach was Saul Cherniack, the minister for urban affairs, but the rest of the cabinet was considerably less enthusiastic.[33]

The compromise provisions that emerged were only a token gesture in the direction of participatory democracy. In the words of the government's consultants: 'Although the government was prepared to go a long way to improve the *representative* model, and did so in the legislation, it provided little statutory base for the development of a *participatory* model ... The Act's contribution to the definition and development of a participatory political relationship in Winnipeg was mixed and on the whole, rather weak ... What ultimately emerged from the debate was an affirmation of the traditional approach to political structures and relationships – albeit improved and strengthened, it was still some distance from acceptance of the idea of a participative model. The status quo was more or less successfully defended in arguments that flowed between ideological commitment and a political sense of what was possible and what was not.'[34]

Thus, contrary to conventional assumptions, the Winnipeg 'reform' experience can provide us with little empirical evidence on the efficacy of institutional reform.[35] Major institutional reform has not even been attempted in Winnipeg. However, the reforms are probably as radical as any that the Canadian political culture is capable of digesting. For even if the divisions that beset the cabinet had not been barriers to a more coherent and radical approach, external, contextual factors would prevent such an outcome. Those factors might be regarded as consequences of the situation of the Canadian state within a capitalistic economy and, accordingly, within the intellectual traditions of Western liberalism. Any institutional reform in Canada that might challenge such concepts as the inviolability of private property or the supremacy of electoral (as opposed to participatory) politics is unacceptable to the public. This same public elects the provincial governments that possess the constitutional power to reform the structures of local government, and the foregoing suggests rather clearly the bankruptcy of institutional reform as an agent of political change.

QUIESCENCE COMPOUNDED: THE ROLE OF THE ICEC

Whatever impact the institutional modifications might have had was dissipated when, predictably, control of the new structure passed into the hands of the ICEC. The ICEC was formed in 1971 to contest the first Unicity elections and is the current incarnation of a long line of anti-socialist local political coalitions that have dominated Winnipeg politics since the General Strike of 1919.[36] Its electoral strength was in suburban middle- and upper-middle-class wards, and with the distribution of Unicity council seats heavily skewed in favour of suburbia (roughly thirty-four of the fifty seats were suburban), its victory was virtually foreordained. Two themes have consistently characterized the ICEC and its precursors: hostility to policies and groups perceived as socialist and a dogmatic opposition to partisan politics.

The ICEC has elevated its putative non-partisanship to the status of a virtue and indeed has made it its chief election issue, as these excerpts from its campaign advertising suggest: 'We need councillors who will put public interest ahead of old party loyalties ... Independent Citizens' Election Committee candidates answer to no political party: they answer to YOU.'[37] 'I.C.E.C. candidates are concerned, dedicated people whose objective would be to strive for the City's best interests and your best interests without partisan political commitments ... The I.C.E.C. is an experienced team that answers only to you.'[38] Precisely what the ICEC understands by 'the City's best interests' is never revealed. Instead, substantive platforms are scrupulously avoided, and the voter is confronted instead by a chance assortment of 'independent' ICEC candidates campaigning on purely personal appeal.

It is important, however, not to confuse the absence of a well-articulated, explicit program with the absence of objectives. The ICEC's most important goals remain almost entirely implicit. Its single overriding objective remains identical with that of its predecessors in 1919: namely, the preservation of the socio-economic status quo through the continued dominance of the city's business and professional élite.[39] The ICEC has systematically tried to depoliticize urban politics by resisting any expansion into contentious new fields such as low-income housing and by convincing the public (and, in some cases, its own members) that there is nothing 'political' about those limited municipal responsibilities it acknowledges as legitimate. The dialectic of class conflict, a central if underlying motif of Winnipeg politics since the General Strike, has thereby been almost entirely submerged. The ICEC has managed to neutralize most local issues and thereby to obscure their class origins. The group's obeisance to business and development interests is camouflaged as simply prudent, efficient municipal administration.

However duplicitous this strategy, it has proven remarkably successful at the polls. In the first Unicity election in 1971, the ICEC captured thirty-seven of the fifty seats, and gained additional, albeit reduced, majorities again in 1974 and 1977. It completely dominated the key council committees.[40] Its chief rival, the municipal wing of the NDP, won only seven seats in 1971, nine in 1974, and four in 1977. This failure (throughout this period the NDP was in power at the provincial level) was partly due to a distribution of seats that minimized inner-city representation, and partly to poor organization. The generally mediocre calibre of NDP councillors, combined with the surprising range of their views, prevented the caucus from mounting a coherent critique of the ICEC. As a result, the ICEC enjoyed a virtual political monopoly over the first three councils.

Council has degenerated into an almost random collection of ICEC candidates elected as individuals, and the group as a whole has evaded responsibility for council decisions, although it enjoyed a majority and controlled all the crucial committees. The public's ability to identify clearly the actors responsible for policy decisions is the first and most rudimentary precondition for the emergence of accountable, responsible, and politicized local government: '[The ICEC and its precursors] have been enormously successful, never losing control of Winnipeg City Council for the past 57 years. But control implies responsibility, and it seems to have been evaded. The result has been not effective leadership, but as the roll-call votes make clear, interest protection. There is nothing wrong with this situation *per se*, if the electorate had been able to assign group responsibility and judge accordingly. The clearest charge against the ICEC has been their failure to acknowledge the political responsibility which their position of power surely entails.'[41] Thus, local politics has been characterized by the existence of a covert party system, but without clear lines of responsibility and accountability.

The consultants had sought to broaden debate in council to include the active participation of citizens through the RAGs, but the legislation did little more than pay lip service to such a model. Even this, however, was too much for the ICEC. If the extension of even the traditional, representative political system to the local level was resisted by the ICEC, a more radical, participatory model was absolute anathema. Although the act had given the RAGs neither power nor resources, their mere existence was a threat to the traditional representative system to which the ICEC was wedded. Any reform that would adulterate the councillor's right to make decisions as he saw fit was to be rejected. In the ICEC's view, all the accountability required was available every three years at the ballot box. Accordingly, it acted swiftly to neutralize whatever minimal potential the act had originally accorded the RAGs.

In 1973, the federal government, through the secretary of state, had offered council a grant of $230,000 to create a research staff capability for the then-embryonic RAG system. In what must surely be the only known case of a Winnipeg city council declining unsolicited funds from a senior government, council's executive policy committee voted to reject the offer. (At that time, the ICEC occupied ten of the eleven EPC seats). A funding opportunity of this magnitude would never again present itself; its refusal was a blow from which the RAGs have yet to recover.

The second tangible manifestation of the ICEC's aversion came in 1976. The community committees did exercise some discretion in the reallocation of their block grants from council to various community cultural and recreation groups. Although the global allocations were modest (at that time each committee was given roughly $10,000), they did provide for some slightly more decentralized decision-making. However, in January 1976, council went to the extraordinary extent of passing a resolution expressly prohibiting the committees from reallocating any of their funds to the RAGS.[42] Of the twenty-three votes cast in favour of this motion, twenty came from the ICEC; conversely, five of the six NDP councillors present voted in support of RAGS. Not only were the RAGS deprived of the funding necessary to develop the research capability necessary to making a more informed and active contribution, but even the most elementary secretarial and reproduction services could not be assured. In 1981, council was allocating RAGS on average the derisory sum of $400 each, which had to cover typing and photocopying as well as the cost of providing meeting space.

Most RAG chairpersons have come to regard the chronically parlous condition of RAG finances as somehow 'natural,' inevitable, and perhaps even appropriate.[43] It is none of these. It is the consequence of the ICEC's systematic if implicit policy of starving the RAGS of the funds necessary for them to become effective. It is hardly surprising that the RAGS have failed to fulfil even the limited potential inherent in the Unicity legislation. In sum, then, not only were the structural reforms of Unicity themselves intrinsically incapable of politicizing local government, but even such modest measures as were taken were frustrated by the hostility of the ICEC and the absence of any effective opposition on council.

BILL 62: A SECOND OPPORTUNITY MISSED

This situation was made worse by a further set of major structural reforms undertaken by the NDP government in 1977. The original legislation had provided that a comprehensive review of the new system be undertaken after five years. A three-man expert committee was set up under the chairmanship of Judge Peter Taraska and issued its report after extensive hearings and deliberation.

The committee diagnosed the chief failure of the new system to be a lack of leadership, accountability, and policy direction on council; in short, the absence of politicized government.[44] This, in turn, was directly ascribed to the failure of the original legislation to deliver more than a feeble version of a parliamentary structure.

The committee proposed a number of steps for the emergence of a politically active and responsible local polity. It reiterated the white paper's original insistence on the mayor's being selected by council.[45] This would require that the mayor enjoy the confidence of a majority on council and would link more cohesively the two most critical elements of the structure. It would be but a short step to the emergence of a party system, as contending political factions began to nominate mayoralty as well as aldermanic candidates.[46] In addition, the committee sought further to focus political responsibility on the mayor by according him the power to select the chairmen of council's standing committees. While devoting most of its attention to the failure of the full council to evolve into the kind of politicized forum contemplated by the white paper, the committee also criticized the absence of a decentralized, participatory dimension. It ascribed the moribund state of the community committees and their RAGs to the absence of both a meaningful mandate and the requisite powers with which to discharge it. Taraska recommended that this deficiency be redressed by giving the community committees express statutory responsibility for the preparation of local plans.[47]

Whether or not such structural alterations would have produced changes in its political behaviour must remain a moot point. The government's response was to ignore most of the recommendations that would have politicized Unicity and accept only those that militated in the opposite direction. The government's amendments, passed through Bill 62 in 1977, represented a retreat from even the incremental reforms of the original legislation. The recommendation regarding the manner of the mayor's selection and the broadening of his powers was flatly rejected in favour of perpetuating the status quo. Furthermore, council was reduced from fifty to twenty-nine members, and the number of community committees and RAGs was cut from twelve to six.[48] This reduction in council size sacrificed that low ratio of constituents to councillors on which the government had prided itself in 1971.[49] This change represented the clear triumph of decision-making 'efficiency' over political sensitivity and accountability. It was now reasoned (or at least argued) that the new, smaller council would be more 'manageable' than its predecessors. On the contrary, what might have imposed some coherence was not a reduction in size but rather political discipline and public accountability through a parliamentary, party system.

More devastating still was the telescoping of twelve community committees and RAGs into six. This modification was unaccompanied by any substantial increase in powers or resources. By effectively doubling both the geographic area and the population represented by each community committee and RAG, the immediacy and familiarity with local issues that had previously been their greatest strength was irretrievably lost. In the case of the

RAGS, the amalgamation resulted in the forced marriage of two and sometimes three distinct groups. Differences of personality, style, and political philosophy produced friction that reduced the RAGS' limited effectiveness still further.[50] The recommendation that community committees and their RAGS be given specific planning responsibilities also went unheeded.

Thus, the 1977 amendments ended a decidedly equivocal commitment by the government to politicize local government and to reconstitute it along more decentralized, participatory lines. The high-minded rhetoric of the original white paper was never accompanied by legislative provisions to give it effect. Even the original legislation stopped well short of providing the structural means of politicizing local government. Certainly by 1977, the minimal reformist zeal was gone. The 1977 amendments represent an abandonment of the government's original objectives in favour of the more traditional goals of local government reorganization: efficiency and rationalization.

In 1971 and 1977, the NDP government faced two distinct options for politicizing local government. The more conservative would have involved structural reforms that encouraged the adoption at the local level of the party system already operating at the provincial and federal levels. This could have been accomplished by requiring the mayor to be elected by council from among its number and empowering him to appoint the chairmen and members of key committees. A more radical alternative would have been to play down the legitimacy and hence the importance of parliamentary, electoral politics,[51] and instead to devolve decision-making power on the grassroots level, perhaps to local resident committees, as was implied in the original white paper.

The government did neither, and both the original and the amended legislation represent a curious hybrid that may contain the worst of both worlds. It is closer to the traditional, parliamentary model, but stops well short of creating a parliamentary forum for local debate. At the same time, it merely creates and then dashes the expectation of a truly decentralized model that might have been 'political' in an even more fundamental sense. While there were a number of pragmatic and philosophical impediments to the government's adopting one or the other of these models unequivocally, its failure to do so cost it the opportunity to break the ICEC's hegemony over council. Even the more conservative parliamentary alternative would probably have forced a greater crystallization and polarization of political views on council, to the undoubted detriment of the ICEC's monopoly and the consequent benefit of the municipal NDP. The more radical, participatory system would have been far more consonant with NDP philosophy and, accordingly, could have served as the vehicle for a frontal assault on the ICEC. Instead, equivocal reform allowed the ICEC to continue both its domination of council and its perpetuation of an anti-political ideology of local government.

All the foregoing is to argue not that institutional reform is itself intrinsically incapable of reforming local politics in Winnipeg (although one must remain extremely sceptical about this possibility) – simply that it has never been attempted. Although there have been discernible changes in Winnipeg politics during the past decade, the most critical have their genesis entirely outside structural reform. The most significant feature of any local political system is probably its substantive policy outputs, and at this level, rather than at the level of structural innovation, the most profound developments in Winnipeg politics seem to be emerging.

THE PROSPECTS FOR NON-INSTITUTIONAL REFORM

For decades, one of the most compelling issues in Winnipeg has been the disparity between its core-area residents and their more affluent counterparts in the suburbs. The proportion of core-area families below the poverty line is nearly five times that for the rest of the city.[52] Unemployment in the core is twice the city average, and the average income of those who are employed is 32 per cent lower than the average.[53] The proportion of deteriorated housing in the core area is nearly double the average; in some subareas as much as 40 per cent of the housing is in poor condition.[54] In the words of one recent study of conditions there: 'The core area contains the highest concentrations of each [type of] high-need household. In effect, there is an overlay within the same areas of one-parent families with young children, low-income, unemployed households, elderly households, and native households. *Furthermore, it is the most disadvantaged of each of these groups that are concentrated in the core area.*'[55]

This situation is of long standing, and the government and its consultants consciously sought to ameliorate it through the unicity reforms.[56] The principal vehicle for reducing these disparities was to be an automatic equalization of municipal tax rates throughout the metropolitan region. It was hoped that this would end the previous inequitable situation whereby the wealthiest municipalities tended to pay the lowest tax rates. Not only did these fiscal reforms fail to achieve their intended result,[57] but, ironically, the system seems to have worsened the problem. When the suburban-dominated ICEC gained control of the structure, it was able to translate suburban priorities into those of the council as a whole. As a result, the neglect of the core area continued and perhaps even intensified. An analysis of council's 1977 and 1978 capital budget by the city's Planning Department revealed that 40.5 per cent of the capital expenditures of $74.8 million had been made directly for the facilitation of suburban growth.[58] Winnipeg's population growth rate of only 0.8 per cent per year requires an annual addition of just 2.7 per cent to the city's housing stock,[59] which reveals the true extent of council's suburban bias. Fully 40.5 per cent of the capital budget was thus spent to facilitate the addition of less than 3 per cent of the housing stock, while the remaining 97 per cent of the built-up city received just 60 per cent. An examination of the city's recent budgets confirms the strong suburban bias in council's spending patterns. Unfortunately, the only component that is disaggregated on a geographic basis is the culture and recreation component, but even this one area is suggestive. In 1980, although the inner city comprised 36 per cent of the city's permanent population and considerably more when the daytime work-force is included, it received only 17.4 per cent of council's $15.5 million allocation for culture and recreation.[60]

Such suburban dictation of the priorities of the urban region has characterized Winnipeg politics for decades, and structural reforms have failed to lessen it.[61] Recently, however, there have been strong indications that council's historic neglect of the core area may be ending. If so, it will mark the most significant shift in the political system in years, although the origins of such changes are totally unrelated to structural reform.

There are two principal indications that the interests of core-area residents may finally be accorded greater primacy. The first is the nature and orientation of the city's new general development plan. That plan, which has been under provincial-municipal study for some time, has as its major focus the regeneration of the core area after years of preoccupation with suburban growth.

At one point the plan states unequivocally: 'The major issue to be faced within the context of long-range development planning has become: what is the most effective strategy for encouraging the maintenance and revitalization of older, established neighbourhoods?'[62] The emphasis is on containing suburban growth and on redirecting resources towards the revitalization of the core area. The plan would effectuate a quantum shift in local government priorities.

The low status of such general planning documents generally confines their ultimate effect to the realm of rhetoric. However, even a rhetorical commitment to the rejuvenation of the inner city is unprecedented in Winnipeg politics and is of a certain symbolic value. Moreover, there has emerged a second and far more tangible expression of council's willingness to confront the pathology of the inner city. In the summer of 1981, council signed an agreement with the provincial and federal governments that calls for the expenditure of over $96 million in Winnipeg's core area over a five-year period.

This undertaking, the Core Area Initiative, subsumes a complex of interrelated programs aimed at the social, economic, and physical revitalization of the inner city. It includes $10 million for job training and employment programs geared to the special needs of disadvantaged core-area residents, as well as nearly $18 million for housing rehabilitation and the construction and improvement of related community infrastructure.[63] The city's contribution will be $32 million. How could a council with a power base and spending priorities firmly embedded in suburbia be induced to adopt a development plan with a focus on the inner city and then agree to spend an additional $32 million there?[64]

This shift in the political centre of gravity of council was entirely unaccompanied by institutional reform and is totally unrelated to it. Instead, it has its genesis in two complementary developments within the Winnipeg political system in 1980. The first and most obvious was the end of the hegemony of the ICEC. The 1980 election marked what may prove to be a watershed: for the first time the ICEC failed to gain a majority, winning only twelve of twenty-nine seats. Its chief rival, the municipal wing of the NDP, increased its standing to seven seats, and nine independents were elected.[65]

There were several reasons for the ICEC's electoral reverse, but most stem from the successful efforts of its critics to strip away the group's facade of apolitical neutrality. A number of writers had mounted increasingly strident attacks on the ICEC, penetrating its anti-partisan veneer and drawing explicit linkages between the group's actions and the protection of privilege and of business and development interests.[66] Other, less conspiratorial critiques contented themselves with indicting the group's apparent lack of leadership and policy direction.[67] In addition, several ICEC councillors had become involved in minor but damaging conflict-of-interest scandals. The cumulative effect of this was to erode public confidence in the ICEC, with a resulting loss of the group's majority.

It is important, however, not to overstate the impact of the ICEC's relatively poor showing in the 1980 election. A superficial examination of the results indicates a marked lessening of the ICEC's monopoly, but the balance of power appeared to be held by the heterogeneous cluster of self-styled 'Independents,' only two of whom represent any kind of challenge to the traditional ICEC priorities. Of the five independents who served on the previous council, four voted regularly with the majority. Indeed, two of them supported ICEC motions more consistently than most ICEC members![68] Moreover, even the improved showing of the NDP represents somewhat less of a challenge than might be supposed. While the NDP was able to parlay its seven inner-city seats into a greater concern by council with the problems of the city's core area, its differences of political philosophy with the ICEC are surprisingly slight. The NDP municipal caucus was a remarkably right-wing group to be campaigning in 1980 under the standard of a social democratic party, much less to be the heirs of a series of labour coalitions dating back to the General Strike. The views of a number of veteran NDP councillors on such issues as rates of welfare payment, the legitimacy of local government intervention in the housing market, and citizen participation are similar to those of the ICEC faction, despite official policies to the contrary. Thus, superficial shifts away from ICEC candidates do not in themselves signal an imminent departure from the kinds of priorities that have characterized council.

The second recent shift in Winnipeg politics, though more subtle than the first, may ultimately have a far more profound impact on the local political calculus. As early as 1979 it was possible to discern a substantial change within the internal dynamic of the ICEC itself, a shift that has heralded the ascendancy of an entirely new breed of ICEC politician. In anticipation of what it correctly saw as a strong NDP challenge in 1980, the ICEC began a concerted campaign to improve its public image. Party strategists saw that it was imperative for the group to project at least the appearance of greater progressiveness. Accordingly, a number of young, talented, and distinctly more liberal candidates were recruited. Several won by-elections in 1979 and immediately began to make their presence felt both within caucus and on council. Indeed, the ICEC strategists may yet come to regret their recruitment; several have begun reordering the ICEC's priorities.[69] Their views represent an increasingly successful challenge to the previously dominant conservative element within the ICEC. There is compelling evidence that the presence of this new liberalizing force will permanently alter the ICEC's adherence to a minimalist and fundamentally anti-political interpretation of local government. The influence of the new group is clearly discernible in council's support for both the new development plan and the Core Area Initiative. In addition, the group was instrumental in a recent council decision to reactivate its dormant non-profit housing corporation.[70] The corporation had successfully been opposed by a faction on council led by hard-line conservative (and suburban) ICEC councillors. Whatever the future fortunes of the ICEC vis-à-vis other political groupings on council, the internal changes seem certain to presage a new era in Winnipeg politics.

Such changes in policy may not be the only significant consequence of this transformation. There exists at least the possibility that they may lead to the restoration of class politics in Winnipeg. The ICEC repressed and denied the class content of local politics.[71] However, the recent emergence of an embryonic progressive faction within the ICEC may revive class politics. While none of these new 'progressives' brings anything approaching an explicit class analysis to bear on local issues, their efforts are a critical first step in the reconstruction of a political epistemology of urban politics – the recasting of urban issues in political rather than technocratic idioms.

To begin with, the progressives have quarrelled openly with the ICEC's historic insistence that local government is apolitical. The destruction of this myth is essential to a reinterpretation of local governance along political lines.[72] Such an interpretation would commence with the proposition that even traditional activities such as building bridges and roads have differential distributional impacts. Their costs and benefits are seldom distributed uniformly, and generally the same groups end up as victims and beneficiaries respectively. By piercing the ICEC's facade of impartiality, the progressives have made possible a re-evaluation of the delivery of even the traditional municipal services according to their distributional, i.e. political impact.

The progressives have successfully advocated the reform and democratization of the ICEC's internal process of selecting candidates. ICEC candidates had always been picked by a small coterie of virtually anonymous party strategists. A non-partisan ideology made such a system virtually inevitable; since the group denied its party status, it could hardly have membership lists, nominating conventions, and the other trappings of partisan life. However, public criticism was mounting against what was seen as a clandestine, élitist process of recruiting. In response to this and to reinforce their efforts to politicize and render more accountable their own party and local politics, the progressives have introduced potentially revolutionary changes to the selection process. The ICEC has agreed to promote and sell party memberships and to select its candidates at open, public meetings through an apparently unrestricted franchise. In two recent suburban by-elections, however, the two ICEC candidates displayed priorities entirely consistent with the party's conservative wing. This may be less an indictment of the new process than simply a reflection of the upper-middle-class suburban ridings in which the elections were held. Reforms in the ICEC may ultimately have a profound impact on the breadth and nature of its political base, on its public accountability, and, as a consequence of these, on its policy.

Moreover, as a direct result of the progressives' efforts, the ICEC will probably concern itself with an ever-broader range of issues. The progressives have broadened both the ICEC's and council's perceptions of the responsibilities of local government to include the alleviation of disparity in the city's core area through municipal provision of low-income housing and a number of job-creation and training programs. These interventions are more controversial than the traditional municipal activities and promise to accelerate the repoliticization of local government in Winnipeg.

CONCLUSION

It has been argued throughout this article that, despite the claims of its proponents, the institutional reform of Winnipeg's local government failed to produce discernible changes in policy or in politicization. The most significant recent developments in Winnipeg city politics resulted from changes within the internal dynamic of its political and ideological *substructure*.

One might conclude that the reforms were too modest to permit a valid test of the efficacy of structural reform. Certainly the Winnipeg reforms were timid, but on the evidence of Winnipeg's experience, institutional reform may well be intrinsically incapable of producing major political change.

Winnipeg in 1971 had a favourable climate for reform. The NDP had just won a stunning majority in the province, having campaigned on a platform that included the reorganization and politicization of local government. Its appetite for reform had not yet been blunted by lengthy tenure. There was considerable public dissatisfaction with Winnipeg's local government structure, with a correspondingly strong consensus for change. That even in such an environment the reforms had so little impact challenges the usefulness of institutional reform as an agent for change. Such scepticism has two basic causes.

The first can be inferred directly from the bankruptcy of the reforms themselves. That reforms undertaken in such a favourable climate were so timourous suggests that reform efforts in other Canadian cities might well be more modest still. Factors inherent in the Canadian political culture make reforms more radical than those attempted in Winnipeg virtually unthinkable. Undoubtedly, the most fundamental factor stems from the situation of the entire Canadian political system within an overwhelmingly capitalistic set of economic, social, and property relations. More specifically, and closely related, class politics has failed at all three levels of government in Canada. Together, these factors place any truly radical reforms (those that would, for example, alter the balance of class forces or redistribute wealth) well beyond the pale. The same applies to even more modest efforts to politicize local government. The history of Canadian local government, including that of Winnipeg, bears ample testimony to public resistance to even the introduction of party politics. The ethos of anti-partisanship dies extremely hard – if it can be induced to die at all. If one were to attempt to go further and graft a truly decentralized, participatory system onto the existing representative one, there is every indication that neither the general public nor their local politicians would accept it. For the dominant ideologies of local government, and indeed of governance generally in Canada, confer legitimacy only on conventional electoral politics, which are ultimately incompatible with a truly participatory system. It is virtually inconceivable that there could ever be the consensus in a provincial cabinet to pass legislation sufficiently radical to have even the potential of effecting major change in local politics.

Secondly, even were this not the case, there would remain the obstacles posed by the limitations of institutional reform itself. Winnipeg's experience demonstrates very clearly the inability of purely institutional changes to modify the behaviour of individuals philosophically disinclined to accede to them. As a result, the most significant developments in the local political system tend to originate in processes entirely unrelated to the reform of its institutional superstructures. Instead, these developments are rooted in the internal dynamic of local politics and, ultimately, at the level of ideological change. In Winnipeg, perhaps the most consistent single generator of political change has been the conflict between the political and anti-political ideologies of local government. Indeed, so powerful has been its influence that it has determined the course of institutional reform rather than vice versa. Given our previous contention that contextual factors forbid reforms more radical than those attempted in Winnipeg, this relationship is not likely to change.

Thus, it is highly unlikely that reforms any more radical than Winnipeg's will occur, and even if they did, their capacity to change the behaviour of actors wedded to contrary ideological notions seems virtually non-existent.[73] For this reason, those who seek to produce truly significant change in Canadian local government would do well to raise their sights beyond tinkering with its institutional superstructures. The latter will only be capable of producing reform if preceded by major changes in the internal dynamic or ideological substructure of local government. It is here that change, if it is to occur at all, must begin.

SUGGESTED FURTHER READING

Artibise, Alan *Winnipeg: A Social History of Urban Growth, 1874–1914* Montreal 1975

– 'Divided City: The Immigrant in Winnipeg Society, 1874–1921' in G. Stelter and Alan Artibise ed *The Canadian City* Toronto 1977

Axworthy, Lloyd 'A Test for Institutional Innovation: Winnipeg's Unicity' Institute of Urban Studies, Winnipeg, mimeo, 1976

Axworthy, Lloyd, and Jim Cassidy *Unicity: The Transition* Winnipeg 1974

Brownstone, Meyer et al *Politics and the Process of Reform of Urban Government: The Winnipeg Experience* Ottawa 1975

Committee of Review, City of Winnipeg Act (Taraska Committee) *Report and Recommendations* Winnipeg 1976

Community Planning Association of Canada *Unicity: A Preliminary Study of Formally Structured Citizen Participation*. Winnipeg 1974

Cook, Gail, and Lionel Feldman 'Approaches to Local Government Reform in Canada: The Case of Winnipeg' *Canadian Tax Journal* XIX 3 (May–June 1971) 216–25

Government of Manitoba *Proposals for Urban Re-organization in the Greater Winnipeg Area* (white paper) Winnipeg 1970

Government of Manitoba, Department of Urban Affairs *Background Paper on the Operation of the City of Winnipeg Act, Community Committee and Residents' Advisory Group Sections* Winnipeg 1975

Kiernan, Matthew 'The Fallacy of Planning Law Reform' *Urban Law and Policy* V (1982) 173–215

– 'Ideology and the Precarious Future of the Canadian Planning Profession,' *Plan Canada* XXII 1 (March 1982)

Levin, Earl 'Problems of Planning in the Metropolitan Framework' mimeo, 1968

Lightbody, James 'Electoral Reform in Local Government: The Case of Winnipeg' *Canadian Journal of Political Science* XI 2 (June 1978) 307–32

– 'The Reform of a Metropolitan Government: The Case of Winnipeg, 1971' *Canadian Public Policy* IV 4 (autumn 1978) 489–504

Lorimer, James et al 'Reform Politics in Winnipeg: Opening Things up' *City Magazine* I 3 (February–March 1975) 28–36

Morton, W.L. *Manitoba: A History* Toronto 1957

Newman, David 'Citizen Participation through Community Committees: The Winnipeg Experience' paper presented to the annual meeting of the Canadian Bar Association, Quebec City, August 1975

Rea, J.E. *Parties and Power: An Analysis of the Winnipeg City Council 1919–1975* appendix IV to the Taraska report (Winnipeg 1976)

Walker, David C. *The Great Winnipeg Dream* Oakville, Ontario, 1979

Wichern, Philip 'An Election Unlike – and Very Much Like – the Others' *City Magazine* III 4, 5 (May–June 1978) 20–9

– 'Patterns of Public Participation in Canadian Urban Policy-making: The Case of Winnipeg's Residents' Advisory Groups' paper presented to a meeting of the Atlantic Provinces Political Science Association, Antigonish, Nova Scotia, October 1975

NOTES

1 See, for example, Norman Penner ed *Winnipeg 1919: The Strikers' Own History of the Winnipeg General Strike* (Toronto 1973), Tom Peterson 'Manitoba Ethnic and Class Politics' in Martin Robin ed *Canadian Provincial Politics* (Scarborough 1978) 61–119, and J.E. Rea *Parties and Power: An Analysis of Winnipeg City Council, 1919–1975* appendix IV to the 1976 report of the (Taraska) Committee of Review, City of Winnipeg Act (Winnipeg 1976). For a more recent analysis that draws similar conclusions, consult James Lightbody 'Electoral Reform in Local Government: The Case of Winnipeg' *Canadian Journal of Political Science* XI 2 (June 1978) 307–32.

2 Consult the Appendix for a detailed demographic profile of Winnipeg's population. Moreover, it should be borne in mind that the census data understate the city's ethnic diversity. Not fully reflected in the census statistics is the more recent influx of both native people migrating from rural Manitoba and of Asian immigrant groups. In addition, the census figures over-represent the proportion of anglophones – many of the original ethnic migrant groups have now assimilated (at least in language) after two generations.

3 Derek Hum 'The Future Economic Prospects of Winnipeg: An Analytical Speculation' in Tony J. Kuz ed *Winnipeg 1874–1974: Progress and Prospects* (Winnipeg 1974) 239, 240 and David C. Walker *The Great Winnipeg Dream* (Oakville, Ontario, 1979) chap 1

4 For a much fuller discussion of the multiplicity of factors responsible for Winnipeg's economic decline, consult Kuz *Winnipeg: Progress and Prospects*.

5 Winnipeg Tri-level Committee on Urban Affairs *Economic Base Study* a background technical report to the Winnipeg Development Plan Review (Winnipeg 1978) 64

6 Ibid 59

7 Ibid 63

8 Ibid 103

9 Exploratory Sub-committee on the Organization of Local Government Service in the Greater Winnipeg Area (*Manitoba Provincial-Municipal Committee Report* (Winnipeg 1953) 83

10 For a more detailed account of this period, consult Meyer Brownstone et al *Politics and the Process of Reform of Urban Government: The Winnipeg Experience* (Ottawa 1975) 22–9. The book provides an insightful, insiders'

account of the Unicity experiment by the four consultants who designed the new structure of local government at the invitation of the provincial cabinet.

11 We use the term 'substructure' throughout this essay to refer to that constellation of political and ideological thought and activity that invariably underpins the urban polity but that does not necessarily (and indeed usually does not) have analogues in the formal institutional 'superstructure' of local government, for example, in its council or committee structure.

12 Although extensive, Metro's planning powers were severely compromised in at least two respects. First, the lower-tier municipalities retained most of the development powers in fields such as housing. Without such developmental powers, regional plans (such as Metro's ill-fated downtown plan) became meaningless. Second, even in areas where Metro did have development powers, the lower-tier municipalities could prevent regional plans by withholding minor but essential approval for items such as sewer connections.

13 On this point see James Lightbody 'The Reform of a Metropolitan Government: The Case of Winnipeg, 1971' *Canadian Public Policy* IV 4 (autumn 1978) and Brownstone et al *Politics and the Process of Reform*.

14 E.C. Banfield and James Q. Wilson *City Politics* (Cambridge 1966) 20

15 The most prominent of these was the Zoning Board of Adjustment, composed entirely of appointed members. While ostensibly limited in its mandate to approving small exemptions from the provisions of zoning by-laws, the board enjoyed such sweeping powers that it exercised a virtually legislative function with respect to land use. Unfortunately, the board lacked the public accountability normally and properly associated with such powers.

16 For an analysis of both the genesis and the indifferent results of the NDP's policy on municipal tax equity, consult James Lightbody 'The Reform of a Metropolitan Government.' For a detailed discussion of the nature and ultimate emasculation of the new planning powers, see Matthew Kiernan 'The Fallacy of Planning Law Reform' *Urban Law and Policy* V (1982) 173–215.

17 Interview with Saul Cherniack (minister of urban affairs at the time of the Unicity legislation), Winnipeg, 15 January 1980, and discussions with Professors Meyer Brownstone and Dennis Hefferon, two of his key advisers.

18 See, for example, T.J. Plunkett 'Structural Reform of Local Government in Canada,' and four studies by Lloyd Axworthy: *The Future City* (Winnipeg 1971), 'The Best Laid Plans Oft Go Astray: The Case of Winnipeg' paper presented to a conference on alternative forms of urban government, Banff, Alberta, 10 May 1974, 'A Test for Institutional Innovation: Winnipeg's Unicity' unpublished 1976, and 'Winnipeg: An Experiment In Innovation' *Canadian Forum* (May–June 1972) 31–5. This flattering view of the Unicity experiment is not restricted to external commentators; the consultants who advised the

Manitoba government also shared this understanding. See Brownstone et al *Politics and the Process of Reform* 217–19.

19 Memorandum from Meyer Brownstone to provincial cabinet committee, 3 June 1970, quoted in Brownstone et al *Politics and the Process of Reform*

20 13, 14, 24

21 Saul Cherniack in Legislative Assembly of Manitoba *Debates and Proceedings* 3 June 1971, 1464–5

22 City of Winnipeg Act *Statutes of Manitoba* 1971 chap 105 sec 21

23 See, for example, Institute of Urban Studies *Meeting the Problems and Needs of Resident Advisory Groups* (Winnipeg 1873), Axworthy 'An Experiment in Innovation,' and Community Planning Association of Canada *Unicity: A Preliminary Study of Formally Structured Citizen Participation* (Winnipeg 1974).

24 See, for example, the interview with Saul Cherniack in the *Winnipeg Free Press* 12 January 1971. His interpretation has been at least partially endorsed by Lightbody; see Lightbody 'The Reform of a Metropolitan Government' 489–504.

25 The 1960s had seen incessant conflict between Mayor Juba and the senior Metro tier as the two levels of government struggled for control. Such was Juba's mastery of the media, however, that Metro was consistently vilified as the cause of any problems. As a result, there was considerable public support for the abolition of the Metro system. The NDP was able to exploit that support to bring about a newly unified city government, and Juba became its first mayor. For an excellent account of the public debate preceding the passage of the Unicity legislation, consult Brownstone et al *Powitics and theProcess of Reform* 35–9

26 On this point, see Matthew Kiernan 'Ideology and the Precarious Future of the Canadian Planning Profession' *Plan Canada* XXII 1 (March 1982) 14–24.

27 See Lightbody 'The Reform of a Metropolitan Government' 493–503, Department of Environmental Planning, City of Winnipeg *Suburban Growth and the 1978 Capital Estimates* mimeo, February 1978, and Kiernan 'The Fallacy of Planning Law Reform.' We shall return to this point later.

28 See n 18 above. James Lorimer was one of the consultants advising the cabinet on the amalgamation plan, but his proposals were rejected as excessively radical and he left the group. In a subsequent series of newspaper articles he criticized the Unicity legislation sharply for what he perceived to be its grossly inadequate devolution of power to the neighbourhood level.

29 Brownstone et al *Politics and the Process of Reform* 193

30 The original City of Winnipeg Act sec 22(1)

31 *Statutes* 1971 chap 105 sec 22(6) (as amended)

32 City of Winnipeg Act sec 621

33 For a detailed account of the cabinet deliberations from the consultants who were direct participants in them, see Brownstone et al *Politics and the Process of Reform* especially 63–8.
34 Ibid 67, 196 (emphasis added)
35 This debate is one of the most central and persistent in the literature on Canadian urban politics. Supporting the contention that the structures of local government determine political outcomes are such traditional scholars as Rowat and Plunkett. Their perspective has more recently received support from contributions by Higgins and, in an indirect way, Lightbody. The writers of the Canadian 'reform' group, led by James Lorimer, have argued that what is important is the ideologies and interests of the actors who control the structures.
36 For an excellent account of the history of the ICEC, consult Rea *Parties and Power*.
37 *Winnipeg Free Press* 2 October 1971, 17
38 Ibid 5 October 1974, 7
39 The process by which the ICEC and its precursors ensured the primacy of business interests has been extensively documented and lucidly described by Rea. For an account of the extent to which these values continue to dominate the ICEC, see Kiernan 'The Fallacy of Planning Law Reform.'
40 From 1971 to 1980, the ICEC occupied all but one seat on the powerful Executive Policy Committee and had strong majorities on all of its standing committees.
41 Rea *Parties and Power* 23
42 Council minutes, 7 January 1976, 274
43 All six RAG chairpersons were interviewed by the author between June and August 1980. As the weakness of the RAGS' position has become apparent, the dynamic, occasionally confrontationist RAG leaders of the early 1970s have dropped out and have largely been replaced by more conservative individuals with more modest expectations of the local government system.
44 Committee of Review, City of Winnipeg Act (Taraska committee) *Report and Recommendations* 16–19 (hereafter Taraska report)
45 Ibid 55–60, 134. The Taraska committee evidently assumed that structural changes could transform the behaviour of the system.
46 This is not currently the case in Winnipeg politics. Largely because of the dominance of Juba for more than twenty years, the ICEC has never advanced a mayoralty candidate. The current mayor, William Norrie, dropped his previous ICEC affiliation when he contested the mayoralty in an apparent recognition of the lingering strength of the anti-partisan ideology in Winnipeg.
47 Taraska report 136

48 The Taraska committee had recommended a reduction in both the size of council and the number of community committees and RAGs. These recommendations are curious, given the committee's otherwise pervasive concern with political sensitivity and accountability and run counter to the general tenor of its report.

49 Another consequence of this structural modification was a further decline in class politics. The new, larger wards tended to submerge minority, working-class, and ethnic candidates who had fared much better under the system of smaller, more homogeneous wards.

50 While purely quantitative indices are of limited use, and while the 1977 amendments are by no means the only relevant factor, attendance at the annual community conferences where the RAGs are chosen declined from 4,500 in 1972 to less than 300 in 1979. For a qualitative assessment of the performance of the RAG system in the area of urban planning, see Kiernan 'The Fallacy of Planning Law Reform.'

51 A number of neo-Marxist writers have emphasized the bankruptcy and duplicitousness of electoral politics, arguing that it serves simply to distract public attention from the impotence and subservience of the entire formal political system to non-elected, capitalist interests. See, for example, Jurgen Habermas *Legitimation Crisis* (Boston 1975).

52 Institute of Urban Studies *Housing: Inner City Type Older Areas* (Winnipeg 1979) 6

53 Institute of Urban Studies *Core Area Report: A Reassessment Of Conditions In The Inner City* (Winnipeg 1979) 53

54 Institute of Urban Studies *Housing: Inner City Type Older Areas* iii

55 Social Planning Council *An Analysis of Social Problems, Needs, and Trends for Winnipeg* (Winnipeg 1980) 55 (emphasis added)

56 That the problem of socio-economic disparities was of great concern to the consultants is evident from their own account of the Unicity experience. See Brownstone et al *Politics and the Process of Reform* 299. That the provincial cabinet shared this concern is indicated in the white paper at 5.

57 On this point see Lightbody 'The Reform of a Municipal Government.'

58 Department of Environmental Planning 'Suburban Growth and the 1978 Capital Estimates' mimeo, February 1978

59 Figures from the current files of the Department of Environmental Planning, Research Branch

60 City of Winnipeg *Current Estimates, 1980*

61 On this point see Rea *Parties and Power* passim, Kiernan 'The Fallacy of Planning Law Reform,' and Lightbody 'The Reform of a Municipal Government.'

62 City of Winnipeg *Plan Winnipeg: Final Report and Recommendations of the Study Team* (Winnipeg 1980) EP6 (emphasis added)

63 *Canada-Manitoba-Winnipeg Tri-partite Agreement for the Winnipeg Core Area* agreement signed 3 September 1981. The author, Matthew Kiernan, is assistant general manager of the Core Area Initiative.

64 The city's share of the Core Area Initiative represents incremental funds over and above those normally spent in the inner city. The Initiative represents a shift not only in council's geographic focus, but in its substantive one as well. The Initiative will involve council in many innovative social programs, most of which lie well beyond its traditional interpretation of its mandate.

65 The remaining seat was won by Joe Zuken, a long-time Labour Election Committee (Communist) alderman.

66 See, for example, James Lorimer 'Reform Politics in Winnipeg: Opening Things up' *City Magazine* III (February–March 1975) 28–36, Rea *Parties and Power*, David C. Walker *The Great Winnipeg Dream*, and Philip Wichern 'An Election Unlike – and Very Much Like – the Others' *City Magazine* III 4, 5 (May–June 1978) 20–9.

67 The most coherent and sustained criticism can be found in the Taraska report.

68 The two independents displaying the greatest solidarity with the ICEC were councillors Ragsdill and Rizutto, who supported the ICEC majority 79 per cent and 77 per cent of the time, respectively. Only three ICEC members supported their own caucus more consistently. See Jon Fedorowicz 'An Analysis of 57 Non-Procedural Votes Taken between November 1978 and November 1979' MA paper in political studies, University of Manitoba, March 1980.

69 Perhaps the most conspicuous example of this trend was the ICEC's recruitment and the subsequent election of Bill Neville. A professor of political science, Neville's positions on issues ranging from historic buildings to welfare rates exhibit a marked departure from the conservatism of the ICEC. Other members of this emerging liberal rump within the ICEC include councillors Harold MacDonald, a minister, and Larry Fleisher, an executive of a social service agency.

70 Council minutes, 5 December 1979

71 The ICEC's precursors had been much more explicit. For example, in 1948 the Greater Winnipeg Election Committee admonished the voter to 'Guard your liberty! Don't let Communists and Party Politicians run our city. Elect independent candidates' (*Winnipeg Free Press* 23 October 1948, 8). The ICEC perpetuated this denunciation of partisan politics, but abandoned the crude attempts of its predecessors to equate partisanship with Communism in favour of more subtle but no less effective strategies.

72 For an amplification of this point, consult Kiernan 'Ideology and the Precarious Future of the Canadian Planning Profession.'

73 For an amplification on this point, consult Kiernan 'The Fallacy of Planning Law Reform.'

JAMES LIGHTBODY

Edmonton

Edmonton is a solid bourgeois city. For the greater part of the twentieth century its commercial community has discreetly directed civic affairs. While this exercise of influence has been quite unlike the crude control displayed by the business sector in Winnipeg, it has been none the less effective. There have not been many successful competitors in Edmonton politics; since the Second World War, the municipal arena has not witnessed any significant clash of ideologies. Perhaps the city's motto, adopted in 1949, best defines the ethos: 'Industry, Integrity, Progress.' It must be conceded, however, that in the 1970s neighbourhood reaction to metropolitan freeway designs did spawn active interest in an alternative direction for civic policy and some measure of electoral competition for the business interest coalition.

Edmonton is also very much a twentieth-century city. Until the general urbanization impelled by the Second World War it was, despite pretensions, essentially a very small city. Social and civic life were dominated by an Anglo-Ontarian élite until the 1950s. Civic institutions had been strongly influenced by the American municipal reform movement, best summarized by the twin phrases of 'municipal management' and 'civic non-partisanship.' The city has been organized along council-commission lines since its incorporation. Its politics has been affected as well by the general environment of western Canada, and it is not surprising that Alberta's political culture and partisan, personal rivalries have played a role in Edmonton. While the city's institutions were depoliticized early, the anti-party feelings afoot in the province during the 1930s firmly reinforced local non-partisanship. More broadly, of course, national and international events, political and economic, have had a direct impact upon the city's growth and the nature of local political demands.

These several themes may conveniently be considered by dividing the city's political history into two eras, with the Second World War marking the watershed.

FOUNDATIONS: 1795–1946

As with other Prairie cities, Edmonton's origins lay in the fur trade. In 1795, the Northwest Company and the Hudson's Bay Company established competing posts – Forts Augustus and Edmonton – on the North Saskatchewan River about thirty kilometres from the present core city. With advantageous access to the Yellowhead pass, both posts flourished and were rebuilt on Edmonton's present location in 1802. The settlements were abandoned in 1810 in the belief that the Blackfoot Indians intended to burn them to the ground. Once the posts were abandoned they did. But by 1819 both companies were ensconced within a common stockade at the heart of the present city. The disappearance of the Hudson's Bay's rival in 1821 not only ensured its monopoly commercial position, but also some seventy years as Edmonton's dominant actor, until the arrival of the Canadian Pacific Railway in 1891.[1]

Edmonton stood at the centre of the company's northwest trading empire but, as late as 1867, its permanent population still hovered about 150. Such local administration as was necessary was at the discretion of the company's chief factor whose concerns were more usually focused upon the security of the settlement, American penetration of the northwest, and the regulation of spirits. The cession of Rupert's Land to the new Dominion of Canada marks the beginnings of the Edmonton settlement, for it was not until the 1870s that substantial dwellings were erected beyond the confines of the fort. The cession agreement also permitted the company to retain 3,000 acres surrounding each post, easily making it the most significant land-owner. In December 1880, Frank Oliver launched the settlement's first newspaper, the *Bulletin*, and by this time the community's indigenous commercial establishment, based on timber, coal, and small-scale agriculture, had started to develop.[2]

In anticipation of the arrival of the CPR spur line from Calgary which was begun in 1890, and in sudden realization that the railway company had bought land on the south side of the North Saskatchewan to create a rival South Edmonton community around its terminus, members of Edmonton's board of trade moved quickly to incorporate their small village as a town. They had no wish to play Selkirk to South Edmonton's Winnipeg. Prior to incorporation, matters of municipal import had generally been resolved informally through open town meetings by what J.P. Day calls the 'old social elite.'[3] Despite CPR opposition, the incorporation was supported by the territorial legislature, which had been persuaded by the area's two members, Oliver (Liberal) and Dr H.C. Wilson (Conservative). The first town council, to be elected at large annually, was drawn essentially from the board of trade and was entirely Anglo-Ontarian in ethnic background: the mayor was Matt McCauley, a close political associate of Oliver.

J.P. Day well describes the issues of the period and the personality clashes associated with their resolution as the town struggled to establish basic services and to cope with the short-lived boom (1896–1900) of the Klondike gold rush and the bust of the 1890s recession. While he characterizes the various cliques as 'Professionals,' 'Populists,' and 'Commercials,' Day, with his wealth of detail, fails to bring home the fact that the business and professional community was generally in control and governing in its own interest. The major personality clashes were between Oliver's adherents and Wilson's. Opposition was sporadic and based on single issues.[4] (Alan Artibise is correct in his assessment that local decision-making was both relatively simple and controlled by a small, interlocking élite.[5]) Oliver's election to Parliament in 1896 ensured that Edmonton's business community was both in step with Laurier's new Liberal government and would have a powerful voice in shaping its policies.

The city's foremost citizens were unabashed boosters. Municipal government was to be run professionally on business principles, and, to ensure development to attract growth, the municipal leaders also pressed for municipal ownership of utilities. The city's private electrical company established in 1891 proved timid: it was bought out in 1904. Streetcars were seen to be a necessary adjunct of realty development. The city-owned telephone system, taken over in 1904, functioned like any other private concern. An ambitious waterworks and sewage system was initiated by by-law in 1902.[6] Edmonton became a major municipal corporation and its civic leaders finally brought the CPR across the river via a federally funded bridge.[7] The process culminated in 1904 when, by territorial charter, Edmonton was incorporated as a city, employing principles of government then being advocated in the United States by the National Municipal League. In short, the city was to be governed by a small six-member council plus the mayor and to be administered by two commissioners at the head of a professional public service.[8] Reflecting the spirit of the times, the franchise was given to male property-owners; those with property assessed at more than $100 also had voting rights in plebiscites on money by-laws.[9] Mayor Short thought that businessmen should run city hall, otherwise anyone could be chosen: 'the hail fellow, well met ... Or it may be that the trades unions' political party may place a man in the council irrespective of his fitness.'[10] In an expansionist era, all was in place to govern in an orderly and business-like fashion.

Edmonton's civic leaders had long resented the CPR decision to by-pass them in favour of Calgary, which had permitted the latter to develop an extensive commercial empire across the southwest part of the Northwest Territories. In 1891 Calgary's population was ten times Edmonton's. The long and sometimes bitter rivalry was still alive in the 1980s.[11] But in October 1904, Laurier promised that if he were re-elected he would bring provincial status to the West; he also promised to sustain the Grand Trunk Pacific Railway in its plans to build a trans-continental line across the northern Prairies. Laurier was returned and Frank Oliver was to become his minister of the interior. In the opening of the American west the move from territorial to state government had meant fierce competition among cities for the location of three institutions: the state capital, the state university, and the penitentiary. Almost without exception no centre gained all three. Edmonton's boosters wanted all three and, of course, the railroad main line. Booster Calgarians had similar designs but, unfortunately, their voters had returned an opposition member. Oliver's personal lobbying gained Edmonton the provisional capital site in the Autonomy Bill of 1905, and when he was handed the task of deciding upon the electoral divisions of the new province he also ensured a northern Alberta majority in the legislature, through the creative use of mathematics. The Alberta Act established Edmonton as capital until an order-in-council might decree otherwise. None ever did.[12] In 1906 the federal penitentiary was established on what is now the site of Clarke Stadium. On 6 April 1907, Premier Rutherford, a Liberal, announced that the University of Alberta would be located in his south-side city of Strathcona. Finally, in November 1905, the arrival of the CNR, following negotiations and the usual civic tax concessions and incentive grants ($100,000), had officially provided Edmonton its trans-continental link. Edmonton entered a spectacular boom era that was to last only until the crash of 1913.

Unrestrained growth appeared certain following revitalization of the lumber industry and the western policies of Laurier. Between 1901 and 1911 the city's population grew from 2,626 to 24,900; assessment rose from $1.3 million to $46.4 million. Capitalizing on the excitement, the Hudson's Bay Company subdivided half its reserve lands in 1912, announcing that it would hold a public lottery to permit 1,500 investors to buy four lots each.[13] Hucksterism was in the air, and minor municipal scandals normally associated with the extension of services surfaced periodically. In 1913, for instance,

Edmonton's most colourful populist, 'fighting Joe' Clarke, self-professed friend of the working man, defeated Mayor W.J. McNamara (accused of permitting police tolerance of widespread prostitution and gambling), in the process of which the antagonists brawled in council chambers. It was a fool's paradise; the long depression that began in 1913 did not loosen its grip until the Second World War and severely shook the city. None the less, until 1914, the civic mood was aggressively expansionist. The amalgamation, in 1912, with the city of Strathcona on the south side of the river[14] was only the most significant of a series of annexations and amalgamations with small suburbs that occurred until 1917 and increased the city's size from 7.17 square miles to 41.16.[15] The population peaked at 72,516 in 1914, declined to 51,000 in 1917, and did not reach pre-war levels again until 1929.[16] Property assessment rose from $1.3 million in 1901 to $188.5 million in 1913, and then plunged to $54 million in the heart of the Depression (1936): assessment did not again reach 1913 levels until the mid-1950s.[17] The value of building permits issued in 1912 ($14,447,000) was not equalled until 1948.

In the growth decade the municipal role in this 'St Louis of the north' was straightforward: it was to establish the infrastructure to facilitate growth. Between 1912 and 1914, for example, 'the mileage of paved streets had increased from five ... to thirty-five, while that of graded streets had grown from twenty-six to 181. The miles of sidewalk had doubled, to reach 140, while the length of water main had likewise doubled, to 128 miles.'[18] The pipe mileage would not again double until 1944.[19] The price of this expansion would have to be met in the troubled years ahead. Artibise observes that the per capita debenture debt of Edmonton in 1917 was $359, compared to $150 in Toronto and $96 in Ottawa.[20] The political struggles of the next three decades would most often centre upon the difficulties of servicing and reducing this debt while struggling to maintain at least the existing physical plant. Speculators would forfeit holdings rather than pay taxes. In its later attempt to explain Edmonton's heavy debt load in the 1950s, the McNally commission found that 'during the depression and war, little maintenance or capital work had been carried out, and city debt actually declined considerably. The [city] had to some extent run down, and a 'backlog' of deferred public works had accumulated which had to be cleared out of the way.'[21] In 1918, cumulative tax arrears amounted to $8 million;[22] during the 1920s, 43 per cent of the city's area reverted to the municipality for tax purposes.[23] These financial straits undoubtedly contributed to the civic administration's niggardly attitudes during the worst of the Depression.

Notwithstanding the desperate economic climate, it was during the inter-war period that Edmonton's mercantilists successfully developed a northern commercial empire and promoted the city as the 'gateway to the north.'[24] Three factors contributed to this role. Edmonton was the natural supply centre not only for its immediate agricultural hinterland but also, via rail, for the burgeoning Peace River country. As well, by 1924, Edmonton became the supplier to the Mackenzie River system with the Alberta Great Waterways rail link to Fort McMurray. The northern orientation was supported by council, which in 1929 voted the funds to develop the first licensed municipal airport in Canada (Blatchford field). In 1942, Edmonton became the operations base during construction of the Alaska highway and the Canol pipeline.[25] Finally, even the limited northern Alberta petroleum exploitation prior to Leduc in 1947, such as Imperial Oil's Fort Norman discovery in 1920, laid the groundwork for Edmonton's becoming one of the largest oilfield supply centres in Canada. The Viking natural gas field, proved in 1914, had become the city's major source of residential energy by 1924.

The city had entered the years of the First World War with a 'clean government' business council and ended them with the same labour strife that shook other Prairie cities. Capitalizing upon the situation was the indefatigable Joe Clarke,[26] who translated his labour sympathies and anti-eastern sentiments into the mayor's chair. Rising labour success, as represented by Clarke, sparked a resurgence of business interest in civic politics. The resultant mobilization of conservative interests produced the Citizens' Progressive League and Clarke's defeat in 1920 by D.M. Duggan, subsequently an MLA and provincial Conservative leader (1926–42). In the aftermath of these campaigns, Edmonton's municipal political system more or less congealed: the elections of 1922 produced a collective attempt by organized labour to capture city hall by campaigning against the other independent candidates. Its slate of four relatively conservative candidates[27] yielded two winners and a continuing labour minority on council until the election of 1928. This forced a resurgence of the good burghers, initially in the form of a revived Citizens' League and for the 1923 elections in the form of the Civic Government Association (CGA), which campaigned on slogans of 'sound business government' and representation 'of all classes of our citizens.' The north and east were predominantly labour; the south, central and west, CGA. The CGA retained a slim majority on council until 1929 and held the mayoralty until labour's smashing victory in 1931. The declining fortunes of the CGA initially reflected internecine divisions but, as the Depression worsened, the electorate clearly sought an alternative.

Labour held a majority in council in 1933–4. The pressure during these early years of the Depression was unrelenting: tax revenues declined while forfeitures rose, municipal services had to be reduced and the unemployed shipped out, senior levels were insensitive to municipal desperation, and even ambitious debt-financing schemes merely deferred the inevitable. The voters required a scapegoat, and labour complied. There was little alternative: 'There is not much scope for civic statesmanship when the consideration is how to make seventy-five cents do duty for a dollar.'[28] Internal conflict within the labour group on the issue of expansion versus retrenchment meant rival slates and severe defeat in 1934. Clarke was mayor once again, and the CGA (which narrowly lost the mayoralty by 400 votes) controlled the council.

Municipal elections since 1934 have revolved around the slate-making activities of the Citizens' Committee, the name of the CGA from 1936 to 1959.[29] Its executive, according to George Betts, included 'representatives of real estate and insurance, investment corporations, gas board directors and employees, an office equipment firm, meat packing, a tyre firm, iron and steel firm and countless lawyers.'[30] Almost all were members of the chamber of commerce. As we shall see, the success of the Citizens' Committee was staggering: from 1934 to 1960, 87.5 per cent of successful candidacies were on the slate. It was also, until the late 1940s, overwhelmingly British, as roughly 80 per cent of successful candidacies stemmed from this ethnic community.[31] Its first mayor, John W. Fry (mayor 1938–45), defeated Clarke by 3,000 votes in 1937, by 6,600 in 1938, and generally had no major electoral difficulty in succeeding elections.

Several unsuccessful attempts were made to dislodge the hegemony. In 1935, for example, the nascent Social Credit movement, at the instance of its advisory board (attempting to build a 'grass roots' movement), elected all three candidates it nominated, but, by then at the provincial controls, the movement failed to organize at the local level. In 1936 it lost all three nominated to the revitalized Citizen's Committee and, in 1937, gave up the municipal ghost with its members either supporting an umbrella coalition, the Progressive Civic Association (PCA) (1937–43), or campaigning as independents. The Citizens' Committee swept the field.[32] On the left, the Trades and Labour Congress of Canada in 1938 recommended 'neutrality in politics,' which policy was adopted by the Edmonton branch. But, in a 1942 provincial by-election in the city, party president Elmer Roper was successful as a CCF candidate, and a municipal foray seemed in order. To avoid a split in the 'progressive' vote, the CCF and the PCA agreed to run partial slates. The results were hardly encouraging; the Citizens' Committee never failed to gain a majority of the popular vote, and all its candidates but one were elected to council from 1942 to 1944. The Edmonton *Journal* was an implacable foe of the CCF, and at a September 1945 membership meeting it was determined that national and provincial priorities must necessarily command the party's first attention.[33] The CCF's sole successful alderman, the immensely popular H.D. Ainley, narrowly won the mayoralty in 1945 (by 1,850 votes) and consolidated his personal position in 1946 and 1947.[34] But his slate, the Civic Democratic Alliance (1945–7), elected only two aldermen in 1945 and none subsequently. Other sporadic challenges from the left, and from various sectional interests, were simply not successful.

But, in practical terms, it did not much matter. Declining assessment, tax defaults, and a crippling municipal debt left little scope for creative policy initiatives. Even labour, when in power, attempted little that would distinguish it from the CGA. As a result it too was burdened with blame for the municipal impact of the Depression. Edmonton's local government became a holding action until the Second World War.

The war initiated Edmonton's economic resurgence. A business-minded municipal government was firmly entrenched, the electorate was reasonably passive, and members of the city's ethnic minorities were beginning to crack the socio-political élite as they had the economic. During the Depression, councillors had tended to view unemployment as a temporary aberration to be dealt with best by stop-gap measures; Leduc Oil Well No. 1, on 13 February 1947, wrote 'paid' to those and other concerns.

GROWTH AND EXPANSION: 1947–80

Edmonton entered the post-war period as a small city of some 112,000 with an area of 25,845 acres. By 1981 its population had quadrupled to 515,800 and its size increased to just under 150,000 acres. This tremendous growth, spurred by the petroleum boom and the location of major refining and manufacturing plants in the Edmonton area, meant a number of things for civic government. A highly mobile and, in many instances, transient population weakened the community ties and established neighbourhood leadership, which in turn reinforced the commercial dominance of municipal politics through low electoral turn-outs and suffused issues. But the ethnic heterogeneity of the community increased to the point where the Anglo-Ontarian group was no longer the majority. Population changes led to a growing successful involvement in public affairs of non-Anglo citizens, most prominently William Hawrelak (mayor 1951–9, 1963–5, and 1974–5), whose policies typified the earlier part of this era. Efficient management, support for growth, and 'common sense' became the dominant themes for a generation of civic leaders.

Demand for development and the extension of city services thus met a generally sympathetic response from city politicians and the civic administration, both buttressed by a zealous booster press. Rapid city expansion and suburban developments complicated inter-municipal relations within the region, ultimately prompting reluctant provincial authorities to attempt metropolitan planning and land assembly schemes. The last and most dramatic chapter in these latter struggles was not written until June 1981.

This post-war era ought properly to be considered as two periods. After the war Edmonton could be considered the model of the American 'reformed' city, based upon the belief that there exists an objective public interest pertaining to the community as a whole. Government is then to provide 'the businesslike management of essential public services.'[35] The package, institutionally, required a small council, elected at-large, on a non-partisan basis. While this council of 'best-qualified citizens' devised 'policy,' the administration of that policy was entrusted to competent, trained professionals – ideally a city manager. Formal city planning became a key program plank around the time of the First World War. Edmonton conformed to this model until the end of the 1960s, when the political culture had evolved to permit more competitive elections and more widely participatory decision-making. While the watershed is imprecise, the policy controversies culminating in the 1974 elections may mark the break for our purposes here.

The Non-partisan Council

It would be hard to overstate the control of public decision-taking exercised by the Citizens' Committee and its several acronymic successors. Betts makes the essential point when he observes that for the period 1934–60, the committee 'never failed to have a majority of its candidates on the City Council or Public School Board.'[36] The committee proper held *all* council seats between 1945 and 1959. During this period the most dominant and colourful Citizens' Committee leader was Hawrelak. He had arrived in Edmonton in 1945, after having successfully managed the family farm through the Depression. Starting as proprietor of a bottling firm, he soon moved into real estate and was so successful that, at his death in 1975, his estate was valued at $14 million. After suffering defeat as a Citizens' Committee aldermanic candidate in 1948, he returned to politics the following year and this time was elected. He was mayor from 1951 to 1959, enjoying two acclamations. His resignation in 1959 followed a verdict of gross misconduct in a land deal with his brother-in-law. A dramatic public apology led to his re-election in 1963 and 1964, but once again questionable land dealings forced him from office. On this occasion he was ultimately cleared by the Supreme Court of Canada. His legal vindication led to a final successful mayoralty campaign in 1974, but a year later he died.[37] Although Hawrelak's entanglements with the law in the 1960s and 1970s caused much public controversy, his eight-year period in the 1950s at the head of a council made up solely of Citizens' Committee members was ultimately more significant.

Following Hawrelak's first departure in 1959, the Citizens' Committee splintered, with different sections choosing new names. The most prominent fragment reverted to the old pre-1963 label, the Civic Government Association (CGA). New names and new groups were invented with increasing regularity. By 1971 fragmentation had become so great that local parties effectively no longer existed. However, aldermen sharing a business orientation retained total domination of the council.[38] The disappearance of the CGA slate was due to several factors, not excluding atrophy. Hawrelak was no longer a credible organizational focus. Moreover, several stalwarts retired from the fray. Also, the provincial Conservative victory in August 1971 had pulled both candidates and organizational talent out of the civic arena: fully half the new council were rookies.

We may well ask how such domination over a generation of municipal politics was maintained. Not withstanding the political scientist's concerns with classifying 'pure' and 'adulterated' systems of non-partisanship,[39] the Citizens' Committee ran so well by claiming that it was not a party and by discrediting opposing slates for their party-like behaviour.[40] These activities certainly contained a subliminal appeal to the anti-party ethos underpinning the provincial system of the period and thus played to a sympathetic audience. Almost 60 per cent of Edmonton electors surveyed in 1968, for example, 'opposed having political parties in local elections in Edmonton.'[41] The facade of non-partisanship was reinforced by the pure cadre behaviour of the committee. Betts says: 'The original idea of CGA had been that it be strictly a non-partisan organization, active only around election time to persuade the best possible men to stand for civic office and to put the weight of an organization behind them.'[42] Given the absence of a visible, continuing party structure between elections, it was possible to maintain the myth of the non-party.

At the same time, and characteristically for business-oriented local slates in the West, the committee/association never presented a well-formulated policy program of its own. Typically the call was for the 'most efficient and progressive civic government possible,'[43] or 'dynamic growth for the city.'[44] In consequence Citizens' Committee aldermen were able to behave as independents without betraying the integrity of any platform; no consistency in voting blocs emerged. Such random behaviour is probable in municipal legislatures devoid of any significant ethnic or ideological cleavage that would serve to marshal allies consistently on issues of substance. Shifting votes on technical matters concerning the erection of a domed stadium are insignificant if no councillor raises the fundamental question of whether one is desirable at the expense of, say, a massive program of public housing.

In this type of arena public visibility is a must. Councillors have tended to accentuate their 'independence' and 'common sense' as a reliable vote-getting tactic. Incumbency has proven the most potent of political resources: for the period 1948–71 only four of eighty incumbents seeking re-election were denied at the polls.[45] Even in the three more competitive elections from 1974 to 1980, twenty-one of twenty-three incumbents who stood were re-elected. Community groups, normally operating at a disadvantage within an at-large electoral system, are further handicapped if little electoral pressure can be applied. After interviewing all councillors for the period 1964–7, Donald Blake concluded: 'The large majority of respondents admit that incumbency virtually guarantees re-election, making the currying of group favour apparently unnecessary.'[46] For this period, group 'pressure' ran counter to the norms capitalized upon by the Citizens' Committee.

The Citizens' Committee in its public policies ran the city as a business and in the interests of the business community. After the war municipal expenditures were disproportionately highly directed to public works rather than expanded social services.[47] The Citizens' Committee was never a large group: when founded in 1936 it comprised forty-one professionals and businessmen led by the president of the chamber of commerce, and at its nominating meeting in 1962 only twenty-seven members were present, including candidates.[48] Activities were structured by a small, business-oriented executive – most prominently William Hawrelak – with strong social and economic links to the leaders in the commercial world.[49] The latter were not forced to meddle directly in the sordid world of *realpolitik*; the gladiators in the Citizens' Committee and the CGA tended their best interests. As well, the Citizens' Committee never failed to accumulate sufficient resources to fight a respectable campaign since donations were subscribed by commercial firms not individual memberships.

The Citizens' Committee was also able to capitalize upon the overwhelming booster spirit of the period. Unbridled optimism fed upon the apparent absence of limits to either economic growth or the spatial expansion of the city. In his enthusiastic history of the city, J.G. MacGregor reflects this tone: 'As if to make up for the seventy years when time after time Edmonton's oil seekers suffered failure and frustration, now, month after month fate filled their flare lines with oil and gas. Edmontonians lived in a dream world. Every month brought some fresh discovery, and every month saw more drilling rigs and seismic trucks coming in.'[50] It was an era in which each successive year established a record for the value of building permits issued. William Hawrelak, returning to political prominence after his 1959 resignation, captured the mood in 1963 with his slogan – 'Keep Edmonton Rolling.'

But to cash in on the ethos, the Citizens' Committee needed a medium as well as a message. In this instance, the role of handmaiden fell to the *Edmonton Journal*. Unashamedly a booster press, the *Journal* suffered the happy good fortunes of monopoly for nearly thirty years following the collapse of the Edmonton *Bulletin* on 20 January 1951.[51] The *Journal* was very much a part of the civic system on which it reported and normally it endorsed the Citizens' Committee or its Civic Government successors.[52] Its penetration of the Edmonton market made it a formidable vehicle in the dissemination of politically relevant information: Gilsdorf's survey in 1968 indicates that '83 per cent of the respondents reported that they read the *Journal* every day.'[53] While the evidence is insufficient to 'prove' that the *Journal* was able to structure electoral choice, judging by results we can conclude with some certainty that the environment was scarcely conducive to the emergence of an effective challenge to the Citizens' Committee.

The Citizens' Committee maintained its dominant position through the successful co-opting of ethnic and political minorities. George Betts, in discussing the re-establishment of the Civic Government Association in 1960 out of the post-Hawrelak shambles of the Citizens' Committee, outlines the central philosophy: 'The CGA contained experienced people from different political parties. There was no reason why, although in different camps at the higher level, they should not pool their experience with campaigning and electioneering to win the election for the CGA by party techniques at the municipal level.'[54] Throughout the 1950s, the Citizens' Committee was extensively infiltrated by Liberals who employed their federal organization to advance municipal candidates, perhaps as a surrogate to realistic hopes elsewhere. None the less, there always appeared to be room on the slate for a few prominent Social Credit or Conservative devotees. In the 1960s the slate was expanded to provide support for a popular, but conservative, CCF mayor, businessman Elmer Roper. The city's largest ethnic minority was assiduously courted by the highly personalized politics of William Hawrelak who, it was frequently observed, was the first Ukrainian mayor of a major Canadian city. The Jewish and francophone communities were similarly and carefully represented within Hawrelak's personal network.

Why was Hawrelak so eminently electable? Quite apart from his amiable personality, Hawrelak was successful. As a tough and thriving entrepreneur his links to business were secure. He was a federal Liberal in a city with a Liberal tradition. He was a ward-heeler in the classic sense.[55] In short, he was the type of man his constituents aspired to be. Even when he lost the mayoralty in 1966 he received 55,544 votes and provoked the city's highest voter turn-out (59.2 per cent) since the Joe Clarke-CGA-labour campaign of 1934 (60.7 per cent).

Before considering the changes of the 1970s a question must be confronted: what more generalized conditions than these specific strategies and personalities permitted the ascendancy of the Citizens' Committee? Under what circumstances might we expect city politics to be premised upon the politically neutral concepts of business administration? There appear to be at least three.

First, there must exist a strongly embedded sense of non-partisanship or anti-partyism; whatever else they may do, parties *do* organize issues during elections and provide policy leadership between elections. As observed, these beliefs did exist locally, sustained as much by the anti-party myths underpinning the Social Credit movement as by the middle-class ethos of the civic political culture.

Secondly, there must also exist an environment in which social and economic cleavages are either disguised by an ubiquitous sense of social equality or are organized out of political prominence institutionally. Edmonton possessed both factors. The city's lowest-income sector has never been as concentrated and visible as in other similarly sized cities and, in the easy affluence of the 1950s and 1960s, was quietly overlooked. Additionally, the at-large electoral system muted the potential impact of such geographically focused cleavage as did exist; consequently, the voice of the city was that of the very small, middle-class proportion who turned out to vote.[56] In essence, Edmonton turned itself into a small, socially homogeneous suburb.

Third, there must exist an apparent high level of consensus about the desired objectives for the local political system, for under these circumstances political problems become essentially managerial ones. While it is not possible to document with certainty the extent of consensus, some circumstantial evidence might be drawn from recent, and controversial, plebiscites. In 1966, for example, 69.7 per cent of the electorate supported the Capilano freeway bridge across the North Saskatchewan.[57] Two years earlier the commission board had been requested by council to list those opposing the MacKinnon Ravine freeway: 'The commissioners responded with the names of three individuals and one community organization.'[58] Even as late as March 1974, citizens supported expenditures for Commonwealth Games facilities by a ratio of three to one. 'The issue,' editorialized the *Journal*, was simply this: 'does Edmonton want to take a forthright step forward?'[59]

In retrospect, the extent of consensus may have been more illusory than real and founded in political inefficacy rather than a complete satisfaction with the civic administration. None the less two factors worked to maintain the image. First, the civic political culture did not sustain a clearly defined, cohesive, countervailing local élite to provide leadership and expertise for challenges to the direction of city policy. Thus opposition tended to be sporadic, ill-defined, and issue-specific. For instance, probably the most contentious issue of the early 1960s was the implementation of a comprehensive zoning by-law for the city that was strenuously opposed by a variety of small developers and landholders.[60] Their pressure group, the Civic Rights Protection Association, contested the 1962 municipal election, received slightly over 7 per cent of the vote, and disappeared from the scene. Also short-lived were the Save Our Parks Committee (an anti-expressway group) of the late 1960s and the Edmonton Taxpayer's Association, which opposed the Commonwealth Games facilities in 1974. The CCF-NDP has not demonstrated any serious local interest since being crushed in the 1944 municipal election.

Second, there was an absence of sophisticated organization, co-ordination, and communication among local groups that might, in different circumstances, be logically expected to be in opposition to the general drift of city policy. For example, there was no equivalent in Edmonton to Toronto's Confederation of Resident and Ratepayer Associations. In Edmonton, the community leagues flooded the rinks. Edmonton's community leagues (the first was established in 1917; there are now more than 120) *have* provided the city an invaluable volunteer community recreational service over the years, but, except as a springboard for aldermanic aspirants, were not, until recently, a vital part of the political process. When Don Blake asked aldermanic incumbents about active interest groups in 1967 he found that 'business groups were mentioned most frequently (e.g., Chamber of Commerce, Retail Merchants Association), with 'single-purpose' groups (groups springing into action on specific issues such as fluoridation or bridge location, then disappearing when these issues are resolved) next ... Labour groups, recreational associations, and advisory groups (e.g., Edmonton Welfare Council) merited few responses.'[61] Although the Edmonton Federation of Community Leagues hovered on the fringe of issues such as the ward system, or the proposed downtown coliseum, it was not able to command the allegiance of its constituents who, in any case, were more concerned with the expansion of recreational services to their rapidly growing clientele. It was not until the late 1970s that the federation, and such bodies as the Edmonton Social Planning Council, were invited by a city council operating within a new political climate to participate in policy development such as the preparation and implementation of a new general plan for the city.[62]

The New Era: A Policy Challenge

The political atmosphere of Edmonton has evolved considerably during the last decade. The catalyst emerged with the development of a countervailing expertise with the competence to challenge the civic administration both technically and organizationally. The source of this challenge was an unintended consequence of the rapid expansion of the University of Alberta's faculty (which tripled in size) and the research staff at other agencies such as the Research Council of Alberta. By far the greatest number of recruits for these institutions were either American by birth or Canadians who had received their post-graduate education in the United States. They were not only highly qualified but had also been subject to the experience of major freeway systems, the critical attacks upon the 'concrete jungle' way of life, and the rhetoric of direct citizen participation then associated with the American war on poverty programs. In short, many were technically competent and ideologically prepared to provide leadership for whatever latent discontent did exist.

The initial focus for dissent was the Metropolitan Edmonton Transportation Study (METS), released in February 1964. The study proposed five new freeways to the core, six new bridges, and a downtown freeway loop. But it was a provincial statute that became the unintended catalyst for citizen opposition. The province now required that municipal applicants for conditional grants in support of transportation designs hold public hearings prior to approving a general transportation by-law. Hearings on the METS proposals served to spark a citizen revolt. In contrast to the three individuals opposed to the MacKinnon freeway in 1964, twenty-two groups or individuals remonstrated before the meeting in 1971 'which lasted through the late afternoon and resumed in the evening after a dinner break.'[63]

The citizen reaction sparked three changes in city politics. First, it forced an immediate rewriting of the transportation by-law, during the course of which some fifty-seven groups and individuals were heard; the public hearing lasted three days.[64] Second, it mobilized a vigorous anti-freeway lobby from among neighbourhoods likely to be most directly affected and from the community of experts outside the civic administration. The latter found a focus in the University's extension 'Practicum in Community Analysis,' which quickly became enmeshed in the transportation debates. The group produced a professional, and technically competent, critique of the METS scheme, including a much less rosy financial projection than had the commission board, and, importantly, proposed an alternative – light rail transit (LRT).[65] This report, combined with information leaked from within the civic bureaucracy, provided a basis for highly effective lobbying of council, largely co-ordinated by the practicum's convenor, Gerry Wright (ultimately elected to council on his third try in 1980). The revised transportation policy of 1973 de-emphasized expressways and permitted construction of an LRT system, the first line of which was opened in conjunction with the 1978 Commonwealth Games. While Leo is probably right to conclude that the response was 'less to the representations of citizens than to the financial stringencies which were already evident in the mid-1960s,'[66] he discounts too greatly the role of the citizen groups in publicizing the costs (social as well as economic) and forcing the issue by offering a viable alternative.

Third, municipal slates reappeared. Just as the Electors Action Movement (TEAM) in Vancouver grew out of upper-middle-class opposition to freeway and major development projects in 1968,[67] the Urban Reform Group of Edmonton (URGE) resulted from a coalition of groups opposed to the METS proposals. By 1974 URGE was committed to contesting municipal elections and to lobbying for a more humane and open municipal system. URGE has mounted coherent campaigns with modest success (see Table 1), emphasizing policies of 'citizen participation,' neighbourhood decentralization, and, generally, more cautious development. The activists now appear to be essentially progressive Liberals and conservative New Democrats. It is not a party of radicals. Don Higgins makes this relevant observation: 'So much depends on the *context* of the particular city. For example, it struck me that the four fairly clear progressives on Edmonton's city council ... would in the context of Toronto's city council most likely be of the soft-middle variety.'[68] Although William Hawrelak defeated incumbent mayor Ivor Dent decisively with 49.2 per cent of the votes to Dent's 20.6 per cent in 1974, the URGE candidates won two seats and the party's share of the popular vote has risen to 16 per cent in 1977 and 33 per cent in 1980. In no election has URGE yet advanced a mayoralty candidate. Its active presence in the 1977 election prompted an ineffective attempt to resurrect the CGA, in the form of a slate of four fairly conservative incumbents and five prospective colleagues: six were successful.[69] The group disappeared after the election. URGE, in contrast, has been reasonably successful, to the point where it can now legitimately claim some 1,000 members and a comprehensive urban policy package from a centrist-left perspective.[70] In several important instances, URGE has fulfilled an innovative function for the system as issues they have espoused gain currency through being adopted by other influential actors.[71]

TABLE 1
Slates and affiliations on Edmonton city council* 1971–80

Year	CGA†	URGE	EVA	Independents	
				Conservative	Progressive
1971	8	0	0	3	2
1974	8	2	1	1	1
1977	7	3	0	1	2
1980	6	4	1	1	1

* Council included twelve aldermen and the mayor.
† An official slate was designated by the CGA only in 1977, but those incumbents, plus others with previous attachments or strong linkages, have been listed for the other years.

Orthodox socialists have not been so successful, although a small fringe has persisted. As noted above, the NDP has not openly participated in civic elections since the Second World War, although prominent members have served as 'independent' mayors (Elmer Roper, Ivor Dent) and party officials apparently hope for progressive voting coalitions.[72] Members participated as individuals, behind the scenes, in 1980. Somewhat more persistent has been the Edmonton Voters' Association (EVA). This group was formed in January 1957 to speak politically for the Edmonton and District Labour Council and to compete with Mayor Hawrelak's gang. EVA ran a full slate, including a mayoralty candidate in 1957 and 1958 and lost everything; in 1959 three candidates ran and lost; in 1960 EVA activities ceased.[73] In the elections between 1963 and 1968 a small group of populists and progressives produced a partial slate under the United Voters Organization banner, but only abetted the re-election efforts of two opposing incumbents. An avowed socialist, David Leadbeater, won accidental election in 1974 and, seeking a vehicle to help advance his policy interests, was instrumental in re-creating EVA.[74] Leadbeater did not seek re-election, but in 1977 EVA fielded five candidates for 6.7 per cent of the vote but no victories. In 1980, one of three candidates was elected (the slate won 3.3 per cent of total vote). EVA has had no significant impact on Edmonton's local government.

One final note ought to be made. As in other major Canadian cities, municipal elections are essentially a middle-class sport. Table 2 reveals the familiar pattern[75] and demonstrates vividly what powerful gatekeepers the political resources of time and money can be. For the decade commencing in 1974, 87 per cent of *successful* candidacies have come from professional (including

TABLE 2
Occupations of recent Edmonton municipal candidates by percentage

Occupation in election year	1974 Candidates	1974 Elected	1977 Candidates	1977 Elected	1980 Candidates	1980 Elected
Law	7.5	15.4	–	–	–	–
Business	35.8	46.2	50.0	46.2	37.5	53.9
Professions	18.9	30.8	15.8	30.8	18.7	15.4
Teachers	9.4	–	5.3	7.7	10.4	–
Other white-collar	13.2	7.7	13.2	15.4	14.5	7.7
Blue-collar	7.5	–	15.8	–	14.5	7.7
Others	7.5	–	–	–	4.1	15.4
Number	53	13*	38	13	48	13

* Council included twelve aldermen and the mayor.

teachers) or business ranks. Patently, such crude data tell nothing of the ideological orientation of the councillors or of their positions on neighbourhood versus city-wide policy issues. The party system is not sufficiently sophisticated to command cross-tabulation on that basis, except for the observation that at least six of the eight EVA candidates were 'blue-collar' workers. What is starkly revealed in the table is a systematic pattern of exclusion for that 24 per cent of Edmonton's working population that, in 1971, could be considered its blue-collar class.

The Electoral System

Edmonton began the era with at-large elections to a ten-person council, following the not-unusual practice of electing one-half its membership annually. In 1947, following a plebiscite, the annual election of the mayor was abandoned in favour of a two-year term. A plebiscite in 1962 narrowly supported a move to have the entire council elected every two years which held until 1968; since then mayor and council have been elected for three-year terms. Council was itself enlarged from ten to twelve for the elections of 1963 to reflect the growth in city population. Elections have been computed on a simple plurality basis since the city abandoned proportional representation (which was in effect 1923–7 inclusive), and no partisan affiliation is permitted on the ballot.

The question of wards has not proven controversial for Edmonton. Although some pressures for a move away from the general vote began to emerge in the early 1960s, largely to emulate Calgary which had moved to a ward system in 1960, the dominant CGA rejected any such action as premature and detrimental to the best interests of the city as a whole.[76] But the system became increasingly unmanageable as the candidate lists swelled (forty-four in 1966 for example) and the costs of city-wide campaigning escalated. A reasonably non-controversial plebiscite in 1968 supported (61.64 per cent in favour) the concept of a ward system to take effect for the elections of 1971, and council moved to devise a scheme to minimize electoral disruption.

As in Toronto in 1969,[77] Edmonton's new wards were suggested by a civic official who 'certainly had a strong sense of political reality and knew that he was not being asked to prepare a map which would make the task of re-election for the sitting aldermen any more difficult than necessary.'[78] The proposal was for the creation of four strip wards running the length of the city, completely ignoring community, economic, and ethnic cleavages and each electing three councillors. Jack Masson sizes it up accurately: 'By establishing four wards completely heterogeneous in terms of socioeconomic composition, the council in effect provided four at-large elections (at) every municipal election'[79] – but at a quarter of the cost! The important difference with the Toronto case was the absence of well-organized and articulate opposition, rooted in political cleavage, to force consideration of a more realistic ward arrangement. The system, incidentally, had the desired impact: of incumbents seeking re-election only one was upset and he by a recently retired city commissioner. A plebiscite in 1974, prompted by the more conservative council faction, ratified a continuation of the ward system (53.39 per cent support).[80]

In 1979, in response to pressure for a thorough examination of municipal institutions with an eye to improving representation and 'constructive citizen participation,' city council appointed a task force on city government. To date, the most significant of its recommendations to be implemented was ward revision for the 1980 municipal elections. The new wards (six, electing two councillors apiece) have more of a 'block' nature, but are still sufficiently large (81,900 people) to defy description as neighbourhood constituencies. In 1980, of nine aldermen seeking re-election only one was upset. However, while it is premature to judge the effects of the new system, the 1980 results strongly suggest that a local community attachment will play an increasing role in successful candidatures. Of the twelve aldermen it might reasonably be said that at least six are oriented towards neighbourhood, at the expense of 'city-wide,' interests. The nine-person school board is elected at large, by simple plurality, employing a non-partisan ballot.

The Municipal Administration

The city's municipal structure is of the council-board of commissioners form. Essentially a western Canadian adaptation of the city manager model, under this arrangement 'a council may, by by-law, provide for the delegation of any or all of its executive and administrative duties and powers to one or more municipal commissioners.'[81] The mayor is *ex officio* a member of the board[82] and chairs its meetings. Although council is legally accountable for both the development of policy and its implementation, administrative responsibilities have increasingly devolved upon the board as the volume and pressure of civic business have exploded since the war. Operating expenditures in 1954 were $19,033,101; in 1981 the city budgeted for current expenditures of $329,463,000 and a capital program of $556,654,000.[83] The board is the general management arm of the city, which is itself one of the largest Alberta corporations, being collectively and directly responsible to council for all civic departments and agencies.

Until the reorganization of the system in 1968, three commissioners (and the mayor) comprised the board, with the commissioners exercising line authority over the various municipal departments. The board directly managed policing, civil defence, and legal affairs. The reorganization prompted a shuffling of responsibility for departments into three more functionally compatible groupings – public affairs, economic affairs, and utilities and engineering – and added the office of chief commissioner. Corporate policy planning has, in recent years, become an increasing responsibility of the last.

The commissioners are responsible to the council for the proper functioning of departments within their individual purview. Departments normally report to council through their respective commissioner. Policy initiatives from the departments are vetted by the board and, if approved, are presented directly to council. In the case of a disagreement with a departmental recommendation, the board must prepare an alternative proposal (with the assistance of the department) and present both to council for determination.[84] Not surprisingly, most council business originates from commission board reports, which have a considerable impact in the structuring of political choice.

Paul Hickey is correct to assert, in his comparative study of local decision-making, that 'the development of Western Canada's council-commissioner system represents a significant Canadian contribution to the art of local government.'[85] It is a highly efficient bureaucratic form, well suited to the administration of a major corporate enterprise. But, as such, it also represents a concentration of power based upon technical expertise and, in a political system that does not put forth competitive technical élites, council is all too dependent upon the considered views of the board. It is also a closed hierarchy for, in much the same way as the environment of the newsroom rewards consistency with the general editorial orientation of a newspaper, upwardly mobile civic managers do not upset applecarts in Edmonton. Rarely do internal struggles over policy alternatives reach the public ear, even though some have been fierce. The internal structure of the hierarchy, based as it is upon integrating activity into comprehensive but multifunctional divisions, holds considerable potential for generating conflict. For example, land-use planning (and parks) lie in the realm of 'Public Affairs' while long-range transportation planning is the responsibility of 'Utilities and Engineering.' Fundamental policy differences are intended to be resolved internally, not infrequently at board level. Only once, despite the intense public controversy surrounding the development of the city's transportation policy in the 1970s, were internal documents critical of the METS program 'leaked' to the media by anonymous officials in an attempt to discredit the engineering schemes.[86] The commissioners instigated a comprehensive interrogation to prevent a recurrence.[87] The lesson was learned. Commissioners have usually been recruited from the world of the hard services and, by virtue of their training, have not been overly sympathetic to the direct intrusions of citizen amateurs into civic policy-making.

Despite its preoccupation with physical development, the city has in recent years been forced to become more active in the social services. By 1978 there were some thirty programs, ranging from day care and family aides through home services for seniors. In public housing the city now owns in excess of 1,000 units, assumes the operating costs of senior-citizen lodges, provides land for non-profit housing at 50 per cent of cost, and requires a land dedication for community housing purposes sufficient to accommodate 5 per cent of the population in new subdivisions. The tax levy now carries the operating deficits of a dozen major cultural and athletic installations such as the conservatory, planetarium, aquatic centre, and stadiums built over the last two decades. By the late 1970s the programs, staff members, and territory of the civic administration had grown to the point that comprehensive decentralization of the 'Human Service Delivery System' in response to community-generated demands became necessary. This is now being implemented, prompting complementary demands from a variety of sources for a parallel political decentralization to ward councils, which is not.

Provincial-Municipal Relations: The Metropolitan Question

Since the Second World War the population of Edmonton has quadrupled. Problems resulting from this growth have been legion, but both Social Credit and Progressive Conservative provincial administrations have generally turned a blind eye to difficulties that were emerging on their doorstep.

Most of the structural adaptations to metropolitan growth have come about through the annexation of peripheral properties, normally at the instigation of land-owners and developers desiring the extension of urban servicing capabilities.[88] There were no annexations during the period 1917–47, because of the post–First World War recession, the Great Depression, and Edmonton's earlier over-expansion during the heady years of the century's first decade. But from 1947 to 1980 there were nineteen separate annexations encompassing a total of 55,474 acres.[89] The metropolitan region as well had to respond to growth pressures. In the 1950s small towns adjacent to the city grew, but as provincial highways were upgraded, the city's commutershed was enhanced considerably. The metropolitan population ballooned from 234,000 in 1951 to 660,000 in 1978; the small, formerly French-speaking town of St Albert, northwest of the city, grew from 1,300 in 1956 to 28,000 in 1978; and the tiny unincorporated hamlet of Sherwood Park (to the east) from 60 to 26,500. Both now are classic 'dormitory' suburbs.

The first, half-hearted provincial attempt to come to grips with the question of metropolitan development occurred with passage of the Town and Rural Planning Act in 1950, which permitted cabinet to establish district planning commissions designating area, municipal membership, and levies in support of costs. Various provincial departments also appointed members.[90] The crucial problem with the Edmonton District Planning Commission was simply that, until 1957, its decisions were advisory. As well, the act contained this provision: 'No business relating to any matter of special concern to a particular municipality shall be transacted at any meeting which is not attended by at least one representative of that municipality.'[91] On two important occasions, including the creation of Sherwood Park, municipal districts withdrew from the EDPC in order to implement, unilaterally, their concepts of metropolitan planning.[92] On the issue of Sherwood Park, the McNally commission was later to observe: 'In itself, [it] may be a good project, but from the point of view of orderly development and district planning its location is a metropolitan tragedy. It is also a testimonial to the failure of voluntary joint area planning.'[93]

To avoid acting precipitously in response to urban development, the Social Credit administration struck an investigatory commission (McNally) in 1954. The commission specifically rejected two-tier federation (à la Toronto) and government by special purpose districts (Vancouver) and recommended the amalgamation of Calgary and Edmonton with their immediately adjacent industrial and residential suburbs.[94] Since its report in 1956, successive civic administrations have consistently sought to realize McNally's boundaries. The recommendations were not enthusiastically received by a provincial administration that believed, rhetorically at least, in 'local autonomy.' It did not disturb boundaries but increased substantially direct financial assistance to municipalities, modified the planning commission structures along the lines suggested by McNally, and required the preparation of a regional plan.[95]

Faced with obvious provincial indifference, Edmonton itself attempted to gain the McNally boundaries by lending a sympathetic ear to annexation requests. In 1961 the small town of Beverly amalgamated with the city, and in 1962 Jasper Place, also hard pressed to provide public services, formally applied to the Local Authorities Board (LAB) for amalgamation. Although Edmonton's council was unimpressed with the prospect of upgrading municipal services, it supported the town by arguing the McNally case and called for the annexation to it of 'Refinery Row' to offset costs.[96] The LAB annexed the town and some rural lands to the city, but not the industrial complex.

Other post-McNally annexations added some 28,400 acres to Edmonton by 1967. Foreseeing no end to piecemeal annexation, the city again took the initiative by retaining Dr Eric Hanson, who very shortly (1968) recommended unitary government, but for a much larger territory.[97] Hanson's report was adopted by Edmonton, but a delegation received a distinctly cool reception from the premier, and a meeting of area municipalities convened by the minister in late 1969 proved completely inconclusive.[98] At the same time, the province was secretly assembling a massive land bank for housing purposes.[99] Mill Woods, the largest land bank at that point in Canada, comprising some 5,500 acres, was annexed to the city (along with 9,600 acres elsewhere) in 1971, and by 1974 about 4,000 serviced lots had been marketed.[100] Edmonton's housing crisis had been eased, but the metropolitan problem remained unresolved. Moreover, metropolitan planning was not abetted by the existence of the Edmonton Regional Planning Commission (ERPC), on which the city had but three of twenty-two votes despite representing 75 per cent of the population in the 5,500-square-mile jurisdiction. Although member municipalities could no longer opt out of decisions affecting them, the intermunicipal log-rolling of rural and suburban municipalities prevented effective action: 'The ERPC ... has been little more than a public forum in which an inter-municipal land rush is fought out.'[101]

In 1971, thirty-six years of Social Credit provincial administration ended; the city was inspired to try again, submitting a modification of the Hanson line directly to cabinet with a request for action. There was no response.[102] However, between 1974 and 1976 the provincial Department of the Environment unilaterally imposed restricted development areas (RDA) on the periphery but beyond the boundaries of both Edmonton and Calgary. The

Edmonton RDA (generally a half-mile-wide strip surrounding the city) is clearly intended to be a utilities and transportation corridor, but city officials saw it as a potential barrier to future expansion. This concern, plus the frustrations built into the planning process by continued small-parcel annexations, led the city to approach cabinet in 1977 requesting immediate annexation of all lands within the RDA (including Refinery Row) and a royal commission study. In the legislature, in May 1978, the minister told the city to pursue any land acquisition via the LAB route.

In March 1979, the city applied to annex 467,200 acres to its then-existing 80,000, including St Albert and the entire county of Strathcona.[103] In December 1980 the LAB essentially awarded the city Hanson's boundary, which encompassed the area most subject to urbanizing pressures. But in Alberta, the lieutenant-governor in council has the power to vary LAB orders, and, accordingly, MLAs were bombarded with worried pleas from those about to lose their municipal identities. In June 1981, the cabinet issued a revised order, awarding the city some 86,000 acres of land but not its dormitory suburbs. Included in the territory was a mysterious 17,000 acres to the northeast of the city which was beyond the border ordered by the LAB and in which Royal Trust, acting for a secret buyer, was the major landholder. It has since been revealed that Royal Trust acted for the province, which owns 41 per cent of the area.[104] The cabinet also decided to replace the ERPC with a new Edmonton Metropolitan Regional Planning Commission. The latter seems destined to fail because the city, with about 80 per cent of the area's population, has but one-third of the votes, while the remaining municipalities, all in competition with the city and among themselves for commercial, industrial, and residential development, have the remainder.[105]

Several questions emerge from Edmonton's metropolitan odyssey. Why, for instance, has the city been so persistent in its amalgamation attempts given the obvious indifference of successive provincial governments? One explanation may lie simply in the city's administrative structure. Since Edmonton has generally conformed to the American model of the 'reformed' city, its leaders (as noted) have expected municipal government to provide effective management. Governmental fragmentation of the metropolitan area is then perceived as 'inefficient,' a barrier to economies of scale and the implementation of higher levels of technology, a source of unnecessary bureaucratic duplication, and a nuisance because of the often complex bureaucratic (and political) negotiations that must often precede regional decisions. Thus, the commissioners have pressed for 'rationalization' of the city's boundaries over time, and their link with council, i.e. the mayors, have successively been among the strongest city expansionists: they have, in short, kept the issue on the front burner.[106] But why continue to approach the cabinet and not earlier employ the LAB route?[107] Apparently, following the release of the McNally report, Calgary had prepared an elaborate LAB application to realize those boundaries. In those more frugal times, they were told clearly by provincial authorities that the application was too expensive and unnecessary: they should apply directly to the executive council. In the Edmonton area, at the same time, the premier also indicated that a provincial policy would be enunciated. Of course it never was, except to the extent of a calculated indifference, but the belief that a direct approach to cabinet was the route to follow stood as conventional political wisdom until clearly refuted in the legislative assembly in 1978.

Why were the two governing parties so unexcited about metropolitan reorganization, given developments elsewhere in Canada during this period? From one perspective the answer is clear: there has been no crisis in servicing or planning of sufficient importance to force the provincial hand, especially during a time in which other policy areas have compelled close provincial attention. Political motivations are less clear. The available evidence does suggest, however, that both régimes have believed the pieties of their respective rhetoric. Thus, Social Credit sought to avoid intervention in local affairs and, in true laissez-faire style, reacted to events rather than initiating them. The Lougheed administration asserts a strong commitment to an ill-defined concept of economic decentralization within the province, which it mistakenly applied to justify the urban sprawl adjacent to Edmonton. The recent decision concerning metropolitan governance was reached during an intense period of federal-provincial confrontation over energy and constitutional concerns. There was widespread concern in the government caucus that federal authorities sought to diminish provincial powers. How could this champion of provincial rights trample underfoot the rights of municipalities to an independent existence? Also lurking in the background may have been some harsh political calculations. With the exception of Manitoba, no provincial government has been eager to institutionalize a competitive political force by unifying the government of their major population centres. Leaving the capital city area fragmented governmentally meant no single mayor could present a unified set of demands and claim to represent a quarter of the province: continued intermunicipal bickering further diverts attention from more serious policy concerns. With very minor, short-term exceptions no Edmonton mayor of the last three decades has been a prominent member of the party in office provincially.

CONCLUSIONS

It is too easy, perhaps, to be critical of what has been accomplished in Edmonton. The city's site atop the high banks of the frigid North Saskatchewan is striking, and, despite the mild climatic 'pocket' that encircles the metropolitan region, the ability of the city's founders to sustain a vigorous community is remarkable. Edmonton is a modern city with few visible signs of decay, bubbling with energy and wealth, and enjoying the happy combination of cultural abundance, high-level community services, and low-level taxation; for most citizens it is a humane and hospitable environment, despite the deplorable winters. The city's relative youth, as much as initiatives in urban regeneration, has also inhibited a flight of Edmonton's social upper crust from the core city: 'They have been left behind rather than leading the suburbanization of residential development.'[108]

None the less, it is also easy to overlook what the early years were all about. Local raconteurs – Tony Cashman and others – write excitedly about 'men of vision' and so forth.[109] In this nostalgia it is forgotten that Edmonton was established for commercial purposes and that intensely interpersonal politics disguised a common goal of employing municipal institutions to attract enterprise and to ward off competitors. These themes emerged again in the post-1947 period. Municipal initiatives led to the urban renewal of the downtown 'civic centre' in the late 1950s and the 1960s (focused on the city hall completed in 1956 and declared a municipal historic site in 1981) and the quest for major league sports facilities and a convention centre in the 1970s and 1980s. Inevitably over the years a few civic officials have been tainted with scandal; it is remarkable there have been so few. Municipal institutions (employing the American reform package) and processes (the non-partisanship ethos) have been employed to suffuse latent cleavages in the community and to generate a commonality of purpose in support of growth and development. Direct business 'pressure' at city hall has tended, it appears, to be related to development rather than interventionist on a broad range of issues. It is not surprising that the mayor customarily delivers his annual 'state of the city' address before the city's chamber of commerce.

If Edmonton's local politics is unique in Canada in any significant respect, it would be for the long period of unchallenged dominance of the Citizens' Committee and its successors. The obvious question is whether the Citizens' Committee engendered the conditions that gave rise to it or rode the crest of public sentiment. The answer is a bit of both. Despite internal squabbles among the gladiators, the public ideology of Edmonton has equated progress with growth and development and this, in turn, has become the 'common sense' to which municipal boosters constantly appeal. Youth, wealth, and high residential mobility made the image easy to sustain and the Citizens' Committee capitalized. Until very recently there has been no basis for an effective challenge to this vision.

All this is not to suggest a civic administration that is insensitive to the needs of the non-commercial community. Particularly over the last generation, Edmonton's municipal governments have placed greater emphasis on developing services to people, as well as traditional services to property. As the city has moved to provide public transit for the disabled, to improve levels of publicly supported day care and social services generally, to require 'community' housing in new subdivisions, to develop cultural and recreational facilities in pace with population expansion, and the like, it has heightened tension in municipal-provincial relations. The Lougheed government has shown little inclination to employ its vast financial resources in materially assisting such progressive and expensive policies.

If we can look ahead with any degree of reliability we may anticipate an increasingly politicized electorate to pressure councils (themselves changed in orientation) to upgrade human services. Subtle but effective pressures from developers anxious to bring the newly annexed lands 'onstream' through service extensions will continue to be felt, depending always upon the national economic climate. The freeway debates will again follow in consequence. If the shift to a 'progressive' majority in council persists, we may also expect to see future rancorous debates about the influence of the commissioners in policy development. The unquestioning acceptance of their role will almost certainly remain a thing of the past.

SUGGESTED FURTHER READING

Artibise, Alan F.J. 'Patterns of Prairie Urban Development: 1871–1950' in David Jay Bercuson and Phillip A. Buckner ed *Eastern and Western Perspectives* Toronto 1981

Betke, Carl 'Urban Social Developments in Edmonton, 1898–1930' PHD thesis, University of Alberta, 1981

Bettison, D.G., J.K. Kenward, and L. Taylor *Urban Affairs in Alberta* Edmonton 1975

Betts, George M. 'The Edmonton Aldermanic Election of 1962' MA thesis, University of Alberta, 1963

Blake, Donald E. 'Role Perceptions of Local Decision-Makers' MA thesis, University of Alberta, 1967

Dale, E.H. 'The Role of Successive Town and City Councils in the Evolution of Edmonton, Alberta, 1892–1966' PHD thesis, University of Alberta, 1969

– 'Decision-Making at Edmonton, Alberta, 1913–1945: Town Planning without a Plan' *Plan* XI 2 (1971) 134–47
Day, John P. 'Edmonton Civic Politics, 1891–1914' *Urban History Review* 3–77 (February 1978) 42–68
Diemer, H.L. 'Annexation and Amalgamation in the Territorial Expansion of Edmonton and Calgary' MA thesis, University of Alberta, 1975
Gilsdorf, Robert R. 'Cognitive and Motivational Sources of Voter Susceptibility to Influence' *Canadian Journal of Political Science* VI 4 (December 1973) 624–38
Hanson, Eric *Local Government in Alberta* Toronto 1956
Kilpatrick, Alexander Bruce 'A Lesson in Boosterism: The Contest for the Alberta Provincial Capital, 1904–1906' *Urban History Review* VIII 3 (February 1980) 47–109
Lightbody, J. 'Edmonton Politics: Business as Usual' *Canadian Forum* LII (December 1972) 8–9
MacGregor, J.G. *Edmonton: A History* Edmonton 1975
Masson, Jack K. 'Decision-Making Patterns and Floating Coalitions in an Urban City Council' *Canadian Journal of Political Science* VIII 1 (March 1975) 128–37
– 'The Demise of 'Alphabet Parties'; The Rise of Responsible Party Politics in Cities' Occasional Paper 4, Department of Political Science, University of Alberta, 1976
– 'Edmonton: The Unsettled Issues of Expansion, Governmental Reform and Provincial Economic Diversification' in L.D. Feldman ed *Politics and Government of Urban Canada* 4th edn Toronto 1981, 431–47
Plunkett, T.J., and James Lightbody 'Tribunals, Politics and the Public Interest: The Edmonton Annexation Case' *Canadian Public Policy* VIII (spring 1982) 207–21
Smith, P.J. ed *Edmonton: The Emerging Metropolitan Pattern* Victoria 1978
Weaver, John C. 'Edmonton's Perilous Course: 1904–1929' *Urban History Review* 2–77 (October 1977) 20–32

NOTES

I am pleased to acknowledge the research support of D. Young, T. Swanky, and R. Hatfield, the co-operation of the City of Edmonton Archives and the City Election Office, and the critical comments of professors G. Pyrcz and I. Taylor. Any errors of fact or interpretation are my own.

1 A colourful history of personalities and events during this period is provided by J.G. MacGregor *Edmonton: A History* rev edn (Edmonton 1975) 17–102. The name Edmonton, incidentally, appears to derive from the birthplace of Sir James Winter-Lake, deputy governor of the Hudson's Bay Company, in Edmonton, Middlesex, England.

2 But the settlement was still small. In January 1881, it was calculated to include 263 people; ibid 91–3.
3 A more detailed history of personalities and politics up to the First World War is provided in John P. Day 'Edmonton Civic Politics, 1891–1914' *Urban History Review* 3–77 (February 1978) 42–68.
4 For example, two French-Canadian candidates fared badly; the fire brigade usually nominated a single-issue candidate; ibid 56.
5 Alan F.J. Artibise 'Patterns of Prairie Urban Development, 1871–1950' in David Jay Bercuson and Phillip A. Buckner ed *Eastern and Western Perspectives* (Toronto 1981) 115–18. These close linkages are examined by Carl Betke 'Urban Social Developments in Edmonton, 1898–1930' PHD thesis, University of Alberta, 1981.
6 For more detail consult John C. Weaver 'Edmonton's Perilous Course: 1904–1929' *Urban History Review* 2–77 (October 1977) 23–6. The utilities were later to provide a vital cash flow to city coffers during the Great Depression. See also R.G. Ironside 'Locational Adjustments in Public Service Facilities' in P.G. Smith ed *Edmonton: The Emerging Metropolitan Pattern* (Victoria 1978).
7 For fascinating details see MacGregor *Edmonton* 122–3.
8 The city operated under its own charter, as did Calgary, until brought under a general city act on 1 January 1952.
9 Hence, the charter permitted property-owners with an assessment of $2,000 or more four votes; $1,200 to $2,000 meant three; and $600 to $1,200, two. On this point note John C. Weaver *Shaping the Canadian City: Essays on Urban Politics and Policy, 1890–1920* (Toronto 1977) 67–8. The system ended in 1931. Tenants were not permitted a vote until a change in provincial legislation in 1911.
10 As quoted in ibid 63–4
11 Even in the late 1970s, for example, senior civic officials complained in private of not-so-subtle pressures from the Lougheed administration (he being from Calgary) upon corporate head offices to locate in Calgary in preference to Edmonton. Sour grapes or not, it is believed; personal interviews.
12 This discussion is based upon the extensively detailed commentary of Alexander Bruce Kilpatrick 'A Lesson in Boosterism: The Contest for the Alberta Provincial Capital, 1904–1906' *Urban History Review* VIII 3 (February 1980) 47–109.
13 MacGregor *Edmonton* 191–5. The company realized a paper profit of $4,343,000, and purchasers from as far away as England were among the speculators.
14 There was virtually no opposition to the amalgamation. By the terms of the legislative act the south side was to be guaranteed representation by the practice of having the three top vote-recipients with south-side assessment declared elected before the overall plurality winners.

15 J. Suski *Edmonton* (Edmonton 1965) 10. The amalgamations were with villages such as Calder and North Edmonton. As evidence of the recession it might be noted that no further annexations to the city occurred until 1947.
16 The impact of the war and the out-migration is reflected by the size of the electorate. In 1914 32,246 were enfranchised exclusive of burgesses; this fell to 10,825 in 1918; calculated from files in the City Election Office.
17 Artibise 'Patterns of Prairie Urban Development' 127–9
18 MacGregor *Edmonton* 202
19 Ironside 'Locational Adjustments' 238
20 Artibise 'Patterns of Prairie Urban Development' 126
21 *Report of the Royal Commission on the Metropolitan Development of Calgary and Edmonton* (Edmonton 1956) chap VI 41. This report is commonly referred to by the surname of the chairman of the commission, G.F. McNally, and will be so cited here.
22 Artibise 'Patterns of Prairie Urban Development' 129
23 E.H. Dale 'The Role of Successive Town and City Councils in the Evolution of Edmonton, Alberta, 1892–1966' PHD thesis, University of Alberta, 1969, 158–67. For example, between 1918 and 1921, 44,348 land parcels became city property; Weaver 'Edmonton's Perilous Course' 28. Tax collections in 1916 were only 49 cents on the dollar.
24 George A. Nader *Cities of Canada* II (Toronto 1976) 354–77 ('Edmonton')
25 Nader observes that this pipeline from Norman Wells on the Mackenzie was to supply a Whitehorse refinery that in turn would fuel the American fleet in the event of a Japanese attack. In 1948, the dismantled refinery was relocated to become metropolitan Edmonton's first, ibid 358. It was located adjacent to, but outside, Edmonton's municipal boundary. Edmonton's population increased 22.4 per cent in the five years 1941–6.
26 A university classmate of Mackenzie King, a deserter from the Mounted Police, and a participant in the Klondike gold rush, he was to contest the mayoralty or a council seat some twenty times between the war and 1940.
27 Opponents of the One Big Union had a clear majority in the Edmonton trades council and the craft unions (and Alfred Farmilo, subsequently an alderman 1926–30) worked effectively to oust OBU supporters; David J. Bercuson *Fools and Wise Men* (Toronto 1978) 110–11. Edmonton's general strike in sympathy with Winnipeg in 1919 commenced 22 May with strong initial support. But civic services were resumed within a week and everything was back to normal within a month. W.R. Askin attributes the lack of civic disruption to the conservative leadership of the trades council; 'Labour Unrest in Edmonton and District and Its Coverage by the Edmonton Press: 1918–1919' MA thesis, University of Alberta, 1973.

28 Editorial comment *Edmonton Bulletin* 12 November 1931
29 George M. Betts 'The Edmonton Aldermanic Election of 1962' MA thesis, University of Alberta, 1963, 26ff
30 Ibid 27
31 These and succeeding calculations have been derived from the official election tally compiled by the City Election Office.
32 Betts 'Aldermanic Election' 40–4
33 Ibid 32–9. Roper held his provincial seat until 1955.
34 Ainley's plurality was 20,971 in 1946 and 15,394 in 1947. In the latter year a plebiscite narrowly approved a two-year term for mayor. Ainley had lost as a labour mayoralty candidate in 1936 and as a PCA aldermanic hopeful in 1937.
35 E.C. Banfield and J.Q. Wilson *City Politics* (Cambridge, Mass, 1963) 139
36 Betts 'Aldermanic Election' 70
37 For a more detailed account upon which this is partly based consult *St. John's Edmonton Report* 24 November 1975 and 14 June 1976.
38 J. Lightbody 'Edmonton Politics: Business as Usual' *Canadian Forum* LII (December 1972) 8–9
39 For a satisfactory summary of these concerns, note Robert R. Gilsdorf 'Cognitive and Motivational Sources of Voter Susceptibility to Influence' *Canadian Journal of Political Science* VI 4 (December 1973) 624–38 and James D. Anderson 'Non-partisan Civic Politics in Canada and the United States' MA thesis, University of Alberta, 1971
40 See, for example, Jack K. Masson 'The Demise of "Alphabet Parties"; The Rise of Responsible Party Politics in Cities' Occasional Paper 4, Department of Political Science, University of Alberta, 1976, 8–9
41 Gilsdorf 'Cognitive and Motivational Sources' 626
42 Betts 'Aldermanic Election' 68
43 Ibid 112
44 Jack K. Masson 'Decision-Making Patterns and Floating Coalitions in an Urban City Council' *Canadian Journal of Political Science* VIII 1 (March 1975) 130
45 Gilsdorf 'Cognitive and Motivational Sources' 625
46 Donald E. Blake 'Role Perceptions of Local Decision-Makers' MA thesis, University of Alberta, 1967, 92
47 Mayor Hawrelak's obituary probably makes the point: 'He could take credit for begetting or pushing development of the main library, the city hall, the Riverside golf course, the Royal Alexandra hospital complex, Mayfair Park, Borden Park ... and Storyland Valley Zoo'; *St. John's Edmonton Report* 24 November 1975.
48 Betts 'Aldermanic Election' 69–72

49 After his first mayoralty victory in 1951, Hawrelak put it this way: 'I am overwhelmed with the results at the polls and I take it to mean that citizens of Edmonton have chosen the man they expect to handle the civic duties in a business-like manner necessary in such a large corporation as the City of Edmonton'; *Edmonton Journal* 8 November 1951.
50 MacGregor *Edmonton* 274
51 For some brief comments on the chain of events, see Charles Bruce *News and the Southams* (Toronto 1968) 313.
52 Betts 'Aldermanic Election' 38ff, 154ff; Gilsdorf 'Cognitive and Motivational Sources' 629–30
53 Gilsdorf 'Cognitive and Motivational Sources' 629–30
54 Betts 'Aldermanic Election' 145
55 'Mr Superstein' was the first, but by no means the only, to repeat stories of the mayor's generosity and his willingness to see anybody who had a problem: 'Someone will come in off the street, out of a job; Bill will reach in his pocket and slip me ten dollars and say, "Jake, you give it to him – it wouldn't be right for me, so you do it." Sometimes it was a twenty'; *St. John's Edmonton Report* 24 November 1975.
56 In the 1950s, for instance, turnout regularly hovered between 10 and 15 per cent with but two exceptions.
57 Christopher Leo *The Politics of Urban Development: Canadian Urban Expressway Disputes* (Toronto 1977) 55
58 Ibid
59 *Edmonton Journal* 21 March 1974
60 Dale notes that 'it can be convincingly argued that up to the end of 1966 the City of Edmonton had no 'core concept' of municipal planning, for though it had a Preliminary General Plan it had no official master plan'; 'Decision-Making at Edmonton, Alberta 1913–1945: Town Planning without a Plan' *Plan* II 2 (1971) 134.
61 Blake 'Role Perceptions' 87–8
62 The degree of the change can be debated. In a survey undertaken for the mayor in 1979, the university's Population Research Laboratory found that, although citizens were strongly supportive of 'citizen involvement' (85 per cent), 'most of the strategies proposed [by them] are passive ones with the onus for implementation resting with public officials'; *Citizens' Concerns in Edmonton* (Edmonton 1979) 25.
63 Leo *The Politics of Urban Development* 58
64 Ibid 59
65 *The Immorality of the Motorcar*, University of Alberta Department of Extension, 1971

66 Leo *The Politics of Urban Development* 61
67 Paul Tennant 'Vancouver Politics and the Civic Party System' in M.O. Dickerson, S. Drabek, and J.T. Woods ed *Problems of Change in Urban Government* (Waterloo 1980) 24–5.
68 Donald Higgins 'Progressive City Politics and the Citizen Movement: A Status Report' *City Magazine Annual, 1981* (Toronto 1981) 87–8
69 Despite its Lazarus endeavours the group never numbered more than a few dozen members, was not as well funded as the earlier group, and took pains not to appear as a party: 'The only control the association will have over candidates once they're elected is continuing financial support at the next election'; *Edmonton Journal* 1 November 1976, 13 October 1977.
70 Ibid 30 October 1980. The membership appears to reflect a pre-election 'high' however. Continuing membership is under 300 and 'active' members number about two dozen; personal interviews.
71 URGE President Iain Taylor was blunt with the press: '"[Mayor] Purves stole our shirts in 1977," ... Taylor charged yesterday. "He didn't know anything about citizen participation before then"'; *Edmonton Sun* 23 September 1980.
72 *Edmonton Journal* 9 December 1976, 14 February 1977
73 Betts 'Aldermanic Election' 52ff
74 His election was 'accidental' insofar as none of the three incumbents stood for re-election in the ward and in a non-partisan contest, where name recognition is important, many voters undoubtedly thought they were voting for his father, a very prominent Anglican clergyman. Mr Leadbeater received 8.93 per cent of the total votes cast. His EVA successor in 1977 received but 2.7 per cent.
75 For comparison, the case of Winnipeg is presented in James Lightbody 'Electoral Reform in Local Government: The Case of Winnipeg' *Canadian Journal of Political Science* XI 2 (June 1978) 326–32. See also P. Silcox ed *Parties to Change* (Toronto 1971) 56–7.
76 Betts 'Edmonton Aldermanic' 204. A 'form' of sectional representation did exist until the election of 1962, with top south-side vote-getters being elected to council regardless of overall position. A plebiscite in 1960 produced a rejection of the practice by two-thirds of the votes cast.
77 James Lorimer *The Real World of City Politics* (Toronto 1970) 37–52
78 Ibid 38
79 Masson 'Decision-Making Patterns' 128
80 On the general question of the ideological underpinnings of electoral reform note Lightbody 'Electoral Reform' 307–32
81 Alberta *Revised Statutes of Alberta* 1970 chap 246 sec 87.1
82 Ibid 1970 chap 246 sec 89

83 Alberta *Municipal Statistics* (Edmonton 1952), City of Edmonton *Tax Information, 1981*

84 For a more extensive discussion of the process see Andre Bernard, Jacques Leveille, and Guy Lord *Profile: Edmonton* (Ottawa 1974) 27–33 and Paul Hickey *Decision-Making Processes in Ontario's Local Government* (Toronto 1972) 213–16.

85 Hickey *Decision-Making* 221

86 *Edmonton Journal* 19–27 October 1973

87 Ibid 24 October 1973. 'Aldermen were told by acting chief commissioner George Hughes that all departments connected with the working paper ... have been interrogated, and that an investigation of the leak was continuing. 'If we find out who did it, they will be suspended,' he said. Mr. Hughes told council there was a standing rule governing the city administration that makes leaking documents to the press subject to dismissal.'

88 In Alberta, the annexation process may be initiated by either a land-owner or a municipality (usually the former) who makes application to the local authorities board to annex land immediately adjacent to an urban centre. For a discussion of the process and a unique case, see T.J. Plunkett and James Lightbody 'Tribunals, Politics and the Public Interest: The Edmonton Annexation Case' *Canadian Public Policy* VIII (spring 1982) 207–21.

89 A more comprehensive discussion than the one here is provided by D.G. Bettison, J.K. Kenward, and L. Taylor *Urban Affairs in Alberta* (Edmonton 1975) 257–318. For a more recent discussion of the problem, from a perspective different from my own, note J.K. Masson 'Edmonton: The Unsettled Issues of Expansion, Governmental Reform and Provincial Economic Diversification' in L.D. Feldman ed *Politics and Government of Urban Canada* 4th edn (Toronto 1981) 431–47.

90 Bettison *Urban Affairs* 95ff. See also Andre Bernard *Profile: Edmonton* 77–94. The province was deeply interested in municipal administration at this time. For example, the Alberta County Act of 1950 created a unique multifunctional governmental unit for rural areas of the province.

91 *Statutes* 1950 chap 71 sec 11(2)

92 McNally *Report* V 28–33

93 Ibid XIV 27

94 Ibid XIII 1–11. Summarizing the 'two fundamental principles' that guided their recommendations, the commissioners said (XII 5): '(a) It is unjust and inequitable that wide variations in the tax base should exist among the local governing bodies that comprise a metropolitan area where that area is in fact one economic and social unit. (b) A metropolitan area which is in fact one economic and social unit can ordinarily be more efficiently and effectively

governed by one central municipal authority than by a multiplicity of local governing bodies.'

95 Ibid XVII; Bettison *Urban Affairs* 191–4. The intensity of the squabbling among municipalities that resulted is perhaps measured by the fact that the *Draft Edmonton Regional Plan* was not approved for release until 16 October 1978, although the 'Metropolitan Part' has been in existence since late 1968.

96 Refinery Row was an area of some 2,400 acres (in 1956) immediately adjacent the eastern boundary of the city in the county of Strathcona and occupied principally by major refineries and oil-related heavy industry. The industries wished to locate near Edmonton but outside its boundaries in 1947 and provided a windfall for Strathcona. McNally notes (*Report* XI 1) that the county's assessment increased by 420 per cent from 1947 to 1954.

97 Eric Hanson *The Potential Unification of the Edmonton Metropolitan Area*, City of Edmonton, 1968

98 First Meeting of the Provincial-Municipal Committee on Boundary Change for the City of Edmonton *Transcript of Proceedings* Edmonton, Legislative Assembly, 20 October 1969

99 It appears that only four senior officials were aware of the details of the assembly: the minister of municipal affairs, F.C. Colborne; Mayor Dent of Edmonton; the city's chief commissioner, P. Bargen; and the head of the Alberta Housing and Urban Renewal Corporation, R. Orysiuk; ibid 33. Mr Orysiuk was subsequently convicted for accepting kickbacks in connection with the assembly, fined $121,369, and sentenced to three years in prison; *Edmonton Journal* 12 December 1981.

100 Nader *Cities of Canada* II 376–7

101 Lloyd Axworthy and James Lightbody *The Reorganization of Local Government in the Metropolitan Edmonton Area* City of Edmonton, 1979, 32. Others observe that the commission's 'main concern has been to create a permissive environment through its master plans and its development approval procedures'; Bernard *Profile: Edmonton* 81.

102 For yet another view on the 'unresolved issues' see P.J. Smith and H.L. Diemer 'Equity and the Annexation Process: Edmonton's Bid for the Strathcona Industrial Corridor' in Smith *Edmonton* 263–89.

103 Details on the process and conduct of the case are presented in Plunkett and Lightbody 'Tribunals, Politics and the Public Interest.' The hearings, however, extended from September 1979 to the end of June 1980, entailing 106 days of testimony, the hearing of about 200 witnesses, the examining of 299 official exhibits, and the production of 12,235 pages of transcript. The process cost in excess of $6 million. I was involved as a consultant retained by the city of Edmonton.

104 *Edmonton Journal* 23 June 1981

105 Alberta *Report and Decision Concerning the Edmonton Annexation Application*, Edmonton, Municipal Affairs, 1 June 1981, 5, 8

106 Some years ago, for example, T.R. Dye found a strong, direct correlation between success of annexation and the city manager form of government; 'Urban Political Integration: Conditions Associated with Annexation in American Cities' *Midwest Journal of Political Science* VIII (November 1964) 430–46.

107 Prior to amendments in 1975, LAB orders had been final and binding, but in that year the executive council was given the power to approve or disallow. In 1978 the process was again amended to permit the cabinet to vary orders and to attach conditions; Plunkett and Lightbody 'Tribunals, Politics and the Public Interest.'

108 Kenneth J. Fairburn 'Locational Changes of Edmonton's High Status Residents, 1937–1972' in Smith *Edmonton* 225.

109 For but one example note Tony Cashman 'Thank 9 Edmonton Men of Vision for Alberta's Classy First Birthday' *Edmonton Journal* 28 August 1980. Or see his *The Best Edmonton Stories* (Edmonton 1976).

ANDREW SANCTON

Conclusion: Canadian city politics in comparative perspective

Political scientists studying any political system are faced with a set of important and related questions. What is the nature of the political conflict within the system? To what extent is it based on class, ethnicity, or other social variables? Is it overt or disguised? Is it part of a wider pattern of conflict or is it relatively unique to the system in question? These issues have generally been avoided in Canadian works on urban politics, and, as a result, most have been of interest only to those social scientists involved in the specialized field of municipal government.

In the past decade or so, a new group of Canadian scholars has at least opened a debate about the nature of political conflict within Canadian cities. Following the lead of their American counterparts, Canadian urban historians have shown how business sponsorship of much of the urban reform activity early this century served to adapt municipal government to business interests and practices.[1] In the view of these historians, the urban reform movement was a crucial part of the political process whereby the interests of large-scale industrial and commercial capital overcame the debilitating effects of entrenched local politicians and their clientele of contractors, ethnic organizations, and other apparently retrogressive forces.

In a more modern context, James Lorimer has tried to show that municipal politics is little more than the arena in which 'the property industry' manipulates municipal regulations and expenditures to serve the interests of property-owners – especially those who hold major parcels of land for development purposes.[2] Other commentators, most of whom share many of Lorimer's assumptions and loyalties, are much more systematic in their discussion of how business interests pervade not just the internal politics of local government, but also the political process at the provincial level by which the structures and functions of local government are legally established.[3] Taking their lead primarily from European scholars, proponents of this view use a Marxist framework to show the particular ways in which urban politics is part of the continuing struggle between capital and labour.

All of these views have one thing in common: they assume that the study of urban politics is above all the study of business dominance. None of the contributors to this book deliberately began with such an approach. A number of us consciously set out to show that municipal politics in Canada is much more rich and complex than some of the more simple-minded descriptions of business dominance seem to have suggested. Given his previous work on Vancouver,[4] it is not surprising that Donald Gutstein places the greatest emphasis on the role of business. His descriptions of the powerful role of the CPR and of the way in which business interests dominate the influential Non-Partisan Association are potent arguments in support of this approach.

Similar analyses of the connection between business interests and allegedly non-partisan local formations can be found in the essays on Edmonton and Winnipeg. Nevertheless, all three essays also describe the increasing threats to business hegemony. In Vancouver, the importance of the CPR has declined, and, for the moment at least, the NPA has been defeated. Lightbody concludes that in Edmonton 'business pressure at city hall has tended, it appears, to be related to development rather than interventionist on a broad range of policy issues.'[5] He also concludes that the level of political conflict on the local council is bound to increase. The essay by Kiernan and Walker on Winnipeg suggests that although the pro-business ICEC still prevails over the NDP, older elements within the ICEC are now giving way to a more moderate group of younger city councillors who are not unquestioning servants of the traditional business approach.

If these apparent trends continue, local politics in our western cities would become more similar to local politics in the eastern cities of Toronto, Ottawa, and Halifax. Local councils would contain a substantial diversity of interests, and political control of the city would depend on shifting coalitions involved in genuinely competitive municipal elections. In many respects, Vancouver already clearly fits this model; only the continued existence of its small eleven-person council and its at-large elections suggests cause for hesitation. Because the three western cities already have municipal political party systems in place, it can be argued that they are now better prepared for genuinely competitive local politics than are eastern cities.

In this discussion of business dominance in Canadian local politics, Montreal, as usual, seems to be a special case. Mayor Drapeau – who presides over a city in which planning and zoning controls are extremely weak and who has worked closely with the private sector in many ways – has completely dominated local politics for more than twenty years. If the analysis were to end here, Montreal would seem a prime candidate for the 'business dominance' category. The problem, of course, is that, although most of his projects have benefited many firms in the private sector, their overall effect has been to create huge levels of public expenditure and, in one form or another, increased levels of taxation. This is decidedly not something of which business generally approves – and Drapeau, though recognized as a visionary, is also perceived by business as among the more profligate of the country's spendthrift politicians.

Drapeau cannot be analysed on a 'pro-business–anti-business' continuum. He is not in municipal politics to defend or attack business, but rather to preserve Montreal's status as a major North American city and to proclaim its virtues around the world. He is not unlike municipal politicians throughout the country, but simply operates on a grander scale and with fewer financial constraints imposed by grateful electors.

The reality is that Canadian municipal politicians have little choice but to build their political careers on policies designed to make their city more prosperous, more appealing, and more pleasant than other competing cities.[6] In the general absence of politically salient cleavages based on class, ethnicity, or even neighbourhood, they are rarely in a position to profit politically by mobilizing one sector of the community against another. A candidate's path to victory involves convincing the electors that his or her policies and capabilities are best suited to promoting the general well-being of the whole city. To be sure, there can be dramatically different conceptions of what this general well-being might involve, but there have been few, if any, successful local election campaigns fought on the basis of conscious appeals to class, ethnic, or neighbourhood solidarity. Any such successful appeal would risk driving the losers elsewhere or otherwise reducing the resources of the city as a whole in its struggle to maintain or advance its relative attractiveness.

This means that Canadian city politics is, above all, about boosterism. Although it is undoubtedly a characteristic of local politics everywhere, in Canada it seems all-pervasive. Local politics in Drapeau's Montreal is the most obvious example, but other cities demonstrate this same characteristic in other ways. 'Business dominance' in Winnipeg, Edmonton, and Vancouver is perhaps little more than the expression of the fact that economic prosperity in these cities is based primarily on private-sector entrepreneurship. Since Vancouver and Edmonton have been remarkably successful in achieving this prosperity, we might now expect the focus of local politics to turn to other issues, hence lessening the influence of the business interests. Conversely, in Winnipeg, where economic growth is low, the business element was clearly dominant in the ethnically based boosterism of Steven Juba and still seems unlikely to be seriously threatened, even if it is now beginning to express itself in a more sophisticated manner.

Because the economies of Ottawa and Halifax are comfortably built on the activities of senior levels of government, there is little need for the aggressively pro-business boosterism found in the western cities. Local politics seems pluralistic and diffuse in both cities and politicians can indulge what Caroline Andrew refers to as the consumer-oriented interests of the voters. Toronto seems similar, except that its prosperity is now firmly based on its role as the financial centre for Canadian big business, an economic base that is just as secure as that provided by big government.

The example of Toronto is especially instructive. When David Crombie and the new reformers gained control of city council in the early 1970s, their policies were seen as anti-development and anti-business. To the extent that these policies prevented the total redevelopment of central Toronto, this observation was true. It is also true, however, that, although the advent of the new reformers might have hurt certain development companies and speculators, the overall effect of their actions was to preserve and enhance the long-term value of existing buildings and land. By protecting the diversity of the core area, they ensured that Toronto remained an attractive location for real estate investment. Crombie became a new type of booster: Toronto for him was becoming the most liveable of major North American cities. It was seen as especially attractive to people who place high priority on the quality of urban life and who can pay for both their own comforts and for the subsidization of the less wealthy, some of whom were still needed in central Toronto even though they were increasingly less able to compete for housing space on the open market.

If boosterism – including its modern Toronto-style variant – is at the heart of Canadian local politics, and if it explains much of the apparent 'business dominance,' it follows that there is more competition among Canadian cities than within them. The implications of this observation will be explored later. For now, however, we must look at the nature and extent of the political conflict that takes place within the general ethos of boosterism.

Could it be that boosterism faces a challenge from the modern descendants of the 'cutters' who were described in the introduction? The Proposition 13 movement in California does not seem to have had much influence in Canada. This is doubtless because of generally higher provincial subsidies (especially to school boards) in Canada and our lesser degree of local autonomy. Even if committed cutters did gain control of Canadian local councils, they would find numerous provincial laws preventing them from lowering standards and expenditures below certain minimum levels. None of our contributors explicitly considered anti-tax groups as a force to be reckoned with, although such sentiments are obviously part of the appeal of such generally right-wing groups as Vancouver's NPA, Edmonton's CGA, and Winnipeg's ICEC. Recently formed anti-tax groups in Montreal merit close observation, but because they began to gain strength only in early 1982, it is too early to judge their significance. Serious challenges to the high-spending Drapeau have hitherto always come from the left rather than the right. Perhaps he will find that he is vulnerable on the tax issues – but as long as Montreal remains primarily a city of renters, this seems unlikely.

The main line of cleavage in Canadian municipal politics involves attitudes towards urban development. Proponents usually cite the need for economic growth; opponents – the new reformers – take their position on grounds of 'quality of life.' This corresponds to Andrew's description of the cleavage between producer and consumer interests. It also closely corresponds to the suburban–city centre cleavage that was documented in our essays on Toronto, Winnipeg, Ottawa, and Vancouver. In all these cases suburban politicians have argued within two-tier metropolitan authorities (within Unicity in the case of Winnipeg) that suburban development should be encouraged and that new transportation facilities, especially expressways, should be built to provide easy accessibility to jobs and services in the central city. Relative to their suburban counterparts, centre-city politicians in these cities have been less likely to support unrestrained development and have certainly been reluctant to expropriate centre-city homes to accommodate new expressways.

Montreal and Edmonton both include central municipalities that contain a majority of the population within their respective metropolitan authorities (the Montreal Urban Community and the Edmonton Metropolitan Regional Planning Commission). In both these cases the central municipality includes within its boundaries many neighbourhoods that are essentially suburban. The conflict with the suburban municipalities has therefore been not so much about particular development or transportation issues but rather about the strength of the central municipality within the metropolitan planning process. In both cases the central municipalities have not been successful at the provincial level in attaining sufficient political authority to impose their particular planning objectives on the still remaining autonomous suburbs.

Virtually all conflict in Canadian urban politics can be located on a pro-development–anti-development spectrum. This seems to hold true even for Toronto and Winnipeg, where the NDP is a significant municipal force and might therefore be expected to extend the scope of local political debate. Magnusson has described the ambiguous role of the NDP in Toronto politics while Kiernan and Walker have concluded that in Winnipeg 'the NDP municipal caucus was a remarkably right-wing group to be campaigning in 1980 under the standard of a social democratic party.'[7] The 'reform caucus' in Toronto in the early 1970s made an attempt to raise more fundamental issues, but foundered on ideological disputes and personality conflicts, not the least of which was the desire of John Sewell to remain independent. His populist radicalism raised important questions for public debate but he has not proven successful in mobilizing widespread political support around a coherent program for change.

In Montreal, genuinely radical local political alternatives have been provided by the Front d'Action politique (FRAP) and later by the radical wing of the Montreal Citizens' Movement (MCM); in Vancouver the Committee of Progressive Electors (COPE) has served a similar purpose. Except for strong showings by the MCM in 1974, COPE in 1980, and both in 1982, these groups have not experienced significant electoral success.

What are the implications of the conclusion that Canadian city politics is structured almost completely along a pro-development–anti-development spectrum? First, it confirms one of Lorimer's earliest observations: above all, municipal politics in Canada is about property. Within municipal councils, issues not related to property are generally peripheral. For example, people concerned with local social issues generally do not see municipal politics as a useful focus of their efforts. Because they tend to view municipal politicians as having no concern for social policy, they often work actively to keep such issues as day care, preventive public health, and protection of children outside the direct jurisdiction of municipal government. This attitude, of course, serves to reinforce the separation between municipal politics and these pressing social issues. The end result is that they are dealt with either by the province or by various local special-purpose bodies subject to strong provincial and professional influence.

This restriction of municipal councils to property issues is yet another manifestation of the split-level attitude to politics often observed in Canada. Voters clearly and consistently vote for different parties at the federal and provincial levels. Much political discourse is conducted in terms of jurisdictions. Debate is not so much about which policy to follow but rather about which government should have the jurisdiction to implement it. Similarly, at the municipal level, local political systems are not small-scale replications of the provincial political system. They occupy a jurisdiction all their own: the control and servicing of property. This generates a form of politics quite distinct from that found at other levels in Canadian politics.

Because local politics is concerned primarily with property, it is quite normal that, among business interests, it is such people as developers, real estate agents, property investors, building contractors, and local lawyers who are going to be particularly attracted to the local political arena. In describing the role of the 'property industry' in Canadian cities during the 1960s, Lorimer effectively documented their involvement. What he was unable to prove was that the property industry could sponsor and maintain a development boom in all major cities over an extended period of time. Magnusson has shown that, for Toronto at least, the development boom of the 1960s was an aberration and did not reflect the traditional pattern of cautious physical expansion. Our other contributors have cited numerous examples of the ways in which various kinds of citizen groups emerged to oppose and defeat large-scale development proposals: Quinpool Road in Halifax and expressways in Edmonton and Vancouver.

In most Canadian cities local politics is now genuinely competitive. The political representatives of the property industry no longer control the municipal councils of the country's major cities. Open political conflict in big-city councils is now much more common. Property and land-use issues remain at the forefront of debate, but now the owners are being challenged by the tenants, the contractors by the conservationists, and the private developers by the advocates of co-operatives and other forms of non-profit housing.

Different economic circumstances in different cities will provoke different alignments of power, and these will generally fall along the pro-development–anti-development spectrum. Just as there will always in a capitalist system be those who want to accumulate capital through property investment aimed at maximizing their return, so will there be others who wish to defend the utility (and probably the value) of their own property by limiting such further investment on the part of others. There will be many more who, while standing to gain indirectly through investment in their city's land, will be anxious to preserve property in its present form so as to protect rent levels, to preserve open space, or simply to cling to the familiar. The outcome of the conflict among these interests eventually determines how urban land is allowed to be used. Such conflict is the stuff of Canadian city politics.

CITY POLITICS: CANADA, BRITAIN, AND THE UNITED STATES

Students of urban politics in the United States and Great Britain have shown how the study of the local political system can enhance our understanding of both national politics and some of the central issues in modern democratic theory.[8] The same cannot be said for Canadian political scientists.

Why is this so? It is not simply because we are a smaller country with fewer university professors – although this is undoubtedly part of the answer. The main reason is that the most important political cleavages within Canada are regional, especially if we assume (as we are increasingly more justified in doing) that the territory of Quebec is now the only significant political base in Canada for the national interests of French Canadians.

Cities are the modern anchors of the various regions that make up the Canadian federation. Because so much of our politics is regional, much Canadian political conflict has to do with the relative strength of various cities within the federation as a whole: Montreal v Toronto, Toronto v Calgary, Halifax v St John's. Canadian cities, unlike those in other industrialized countries, tend not to be arenas in which major national political battles are fought. The only exception is Montreal, where the continuing search for a resolution of the French-English conflict remains as the legacy of English Montreal's domination of both the Quebec and the Canadian economy. Montreal, however, as the new centre of the francophone-controlled Quebec economy, now joins such cities as Halifax, Toronto, and Vancouver in the struggle for economic strength. When powerful provincial premiers battle the federal government and each other for control over resources and economic policy, they are, above all, defending and advancing the economic interests of their major cities.

Britain and the United States – the two countries that inspired the main features of the Canadian system of local government – are not without their own regional tensions. Britain faces discontent caused by economic decline in northern England, recurring waves of Celtic nationalism in Scotland and Wales, and intractable communal conflict in Northern Ireland. American cities in the northeast and midwest now face desperate problems as they are drained of investment and high-technology jobs by the prospering Sun Belt in the south and west. Nevertheless, politics in Britain and the United States is not dominated by the forces of regionalism to nearly the same extent as in Canada. Despite the obvious importance of numerous other factors, cleavages based on class and race still dominate the national political systems of Britain and the United States respectively. More important for our purposes, the political manifestations of these cleavages are seen particularly clearly within the local political systems of each country's major cities.

Although city governments in Britain and the United States deal with roughly the same range of property-related issues as those in Canada, they also are more closely involved in the administration of a wide variety of other governmental functions, the most notable being housing, education, and social welfare. Having noted these wide-ranging functions of local government, some commentators have claimed that urban politics is really about the 'production and consumption of the goods and services provided by state agencies in non-commercial forms.'[9]

This 'collective consumption' approach suggests that urban politics is not merely the politics of municipal government; it includes important aspects of decision-making at other levels as well. Nevertheless, the approach assumes that multifunctional local governments are administering much of the apparatus of the welfare state. In Canada, this is simply not a valid assumption. Our urban governments – preoccupied as they are with property issues – are not crucial pillars in the structure of the welfare state. This then is one more reason why the usual kind of political conflict engendered by the welfare state is not a central feature of Canadian urban politics.

RACE AND CITY POLITICS

In the early 1960s two well-known commentators on American city politics wrote: 'In many Northern cities, the question of where Negroes are to live lies behind almost every proposal for civic action. Will locating a major highway here prevent them from "invading" that white neighbourhood? And where will those Negroes who are displaced by an urban renewal project resettle? If a school or a hospital is placed here or there, will it bring Negroes to the neighbourhood? And if it does, will the neighbourhood "tip" and become all Negro?'[13] Twenty years later little has changed, apart from the fact that blacks are no longer referred to as 'Negroes.' Racial issues remain of utmost importance in American cities, so much so that in both political and academic discourse the analytical distinctions between urban problems and racial problems are seldom made.

Race has not always been a central issue in American city politics. It is simply a recent and more dramatic example of the ethnic divisions that have been present in many American cities for at least a century and a half. The arrival of successive waves of Germans, Irish, eastern Europeans, Italians, and eventually southern blacks has been extensively documented. The role of the 'ethnic vote' in the emergence of the great nineteenth-century political machines has also received much academic attention.[10] Less well known is the fact that ethnic differences sparked the incorporation of many independent municipalities even as early as the late nineteenth century. For example, Jon C. Teaford cites the incorporation in 1878 of an almost wholly German and Catholic municipality near an American and Protestant one in suburban Cincinnati.[11] The use of municipal boundaries to insulate one group from another certainly did not begin with the black-white confrontations of the 1960s. It is part of a continuing pattern in the organization of American city government.

Since the migration of rural blacks to the more prosperous American cities, there can be little doubt that the most significant ethnic cleavage with these cities has been based on race. In 1978, blacks made up only 12 per cent of the nation's population; but in the central municipalities of metropolitan areas having populations over one million the figure rises to 28 per cent.[12]

Statistics on the size of the black population become much more dramatic if we look at the figures for some of the larger central municipalities. Chicago, St Louis, and Cleveland all have black populations of over 40 per cent. Washington, Atlanta, Detroit, Baltimore, and New Orleans have black majorities.[13] These statistics confirm that there are two arenas in which the connections between race and American urban politics can be studied: the metropolitan area as a whole, in which middle-class whites have tended to use suburban municipal structures to protect and advance their own positions, and the central municipality, in which the political manifestations of the racial cleavage are more obvious because they cannot be so easily disguised.

In comparison to Canadian census metropolitan areas, the American standard statistical metropolitan areas are characterized by an astonishing number of independent municipalities and special-purpose bodies. The most extreme examples were metropolitan Chicago, with 1,214 local governments in 1977, and metropolitan Philadelphia, with 864.[14] With some notable exceptions,[15] American students of public administration and urban government have been enthusiastic advocates of the kind of consolidated two-tier metropolitan government now exemplified by Metropolitan Toronto. Unlike their Canadian counterparts, they have generally been unsuccessful. Only Miami, Baton Rouge, Nashville, Indianapolis, and Jacksonville have anything remotely similar to the two-tier systems now found in Toronto, Montreal, Vancouver, Victoria, Ottawa, Hamilton, Sudbury, Kitchener, St Catharines, and Oshawa.[16]

A simple explanation for this difference is that Americans are more attached to genuinely autonomous local government than Canadians are. American legislators have generally written state constitutions and state laws in such a way that local governments cannot have their boundaries and functions changed without the consent of the affected residents, usually through some form of referendum. The American literature on local government is littered with accounts of how various plans for metropolitan reform foundered on their inability to attain popular approval. Given what we know about mass political behaviour, it is difficult to imagine that voters defeated these proposals out of devotion to abstract principles concerning the virtues of autonomous local governments. They were usually defeated because people feared that the reforms would bring higher taxes and less local control over the immediate environment. There is every reason to believe that if voters in suburban Canada had been given the same opportunity they would not have behaved much differently. This does not mean, however, that suburban and centre-city interests are the same in both countries.

Metropolitan political conflict in the United States is fundamentally different than in Canada because of the unique role of ethnicity in the pattern of American urban politics. Originally, there was the antipathy between the WASP suburbs and the ethnically based machine politicians of the central city. Later, the cleavage in many cities became more pronounced: it became simply the white suburbs versus the black central city. Even among the suburbs in racially mixed metropolitan areas, there tends to be segregation between white and black. While most suburbs are overwhelmingly white, a few are usually overwhelmingly black. Suburban municipalities in the United States – like all other public institutions – are now constitutionally barred from engaging in any overt form of racial discrimination. Nevertheless, white suburban municipalities have been remarkably effective in preventing the emergence of racially integrated suburban populations.

They have accomplished this mainly through the use of their control over zoning.[17] Because blacks have significantly lower incomes than whites, most cannot afford single-family houses on large lots meeting rigorous building codes. By insisting that only these kinds of residences be built, suburban municipal councils can effectively exclude all but the most prosperous of black city-dwellers. This latter group can be effectively discouraged from moving in by a host of informal actions and suggestions on the part of established residents, real estate agents, and others with an interest in maintaining high property values through resisting the pressures for racial integration. 'Opening up the suburbs' is probably the greatest challenge for contemporary American race relations. It is an issue intimately connected to the seemingly dry, legalistic concerns relating to the structures, functions, and boundaries of local governments.

Although Canadian suburbanites have generally tried to resist either annexation to the central city or metropolitan government, they have done so without the passion or commitment of their American counterparts. The main reason for this difference is the absence in Canada of the racial dimension to metropolitan political conflict. The linguistic cleavage in metropolitan Montreal seems to provide a parallel to the American experience, but close observation shows that, because racial and linguistic differences do not seem to provoke the same psychological effects and because the island of Montreal contains as many French-speaking suburbs as English-speaking ones, the impact of the linguistic cleavage is much more subtle and indirect.

Just as American experts have pointed to the evils of exclusionary zoning, so have a few Canadian studies decried the tendency of some municipalities to zone out low-income housing of various sorts and to insist on 'gold-plated' standards of subdivision development.[18] But, once again, on the Canadian side, the passion and commitment are lacking. Compared to the United States, any problems we might have in this area are scarcely significant. While our experts point to relatively minor abuses on the part of suburban municipalities concerned with keeping taxes low and preserving the sanctity of middle-class life-styles, the concern of American commentators is with a conscious desire on the part of many suburban residents to exclude their black fellow citizens from sharing in the most sacred aspect of the modern American dream – a residence in a peaceful suburb.

While racial or ethnic considerations have not been of major importance in the politics of metropolitan government in Canada, they have had much more significance in the politics of the central municipalities. Here the American experience has been much more similar. The introduction pointed out that some Canadian cities, especially Montreal and Winnipeg, became quite ethnically diverse around the turn of the century and that they accordingly experienced, in some measure at least, the kind of urban political machines based on ethnic group alliances that drew the scorn of contemporary municipal reformers on both sides of the border. Why have Canadian cities never experienced the fully developed political machines of the kind made famous by New York's Tammany Hall or Chicago's Mayor Daley? A partial explanation is that we have fewer locally elected offices, and our municipal elections are not held on the same day as federal and provincial ones. These institutional differences have meant that our big-city mayors have had no need to develop overt connections through political parties to other levels of government, and they have not had the opportunity to pack their city councils and special-purpose bodies with loyal party troops. As a result, our mayors have generally been pale imitations of their American counterparts. Mayor Juba of Winnipeg was notably successful in assembling an ethnic group coalition with the capacity of keeping him in the mayor's office – but he had little power to do much once he was there. The direct election of our mayors is what most distinguishes the structure of Canadian local government from its British ancestors. However, the political weakness of these elected mayors places the Canadian experience in its customary position in relation to things British and American. The Canadian experience seems to draw equally from both.

Once again, Montreal is an exception to the general Canadian pattern as it has emerged in this book. Since early in the twentieth century, voters in the city of Montreal have shown great devotion to three long-serving mayors – Médéric Martin, Camillien Houde, and Jean Drapeau. Only Drapeau has been all-powerful within the municipal political system, and, unlike American big-city mayors, even he has seldom been able to influence the course of federal and provincial politics within his city boundaries. Prior to the election of Médéric Martin in 1914, the mayor's office was carefully alternated between French and English because it was felt that neither of the two linguistic groups could lay claim to permanent political leadership. By repeatedly running for re-election, Martin swept this convention aside and asserted the political dominance, within Montreal, of the French-speaking majority. In many respects this development was analogous to what happened in some major American cities in the 1960s and 1970s. By electing black mayors, black voters in such cities as Detroit and Los Angeles were stating that they were now the dominant political force within the city and that they intended to reap both the real and symbolic rewards that flowed from their numerical strength. In this kind of situation the electoral process no longer involves delicate manoeuvring based on shifting ethnic group alliances but instead becomes an opportunity for members of the group that is numerically dominant, but economically weak, to express their solidarity behind a popular spokesman.

Once blacks gained control of American central cities, they became extremely reluctant to give up their newly found power to metropolitan institutions that would inevitably be dominated by whites. Two-tier metropolitan government is even less likely to be implemented than before. Centre-city black politicians plead for financial assistance from state and federal agencies but vehemently resist giving up any of their hard-won political power. Mayor Drapeau's behaviour in protecting the city of Montreal against losing authority to any form of metropolitan government that he cannot control is remarkably similar.

It is not yet clear if racial differences will ever become as potent a political cleavage in Canada as they eventually became in the United States. Although the problems of native peoples are gaining increased visibility in most western cities, Toronto, with its growing black and Asian population, now seems to be the Canadian city with the greatest potential for racial conflict. Recent problems between the metropolitan police and the visible minorities are clear manifestations of this. Nevertheless, because of the way in which wealthy residential areas have been preserved and regenerated close to the downtown area, it is impossible to imagine Toronto ever developing in such a way that blacks would take over the central city while whites flee to the suburbs. If anything, the reverse is more likely to be the case.

Although it is clearly too early to be complacent, Canadian cities may escape the racial problems experienced in the United States and more recently in Britain. We still must adapt to the increasing presence of native peoples in our cities, but unlike the United States and Britain, we bear neither the burden of past slavery nor the legacy of a coloured empire. Our immigration laws, while now officially 'colour-blind,' maintain our status as an overwhelmingly white nation. However, in the unlikely event Toronto and other cities find themselves with significantly more blacks and Asians than there are now, an argument can be made that we are better equipped, in political terms at least, to cope with the resulting strains. British cities have been unable to adapt to growing numbers of blacks and Asians because their whole political system is structured in such a way as to reflect class interests, not racial or ethnic interests.[19] Americans, with their traditional concern for the rights of individuals rather than of collectivities, have had great trouble adapting to black demands for both legal equality and communal recognition at the same time.

If Canadian constitutional theory and rhetoric are to be believed, our country is better equipped to recognize and accommodate the varying interests of distinct collectivities. The Constitution Act (formerly the British North America Act) of 1867 guarantees collective educational rights for Roman Catholic and Protestant minorities in certain provinces (section 93). The 1982 additions to this act recognize and affirm 'the existing aboriginal and treaty rights of the aboriginal peoples of Canada' (section 35) and provide that the new charter of rights 'shall be interpreted in a manner consistent with the preservation and enhancement of the multicultural heritage of Canadians' (section 27). Canadian history suggests, however, that respect for communal interests has occurred more in theory than in practice. The experience of francophone Catholics in Manitoba and Ontario is ample testimony to this. If the collective rights of one of the so-called charter groups have not been properly protected, what hope is there for native peoples or for other racial, ethnic, or religious groups who might some day seek a form of collective recognition?

Cameron and Aucoin's treatment of Halifax in this book portrays one Canadian city that seems to have been remarkably successful in accommodating one type of cleavage – the historically explosive one between Catholics and Protestants. Arrangements were worked out for what were in effect separate and distinct school systems for each religious group. As the cleavage became less salient, these arrangements were slowly dismantled. All this was done without any original constitutional guarantees for Catholics in Nova Scotia, and hence without any subsequent constitutional amendments. Perhaps this suggests that minority communal interests are best protected by means other than constitutions. A spirit of accommodation among local politicians on such matters might well be more important than solemn declarations in national constitutions. If this is so, Canadian local politicians will eventually face some crucial tests. The Halifax example notwithstanding, we simply do not have enough evidence to predict their behaviour.

CLASS AND CITY POLITICS

On first encountering the British literature on city politics, the Canadian student will inevitably be struck by the fact that virtually all analysts place special emphasis on the importance of social class. This is not necessarily because such writers have explicitly adopted a Marxian framework. It is simply because, in most instances, they are reporting what is surely one of the central features of British society. People who know Britain – either from direct personal experience or through novels, plays, and films – will be familiar with the way in which class cleavages seem to pervade, in an especially obvious way, virtually all aspects of everyday life. The best studies of urban politics in Britain confront the reality of social class and carefully describe and analyse the numerous ways in which it affects virtually all aspects of the local political process. In doing so, these studies are often an especially effective means of understanding not just local politics but British politics in general.

It was not until the twentieth century that the class struggle in local politics became so predominant. Prior to that time, working-class Britons either did not have the vote or were not sufficiently organized to use it effectively. This did not mean that nineteenth-century British city politics was calm and sedate – quite the contrary. There appears to have been a vicious 'contest for power within the urban middle class and between that urban elite and the landed gentry.'[20] These battles took place in many more public political arenas than exist today. Elections for such offices as churchwarden, local improvement commissioner, poor law commissioner, and school board member provoked a level of political involvement seldom experienced in today's local elections.

Generally speaking, longer established Anglican families confronted *nouveau riche* dissenters. It is well known that in parliamentary elections the former group generally supported the Tories and the latter group the Liberals. What is less well known is that these two political parties fought each other just as fervently in local elections. Decisions at the local level concerning taxes for churches, the nature of publicly assisted schooling, and the administration of the poor law were often more crucial to the interests and concerns of the two conflicting groups than what was being debated in Parliament.

In the first decades of the twentieth century, when the new Labour party began running candidates for local office in an attempt to bring about 'municipal socialism,' it was not so much introducing party politics to British local government as it was changing the nature of the party political conflict. By organizing the working-class vote, it forced middle-class interests at the local level to coalesce in self-defence. By openly supporting official Labour party candidates for local office, it caused other parties, notably the Conservatives, to follow its example and to give up the fiction that they stayed aloof from local politics.[21]

Despite fervent activity at the local level in the early years of its existence, the overall impact of the Labour party eventually led to a decline in the political salience of local government. This was not, as its opponents often allege, because it downgraded local government by introducing party politics. It was rather because, by eventually achieving success at the central level, it caused the implementation of numerous central government policies aimed at redistributing wealth, rationalizing public investment, and providing certain basic standards of service. Such policies had the effect of reducing the autonomy of individual local authorities such that the kinds of decisions they were free to make in mid-century did not seem to provoke nearly as much public controversy as was generated a hundred years earlier, prior to the full political mobilization of the working class.[22]

Another reason given for the apparent decline in the salience of local politics in Britain is that, because the Labour and Conservative parties now openly compete against each other in all major urban centres, local elections have become little more than an opportunity for voters to express pleasure or displeasure with the activities of the parliamentary parties at Westminster. There is much evidence to support the validity of this complaint.[23] Anyone concerned with local autonomy and the accountability of local politicians for their actions cringes at the thought of candidates for local office winning or losing their elections as a direct result of unrelated events such as British military successes in the Falkland Islands. Yet this is exactly what happens in every British local election.

Unlike Canadian voters in federal and provincial elections, British voters seem reluctant to vote for one party at one level of government and for a different party at another level. The most obvious explanation for this difference in voting behaviour is that in Britain (unlike Canada), individual party identification is above all related to social class, or at least to perceptions of how one fits into it. If local government were to have little or no jurisdiction over issues that relate to social class, it is possible that British voters might develop the kind of split-level perceptions of parties that characterize Canadian voters. The reality, however, is that British local governments, even more than their Canadian equivalents, do make decisions that are highly sensitive to class considerations. Hence the high correlation between national and local voting behaviour is unlikely to be significantly reduced, because voters' perceptions of social class can hardly be expected to change depending on which level of government happens to be holding an election.

It is precisely because local governments in Britain do make important decisions affecting class interests that we should not dismiss their importance merely due to the apparent arbitrariness of local election results. Despite the centralizing impact of the welfare state and the considerable importance of central financial control, a local council in Britain, in relation to its Canadian counterpart at least, has considerable power, especially in two important policy fields – education and housing.

There have been no local school boards in Britain since 1902.[24] The management of local, publicly financed schools has been under the jurisdiction of the local council. This fact alone gives British local government considerably more functional responsibility than the equivalent municipal government systems in Canadian provinces. Furthermore, in modern Britain (unlike Canada) there has been no general societal consensus on the best pedagogical structure for a public educational system, and there have been no conclusive central decisions forcing local councils to establish one system or another. Instead, local councils have had considerable freedom to choose whatever system or mixture of systems they desire.

The Labour party supports the establishment throughout the country of a publicly financed school system somewhat similar to the normal Canadian model. This involves the establishment of common or 'comprehensive' secondary schools for all students in a given area, regardless of their intellectual capabilities. The Conservatives, in addition to approving of such privately financed élite schools as Eton and Harrow, favour a publicly financed system that streams adolescent students into distinct 'secondary modern' or 'grammar' schools, depending on each individual student's demonstrated intellectual ability. Conservatives claim that their defence of grammar schools is above all a defence of academic excellence and that such schools are open to children of all social classes as long as they have the required ability. Labour claims that there is not equal access to grammar schools and that, anyway, such divisions in the school system both reflect and promote undesirable inequalities of various sorts and that consequently such schools should be abolished. A more important issue affecting the relations between social classes can scarcely be imagined.

While in office at the national level, each party has pursued its favoured scheme by using various devices, including financial incentives, moral suasion, and regulation. Neither party, however, has had either the political will or a sufficiently long period in office to impose its policy throughout the country. Local councils have on numerous occasions successfully thwarted policies emanating from a central government of a different political persuasion. Many local elections in recent years have been fought on the comprehensive school issue, and their outcomes have profoundly affected the nature of local school systems.[25] Who in Canada can cite examples of local school board elections – let alone municipal elections – when the educational stakes have been so high?

Housing is another field in which the actions of British local government are especially sensitive in terms of social class. About 35 per cent of the housing stock in the United Kingdom is owned by local councils.[26] The proportion is, of course, considerably higher in large urban centres. Politically, one of the results of this situation is to ensure that actual and potential 'council house' residents – almost all of whom are of the working class – have a direct interest in the activities of local government. This is not to suggest that many of them become passionately involved in debating the merits of alternative housing policies, but it does mean that, unlike the person who is a passive recipient of cash payments from government, the resident of a council house has a never-ending series of day-to-day complaints about the actions or inactions of local government: rent levels, the state of repair of the dwelling, noise, parking, and all the other vexatious aspects of landlord-tenant relations. Many tenants are also worried about the future availability of council housing for married sons and daughters.

Providing council housing is not like providing welfare cheques: it must be planned, constructed, and allocated – all of which are immensely difficult political and bureaucratic tasks. In Canada, despite considerable hand-wringing on the part of governments at all levels, the provision of family housing remains a function of the private marketplace, even for most long-term welfare recipients and low-wage earners. In Britain, because local government performs much of this function, its political and administrative responsibilities are immensely greater, and its importance for the daily concerns of working-class voters is obviously strengthened.

Not surprisingly, there are those in Britain, mainly in the Conservative party, who are ideologically opposed to such a strong public role in the provision of housing. They have argued their case in both central and local political arenas but it appears that on this issue, which involves difficult questions of principle and large amounts of money, the most important focus of decision is at Westminster. Nevertheless, as with the comprehensive school issue, a decision to either promote or discourage council housing does not lead to immediate results at the local level, especially if the national and the local government in question are of different parties.

When a metropolitan level of government is added to the equation, as is the case in Greater London, the chances of three levels of government pulling in the same direction on housing are even more remote. This has been well documented by Ken Young and John Kramer,[27] who have shown how the Conservative-controlled suburban borough of Bromley in Greater London successfully fought off numerous attempts from above to force it to provide more public housing within its borders. For Conservatives in Bromley, local government proved to have considerable power in protecting their cherished middle-class environment. Meanwhile, other boroughs in poorer areas of the city continued to experience severe shortages of public housing.

The housing issue in Greater London is symptomatic of yet another way in which class considerations relate to British local government. Because working-class and middle-class people tend to live in their own separate territories and because each group tends to support the Labour and Conservative parties respectively, the drawing of local government boundaries has profound effects in determining which party is to control the local council of a given area.

In 1972 Britain's Conservative government substantially reorganized local government boundaries in Britain. The main changes involved the abolition of one-tier local authorities in urban areas and the consolidation of smaller rural ones. Urban authorities, and the new rural ones, were brought together under new two-tier authorities, which, in most instances, were given considerable control over such functions as planning, housing, and education. Many observers have noted that the absorption of central-city areas into larger units of local government has had the effect, intended or otherwise, of considerably reducing working-class control over the inner-city environment.[28]

To study urban politics in Britain without reference to social class is to study form and structure without studying content and without coming to grips with the political reality in which the local government system operates. Parties are important in British local government because they reflect class interests. Education and housing are important issues because they reflect disagreement about how the different classes are to relate to each other. One reason then why urban politics does not seem as important in Canada as in Britain is simply because Canadian urban political conflict is not a crucial aspect of a general pattern of class conflict extending throughout all levels of the political system.

CITY POLITICS AND CANADIAN POLITICS

The systematic study of local politics in Canada has neither been informed by the general literature on Canadian politics nor added to it. Instead, the study of local government in Canada has remained an academic ghetto. Few students of Canadian local government have ever ventured much beyond the subject's original base as a sub-field in traditional public administration. Within this context, many scholars continue to rework the themes of the original urban reform movement at the turn of this century. Others have tried to apply the methodology of the 'American science of politics' to particular Canadian situations. More recently, a European brand of Marxist urban analysis has become popular. None of this work is to be sneered at. Without it, a volume such as this could never have been written.

If the study of local politics has any value for understanding the exercise of power in our society, it must in some way be connected to the study of the general political system of the whole society. One of the characteristics of Canadian city politics that has undoubtedly hampered such a connection in the past is its apparent diversity. How can anything of significance be said about city politics when structures and practices vary so much from city to city and when there are not even two cities in the whole country that share the same local political parties?

One way of approaching the question is to acknowledge this undoubted diversity and to list both the socio-geographic and the political factors that account for the numerous differences from city to city. For anyone familiar with the development of Canadian society, the resulting analysis is quite familiar.

On the socio-geographic side, there is first of all the relative isolation from each other of the major Canadian cities. Even though Ottawa and Edmonton are similar in size, and both are seats of government, they are so far apart that, except for small bands of travelling politicians and civil servants, there is little opportunity for residents of one city to become familiar with those of another. The usual claim that the mass media, especially television, expose us all to common news reporting does not really apply in the case of municipal politics. While many of us might watch the same national newscast dealing with major federal and provincial issues, the audience splinters dramatically when we turn to the 'local' news. In most such local newscasts there is little effort to link local issues of the day in one community to similar problems in other places. There is little serious analysis of local politics at all.

Apart from being geographically isolated, most Canadian cities are culturally quite distinct from each other. The most dramatic examples, of course, are Toronto and Montreal. Here are two metropolitan areas of roughly equal size which, by Canadian standards at least, are quite close to each other. Both cities have substantial numbers of 'new Canadians' from a great diversity of ethnic groups. But Toronto is overwhelmingly English in language and culture while French is scarcely noticeable; Montreal, however, has a French majority and a substantial English minority. Toronto is now the metropolis of English Canada while Montreal adjusts to its new role as the metropolis of an increasingly French Quebec. The ramifications of the differences at the local level are immense and were described in the relevant essays in this book.

Differences in the ethnic make-up of such cities as Winnipeg and Halifax are almost as dramatic as those between Toronto and Montreal. Ethnic diversity in Winnipeg led to the success of Steven Juba – a type of flamboyant politician not known in the quieter politics of Halifax, where the once salient Catholic-Protestant cleavage is now a relic of the past.

Finally, Canadian cities are different from each other in that they perform widely differing economic functions. Despite being the seat of Alberta's growing provincial bureaucracy, Edmonton remains the centre of petroleum exploration, production, and refining, both for Alberta and for much of Canada's northern frontier. Whether Halifax will ever perform such a function for Canada's east-coast petroleum resources is still unclear. If it does, the character of its local politics is likely to change considerably, although, as Cameron and Aucoin point out, local politics in Halifax will always bear the imprint of the city's long history as a military and institutional centre. This past tradition will no doubt prevent Halifax politicians from ever following the blatant boosterism so common in Edmonton. We have also seen how Toronto's secure economic position in the 1960s and 1970s provided the luxurious environment in which local politicians could reject the need to 'attract investment' and turn instead to 'saving neighbourhoods.'

Despite the obvious importance of all these socio-geographic factors, the most powerful factor accounting for the apparent diversity in Canadian city politics is the rise of the provincial state.[29] The dramatic increase in the provinces' importance need not be documented here. What is crucial for our purposes is to understand that provincial power in relation to urban issues has emerged at the expense of both the federal and local governments and that this has helped lead to the breakdown of what was once an important country-wide 'municipal network.'

Federal control over rail and air transport and its ownership of vast amounts of urban land still ensure that the Ottawa government has an important presence in all major Canadian cities, but as an urban policy-maker it is now virtually impotent. Since the Canada Mortgage and Housing Corporation was prevented from intervening directly in the provision of housing and since the much less important Ministry of State for Urban Affairs was dismantled, there are no longer any major federal policies that bypass provincial politicians and bureaucrats and apply directly to the cities. This is quite different from the situation in the United States, where direct federal-city relations in a number of fields are quite frequent and of considerable significance. In Canada, students of city politics do not have the academic luxury of being able to compare the influence of different local political variables by tracing the way in which federal programs are implemented in different cities.

Increases in provincial powers in relation to municipalities have come mainly in the fields of taxation and social services. Prior to the Second World War, some municipalities were supplementing property tax revenues with local sales taxes and even income taxes. Others made a practice of adjusting property assessments, and even tax rates, in order to attract business investment or pursue other kinds of economic objectives. Despite the many good reasons why Canadian municipalities do not now have this kind of fiscal freedom, they are now almost solely dependent on either provincial grants or an inflexible provincially regulated property tax. Municipal councils can now debate only the amount of money to be raised; they have virtually no control over how it is to be raised.

Closely linked to their restricted revenue base, Canadian municipalities now have virtually no control over social welfare. Although a number of municipalities still administer some forms of welfare payments, under strict provincial guidelines, most such payments are now paid directly by the province. From being the main (if ineffective) support for destitute residents prior to and during the Depression, Canadian municipalities are now almost totally excluded from this crucial area of government policy. They have also watched numerous social service agencies in the voluntary sector become increasingly subject to provincial control and financing. As a result, we have seen that municipal political activity has been restricted to a narrow band of issues relating to the control and servicing of property.

The increased strength of the provinces has had a significant impact on the few national institutions we have that are involved in local government. Such organizations as the Federation of Canadian Municipalities and the Canadian Council on Urban and Regional Research have either been weakened considerably (in the case of the former) or completely collapsed (in the case of the latter). Although nation-wide organizations exist for such municipally involved professional groups as planners, engineers, accountants, and lawyers, there are no such groups for general administrators. City managers in Canada are generally affiliated with the American-based International City Managers Association rather than with a purely Canadian group.

A few decades ago a small group of activist mayors, academics, consultants, and employees of national municipal organizations constituted a nation-wide 'municipal network' that, if nothing else, served at least to provide a common municipal orthodoxy in the country as a whole. The existence of this orthodoxy contributed to some degree of national uniformity. For example, it is quite clear that the basic structures and practices of city politics in Montreal and Toronto were much more similar sixty years ago than they are today.

In recent years, the new generation of municipal experts has entered either the narrow specializations of university research or high-ranking jobs in provincial departments of municipal affairs. In both cases, the professional loyalties of the people involved have generally developed in such a way that attachment to the institution of municipal government is not given high priority. While most will applaud the emergence of alternative approaches towards municipal government, the demise of the national perspective also has its obvious drawbacks – not the least of which is that it makes municipal government a more complex and difficult field of study.

While there is so much that is different in city politics throughout Canada, the common concern for property development can never be overlooked. This characteristic of Canadian city politics can enlighten us about two central themes in Canadian political discourse: governmental jurisdiction and economic development.

The Canadian penchant for jurisdictional distinctions between federal and provincial governments is well known. Accustomed to thinking that each level of government has its place, Canadians have been all too quick to link the municipal level with property and refuse to countenance any political connections to senior 'levels.' This pattern is the complete opposite of that in France, where local governments have had even less formal autonomy than in Canada, but where the prestige of local politics has been enhanced by politicians using local offices and local support as bases on which to build their strength in the national political arena. The mayor of Paris, Jacques Chirac, is a key leader of the opposition to the socialist president; the defeated former president, Giscard d'Estaing, is trying to rebuild his political career by being elected to a regional council. How different this is from the Canadian pattern in which local politicians – who often eventually go on to careers in federal and provincial politics – scrupulously avoid any public involvement in partisan politics at other levels.

Partisan affiliation at the local level upsets the already difficult relations between federal and provincial branches of the same party. It is seen to be in violation of the national operation of the properly non-partisan local political process. Without the strong visible presence of organized national or provincial political parties, it is not surprising that municipal politics seem so different from one city to another.

The essays in this book, however, have shown a remarkable similarity both in the subject matter of city politics and in the political forces that predominate. City politics in Canada is about property. Woe to anyone (such as John Sewell) who goes beyond property development issues and raises subjects such as gay rights and the social role of the police – matters that are perceived as not 'suitable' for municipal politicians.

Debates about economic development at the national level usually end up as conflicts among the country's various regions. Regions producing primary goods take on the manufacturing regions; areas of low growth plead for their share of benefits gained in more prosperous areas. It has often been observed that class politics in Canada is a virtual impossibility. Within provinces, political debate revolves more around how to maximize the province's economic position in Canada as a whole, rather than around how benefits and costs are to be redistributed within the province itself.

As the writers in this book have repeatedly noted, politics at the local level in Canada involves a particular form of economic development – the enhancement of the value of urban land. Despite the vast differences among our cities, property issues in each of them have generated remarkably similar political forces. There has been a gradual emergence in our major cities (except possibly Halifax) of a clear split on council between 'right' and 'left.' We might even anticipate that the open emergence of this essentially ideological cleavage will eventually unleash forces that could push municipal politics into fields beyond those associated with the control and servicing of property. Or these same forces might serve as building blocks for a more explicitly ideological form of politics at the federal and provincial levels.

These suggestions are, of course, highly speculative. What is more certain is that to understand Canadian politics in its entirety, one must know about Canadian local politics, especially in our larger cities, where so many of our citizens live. Such knowledge can enrich our awareness of the complexity and diversity of our political life. More importantly, it can demonstrate that, in its most crucial aspects, the local political life of our large cities is remarkably similar. In the final analysis, the study of city politics in Canada suggests that patterns of political behaviour are more alike across the country than studies of politics at federal and provincial levels lead us to believe. In short, it is perhaps at the local level that we can most profitably search for a Canadian political culture having common characteristics throughout the land.

SUGGESTED FURTHER READING:
INTERNATIONAL COMPARATIVE URBAN POLITICS

Cox, Kevin R. ed *Urbanisation and Conflict in Market Societies* Chicago 1978

Dunleavy, Patrick *Urban Political Analysis* London 1980

Lagroye, Jacques and Vincent Wright ed *Local Government in Britain and France* London 1979

Magnusson, Warren 'Metropolitan Reform in the Capitalist City' *Canadian Journal of Political Science* XIV 3 (September 1981) 557–85

Miles, Simon R. ed *Metropolitan Problems* Toronto 1970

Robson, William A. and D.E. Regan ed *Great Cities of the World: Their Government, Politics, and Planning* 3rd edn 2 vols London 1972

Rowat, Donald C. ed *International Handbook on Local Government Reorganization: Contemporary Developments* London 1980

Sharpe, L.J. 'American Democracy Reconsidered' *British Journal of Political Science* III 1, 2 (January and April 1973) 1–28 and 129–68

Sharpe, L.J. ed *Decentralist Trends in Western Democracies* Beverly Hills, Calif, 1979

Tabb, William K. and Larry Sawer ed *Marxism and the Metropolis* New York 1978

Wickwar, W. Hardy *The Political Theory of Local Government* Columbia, SC, 1970

Young, Kenneth ed *Essays on the Study of Urban Politics* London 1975

NOTES

1 See especially John C. Weaver *Shaping the Canadian City: Essays on Urban Politics and Policy, 1890–1920* (Toronto 1977). For another view, see H.V. Nelles and C. Armstrong 'The Great Fight for Clean Government' *Urban History Review* II (1976) 50–66.

2 *A Citizen's Guide to City Politics* (Toronto 1972)

3 For a thorough discussion of this approach, see Warren Magnusson 'Metropolitan Reform in the Capitalist City' *Canadian Journal of Political Science* XIV 3 (September 1981) 557–85.

4 *Vancouver Ltd.* (Toronto 1975)

5 280

6 This is a characteristic of municipal politicians everywhere. See Paul E. Peterson *City Limits* (Chicago 1981).

7 243

8 For example, see Robert A. Dahl *Who Governs?: Democracy and Power in an American City* (New Haven, Conn, 1961), Kenneth Newton *Second City Politics: Democratic Processes and Decision-Making in Birmingham* (Oxford 1976), and L.J. Sharpe 'American Democracy Reconsidered' *British Journal of Political Science* III 1, 2 (January and April 1973) 1–28 and 129–68.

9 Patrick Dunleavy *Urban Political Analysis* (London 1980)

10 For a valuable critique of this literature, see Martin Shefter 'The Emergence of the Political Machine: An Alternative View' in W.D. Hawley et al *Theoretical Perspectives on Urban Politics* (New York 1976) 14–44.

11 *City and Suburb* (Baltimore 1979) 23

12 John C. Bollens and Henry J. Schmandt *The Metropolis: Its People, Politics, and Economic Life* 4th edn (New York 1982) 45–6

13 Ibid 47

14 Ibid 89

15 See the writings of the 'public choice' school. The most useful introduction is Robert L. Bish and Vincent Ostrom *Understanding Urban Government: Metropolitan Reform Reconsidered* (Washington, DC, 1973).

16 Bollens and Schmandt *The Metropolis* 313–28

17 See Michael N. Danielson *The Politics of Exclusion* (New York 1976).

18 *Down to Earth: The Report of the Federal/Provincial Task Force on the Supply and Price of Serviced Residential Land* I 1978 chap 4

19 Kenneth Newton 'Community Politics and Decision-Making: The American Experience and Its Lessons' in Ken Young ed *Essays in the Study of Urban Politics* (London 1975) 22
20 Derek Fraser *Urban Politics in Victorian England* (Leicester 1976)
21 For a detailed account of how this process worked in relation to the Conservatives in London, see Ken Young *Local Politics and the Rise of Party* (Leicester 1975).
22 Fraser *Victorian England* 283–4
23 See L.J. Sharpe ed *Voting in Cities* (London 1967), especially Peter Fletcher 'The Results Analyzed' 319–21, and Newton *Second City Politics* chap 2.
24 The exception is the Inner London Education Authority, which is really a kind of joint education department for fourteen inner London boroughs.
25 This brief account suffers from excessive generalization and simplification. For an account of how this complex issue was dealt with in Birmingham, see Newton *Second City Politics* 203–8.
26 Bruce Walker *Welfare Economics and Urban Problems* (London 1981) 26
27 *Strategy and Conflict in Metropolitan Housing* (London 1978)
28 For a full exposition of this and related arguments, see John Dearlove *The Reorganization of British Local Government* (Cambridge 1979).
29 For details, see Marsha A. Chandler and William M. Chandler *Public Policy and Provincial Politics* (Toronto 1979).

APPENDIX

Comparative statistics

All data in the following tables are compiled from the relevant Canadian decennial census, unless otherwise noted. When 1981 data are not presented, they were unavailable at time of printing. Abbreviation: CMA = census metropolitan area.

TABLE 1
Population 1861–1981

	1861	1881	1901*	1921	1941	1961	1981
Halifax							
CMA			51,000	75,000	99,000	193,000	277,727
City	25,026	36,100	40,832	58,372	70,488	92,511	114,594
Montreal							
CMA			415,000	796,000	1,216,000	2,216,000	2,828,349
City	90,323	140,747	267,730	618,506	903,007	1,191,062	980,354
Ottawa							
CMA			103,000	168,000	236,000	457,000	717,978
City	14,669	27,412	59,928	107,843	154,951	268,206	295,163
Toronto							
CMA			303,000	686,000	1,002,000	1,919,000	2,998,947
City	44,821	86,415	208,040	521,893	667,457	672,407	599,217
Winnipeg							
CMA			48,000	229,000	302,000	477,000	584,842
City	–	7,985	42,340	179,087	221,960	265,429	564,473
Edmonton							
CMA			15,000	87,000	136,000	360,000	657,057
City	–	–	2,626	58,821	93,817	281,027	532,246
Vancouver							
CMA				224,000	394,000	827,000	1,268,183
City	–	–	26,133	117,217	275,353	384,522	414,281

* Estimates for 1901–61 are taken from D. Michael Ray ed *Canadian Urban Trends* I *National Perspectives* (Ottawa 1976) 19.

TABLE 2
Percentage British and Roman Catholic 1881–1971

	1881	1901	1921	1941	1961	1971
Halifax						
British	86.5	88.6	86.3	80.9	72.0	77.4
Roman Catholic	40.7	40.9	39.6	41.2	43.1	41.4
Montreal						
British	41.2	33.7	24.0	20.2	12.4	10.9
Roman Catholic	73.6	75.5	74.3	77.5	81.7	79.9
Ottawa						
British	63.6	60.2	63.2	60.7	55.2	55.2
Roman Catholic	58.0	50.9	47.4	49.4	47.5	49.2
Toronto						
British	93.4	91.7	85.3	78.4	51.7	45.8
Roman Catholic	18.2	13.9	12.4	15.5	34.7	38.6
Winnipeg						
British	83.6	73.8	67.3	58.7	42.8	43.0
Roman Catholic	12.8	12.1	13.5	22.0	21.9	25.9
Edmonton						
British		60.8	77.6	66.9	46.2	44.2
Roman Catholic		29.4	13.2	20.0	22.9	25.1
Vancouver						
British		77.8	79.8	77.3	59.9	53.0
Roman Catholic		11.7	9.2	10.9	17.8	20.5

TABLE 3
Ethnic origin 1971

	British	French	German	Italian	Ukrainian	Jewish	Native peoples	Black and West Indian	Asian
Halifax									
CMA	77.7	8.5	4.9	0.6	0.3	0.7	0.2	0.9	1.2
City	77.4	8.9	4.6	0.8	0.2	1.2	0.2	0.8	1.6
Montreal									
CMA	16.0	64.3	1.4	5.9	0.7	4.2	0.3	0.3	1.3
City	10.9	64.2	1.0	9.0	0.7	4.3	0.3	0.5	1.8
Ottawa-Hull									
CMA	44.9	39.6	3.2	2.6	0.9	1.2	0.2	0.3	1.5
City	55.2	24.9	3.5	4.1	1.1	1.8	0.2	0.4	2.2
Toronto									
CMA	56.9	3.5	4.4	10.3	2.3	4.2	0.2	1.1	2.7
City	45.8	3.7	3.3	12.6	3.2	3.5	0.4	1.6	4.8
Winnipeg*									
CMA	43.0	8.6	11.5	1.7	11.6	3.6	1.2	0.3	1.4
Edmonton									
CMA	44.7	7.2	12.6	1.8	12.6	0.6	1.0	0.2	2.0
City	44.2	6.7	12.4	2.0	13.3	0.7	1.0	0.2	2.1
Vancouver									
CMA	58.6	4.0	8.3	2.8	2.9	1.0	0.7	0.2	5.4
City	53.0	3.4	7.6	4.5	2.9	1.9	0.7	0.2	10.2
Canada	44.6	28.7	6.1	3.4	2.7	1.4	1.5	0.3	1.3

* The 1971 Winnipeg census metropolitan area corresponds almost exactly to the boundaries of the city of Winnipeg (Unicity) as established 1 January 1972.

TABLE 4
Selected population characteristics 1971 and 1981

	Children per family*		Percentage under age 20		Percentage over age 65		Percentage born in Canada	Percentage immigrated after 1945	Percentage French home language	Percentage home language neither English nor French
	1971	1981	1971	1981	1971	1981	1971	1971	1971	1971
Halifax										
CMA	1.7	1.4	38.7	32.0	6.4	7.9	92.8	5.4	1.2	1.4
City	1.6	1.2	34.7	25.2	8.3	11.9	91.9	5.9	1.4	2.0
Montreal										
CMA	1.6	1.3	36.5	28.9	7.0	9.2	85.2	12.0	66.3	8.8
City	1.5	1.1	31.4	23.2	9.0	13.1	81.2	15.6	67.5	13.9
Ottawa-Hull										
CMA	1.8	1.3	39.0	30.6	5.9	8.1	87.5	10.1	33.8	4.0
City	1.6	1.1	34.4	24.1	8.8	12.5	83.7	12.7	17.1	9.4
Toronto										
CMA	1.5	1.3	35.2	29.3	7.5	9.1	66.0	28.2	0.8	17.4
City	1.3	1.2	28.6	23.3	11.0	12.5	56.4	36.4	1.0	29.9
Winnipeg										
CMA	1.7	1.3	35.9	29.9	9.5	11.5	80.1	11.9	3.3	10.2
City		1.3		29.6		11.6				
Edmonton										
CMA	1.7	1.3	40.5	31.9	6.0	6.6	81.7	12.7	1.6	7.7
City	1.7	1.2	39.5	29.9	6.2	7.3	80.9	13.1	1.4	8.4
Vancouver										
CMA	1.4	1.2	34.1	27.2	10.0	11.5	73.5	17.5	0.6	8.0
City	1.2	1.1	27.4	21.5	13.5	15.3	65.6	23.0	0.6	14.3
Canada	1.7	1.4	39.4	32.1	8.1	9.7	84.7	10.9	25.7	7.3

* Includes only children under 25 who have not married and live with one or both parents

TABLE 5
Selected housing characteristics 1971 and 1981

	Occupied private dwellings								Households	
	Percentage owner-occupied		Percentage constructed prior to 1946		Percentage detached houses		Percentage apartments		Percentage non-family	
	1971	1981	1971	1981	1971	1981	1971	1981	1971	1981
Halifax										
CMA	49.8	55.6	34.8		47.9	50.2	40.1	31.9	16.6	25.6
City	44.7	39.1	44.6		42.1	35.2	46.5	46.9	21.6	37.0
Montreal										
CMA	35.3	41.7	31.1		23.7	26.8	50.6	47.2	21.4	28.6
City	19.2	22.0	43.5		5.2	4.7	61.3	67.1	30.4	41.7
Ottawa-Hull										
CMA	50.3	52.3	28.7		46.4	41.7	37.3	33.8	19.0	28.4
City	42.0	39.1	35.3		38.6	30.9	43.9	47.6	26.3	40.4
Toronto										
CMA	54.9	56.5	30.7		45.9	40.3	36.5	39.4	19.7	26.7
City	41.8	40.7	66.5		23.2	20.6	45.9	48.9	34.7	46.1
Winnipeg										
CMA	59.1	58.8	41.5		63.4	59.2	31.5	29.7	21.8	30.8
City		57.9				58.2		30.5		31.3
Edmonton										
CMA	55.3	55.3	18.0		62.3	55.7	30.1	28.9	19.8	29.1
City	52.9	50.2	18.1		60.1	51.4	33.4	33.2	21.1	32.5
Vancouver										
CMA	58.8	58.5	30.8		62.6	57.4	32.9	32.5	24.9	32.4
City	46.9	44.9	45.5		49.7	46.0	47.5	46.2	36.1	45.8
Canada	60.3	62.1	38.0		59.5	57.2	27.7	24.4	18.4	24.8

TABLE 6
Sector of employment, occupations (by census divisions), and income 1971

	Sector of employment				
	Primary (1–4)	Manufacturing (5)	Construction (6)	Transportation and communications (7)	Trade (8)
Halifax					
CMA	0.6	8.3	5.1	8.5	15.7
City	0.4	7.1	4.2	9.3	16.1
Montreal					
CMA	0.6	25.6	4.7	9.5	15.0
City	0.2	25.4	4.3	9.0	14.3
Ottawa-Hull					
CMA	1.0	7.9	5.8	6.2	12.3
City	0.4	5.9	4.6	6.0	11.8
Toronto					
CMA	1.0	26.0	6.3	7.5	16.7
City	0.5	20.9	5.8	7.2	13.5
Winnipeg					
CMA	0.8	18.2	5.1	11.3	18.7
Edmonton					
CMA	3.7	11.4	8.4	9.3	17.3
City	2.4	11.2	8.4	9.5	17.8
Vancouver					
CMA	2.9	16.6	6.8	10.5	18.1
City	2.0	15.1	5.7	10.4	17.2
Canada	12.7	19.8	6.2	7.8	14.7

Sector of employment			Occupations		Income
Finance, insurance, real estate (9)	Service (10)	Public adminis-tration and defence (11)	Professional, managerial (11–33)	Sales and clerical (41 and 51)	Average total income per family (dollars)
5.0	27.6	22.6	21.0	29.7	10,176
5.3	31.4	19.6	23.0	31.4	10,569
5.7	24.5	5.2	19.7	29.8	10,292
5.3	25.9	5.2	16.7	28.4	9,008
4.3	24.9	30.2	25.9	33.0	12,010
4.6	26.1	33.2	27.6	34.9	12,412
6.8	24.1	5.4	19.1	32.7	11,841
7.7	29.3	5.5	19.1	29.0	10,508
5.3	25.7	8.2	18.9	31.3	9,989
4.4	27.6	10.4	19.8	30.5	10,660
4.5	28.3	10.4	19.9	31.2	10,699
5.9	26.9	4.7	17.4	30.5	10,664
6.7	30.6	4.3	17.4	31.2	10,422
4.2	23.7	7.4	17.0	25.4	9,600

Index

Within an entry, the cities are listed in the order in which the articles on them appear in the text; other jurisdictions follow in alphabetical order.

Contributors

Caroline Andrew chairs the Department of Political Science at the University of Ottawa. She is co-author of *Les Élites politiques, les bas-salariés et la politique de logement à Hull* and *L'Urbanisation : une affaire* and has been a member of the Social Planning Council of Ottawa-Carleton and the Participation Advisory Group of the city of Ottawa. She is the 1983–4 president of the Canadian Political Science Association.

Peter Aucoin is director of the School of Public Administration and professor of political science at Dalhousie University. He is co-author of *Knowledge, Power and Public Policy* and in 1981–2 was research director for the Halifax Commission on City Government.

David M. Cameron is professor of public administration and political science and executive director, Policy and Planning, in the Office of the President at Dalhousie University, Halifax. He is the author of *Schools for Ontario: Policy Making, Administration and Finance in the 1960s* and *Northern Dilemma: Public Policy and Post-Secondary Education in Northern Ontario*.

Donald Gutstein is a graduate architect, journalist, community planner, and urban consultant in Vancouver. He has taught at Simon Fraser University and the University of British Columbia. He is a frequent commentator on local affairs and the author of *Vancouver Ltd.*

Matthew Kiernan is assistant general manager of the Winnipeg Core Area Initiative. He has taught urban planning and politics at the University of Manitoba and the University of Winnipeg. His articles on Canadian city planning have appeared in *Plan Canada* and *Urban Law and Policy*.

James Lightbody is associate professor of political science at the University of Alberta. He has written numerous articles on Canadian urban politics and has been a consultant to the city of Edmonton during its recent annexation campaign. He is a member of the Social Science and Humanities Research Council of Canada.

Warren Magnusson is assistant professor of political science at the University of Victoria. Prior to 1979 he taught at the University of Western Ontario, Ryerson Polytechnical Institute, Glendon College of York University, and the University of Toronto. His published articles (most recently in the *Canadian Journal of Political Science*) relate to the political theory of local government.

Andrew Sancton is assistant professor of political science at the University of Western Ontario. From 1974 to 1977 he taught at Marianopolis College, Montreal. He is a member of the federal Electoral Boundaries Commission for Ontario (1982–3) and author of a forthcoming book, *Governing the Island of Montreal: Language Differences and Metropolitan Politics*.

David C. Walker is associate professor of political science at the University of Winnipeg. He is a member of the Social Science and Humanities Research Council of Canada and author of *The Great Winnipeg Dream: The Redevelopment of Portage & Main* and has served as a consultant on local government problems.